AGE OF EXCESS

AGE OF EXCESS

The United States from 1877 to 1914

second edition

RAY GINGER

WAVELAND
PRESS, INC.
Prospect Heights, Illinois

For information about this book, write or call:

Waveland Press, Inc.
P.O. Box 400
Prospect Heights, Illinois 60070
(708) 634-0081

For the late Fritz Pappenheim, scholar, friend

Acknowledgments

Although I have myself worked through a considerable number of primary sources on the United States from 1877 to 1914, this book rests chiefly on the published research of dozens of other historians. My "Essay on Sources" is a hopelessly stingy acknowledgment of my debt to these predecessors and contemporaries. Pertinent data were also dredged up by investigations made by recent students at Brandeis University, and for significant evidence I wish to thank Marc N. Epstein, Judith E. Katz, John D. Levin, and especially David Allan Levine. In addition, many hours of useful labor were contributed by Joan H. Feinson, Linda Levy, and Heidi E. Schuhr. Brandeis University has favored me with a grant in aid of research.

The entire manuscript has been read by four friends: Eugene C. Black of Brandeis University; A. Theodore Brown of the University of Wisconsin at Milwaukee; Herbert G. Gutman of the State University of New York at Buffalo; and Morton Keller of the University of Pennsylvania, presently at Harvard University. Each of them gave generously of his time and knowledge to make helpful suggestions. In fairness I should add that I often did not make the revisions that they proposed.

While I was writing the first version of this work (1960–1964), Evelyn Geiger Farrell spent much energy on the project. During preparation of the Second Edition, my wife Victoria Ginger has been similarly generous in giving her help. My chief debts are to these two women.

R. G.

Contents

PART ONE
1877–1893
Wherein Questions Are Posed

PART TWO
1893–1898
Wherein Some Questions
Are Answered; Others, Evaded

PART THREE
1898–1914
Wherein Americans
Go to Live in the Clouds

ix

List of Illustrations

PART ONE

1877–1893

Wherein Questions Are Posed

CHAPTER 1

Ways of Life at the End of Reconstruction

The national stage of the United States in 1877 held a great variety of actors and actions. The values of Indians opposed the values of white men. The purposes of farmer and banker, of factory worker and industrialist, of railroad president and merchant, often clashed. A person could even find that his own aims contradicted each other. Before we sit down anywhere for a prolonged look, it seems appropriate to glance into several of the theaters. This chapter is deliberately diffuse, for it seeks to explore some ramifications of two features of the country: first, the impact on individual people of certain general conditions of the period—rapid technological change, the growth of the market economy and of organizations, the falling level of prices, the tariff issue; and second, the range of social forms within the United States in 1877, from industrial bureaucracies such as Standard Oil to the hunting cultures of some Indians.

Crazy Horse was a great war chief of the Oglala Sioux. About 35 years old in 1877, he had been a leader of the war party in Wyoming in 1866 that left behind it the corpses of Captain William Fetterman and 80 other soldiers. Through the next decade he fought the white troops, down to that glorious day in June 1876 when he helped to wipe out the entire detachment of Colonel Custer. Most of the Sioux were already in government agencies, but not Crazy Horse. After the Battle of the Little Big Horn he and his lodges went to the Black Hills, sacred to Sioux. Then to the Tongue River, where several couriers from the government came to urge them to lay down their arms. One of the emissaries was Spotted Tail, a great

3

chief, uncle of Crazy Horse, and one of the agency Sioux. At noon on 5 May 1877 Crazy Horse rode into the Red Cloud Agency in Nebraska with 1,100 former hostiles, including 300 warriors. They had only 117 guns.

Even the agency Indians were wary of the army. The Federal government had recently decreed that no more rations would be given to them until they agreed to surrender much of their land including the Black Hills region, even though it had been guaranteed to them in perpetuity by a treaty of 1868. They also had been given a choice of removing to the Missouri River or of going to the strange Indian Territory (Oklahoma).

Crazy Horse brooded. Rumors held that he planned to flee with his warriors. Spies were set on him. His words were distorted in translation. On 4 September a large military force and some agency chiefs started from nearby Fort Robinson to arrest him. He saw them coming and fled to the Spotted Tail Agency. Overtaken, he agreed to go to Fort Robinson. Entering a guardroom there the next day with some other chiefs, he drew a knife from his clothing. Crazy Horse was bayoneted in the stomach. He died that night in the camp hospital. Another chief, his hand on the breast of Crazy Horse, said: "It is good; he has looked for death, and it has come."

An era had died. With the suppression that same year of the Nez Percé, the last of the great Indian wars had been fought. Instead of hostile Indians streaming across the plains, grasshoppers came, across Dakota Territory, Kansas, Nebraska, south to Texas, eastward to Missouri, north into Minnesota. In 1874, and 1875, and 1876, and 1877, when the crops were half grown. The cumulative weight of hordes of grasshoppers broke the limbs from trees. They descended in clouds so dense that chickens thought the sun had set and went to roost. They ate everything: the curtains from windows, bedclothes, plow handles, the sideboards of wagons, and almost anything green. They mowed crops to the ground. Indians could be confined on reservations, but not locusts. Against them, there was no defense. People said two new grasshoppers came to the funeral of every dead one.

The Norwegian immigrant Gro Svendsen, living on a farm in north central Iowa, wrote home to the Old Country in February 1877 "This fall we got 124 bushels of wheat, 224 bushels of oats, and 11 bushels of barley. This is all the locusts left us. They took all the corn, all the potatoes, and all the vegetables we had planted."

She added: "Next month, if God wills it, I shall have another child. This will be my ninth confinement."

A hundred miles to the southwest, in Sioux County, Iowa, the inhabitants of the Dutch farming colony were at Reformed Church services in the old schoolhouse one Sunday when the grasshoppers came. In the air they looked white, and they were clustered so dense that it seemed that snow was falling. They worked such devastation that some farmers sold out and went back east, getting very little for their land. One man in disgust sold 80 acres for $225 and threw into the deal a span of mules, a wagon, and a cow, worth together at least $200. Another sold a homestead the same size and a yoke of oxen for $300; thirty years later the same land was worth some $10,000, selling at $100–145 an acre.

Even grasshopper invasions could have their uses, as when real-estate dealers made them a club to beat down the claims of other areas competing for settlers. The newspaper in Algona, Iowa, in January 1877 carried an advertisement offering to send maps and pamphlets to prospective settlers in Texas. In reply, the editor published an alleged statement by a former Iowan who had gone to Texas. He said grasshoppers were worse there than he had ever seen them in Iowa. Good water was scarce. To Texans "a free country" meant lots of whiskey and sin in general. Women in Texas used all kinds of tobacco, even snuff.

Because Algona believed in "progress" and defined progress chiefly in terms of population growth and rising real-estate values, its leading citizen was a lawyer and real-estate dealer, Asa Call. He had founded Algona in 1855, at a time when a promoter could get government land on borrowed money and sell out in less than a year at a big profit. Soon he was chosen to the county board with the title of Judge. As lawyer and real-estate man, he prospered mightily over the years. In 1876, of 44,000 acres of farmland sold around Algona, 8,000 came from his private holdings. One year he rented out 1,100 milk cows at nominal rates because he wanted to build up dairying to modify the area's current emphasis on wheat. He contributed to the founding of a college in Algona, but it failed —failed, spiteful people said, because the judge had insisted on having it in a part of town where it would increase the value of his real estate.

Asa's brother Ambrose in 1892 built the theater in Algona, and named it after himself. The word "theater" in small Midwestern towns carried with it an aroma of hellfire and brimstone; more dignity attached to the words, Call Opera House. Ambrose Call, too, prospered, as newspaper publisher, real-estate dealer, banker. When he died in 1908 he was president of the First National Bank and owned 2,000 acres of Iowa land.

While the Calls got richer, Eudora Abernethy, a fictional character in Ellen Glasgow's *Barren Ground*, saw her estate dwindle. She was the granddaughter of a retired Scotch-Irish missionary who, soon after 1800, having served his Presbyterian faith in India and Ceylon, had turned to serving himself with 50 slaves on a thousand acres of land in the Tidewater of Virginia. Eudora was his only grandchild. In earliest years she dreamed about "India's coral strand and Afric's sunny fountains." As a young woman she became engaged to an intended missionary. He left for Africa, where she was to join him. She was folding her wedding dress to go in the trunk when they brought news that he had died of fever in the Congo.

While still in mourning Eudora met Joshua Oakley, a poor white. Although he had few merits other than "the eyes of a dumb poet and the head of a youthful John the Baptist," Eudora married him. He worked like a horse; he made noises like a horse when he ate and drank. Every farmer needs a crutch, and his crutch was habit—the kind of habit a horse has. "Well, it's being set in a rut, I reckon, that keeps him going." Year after year he planted the same crops, corn and tobacco, in the same way. The value of the farm fell steadily.

Just before her first son was born, Eudora got the missionary call again. Once more she dreamed at night of "coral strands and palm trees and ancient rivers and naked black babies thrown to the crocodiles." Even after her daughter Dorinda was born, about 1877, Eudora would go for weeks on end in a sort of trance. To keep other folks around Pedlar's Mill from saying she was unhinged, she found an escape.

Work. She worked endlessly, incessantly. It was a disease. She flurried from one task to the next. Exhausted at last, she would lie in her bed through the night, sleepless, her nerves twitching. And for all her labors she had little to show, and the broomsedge crept over her grandfather's land. Almost beautiful as a young woman, Eudora became lean and angular, a haunted stare in her pale eyes, frequent jerks beneath her pale face.

It was a life to age a woman fast. Pedlar's Mill, Virginia, was almost wilderness in 1877, its roads in winter no better than frozen bogs. No place to go anyway. Pedlar's Mill had only the mill where the farmers got their corn ground; the nearest store was way off: at the Court House, and the winter supplies were bought there when you sold your tobacco crop. Just buying coffee and sugar and clothes took all the tobacco money, but to get any coffee and sugar and clothes at all, you had to raise tobacco, year after year.

For days Eudora would get no sign from the outside world, not even an occasional Negro passing along the road. So she worked to keep from losing her mind. She also retreated often into the "kingdom of the spirit." She never stopped liking sermons about the Holy Land and distant places. One of her favorite hymns ran:

> Rescue the perishing, care for the dying,
> Jesus is merciful, Jesus will save.

Her daughter Dorinda felt differently. When as a young woman she rebelled against the monotony of their life, Eudora told her, "There ain't but one thing that keeps you going and keeps a farm going, and that is religion."

"I want to be happy," Dorinda protested.

Her mother replied, "You're too young yet. Your great-grandfather used to say that most people never came to God as long as there was anywhere else for them to go."

The farming areas around Indianapolis were described in early 1879 by the Reverend Myron W. Reed as "missionary ground." He traveled a good deal, sometimes lecturing, sometimes quail shooting; invariably he felt poisoned before he returned home. He thought the diet in Indiana of pork and hot biscuit was sufficient reason for the state's "general democracy and cussedness." Farm wives were "not much better off than slaves," he reported. "It is a weary monotonous round of cooking and washing and mending and as a result the insane asylum is 1/3d filled with wives of farmers."

Reed was canny as well as compassionate. When members of the congregation of a Chicago church were trying to maneuver him into the pulpit there, they asked if he would come preach for them a Sunday or two on a trial basis. "No," he answered, "because of the gossip it would make here." When a friend inquired as to the relative merits of Harvard and the University of Michigan, he replied, "there is a good deal in a name, otherwise Ann Arbor is as good."

* * *

The administration of President Rutherford B. Hayes began on a bitter note for Henry Adams and his circle. Seeking a return from the Liberal Republican debacle of 1872, they had hoped to run a civil-service reformer for President as candidate of an Independent Party. But when the Republicans nominated Hayes, even the eminent Carl Schurz announced that he would support the ticket. The reformers were left high and dry.

This disappointment did not spoil the sardonic pleasure that Mrs. Henry Adams found in Washington society from 1877 to 1881. Henry Adams resigned his post in the history department at Harvard in 1877 and moved to Washington. There his wife Marian organized a busy social life that frequently included President Hayes and Secretary of the Interior Schurz. As befitted a descendant of generations of Massachusetts aristocrats, Marian Adams commented on the Washington scene in well-turned phrases. She also reported gossip: for instance, that the daughter of Secretary of State Blaine referred to the President's family and their associates as "that nasty Hayes set."

One evening, Mr. and Mrs. Adams had dinner at the White House. Marian was both horrified and amused at the new dinner set there—said to have cost $15,000. She found it "intimidating" to eat her soup from a plate whereon one saw "a coyote springing at you from a pine tree," and it seemed *outré* to have ice cream from a dish shaped like an Indian snowshoe.

Such vulgarity would never have been tolerated in the sparsely populated high society of New York. Here the major concerns were to do what "Taste" or "Form" required, to do whatever was "the thing" to do. Whether a given occasion did or did not call for a black tie with evening clothes, whether a man should wear patent-leather Oxfords or pumps—these were grave questions. And the young man Newland Archer, the unheroic hero in Edith Wharton's *The Age of Innocence*, thought them so. He could not imagine brushing his hair except with two silver-backed brushes carrying his initials in blue enamel; he could not appear in society without a flower, usually a gardenia, in his buttonhole. When he attended the opera and heard *Faust,* it seemed indisputable to him that "an unalterable and unquestioned law of the musical world required that the German text of French operas sung by Swedish artists should be translated into Italian for the clearer understanding of English-speaking audiences."

Archer went to formal dinners in private mansions. Equipped with formal visiting cards, he paid social calls on the few other "properly accredited" persons. After dinner he might smoke a cigar in the Gothic library of his home—the only room in the house where his mother permitted smoking. Occasionally he might read something.

Only the charms of Madame Olenska ever tempted Archer to rebel against the code. The cousin of Archer's wife, she had been brought up in Europe, where she had married a count. When she fled from his tyrannies, she was disgraced forever. Nonetheless, Archer wanted to desert his wife and run away with her. Unfortunately, he had earlier persuaded her that "one must sacrifice one's self to preserve the dignity of marriage—and to spare one's family the publicity, the scandal." So she refused to accede to his plan.

In this society it was no necessary cause of proscription for a man to have a mistress, or several, if he did it quietly. But bankruptcy in business called for instant and final banishment.

Such lives of comfortable futility would have seemed foolish if not sinful to men like Joseph Metcalf, treasurer and executive head of the Farr Alpaca Company of Holyoke, Massachusetts. But Metcalf's gaze was fixed elsewhere. In his annual report to the shareholders in 1878 he emphasized that the falling level of prices posed serious problems. The smooth lustrous cloth made by his firm was woven with a cotton warp, but the alpaca for the weft came only from Peru and the adjoining Andes. It had to be bought a year in advance, and the company had to carry a large inventory of raw materials and goods in process. The value of the inventory fell week by week as the general price level declined; a class of wool valued at 73¢ in 1875 was worth only 42¢ three years later. Thus the company bought each lot of raw materials at a price that was high relative to the price at which it sold the goods made from that lot of raw materials.

To make matters worse, the Democrats in Congress were always trying to reduce the import duties on woolens, which would open the gates to competing goods from England. It had been the tariff that had prompted Metcalf's own firm to migrate to the United States in 1873. Located at the time in Canada, the company calculated that its manufacturing costs would be some 10 per cent higher in the United States. But the principal market for their alpacas was in this country, and the Wool and Woolens Act of 1867 had fixed an effective duty on woolen imports of more than 60 per cent. The arithmetic left no choice, and the company crossed the border to relocate at Holyoke.

With it from Canada, or from England, came half of the original labor force of 200, including skilled workers and all of the overseers in the mill. The treasurer continued to suffer because he could not "get help that was accustomed to our work." The shortage of skilled workers aggravated another difficulty—the firm's shortage of capital. Even with an initial capital of $250,000, the company was forced to borrow heavily for working capital to finance full-scale operation, and had no desire to follow what had been the local custom and build tenements for its workers. But when some of the overseers asked the company to build houses for them, Metcalf felt he had to comply.

Some problems were mitigated after Metcalf switched his selling agent in 1876. Besides making large cash advances to the Farr Company, the new selling agent gave astute forecasts about changes in the market. Orders reaching Metcalf's firm were greater than its plant capacity for nearly every year in the 1870's. He saw to it that his plant contained flexible machinery that could be diverted from one line of goods to another as the market shifted. In 1877 the company was making serge linings for coats, worsted coatings for men, cashmeres, mohairs.

Net earnings that year were $44,871, but the firm paid only a 7 per cent dividend and kept $27,000 as undistributed surplus. Metcalf's conservatism also showed in his practice of charging capital expenditures to current operating expenses, so that the firm's net worth was often far larger than its books showed. By 1900 the net worth was more than $1,000,000—on which net earnings for the year were $573,000.

Long before the century ended, the woolen firms had learned that they could not expect to get cheap imports of raw materials if they wanted to keep import duties high on finished goods. Their representatives in Congress needed the support of Congressmen from sheep-raising areas, and vice versa. The result of such mutual back-scratching in the nation's Capital was to maintain or raise import duties on both raw wool and woolen goods, not to mention pig iron, sugar, and thousands of other items.

*   *   *

For three decades the falling price level prompted repeated revolts by farmers and other debtors. The tariff too was a recurrent issue. A new tariff law was more important to Congress in 1890 than was the Federal Elections Bill to protect Negro voters. During the Pullman boycott, President Cleveland was occupied with the tariff. During the furor over Cuba in 1897, President McKinley was occupied with the tariff.

*   *   *

The squatter Plesent raised not sheep but goats. One of the first settlers in the beautiful Santa Ana Mountains of southern California, he introduced the culture of angora goats. Their wool—long and straight and silken, silver or light gold in color—was far more valuable than sheep's wool. Grazing was cheap: at daybreak the bearded buck led his herd from the corral, at night he led it back to the corral. Labor was cheap: the herd was in the care of the Indian, Ramon, still hearty at 70. He played a one-string harp called a *chiote* and sang sad songs.

> The rain refreshed the air for you
> The breezes cooled you
> Mosquitoes did not trouble you
> The fig tree lowered its fruitful branches to you
> Flowers bloomed where'er you stepped
> I loved you, oh, how I loved you
> And yet you have forsaken me

Plesent's worst problem was to protect his herd at night from mountain lions and lynxes. Even a watchdog tied in the corral did not help. Plesent went to Los Angeles and paid $75 in hard cash for an old buck, only to have a mountain lion kill his buck and twelve kids in a single slaughter.

Plesent kept bees in vast number, and used the honey to sweeten his boiled Japan tea. He hunted bear and antelope, and ate their flesh along with kidney beans and fried salt pork. Not yet 40

years old, he lorded it over the Mexicans of the area, partly because of his wealth in bees and goats, even more because of his
Mexican wife whose wisdom was so great she was regarded as an
oracle. Her family had once been wealthy, with vast estates along
the coast, but "more clever, ingenious, and industrious Americans"
now owned what had been Mexican.

The Polish journalist Henry Sienkiewicz lived nearby for
several months, in the coastal area around Anaheim. He heard
from the residents that a certain "Brown or Harrison or Down"
was "extremely poor." Seeking to find out what that meant, he
visited the person in question. He found him living in a comfortable
house with several rooms. One room was fully carpeted, as was
the custom in America, and all were well furnished. The man had
a cow, a horse or two, fields of corn and barley, stands of timber
and fruit trees. He ate meat three times a day and drank wine with
his meals. "Why, then, is he considered poor? Simply because he
does not have on hand a hundred dollars in cash!" Sienkiewicz,
acquainted with Polish poverty, was amused.

But California in 1880 had a per capita wealth of $1,653—the
highest of any state. The squatter Plesent could be glad he had
migrated from his native Louisiana soon after the Civil War.

Shreveport, Louisiana, had its own Henry Adams. He was born
in 1841, the same year as Joseph Metcalf. Metcalf was an Englishman who migrated to Canada as a young boy and was treasurer
of the Great Western Railway by 1867. In 1867, Henry Adams
was barely out of slavery, and was serving in the United States
army. Back in Shreveport in late 1869, after his discharge, he and
others organized a secret colonization society and set themselves
the task of learning how Negroes were making out in various parts
of the South and what would be the best places for Negroes to
settle. Their findings were disheartening: exploitation, poverty, oppression, murders.

In 1874 Negro churches in Shreveport and surrounding Caddo
Parish were not allowed to meet after 9 P.M. Negroes had been
killed in Caddo Parish. Adams and his associates in September
sent petitions for relief to President Grant and to Congress. The
answer was more than two years coming, and then the answer
they got was not the answer they had hoped for. Federal troops
were withdrawn from Louisiana, from all the South. Said Adams,
if the Democrats thought the other party might carry an election

district, "nothing I can make mention of is too mean for them to do."

"In 1877," he said, "we lost all hopes. . . . We said that the whole South—every State in the South had got into the hands of the very men that held us slaves— . . . even the constable up to the governor." They appealed to President Hayes and to both Houses of Congress. No answer. Henry Adams became a leader of a mass exodus that began in January and February 1879. Some 30,000 Negroes, chiefly from Louisiana, fled the South in a few months. Most headed for Kansas.

Negroes were not the only victims of violence in the South. In Mississippi too, after the Radical Reconstruction government was utterly vanquished in 1875, any dissent from the Democratic party was viewed as a threat to white rule. But Judge W. W. Chisholm of Kemper County took his personal animosities to heart. His sworn enemies the Gullys were Democrats, so Judge Chisholm was first a Republican, then an Independent. In the spring of 1877 John Gully was murdered from ambush. A Negro confessed. Chisholm, suspected of conspiring with the Negro, was locked up in the county jail. He feared for the safety of his family, and they were allowed to join him in the jail.

One Sunday at daybreak a mob of at least 100 men appeared with the demand that Chisholm be surrendered to them. The jailer and his deputy fled. With guns from the jail arsenal, Chisholm and two friends shot several of the attackers. The siege force set fire to the jail. As the Chisholm group fled the burning building, the mob shot him down. Also his son, 14 years old, his daughter, 15 years old, and a friend.

Many Southerners regarded such political and personal feuds as puerile. The thing to do, they thought, was to make money. Favored devices for insuring that a large part of what money was made would find its way into a few pockets were sharecropping and the store that gave credit to sharecroppers. The cotton plantation of Dr. Capeheart on Albemarle Sound, North Carolina, used both techniques. Already having thousands of acres, in a single year he added $52,000 worth of land—more than 2,000 acres at $25 an acre. It was divided into 50-acre farms worked by sharecroppers. As rent they paid a third of the crop; if Capeheart supplied the horses and mules, half the crop. Each tenant was required to plant 15 acres in cotton, 12 in corn, 8 in "small crops," and let 15 lie in grass. Tenants were entitled to the surplus herring from the fisheries that were part of the estate. Henry W. Grady, editor of the Atlanta *Constitution,* reported that the tenants were "universally prosperous, and in some cases, where by skill and industry they have secured 100 acres, are laying up money."

A general store at the center of the estate gave credit to tenants, of course charging them considerably more than the cash price. Capeheart's profits were large. He expected to realize rents of $9 annually for every acre that was cultivated. In 5 years at most, the rents would bring back the $52,000 spent in the preceding year for land.

A different picture—poverty, drift—was presented by the town of Milledgeville in central Georgia, where 13-year-old William G. McAdoo lived in 1877. The state capital had recently removed to Atlanta, and the only public institutions left in Milledgeville were the state penitentiary and an insane asylum. The town was aimless, sluggish, still feeling the effects of the Civil War. Its dusty streets held many idlers, whittling sticks, pitching horseshoes, mulling over past glories. The steps of the derelict Capitol were littered with trash. Many of its windows were broken.

Neither McAdoo nor his friends, passionate as they were about baseball, had the money to buy a regular ball. They made their own. A stone in the center, with strips of cloth and rubber wound around it. They made a cover of leather, wet it, and sewed it on. When they heard that a man up North named Vanderbilt had made a big fortune in railroads, McAdoo wrote the Commodore a letter asking to borrow a dollar to buy a baseball. The request was not answered.

McAdoo made 50 cents a week delivering the Augusta *Chronicle and Constitutionalist* to the five subscribers in Milledegeville. Nearly a continent away, a younger boy was doing much better in a financial way. In the summer of 1877 Sam Aaron arrived with his family in Butte, Montana, where it seemed to many men that the ground might be made of silver and copper. Of the 2,500 inhabitants, 90 per cent were miners. Sam saw his chance and grasped it. He bought boxes of apples, shipped in by stage from Salt Lake City. They were tiny things, about the size of crab apples. A box held about 150 apples, and Sam paid $8 a box. After school he peddled the apples to the scurrying miners, two apples for a quarter. Some afternoons he sold as high as two boxes. Cost to him, $16. Receipts, $37.50. Net profit per day, $21.50. Sam Aaron, age 11, was riding high.

So was John D. Rockefeller, age 37. His Standard Oil Company had gained control of nearly all the oil-refining capacity in Cleveland, Ohio. It had absorbed its strongest competitors in Philadelphia, Pittsburgh, New York, and in the Oil Regions of Pennsylvania. It had begun to build up its own sales force to market its illuminating oil, instead of selling to independent jobbers. Now, in the year 1877, it was to score its greatest triumph. Its opponent was a worthy one, the Pennsylvania Railroad, the world's biggest carrier of freight, paying dividends at the time of some $25 million a year.

The Pennsy was intimately tied to the Empire Transportation Company, in which the controlling block of stock was held by Pennsy executives. Empire operated pipelines that carried crude oil from the wells in the Oil Regions to the neighboring railroads. It also owned 5,000 railroad cars, including 1,500 oil tankers. The head of Empire feared that if Standard Oil came to monopolize refining capacity, as it almost did already, it could impose its own terms on the other two chief parts of the petroleum business: oil producing, and oil transportation. To counter this threat, Empire and the Pennsy agreed in January 1877 that Empire would expand its role in the refining of oil. They had misgauged their man.

With his little mouth, the upper lip covered with a droopy mustache, John D. Rockefeller looked almost prim, and he was a Baptist deacon. But in his business behavior he was neither prim nor pious. He and an associate demanded of Pennsy president Tom Scott that he should stick to railroading. When Scott did not comply, Standard Oil struck back hard: it was out to control and organize the oil refining industry, and would not willingly accept competition from such a corporate giant as the Pennsylvania Railroad. Of all oil shipments over the Pennsy, 65 per cent came from Standard, and they were now shipped east over the other three trunklines. Standard cut prices in any market that Empire could reach. Rockefeller bought crude oil for whatever he had to pay. The Erie Railroad and the New York Central, allied with Rockefeller, cut their charges on oil shipments in order to capture the shipments of the remaining independent oil men. The Pennsy cut its rates. Its competitors retaliated. Rates tumbled. In a contract with one shipper in April 1877, the Pennsy agreed in effect to pay 8 cents a barrel for the privilege of carrying his oil. Even so, its share of eastbound oil freight fell from 52 per cent to 30 per cent of the total.

To Tom Scott and the Pennsy, the fight became too expensive. On September 17, they agreed to dissolve the Empire Transportation Company, with Standard buying all its assets except the rolling stock. Those would go to the Pennsy, paid for with money loaned to it by Standard Oil. And all payments to the Empire were to be made in cash. Rockefeller later testified that all the money was raised in New York or in Cleveland. He was in Cleveland, and mid-October found him whirling from one bank to another in his old buggy. He asked at each for its president and urged upon the astonished man: "I must have all you've got! I need it all! It's all right! Give me what you have!"

The negotiations were closed in the little St. George Hotel in Philadelphia. Tom Scott walked in, late, a big soft hat crowning his white hair and clean-shaven face. He smiled, and said, "Well, boys, what will we do?" What they did was this: Standard Oil paid $3,400,000, and loaned the Pennsy another $600,000. Four millon dollars in cash. Standard acquired virtually all of the pipelines in the Oil Region, so that it dominated the routes from the wells to the railroads. It was assured almost total control of refining. The deal also brought some directly profitable properties. One subsidiary, bought for $501,652, had net profits in excess of the purchase price in the next 27 months.

Why had the Pennsy yielded? The depression since 1873, rate wars against its competitors, large bonded debt, high dividends on watered stock—these had left all the railroads suffering financial strain. By the end of July 1877, the price of Pennsy stock had dropped to 27¾—off 20 points since the first of the year. And in mid-July came the violent railroad strikes, set off when all four trunklines cut their wage scales 10 per cent. By July 24 mass rioting, arson, and pillage cost the Pennsy at least $2 million in property damage. Thus did thousands of unruly strikers help to establish a virtual monopoly in oil refining. If Rockefeller ever thanked them, history does not record the fact.

The railroad strikes also influenced a young delegate to the national convention of the Brotherhood of Locomotive Firemen. He was horrified by them, and exhorted his fellow delegates:

> The question has often been asked, Does the brotherhood encourage strikers? To this question we must emphatically answer, No, brothers. To disregard the laws which govern our land? To destroy the last vestige of order? To stain our hands with the crimson blood of our fellow beings? We again say, No, a thousand times No!

This was Eugene V. Debs, who had been a railroader from the time he was 14 until he was 18. Now 21, he was a billing clerk in a wholesale grocery firm in Terre Haute, Indiana. But the Brotherhood of Locomotive Firemen was so weak that the fledgeling ex-railroader was secretary of its local lodge there. In 1880 he was national secretary-treasurer of the union and editor of its magazine. The events of the next two decades beat at him without remorse. By 1900 he was the country's foremost agitator for a sweeping reorganization of American society.

By 1900 Thomas Eakins of Philadelphia was the country's foremost painter, but few knew it. In 1876 he began teaching anatomy, without pay, at the Pennsylvania Academy of Fine Arts. There he tried to impart his conviction that art combines honesty with a capacity for taking infinite pains. Many of his practices with students—immediate drawing with a brush (Nature contains no lines, he insisted, "only form and color"), lack of prolonged study of classical busts, use of live models—were unique or almost so among American art schools of the time. A visiting art critic was stunned to learn that Eakins took his advanced classes to a bone-boiling establishment in suburban Philadelphia to dissect horses. When asked if students did not protest at such repugnant work, Eakins answered, "I don't know of one who doesn't dislike it. Every fall, for my own part, I feel great reluctance to begin it. It is dirty enough work at the best. . . ." But he defended the practice: ". . . no one dissects to increase his eye for, or his delight in, beauty. He dissects simply to increase his knowledge of how beautiful objects are put together to the end that he may be able to imitate them." "Distortion," he insisted, "is ugliness."

At a lecture on the structure of the leg, the critic scoffed, "Do you imagine that the pupil will be able to draw a leg better for knowing all that?"

Eakins replied, "Knowing all that will enable him to observe more closely, and the closer his observation the better his drawing will be."

After describing the course in artistic anatomy, which included some 30 lecture-demonstrations, the critic inquired of his readers, "It quite takes one's breath away, does it not? . . . Must a painter know all this, one asks himself in a kind of awe-struck bewilderment."

In 1877 Eakins finished a major work "William Rush Carving His Allegorical Figure of the Schuylkill River." The central figure was a nude female model on a dais. Nine years later, in demonstrating to a class the action of the human pelvis, he asked a male model to remove his loincloth. Some women students objected. The ensuing scandal persuaded Eakins that he should resign his position, and he did. In 1886, as in 1877, ruling values in the United States placed prudery above art, and money above either.

CHAPTER 2

Making Money

"Get money—honestly if you can, but at any rate get money! This is the lesson that society is daily and hourly dinning into the ears of its members," wrote Henry George in *Progress and Poverty*. Doubtless men tend to think always that an earlier time was a happier time, a more innocent time. But the universality of this apprehension does not prove that it is never true. The Mark Twain who wrote *The Adventures of Huckleberry Finn* was certainly aware of the human evil in the United States before the Civil War. But he recalled that nobody in his youth had worshiped money and that none of the well-to-do men of the neighborhood had been accused of getting rich "by shady methods." Twain, along with other observers so diverse that they would have agreed about little else—Henry Adams, Willa Cather, William Dean Howells, Edith Wharton, Walt Whitman—thought that the acquisitive spirit increasingly held dominion. Not only was the desire to make money checked by fewer other values, but men were able to make vastly more money by exploiting new products and new techniques.

By 1883, five million pounds of Bull Durham smoking tobacco were being sold, and president Julian S. Carr was spending $300,000 a year slapping posters of his famous bull on Egyptian pyramids and elsewhere. The motto of the firm was: "Let buffalo gore buffalo, and the pasture go to the strongest." Less than two decades later, Carr's firm had been swallowed up by the American Tobacco Company of James Buchanan Duke. Buck Duke, a great admirer of John D. Rockefeller, analyzed as follows the policies that had guided his hero to virtual monopoly: "First, you hit your enemies in the pocketbook, hit 'em hard. Then you either buy 'em out or take 'em in with you."

Milton H. Smith, for 38 years the president of the Louisville and Nashville Railroad, said that "society, as created, was for the purpose of one man's getting what the other fellow has, if he can, and keep out of the penitenitary." No personal feeling or humanitarian consideration should be allowed to interfere with the duty of making a profit. Labor relations were not important to the top executives of railroads until the great strikes of 1877 forced such problems on their attention.

State interference was regarded as unjust discrimination. President Charles E. Perkins of the Burlington, disgusted by Iowa regulations, wrote to one of its railroad commissioners in 1885: "Iowa people can make more money in farms and other industries than rrs [railroads]. If this were not true, farmers and merchants and manufacturers and newspapermen, who now put their money into cattle and hogs, manufacturing establishments and business generally would instead invest it in railroads. But they can do better, and it is only the Eastern capitalist, who cannot use his money to advantage at home who is willing to risk it in western railroads and take the low average return which he gets, a return very much lower than the average of other investments in this state."

Even movements to end political corruption in a town were motivated by a belief that a reputation for good government would increase the value of local real estate. To make a town better meant to make it more prosperous, and the essence of the program lay in the hope: "The more prosperous my beloved city, the more prosperous Beloved I!" A town eager to have its own college might want a rise in real-estate prices rather than a rise in civilization locally. Students too were pushed chiefly by commercial considerations. County teacher institutes in the Midwest, inexpensive though they were, were seldom attended for reasons of idle curiosity. An institute usually ran for two weeks or a month in July and August, so as to precede the exams for renewal of rural teaching certificates.

From the Southern Methodist Publishing House in 1885 came William S. Speer's *The Law of Success*. It instructed readers on how to pick wives who would help them get ahead. It stressed "the commercial value of the Ten Commandments and a righteous life." The author, himself an educator, theorized: "The educator of the future will teach his pupils what will pay best. He will teach them the art of thinking, which, for the purpose at hand, I may define to be the art of turning one's brains into money."

A master of this art was Joseph Cook, graduate of Harvard and of Andover Theological Seminary. He was started on the road to fame as a public lecturer when the YMCA in Boston asked him to conduct noon-hour prayer meetings for the benefit of clergymen. In 1876 these became the Boston Monday Noon-Hour Lectures. Cook was a prominent if ignorant participant in the swelling debate about the relations of theology and evolution. The flavor surrounding his ecclesiastical and educational activities can be gleaned from letters written him by his father, William H. Cook, an aging but still diligent farmer in the Lake George region of New York. On 15 Janury 1877: "I like the ring of your last Letter. No more Lectures Short of fifty Dollars. It ought to of been Seventy five dollars, or one hundred occasionally. I dont want you to become a misor or Seek after money. The time is comeing that you will want means to do good. I do not forget for a moment the worth of Souls. . . ." Two months later: "If half the Press Says about you is tru you ought to have Ten thousand for your next year. Say Eight for the Noon lectures, and Two for outside labours. Anything less than this I shall not be Satisfide with. . . . Take care of your means, keep your Surplus on interest and go right Straight ahead. . . ."

It was assumed that a clergyman, so far from being the lifelong shepherd of any specific flock, would harken to the call of a more affluent congregation and a larger salary. The Reverend Jacob van der Meulen joined the Dutch farming colony in Campbell County, South Dakota, in 1889, as pastor of the Reformed Church; only 14 months later he retreated from frontier hardships to a church at Baldwin, Wisconsin. The instability arising from American attitudes contrasts sharply with the example of the Swiss colony at New Glarus, Wisconsin, where in 1884 both the minister and the schoolteacher had held their positions for 18 years. And what of Gallatin, Missouri, which in that year had 6 churches but only 1,250 people? Doctrinal differences were doubtless involved in such splintering, but so was more than one theological imperialist who set out to capture his share of the market.

"Main Street's poor record in the arts," writes Lewis Atherton, "contrasted sharply with its encouragement of some professions. Banking was the outstanding example." It was fitting that so many banks had classic columns and pediments, like temples—the shrine where Americans came to worship.

Those who, in the 16 years after 1877, visited their banks often and deposited large sums were likely to be men who grasped one or more of three crucial developments of the time. The first was the national market, particularly in the growing cities, created by the expanding railroad network. The second was the coordinated nationwide sales force, made possible by railroad, telegraph, and then telephone, often making heavy use of advertising. The third was the augmented power of Federal and state governments, which could be bent to private commercial uses.

The railroad revolutionized farming in Bell County, Texas, some 115 miles northwest of Houston. In 1879, farmers there grew all their own breadstuffs, including 84,267 bushels of wheat, which they took to numerous small local mills for conversion into flour. They grew feed for the stock that did not graze on the open range. They grew little cotton, only 9,217 bales in 1879, for it cost too much to haul cotton by wagon to Gulf ports. But the first patent for the manufacture of barbed wire had been issued in 1875, and it was becoming much cheaper to fence a field to keep livestock out. And, after 1880, railroads entered Bell County. They brought flour of higher purity and reliable quality, ground by mass-production methods in the Minnesota mills of Charles A. Pillsbury or Cadwallader C. Washburn from grain grown in the burgeoning wheat belt on the Western Great Plains, from Kansas or Dakota. By 1889 Bell County was producing only 20,936 bushels of wheat, a decline of 75 per cent in a decade. Cotton, now shipped to market or to the Gulf ports by rail, had become the cash crop. The county's output was 37,473 bales in 1889, four times what it had been a decade earlier. Improved acreage in the county in 1889 was 13 times as great as in 1869. As a greater area was brought under cultivation, more machinery was likely to be necessary. This machinery was often bought on credit, and the farmer relied on the proceeds of his cotton crop to pay his debts. He counted on it too to buy his flour, and Rio coffee, and occasional cans of Columbia River salmon or Boston baked beans, and store-bought pants.

Most of the cotton and flour and other agricultural products flowed into the maw of Northern cities. Chicago, growing from 503,000 in 1880 to 1,100,000 in 1890, was only one dramatic instance of the swelling mass market provided by the cities. In the same decade, the number of people in places of at least 2,500 population went from 14 million to 22 million, of whom nearly 10 million lived in cities with more than 100,000 inhabitants. Mean-

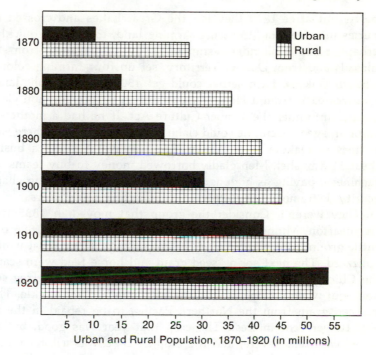

Urban and Rural Population, 1870–1920 (in millions)

while the rural population, although nearly twice as great as the urban population in 1890, went from 36 million to only 41 million.

And yet, some of the growth in rural population was due to migration from the cities. This happened especially during depression years, such as 1876, when immigrant workers might dream of starting a farming town and returning to the peasant existence most of them had lived in the Old Country. Some dreams came true. Catholic priests serving the 20,000 Poles in Chicago started the colony of New Posen, Nebraska. Intending to move there themselves, they negotiated well for the land. Such little towns, with their own churches and parochial schools, resembled towns in Poland. Farmers planted potatoes and sowed wheat as they had done in Poland. A peasant on the Nebraska prairie might weep as he struck his scythe on the whetstone, reminded by the sound of his native village.

But for the most part the frontier was settled by farmers from farther east, whether originally from New York State or from Europe. Hollanders had crossed the ocean in 1847 to find religious liberty, but after 1879 they left the Great Lakes and crossed the prairies into Dakota "to secure farming land, to get rich quickly." Perhaps 5,000 Hollanders, stimulated by propaganda from the railroads and from Dakota Territory, set up four farming colonies in South Dakota. Each settler could get 480 acres of public lands: 160 acres each from a Homestead Act entry, a pre-emption claim, and a claim under the Timber Culture Act. If he had a mother-in-law or an aged parent, he could claim another 480 acres. There were no trees in Dakota to cut down, flax was worth $1.50 a bushel, wheat $1 a bushel. Men gladly borrowed money to buy teams and machinery, paying as high as 60 per cent interest a year on chattel security. Why not? They expected to be rich in a few years.

They weren't. Consider the group that moved in 1885 from Greenleafton, Minnesota, to northern South Dakota. In 1886 only a little ground was planted, and the crop was just fair. That winter, a blizzard. The next spring seed grain and horse feed were scarce. The Chicago, Milwaukee & St. Paul Railroad promised free seed grain, but when it came, it was foul with mustard and cockle. They got seed grain from the Northern Pacific, to be repaid in the fall with 10 per cent interest. The crop that year was good, but the winter was very severe, and the crop in 1888 was a total failure. Many people had to apply to friends back east for help. The next three years the crops were partial failures. In 1892, as threshing was going on, lightning set fire to the prairie, and a swath 12 miles wide was burned out—grain, buildings, stock, machinery. Everybody suffered, and some were left destitute. Again they got help from back east. The next year crops were fair, but prices were so low that the farmer made little or nothing after he counted the cost of hauling the crop 40 miles to market. In 1894 the same story: fair crops, low prices. But the smarter men began to catch on. They learned that dent corn would not ripen in Dakota, but flint corn or squaw corn would yield up to 40 bushels an acre. They fattened hogs on the corn, and began shipping them to Eastern markets. They also turned to raising beeves. The next two winters were mild, so that stock could subsist on the open range, and cattle prices were rising in 1895 and 1896. The Hollanders learned that selling milk to creameries and raising cattle, sheep, and hogs were more profitable than growing wheat and other small grains. It had taken 12 years —plus luck and substantial amounts of aid from back east—to find out how to make money farming the plains in Dakota. Many men had been wiped out and crushed before they had time to learn how to get ahead.

Gustavus Swift learned quicker, in large measure, because he saw the transformation that the railroads were working. Unlike the automobile, which tends to erode cities because it can be used to link together an infinite number of points, the railroads tend to concentrate population in a few places. No matter how many stations are strung along its route, no matter how many branches are built, the railroad works to depopulate the countryside and to build up swelling cities. Swift, a native of Massachusetts, saw the growing market for food in the cities of the East. He also knew that the settlement of the plains would mean a constantly growing supply of meat. Meat could be cured in the West—salted or smoked or canned—then shipped eastward. But such was the demand for meat that beeves were commonly shipped on the hoof. This procedure had grave disadvantages: Cattle lost weight and died en route, had to be fed and watered, nearly 60 per cent of their weight was inedible. Further, if butchering could be concentrated in Chicago, great economies of scale could be gained.

Swift went to Chicago, where Philip D. Armour and others had preceded him in meat packing. He first shipped dressed beef eastward in 1877 over the Grand Trunk using open boxcars, with the carcasses hanging from the ceiling. The next year, with an engineer, he developed an insulated refrigerator car. The cooling agent was ice from the Great Lakes. Railroads, with investments in facilities for shipping live cattle, refused to provide these specialized cars. Swift had to pay for them himself. Now the shippers of live beeves demanded that the railroads juggle their rates to permit them to remain competitive in seaboard markets. The railroads agreed on a principle of "neutrality." But the Grand Trunk, handicapped by a longer route than other railroads, refused to go along; it gave to dressed beef a lower rate. The Trunkline Association in 1884 set a standard Chicago to New York rate: 40 cents a hundredweight for livestock, 75 cents for dressed beef. But every rate agreement was followed by rate wars, and this was no exception.

The decade after 1880 saw Swift's essential effort—the creation of a nationwide sales force built around a network of branches, each with its own storage plant and marketing organization. Having created this network, Swift had to make use of his sales force, so he abandoned his exclusive concern with beef and instituted a "full line" policy: beef, lamb, mutton, pork, and, later, poultry, eggs, and dairy products. To break down consumer bias against eating meat that had been slaughtered weeks earlier and half a continent away, Swift turned to advertising. His firm grew rapidly, and the marketing network needed more goods to sell. He set up new packing-houses in Kansas City, Omaha, and St. Louis. By 1893 he had built a giant company based on vertical integration: handling the product at every stage from raw material to the final sale to the retailer. The chief departments—purchasing of livestock, killing and dressing it, sales, and accounting—were all held tightly in the fist of the main office in Chicago. Swift was the archetype of the age, a systematizer, an organizer, a man who left nothing to chance.

A few men made fortunes by the opposite tactics, by being lone wolves and gamblers. Such a man was Ed Schieffelin, a wanderer and prospector from boyhood. On April Fool's Day in 1877 he reached the Huachuca Mountains in southern Arizona, and he spent the summer canvassing the hills along the San Pedro River. He found the Tombstone claim and the Graveyard claim, but the ore samples he carried back to Tucson did not impress anybody there. The next winter Schieffelin was back on the San Pedro with his brother and a mining engineer named Richard Gird. Staked by the governor of Arizona and by a Tucson gunsmith, the three men found silver ore that assayed as high as $9,000 a ton. They located the Tough Nut Mine, the Lucky Cuss, the Contention, and others. Their backers got two brothers named Corbin, way off in New Britain, Connecticut, to put up $80,000 to build a ten-stamp quartz mill, in exchange for a 12½ per cent interest in the claims. The mill began operation in June 1879, and for the next 27 months the company paid dividends of $50,000 a month.

Long before that period ended, Ed Schieffelin had sold out; he was a prospector, not a mine operator. He and his brother got $600,000 for their half share in the mill and in the Tough Nut Mine. Among the buyers was a Philadelphian named Disston, who had inherited a big saw factory from his father and who was engaged in giant operations in Florida real estate as well as in Arizona silver mines.

Another silver mine was the Anaconda, up in the Butte district of Montana, and Marcus H. Daly took charge of it in 1882 for a syndicate consisting of himself and three other men. (One was George Hearst, whose mining fortune would be diverted by his son William Randolph to newspaper publishing.) In that silver mine, Daly hit the richest vein of copper sulphide yet found, 50 to 100 feet wide, assaying in places 55 per cent copper.

The discovery was perfectly timed. Since the Crime of '73, the Act of Congress that stopped coinage of the standard silver dollar, the market for silver at the U. S. mints had contracted. But a whole congeries of industries based on electricity would form a swelling market for copper. Telegraph wires were following the railroads everywhere. In 1876 Alexander Graham Bell had first transmitted speech through a copper wire; in 1880 Thomas Alva Edison had patented the incandescent light; in 1882 the first electric generating plant to light the streets of New York was opened. Meanwhile copper production in Great Britain, 16,000 tons in 1860, was 3,800 tons in 1881; Chile's output was also declining; production of the United States in 1882 was only 44,000 tons.

Butte in 1882 had no railroad, and proper facilities to reduce the ore did not exist anywhere in this country. Daly shipped the ore by ox team to Corinne, Utah, thence by rail to Atlantic ports, and by ship to Swansea, Wales. Five years later the Great Northern reached Butte, and thereafter it hauled ore to the smelter and refinery at Great Falls, and copper to the Midwest.

The copper and silver mine became the basis of an empire. Daly bought coal lands and coal mines. He bought forests in northwestern Montana to provide timbering for the mines. He set up the Blackfoot Land & Development Company to settle farmers on the land that was logged out. In 1891 the Anaconda syndicate bought the Butte City Water Company from another big mine operator and future United States Senator, William A. Clark. The next year Anaconda produced 100 million pounds of copper, more than twenty times what the whole country had produced a decade earlier.

With his firm the world's biggest copper company, Daly undertook to provide a comfortable home for himself in Butte. He built the Montana Hotel, equipped it lavishly, kept it fully staffed. Often he was the only guest, and ate alone in a dining room that sometimes accommodated 500 guests at a banquet. It was the Dalys and the Clarks and men like them who financed and tried to manipulate two political parties, the Democrats and the Populists, in their effort to recapture the Federal mints as a market for their silver.

Conquer those markets was the watchword, and, then as now, advertising played a part. As early as the 1790's, manufacturers of patent medicines had begun to turn out standardized bottles with a brand name and to advertise their wares widely. The nostrum-makers were true social pioneers pointing toward our own day: the first manufacturers to advertise directly to consumers and to aim for a national market, the first merchandisers to experiment at manipulating psychology. During the Civil War the heavy excise taxes on whiskey gave them a new opportunity, and such products as Drake's Plantation Bitters appeared. Soon its slogan—"S.T. 1860–X"—was appearing in newspapers, on fences, on barns, on billboards, on rocks. It was painted in letters 400 feet high on a mountainside, and then a forest was cut down so the letters could be seen by passengers on the Pennsylvania Railroad. After Drake retired, very wealthy, about 1890, he explained that the slogan meant "Started trade in 1860 with $10."

Some of the consequences of these methods of getting rich can be seen in an entry of 1889 in a diary in Muncie, Indiana: "Elixir of life is all the talk. Claims to make old people feel young, etc. Great many have experienced bad effects of it, sore arms, abscesses, erysipelas, and blood poisoning." But medicine shows continued to tour the country in wagons, and millions of farmers and their wives continued to pay a dollar or so for a bottle of patent medicine (often alcoholic) plus blackface that was played, sung, and joked off the tailgate.

Other manufacturers and retailers were slow to follow the lead of the patent medicine kings, but when Jacques Offenbach made a triumphal tour of the United States he was amazed by the passion for advertising. Everywhere the composer came upon the word "Sozodont," the name of a dentifrice. In an almost inaccessible spot at Niagara Falls he saw a sign:

Gargling Oil
Good for man and beast

In Philadelphia he watched the parade of a voluntary organiza-tion. The bass drummer in the band was pounding his instrument as hard as he could while trying simultaneously to hold it so that spectators could read, in fine black lettering on the skin, an ad for a drugstore. "Decidedly," Offenbach concluded, "the American advertising men play upon the human mind as a musician plays on his piano."

By 1880, manufacturers of durable goods—sewing machines, farm machinery, pianos—were advertising their brands, offering goods on trial to customers, hiring local salesmen, offering agencies to local stores, and otherwise bypassing the retailers. Even so, shopkeepers were glad to see them assume advertising costs, and country editors welcomed them as a source of revenue that would compensate for the decline in political advertising. And customers liked the standardization of quality: as the railroads expanded and thus lowered the transportation costs on flour, Pillsbury and other big manufacturers conquered one market after another by means of advertising and good quality. In less than 50 years they knocked the village flour mills out of business.

Standard Oil, Chase and Sanborn coffee, Bayer aspirin, Wrigley's chewing gum, Postum, Grape Nuts—all were perfecting their sales techniques. But it was tobacco men like Buck Duke who worked on the frontiers of promotion.

His father, Washington Duke, had started a tobacco factory in a log shack near Durham, North Carolina, after the Civil War, and James Buchanan Duke became the father's right-hand man. Although cigarettes in 1881 were still hand-rolled in factories, more than 240 million a year were being sold, and Duke decided to gamble on them. He brought ten Russian and Polish Jews from New York City to roll them. His key salesman Edward F. Small, trying desperately to create a market, got the idea in Atlanta of asking a touring French actress, who was currently the rage there, to endorse Duke cigarettes. She did, and he slapped her picture with the smokes on billboards all over town. He hired lady salesmen to visit tobacco dealers. The chief element in creating trade, he said, was "judicious advertising, especially if the same is novel and astounding in magnitude."

Meanwhile Duke was experimenting with the tobacco machine invented by a young Virginian, James Bonsack. By 1884 they had two machines working well in Durham, each turning out 200 or more cigarettes a minute. They figured they could produce 250,000 cigarettes a day, and the cost should fall from 80¢ per thousand to 30¢. Even more important, Congress in 1883 had cut the revenue tax from $1.75 to 50¢ per thousand. A thousand cigarettes took

3½ pounds of tobacco at 25¢ a pound, and the cost of packing and shipping brought the total cost per thousand to about $1.85. Price to jobber, $4, less a 10 per cent discount. With that sort of margin, Duke could afford to spend money to convince smokers that cigarettes were not effeminate.

He sent his partner to Europe, and in the spring of 1884 Duke went to New York City and started plastering posters and billboards. He offered premiums to retail dealers for selling his product —camp chairs, clocks, crayon drawings. A master stroke was to put a picture of a famous actress or an athlete or a national flag in each pack. The pictures came in numbered sets, and children started pestering their fathers for them. Duke opened a loft factory in New York, installed four Bonsack machines, and jumped his capacity to 500,000 cigarettes a day.

Push that product! Small, directing sales in the Midwest, sponsored a polo club that played on roller skates. He placed street urchins in front of tobacco shops to give a free pack to each person entering the store. Duke topped that by putting men at the Immigration Station in New York to hand out samples to every immigrant. "These people will take our cigarettes all over the country. It's whopping good advertising," he claimed.

He was right. In 1889 the United States consumed 2.1 billion cigarettes, and Duke sold nearly half of them. His gross sales were more than $4 million, and net earnings were 10 per cent of that. He was spending $800,000 a year on promotion, twice his net earnings. He gave secret rebates and cash bonuses to key retailers. He extended his system of premiums to consumers, giving coupons that could be exchanged for prizes ranging from floor mops to gaudy stickpins. And he brought his competitors to the wall. In 1890 he got together with four of them to form the American Tobacco Company, which controlled 90 per cent of the cigarette market.

By guaranteeing to Bonsack's company an annual royalty of $250,000, Duke got exclusive right to use its cigarette machine. He welded the five companies into one. Concentrating manufacture in three plants, New York, Durham, and Richmond, he drove labor costs down to less than 10¢ a thousand cigarettes. Now a virtual monopoly, he could cut promotion costs, and he did, by more than $1 million a year. He bound wholesalers and retailers by contract to maintain the prices he set. Just as Gustavus Swift had moved to set up a full product line, so did Buck Duke, buying a large plug factory, a cigar plant, two manufacturers of chewing and smoking tobacco. The full line cut sales expenses. Duke explained further: "I wanted to make every style of tobacco the public might demand. . . . And I wanted him to take our kind in place of the other fellow's." In 1894, in the midst of the worst depression in the United States up to that time, American Tobacco showed a net profit of $5 million.

Money could be made by using the railroads to reach unexploited raw materials in the West. Money could be made by tapping the urban markets created by railroads in the East and Midwest. Money could also be made by using the power of government to further your own purposes. Milton H. Smith claimed: "The only inducement for railroad companies to enter politics—become parties to the dirty work—is to protect their property." But companies might also enter politics to extend their property, to take money out of other pockets and put it into their own, to, in Smith's words again, "get what the other fellow has, if you can. . . ."

The tariff was a good example. In 1865 the import duty on kerosene—the chief product of Standard Oil two decades later—was fixed at 40¢ a gallon, and domestic producers of kerosene enjoyed tariff protection continuously until 1909. And what protection: The wholesale price of illuminating oil at New York City in 1890 was less than 10¢ a gallon. Or consider steel, in which Andrew Carnegie was piling up his colossal fortune. An act of 1870 fixed the tariff on steel rails at $28 per gross ton. When railroad expansion jumped upward in 1879, American steel men could kick the price of rails sky high without fear that foreign mills would take their customers. In 1881 the price of steel rails in England was about $31 a ton, and a man could pay the import duty of $28 a ton and still make money shipping rails here because the American price was more than double the price in England; it reached as high as $67 a ton. Men like Carnegie were earning net profits of 100 per cent a year and more on the capital invested in their plants. It was not just the tariff, of course: Carnegie and a few others got added help from the government, for they controlled the American patents on the Bessemer process for making steel.

So Carnegie owed a considerable part of his fortune to the generosity of Congressmen who were giving him somebody else's money. It came from the users of steel, from the railroads, from the makers of farm equipment. They priced their products accordingly, raising their freight rates, charging more for a reaper or a plow. So, finally, the consumer paid and the Carnegies got fat. Especially did the farmers pay. The United States had an export surplus in wheat and in cotton and in other farm products, and farmers got no protection from the tariff. It served rather for decades to siphon income and wealth out of the rural areas and into the cities, into the bank accounts of a few men in the cities.

Influence in Washington was good, influence in states and cities could also be good. In 1881 Chicago journalist and reformer Henry Demarest Lloyd commented: "The Standard has done everything with the Pennsylvania legislature, except refine it." But the agents of Standard Oil were not deterred by such remarks. In order to protect its control of the pathways from the oil wells in Pennsylvania to the railroads, Standard Oil opposed the right of eminent domain for pipelines, thus virtually insuring that no competing pipeline could be built. The company reportedly used venal methods in this effort, and successfully so. Pennsylvania in 1882 failed in its effort to collect taxes from Standard Oil of Ohio on the property it owned outside the state; the man who had collected much of the material on the tax case for the state ceased his attacks on Standard Oil. The Billingsley Bill in the Pennsylvania legislature sought to make pipelines into common carriers and to force sharp reductions in their rates for carrying and storing oil. It was defeated in the state senate in April 1887. Its supporters accused Standard Oil of having bribed at least five senators. The following month another Standard Oil executive wrote to Rockefeller that while their firm had met with "unparalleled success in commercial history" its public reputation was "not to be envied."

Access to governmental power was of special importance in the South, where the desperate poverty of the region posed special problems for men seeking their fortunes. But even the general poverty could create glittering opportunities for men who had the political influence to seize them. For instance, poverty made farmers and businessmen receptive to any measure that promised to reduce the taxes they paid. One consequence was the deterioration of the public schools in many Southern states. Another was to make taxpayers amenable to proposals that offered not only to remove from their backs the burden of supporting the state penitentiary but also to convert the prisoners into a source of revenue for the state. Thus arose the convict-lease system—the practice of hiring out the state's convicts to private companies as a conscript labor force.

The larger the conscript labor force, the greater the revenue to the state, and appropriate changes in the criminal laws were made. In 1874 there were 272 prisoners in Mississippi. Then the "pig law" was enacted, defining as grand laceny the theft of any property worth $10 or of any cattle or hogs regardless of their value. Violations brought a prison term up to 5 years. At the end of 1877 the state had 1,072 prisoners—an increase of nearly 400 per cent in 4 years. In Georgia, where the number of convicts rose from 432 in 1872 to 1,441 in 1877, Senator Joseph E. Brown had a 20-year lease that guaranteed him 300 able-bodied convicts to work in his Dade Coal Mines. He paid the state about 8¢ per man per day.

The deal that the Tennessee Coal, Iron, and Railroad Company got from Tennessee was not so good. In 1883 the company leased the entire penitentiary, holding some 1,300 convicts, for $101,000 —over 20¢ a man per day. The company, if not nonpolitical, was certainly nonpartisan: its president was Thomas C. Platt, Republican leader of New York; its general counsel was Arthur S. Colyar, Democratic leader of Tennessee. Colyar explained that his firm had turned to the convict-lease system in large part because of "the great chance which it seemed to present for overcoming strikes."

Considering that the tariff gave Colyar's firm an artificially high price for its output of pig iron, and that the convict-lease system gave it artificially low labor costs, the Tennessee Coal, Iron, and Railroad Company derived much of its profit from these governmental beneficences. Perhaps it even owed to them its survival.

Among the founders of Colyar's company was James H. Inman, who was also president of the largest railroad system in the South, the Richmond and West Point Terminal Railroad. Along with four other directors of Richmond Terminal, including two brothers who were grandsons of the revered John C. Calhoun, Inman bought stock in the Central of Georgia. In 1889 they sold it to Richmond Terminal for $7,500,000—about double what they had paid for it. Less than five years later, Richmond Terminal was bankrupt.

The tactic of looting your own company was no more reprehensible than the various types of industrial blackmail. Such railroads as the West Shore or the Toledo, Peoria, and Warsaw were built not so that their owners could try to operate them at a profit—but so that existing lines would buy them out at an exorbitant price to avoid the threatened competition. The work of launching the construction of telegraph lines so that the partially completed line could be sold to Western Union grew to be an industry in itself. As William H. Forbes, president of the National Bell Telephone Company, explained it: "The Western Union is composed of many companies which have successively been brought forward as competitors. Each of these companies has posed for a time as a public benefactor, organized to fight the Western Union. Under this plea, each has demanded and obtained rights of way and other privileges throughout the country. The footsteps of all lead into the Western Union cave; not one has ever returned."

Businesses whose profits depended on the maintenance of a monopoly position were preyed upon by politicians as well as by other businessmen, and many was the nuisance bill introduced into city councils and state legislatures by men who had no intention of passing it but who wanted to be paid for not passing it.

Although other business strategies might lead to quicker results and more spectacular ones, perhaps the most common route to workaday reputability was that followed by Asa Call in Algona, Iowa, trading in real estate. The United States was growing, and as local communities grew in size, real-estate values moved upward. In Muncie, Indiana, for instance, when natural gas was brought in at local wells in 1886, real estate began to change hands at amazing speed. In 1888 a man hesitated to pay $1,600 for an 8-acre tract on the outskirts of town. He bought instead a 60-day option on the property. Before the option expired, the piece of land was sold 5 times. The last time it brought $3,200.

Industrialist: CHARLES A. PILLSBURY

Pillsbury (1842–1899) became the world's best-known miller of flour. A New Hampshire man and a Dartmouth graduate, he was a commission merchant in Montreal by 1863. Four years later he moved to Minneapolis and ventured his capital in the milling trade. But no leather-aproned country miller was he. By repeatedly modernizing his plant he was able to continually expand his volume, to continually cut costs, and to put many country millers out of business. First he developed the purifier, which produced bread flour of uniform quality, and in 1872 installed the continuous roller process. His "A" mill when opened in 1883 was reputed to be the largest on earth. By 1889 the Pillsbury Mills could grind out 10,000 barrels a day. This enormous volume depended on the railroad network, which allowed him to tap the cheap flood of wheat of the Dakotas, and sell processed flour in the dense markets of eastern and middle western cities.

Some of Pillsbury's beliefs break the stereotype of the manufacturer of his time. Although a notorious plunger on the commodity market, he always gambled on growth, progress, expansion. No freebooter, he scorned to seize booty by mere speculative manipulation, by selling short. In 1892 he testified before Congress for a bill that would prohibit all trading in futures for grain and cotton. Although farmers were his suppliers, he said that his interests and theirs were identical: both would gain from the long-term prosperity of agriculture. He instituted a profit-sharing plan for his employees. Pillsbury even aided another group of suppliers—coopers, who made barrels—in their efforts to start producers' cooperatives.

Equally deviant was his behavior at the time of a strike against the Great Northern Railroad in 1894. At the behest of the St. Paul Chamber of Commerce, the dispute went to arbitration, and Pillsbury became chairman of the panel. The award gave the strikers, with trifling exceptions, everything they had asked for. The industrialist then proposed a banquet to celebrate the settlement. Eugene Debs, the union's chief, replied that $10,000 should not be frittered away on frivolity: let it be spent on calico for the strikers' wives.

CHAPTER 3

How the Struggle for Wealth Reshaped the Economy

Adam Smith contended that competition will act as an "invisible hand" to convert the self-seeking activities of individual men into general if unforeseen consequences that promote the well-being of all. Competition among producers will force them to be efficient and will drive their prices down to reasonable levels.

In the labor markets of the United States, employers competed not only with each other but with the large quantities of unoccupied and cheap land. Although relatively few city laborers had the specialized knowledge and the thousand dollars or so in capital that were needed to succeed as a farmer, there can be no doubt that the frontier kept the general level of wages higher than it would have been otherwise, and far higher than it was anywhere in Europe. This fact had two crucial results. First, it encouraged manufacturers to substitute machinery for labor whenever possible. Although their purpose was to reduce their costs of production, the fruit of their efforts was an increase in the output per man-hour, an increase in efficiency. Since this in turn facilitated increases in wages, the process was self-reinforcing. Second, the relatively high level of wages meant a wide dispersion of purchasing power. Whereas in Europe buying power was in the hands of an aristocracy that wanted individualized and often hand-made goods, the mass market in the United States called for standardized goods turned out by mass production using labor-saving methods. Out of this situation came the industrial supremacy of the United States, which was clearly established by 1892.

From 1877 to 1892 the United States grew—in population, in

wealth, in output per man-hour, in the value of real estate. In these years the economy became industrial. The society became urban. Vast corporate bureaucracies were forged. Power was caught up into the hands of a few men as never before in this country. The men in government were increasingly housebroken, until to many contemporaries they seemed lap-dogs to the barons of business.

The population of the country was 47 million in 1877; 67 million in 1893. The rate of growth was just over 1 million per year in the late 1870's; thereafter until 1893 it was about 1.3 million per year. In most years from a third to a half of the population increase was due to immigration, and much of the growth of the American economy can be attributed to this flow of immigrants. Children were born in Great Britain or Germany or Scandinavia (or increasingly after 1880 in Italy or Eastern Europe), supported and fattened in the land of their birth until they were old enough to go to work, when they would obligingly cross the Atlantic and present themselves at the employment offices of American railroads and factories. Year after year more than 60 per cent of the immigrants were male and more than two thirds of them were aged 15 to 40.

Many of the Scandinavian and German immigrants brought not only their skill as farmers but also modest amounts of wealth with which to establish themselves on the prairies. In the anthracite region of Pennsylvania and other mine fields, many of the foremen and skilled miners had learned their trade in England or Wales. The Farr Alpaca Company had only followed a common practice in the textile industries in importing its skilled workers from Canada

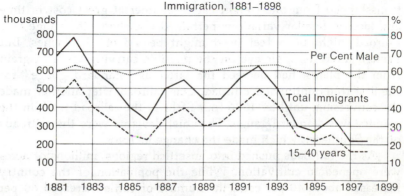

Immigration, 1881–1898

and England. Nor was it the only company to immigrate here, lock, stock, and barrel, because of the tariff. After the McKinley Act of 1890 imposed import duties on tinplate coming from South Wales, thousands of workers there were suddenly without work. Large groups came here, and Welsh manufacturers moved all or part of their factories to such towns as New Castle, Pennsylvania.

Many immigrants were attracted by the unrelenting propaganda of railroads eager to populate the countryside along their recently extended lines. In 1877 the Union Pacific–Central Pacific complex was the only railroad to reach the West Coast. The Great Northern, running out of St. Paul, reached Everett, Washington, in 1893, and by that time the Northern Pacific also had touched the Pacific Ocean. The Southern Pacific, running east from San Francisco, reached New Orleans in 1882. Railroad construction had continued on a small scale throughout the depression of the 1870's, but after 1879 it zoomed ahead. In 1880 10,000 miles of track were opened; the following year, even more; in 1887, a record 13,000 miles. The miles of track in operation doubled from 1877 to 1892.

While the railroad network was being extended, it was also being integrated physically. Most of the railroads in the East before the Civil War were built as short lines to serve the commercial interests of one or two cities. Gradually ownership of several short lines came into a single set of hands, and the lines were integrated into trunk lines such as the New York Central. But each of the three railroad systems serving New York City in 1861 had its rails set a different distance apart. Since rolling stock could not pass from one system to another, goods often had to be transshipped from one freight car to another at great cost in time and money. Similar variations pertained elsewhere: the gauge of a railroad might be 6 feet or it might be 4 feet 8½ inches. But Eastern interests, their eye on the possible carrying trade in grain from the plains, had decreed the latter as "standard guage" for the first transcontinental railroad. One railroad after another made the conversion, until by 1880 four fifths of the railroad track in the country was standard gauge. The chief deviants were the railroads of the Southeast, which made the change in 1886.

As the railroads pushed into unsettled regions, millions of acres were opened to cultivation. While the population of the country increased about 40 per cent, the number of cattle increased 60 per cent and their average value declined 10 per cent. The output of wheat rose more than 50 per cent, and the price of wheat per bushel fell from $1.08 in 1877 to 62¢ in 1892. Such huge increases in many crops resulted not only from virgin land but also from the mechanization of agriculture. An estimated 61 hours of labor were needed to produce one acre of wheat with the hand methods in vogue before the Civil War; with the machine methods of the 1890's the same job could be done in 3 hours and 19 minutes.

The new types of farm machinery were best adapted to use on the open prairies, and thus further increased the competitive pressure on the erstwhile farming areas of the East. Although the industrial cities of New England offered a growing market for farm products, the region had no more persons in agricultural pursuits in 1890 than in 1880, and its farmers were likely to be turning their attention to fruit culture or dairying. In New England as in Texas, flour was coming from the Midwestern mills, and the wheat for it was coming from Kansas or Dakota. The latter had only 135,000 people in 1880. Then a few years of good rainfall there, plus rising real-estate prices in other areas, sent the population shooting upward to 330,000 in 1883.

Such boom stages of growth occurred in more than one place when the coming of the railroad first tied it into the national economy. In Washington state in the decade of the 1880's, for example, population grew over 4 times; value of farms, nearly 5 times; value of farm products, 3 times; value of output of fisheries, 6 times. Manufacturing grew even more rapidly: employment, 17 times; value of output, 12 times. But the number of men involved in manufacturing at the end of the decade was only 17,000, and what manufacturing existed in such a raw if booming area was likely to be chiefly the primary processing of raw materials. Thus the value of the lumber pouring out of Washington sawmills increased 9 times in the 10 years after 1880; this surge accounted for most of the growth in value of manufactures.

Construction of buildings in such boom areas and in the Eastern cities became even more important than railroad construction in furnishing a market for the iron and steel mills—a change symbolized by Carnegie's decision in 1887 to shift the nation's largest steel mill, at Homestead, Pennsylvania, from production of rails to structural steel. The flood of steel into the American economy swelled incredibly, from 569,000 long tons in 1877 to 4,927,000 in

1892. Just as construction of railroads and bridges and buildings created a demand for steel, so did production of steel create a demand for bituminous coal, and the tonnage mined went from 35 million in 1877 to 127 million in 1892, to which we can add 52 million tons of anthracite used chiefly for heating homes.

In those 16 years an industrial society was created. Output of copper rose 7 times; of crude oil, 4 times, passing 50 million barrels of 42 gallons each, of which the major part continued to be refined into illuminating oil, and the major part of the illuminating oil was still being shipped to foreign markets. The electrical manufacturers, who did not even exist before 1875, turned out $23 million worth of goods in 1892. The value of industrial machinery and equipment produced in that year was double what it had been in 1879. The number of active spindles in cotton mills in 1890 was twice what it had been 20 years earlier. Manufacturing production as a whole in 1892 was 2½ times the level of 1877. The number of persons in manufacturing was 2¼ times as great in 1890 as in 1870; in mining, 2½ times; in transportation and other public utilities, 2½ times; in construction, 2 times.

But in agriculture, the labor force increased only 50 per cent, and the United States by 1890 had ceased to be primarily a farming country. In 1870 there were nearly 7 million persons in agricultural pursuits, slightly over 6 million in other activities. In 1890, 13,379,000 were engaged in nonagricultural pursuits, while agriculture could claim fewer than 10 million workers. But developments in different sections were very different. In Massachusetts the number of persons engaged in farming stayed almost constant from 1880 to 1890, while the number engaged in manufacturing rose a third, and employment in trade and transportation rose by half. The same general pattern holds, suprisingly, in Illinois, where employment in manufacturing rose 70 per cent while it doubled in trade and transportation but rose hardly at all in farming. But in the four states from Kansas on the south to North Dakota on the north, employment in farming rose two thirds in those ten years.

Such regional comparisons point to a wavelike process by which the American economy expanded westward. As better farming areas farther west were opened up, Eastern areas lost part of their markets, and the labor force began shifting into manufacturing and other industrial jobs. States such as Ohio and Illinois were passing through this stage in the 1880's. Manufacturing was still growing in New England, but its textile mills were facing increased competition from the cotton industry of the Southern Piedmont. As farming and cotton manufacturing declined in New England, the labor force there shifted increasingly into the service industries.

The development of the American economy showed a second type of wavelike process—the cycle of prosperity and recession. And in the business cycles of the late 19th century, the pace of railroad construction often played a key role. Not only did the railroads themselves employ vast quantities of labor and capital in the expansive years when they added 10,000 miles of new track plus great numbers of new locomotives and freight cars, but they also provided, directly or indirectly, a chief market for the output of other key industries such as steel and coal. This marked dependence of the economy on railroad construction was most unfortunate, for the nature of the railroad business at the time was such that a line's extension was highly erratic.

Many key railroads were dominated by general entrepreneurs; that is, by businessmen whose access to giant amounts of liquid capital gave them the ability to control companies in many different industries. One such man was Commodore Vanderbilt, who multiplied a fortune made in shipping by investing it in the New York Central. Another was John Murray Forbes of Boston, who made money in the years around 1835 in the overseas trade with China, made more money in the early years of cotton manufacturing in New England, made yet more in the Michigan Central Railroad and the Burlington. Another was Jay Gould, who controlled the Erie, left it and acquired first the Union Pacific and then the Wabash. He came to control Western Union and the Manhattan Elevated in New York City. He took over the Texas Pacific. The Northern Pacific was controlled in 1873 by the banker Jay Cooke; it was controlled 15 years later by the former newspaperman Henry Villard.

These men fought intricate wars for control of the future traffic of the Great Plains. Their lines west from the Mississippi paralleled each other, being a hundred or two hundred miles apart. Who would benefit from the traffic that in years to come would pour out of the yet unsettled lands lying between two trunk lines? In prosperous years when money capital could be gotten, each railroad would become afraid that a rival would beat it into a region that either could penetrate. In the effort to get into the region first, each road would plunge ahead. Railroads were built into many areas years before they could reasonably hope to carry any substantial amount of traffic. Much of the construction was financed by issue of bonds, but when the hoped-for traffic failed to materialize, the revenues of the road were not great enough for it to pay interest on its debt. The railroad went into bankruptcy and reorganized its capital structure, the value of its debt being reduced in the process. The bankruptcy of a major railroad or two might trigger a financial panic, leading to a more or less protracted depression in the country as a whole. During a depression, with money capital hard to come by, the general entrepreneurs in command of the railroads felt that their rivals could not finance new construction. Without the threat of competition to force its hand, each railroad slowed its own construction to a standstill.

The results of this process were manifold. First, it forced such roads as the Northern Pacific into bankruptcy repeatedly, and each time millions of dollars in values that had been invested in the road were wiped out in the recapitalization. It is an interesting speculation whether, if we could calculate the total dividends and interest that have been paid on all the capital put into railroads in American history, the average return on the investment might not be negative.

Second, the West was settled much faster than it would have been if the railroads had built only into areas that would clearly be profitable in the near future. Having built a line, the railroad tried desperately to settle its environs quickly. Many a settler was lured by railroad propaganda into a region that did not have enough rainfall in the average year to support farming or that could not be farmed by the methods he knew. After a few years the farmer, beaten, would retreat from the area. As late as 1910, more than half of the farm population of the United States lived on land they had not occupied five years earlier.

Third, the impact of railroad construction on other sectors of the economy tended to lead the entire country into wild excesses. Every prosperity tended to become a runaway boom, culminating in far-reaching collapse, followed by years of bad times. During periods of rapid railroad extension, steel mills worked overtime, coal and iron mines extended their operations, farmers poured into the West, country towns were built and cities grew in the hope of capturing the farmers' trade, thousands of immigrants streamed through New York and fanned out over the country. Then came financial panic, railroad construction slowed, steel mills and coal mines laid off men and cut back production, immigration fell to a quarter of what it had been, urban demand for farm products declined and prices fell.

The longest period of economic contraction in American history —lasting five years and five months—began in the fall of 1873. The banking firm of Jay Cooke, famous for his part in financing the Union armies, had taken on the job of financing the Northern Pacific. Having spent over $15 million, the road had only 500 miles of track in operation in May 1873, and Cooke was trying to float a bond issue of $100 million. But 25 other railroads defaulted in interest on their bonds in the first eight months of 1873, and Cooke was unable to make a deal. He began to borrow money at short term to finance the road, hoping to sell his bonds before the notes came due. This effort failed, and his firm announced on September 18 that it could no longer pay its depositors on demand. Other banks became panicky and called in loans. Stock prices swooped downward. Other banks failed. Businessmen could not get cash to meet their payrolls, and they cut employment. Railroad construction, some 4,000 miles in 1873, was only half that the next year.

Yet, although the ensuing depression lasted a long time, it was relatively mild in terms of actual physical output. Manufacturing output turned upward as early as 1875, and by 1877 railroad investment, construction of buildings, and mining output had all revived. In spite of the long depression, real income per capita rose by a third from 1869 to 1879. But the depression lasted until the latter year because money wages and prices continued to decline.

In 1879 the economy spurted ahead for several reasons. After January 1 of that year all legal-tender notes in circulation could be turned in at the Treasury in exchange for gold; this return to the gold standard, combined with low prices in the United States, tended to reduce imports and stimulate exports. Farmers benefited from the coincidence of bountiful crops here with poor ones in Europe. New farming areas in the West had come into production, and agricultural output by 1879 was 50 per cent higher than it had been in 1873. The resulting increase in railroad traffic brought renewed investment in railroads, and until 1882 there was an orgy of railroad extension. Main lines which had been stopped by the panic of 1873 were completed. More important, feeders and branch lines were built. Repairs and improvements that had been deferred were undertaken.

In the three years from 1880 through 1882 more than 28,000

miles of railroad were built. The stimulus given to industries supplying the railroads was huge, and, as one commentator pointed out,
"every railroad which is constructed, and especially in the West
and South, creates fresh opportunities for investment in agriculture,
mining, mills and foundries." The Louisville and Nashville, for
instance, owned a half million acres of land in central Alabama,
and the road needed more freight. It built lines connecting Birmingham to new coal and iron towns—Bessemer, Helena, Anniston,
Talladega—with spurs to coal mines, iron mines, and mills. It sent
agents everywhere seeking immigrants. By 1888 the tonnage of
minerals and pig iron over the L. & N. was greater than the average
annual weight of the cotton crop of the United States for the
preceding 15 years. The pig iron output of Alabama in 1889 was
more than 10 times what it had been in 1880.

But the national bubble had long since burst. By 1883 capitalists
had become convinced that further investment in railroads would
not prove profitable. The decline in employment in railroad building
from 1882 to 1883 came to 500,000 men, of a total national labor
force of only 18 million. Steel rails, worth $71 a ton in January
1880, were selling for half that in December 1883. Until 1885 the
economy sagged. In that year the Chicago *Tribune* looked back to
1879–1881 and asked:

Why is it that in such a time as that, funds are contributed by all
classes of people for almost any enterprise whose promoters promise
great returns? It is because they see business active all around them,
people in enterprises already established winning large profits, and
everything apparently inviting them to be rich. They are seized with
the craze of money making, and become incapable of reasoning on
any project that is presented for their consideration. It is easy for
unscrupulous men to humbug them at such a time. Even the promoters of enterprises often half-believe the lies they tell, and
partake of the prevailing mania. . . . It is appalling to consider how
many of the corporate enterprises of the country have secured their
capital by taking advantage of these investment—or, rather, speculative—epidemics.

Once again, however, as in 1873–1879, the recession was chiefly
marked by severe reductions of prices and wages, while physical
output was affected relatively little. The preceding railroad extension had opened up many new areas, and construction of new

buildings continued high throughout the recession. This in turn stimulated industries producing building supplies—such as the lumber industry of Washington. In 1885 prospects for profits from railroad investment began to look good again, and the economy in general turned upward, with the result that railroad construction shot upward in 1886 and even more so in 1887. The boom was on once more.

But this one lasted less than two years. From a record 13,000 miles in 1887, railroad construction fell nearly 50 per cent the next year, and building construction fell also. Since the boom had been brief and relatively mild in many ways, so was the downswing that followed, and business revival came in April 1888. The cyclical swings for the next few years continued mild, until a banking panic early in 1893 brought in its train the worst depression that had yet occurred in the United States.

Many features of the crisis that struck American society in the years from 1893 to 1898 can be attributed to the growth of huge corporations in the 16 years before 1893. In trying to get hold of the factors that explain why these corporations developed when they did, it is useful to distinguish between the growth of individual plants to a size where one factory might employ thousands of men, such as the McCormick reaper works in Chicago or the Homestead works, and the growth of multi-plant companies, such as Standard Oil or the Distillers' and Cattle Feeders' Trust.

The appearance of the giant plant can often be traced to the effects of the railroad plus technological changes that gave large-scale production a great advantage in costs over small-scale production. Prior to the railroad, inland transportation costs were so high that only the most valuable and least bulky goods could be shipped long distances. Each plant in an industry tended to serve a strictly limited market, within which it was protected by virtue of the wall of transportation costs. The country was dotted with tiny plants producing pig iron or nails or flour, and selling to a local market.

Railroads changed all that. Freight rates have never fallen to zero, and consequently the competitive disadvantage suffered by a factory still increases as it buys raw materials from more distant sources or sells its output in more distant markets. But the railroad did greatly reduce the margin of this disadvantage for any given distance from raw materials and markets.

The most dramatic reduction in costs came when a region was first connected with the interregional railroad network. The introduction of a railroad into an area might well reduce transportation costs to 10 per cent of what they had been with wagons over poor roads. Thereafter, costs per ton-mile continued to decline as the volume of traffic increased and technical improvements were made. Competition of a railroad with other railroads or with water transportation accelerated the decline in rates on many lines. Thus the cost of shipping a bushel of wheat by rail from Chicago to New York fell from 19¢ in 1877 to 10¢ at the end of the century, but in 1900 the cost by water over the Great Lakes, the Erie Canal, and the Hudson River was less than 5¢. On the Lake Shore and Michigan Southern the average freight charge per ton-mile fell from 1.5¢ in 1870 to 0.5¢ in 1900.

In considering how flour milled in Minneapolis could be sold in markets from Texas to New York, the second principal factor was the advance in productive techniques in flour milling and many other industries. These improvements sometimes greatly increased the economies of large-scale production so that—in the language of the economist—average costs continued to fall until the factory's daily output was very large. When the new technical possiblities were seen in conjunction with the fall in transportation costs, enterprising manufacturers were struck with the opportunity to reach out to ever more distant markets.

To capture a market, a manufacturer had to be able to sell his goods there at a lower price than his competitors. His selling price would consist of his costs of production, plus the cost of delivering the goods to the market in question, plus his profit. The railroad had reduced the cost of delivering his product to distant markets. If he could only get his costs of production somewhat below the cost of firms selling the same commodity in those markets, he could capture them on a price basis. And so it happened.

In industries where the economies of large-scale production were great—sewing machines, farm implements, bicycles, typewriters, sugar, illuminating oil, tobacco, steel—the factories that seized the new technical possibilities expanded rapidly at the expense of those which did not. During the 1880's, for example, the capital invested in the manufacture of farm machinery more than doubled, but the number of companies in the industry declined by half. Meanwhile the number of employees in the industry rose very little. Taken together, these facts suggest that some plants, using more capital for every worker, were able to drive others out of business. The average firm was four times as large in 1890 as in 1880, and by 1890 two Chicago plants together were producing 200,000 harvesting machines per year. As early as 1881 the Singer Company alone was selling an average of 1,700 sewing machines a day. Thereafter the torrent of low-wage Jewish immigrants into New York helped to expand the ready-made garment industry and to build even further the market for sewing machines. To symbolize the triumph, the 47-story Singer Building was erected; when completed in 1908 it was twice as high as any other building on Manhattan Island.

In general, a small plant became a big one by effecting genuine economies in production. As a plant grows in size, each of its elements can be used more nearly to full capacity: machines that are not feasible in a small plant where they would be idle most of the time become economical in a large plant. This makes it possible to extend the specialization of machines and men, both of which often come in indivisible units with a large capacity. Managerial and technical talent can be economized as the size of plant increases; so can generators and railroad rights-of-way. Savings can be effected in buying raw materials, since it costs little more to place a large order than a small one, and since the supplier will find it more economical to fill a large order than a small one.

As we turn to the growth or combination of individual plants into large multi-plant firms, a new range of considerations comes into view. The formation of a large multi-plant firm might bring an increase in the ratio of output to input, for the economy as a whole as well as for the individual firm. But this process in other instances resulted in higher costs and a reduction in efficiency.

Whether concentrated in a single plant or split up among several factories, a large firm enjoyed competitive advantages of several types over small rivals, even though some of these advantages might not be socially beneficial in the sense of increasing the ratio of output to input for the total economy. A large company has more bargaining power to use in buying raw materials, and perhaps also in selling its products. It has advantages in raising capital funds which can be summarized under the rubric, "greater prestige." These advantages in financing may combine with technical talent in a research and development program. Research may lead to patents, and the large company has the financial resources to prosecute (or to defend against) patent suits. Its patents may then become the basis of further growth. This happened conspicuously in the telephone industry and in electrical manufacturing, in both of which multi-plant corporations developed from a process of horizontal and vertical integration.

In electrical manufacturing, for instance, Edison General Electric and Thomson-Houston were some 80 per cent of the industry in 1891, each having sales slightly above $10 million. The product lines of the two companies were in general noncompetitive except in the electric street-car field, and their patents were neatly complementary. The two firms merged in 1892 to form General Electric, which was more than four times as big as its leading rival, Westinghouse.

Crucial to the formation of many multi-plant firms was the growing importance of those costs of production that do not vary as the quantity of output changes—variously called fixed costs, or sunk costs, or overhead costs. If the technical advances of the late 19th century brought increased advantages of large-scale production to many industries, they also, depending as they did on extensive use of machinery, changed the composition of total costs of production, increasing the proportion of fixed costs and reducing the proportion of variable costs. The merchant-capitalists of the early 19th century had hardly known the meaning of fixed costs; John Jacob Astor, during a prosperous time, could have turned all his assets into cash in twelve months without suffering a capital loss. But in railroads and many types of manufacturing this degree of liquidity did not exist. On railroads, in addition to such fixed costs as taxes and the interest on bonded debt, an estimated 55 per cent of the operating expenses were fixed costs. Most of the expenses of a railroad simply cannot be evaded, even if its receipts drop to zero; conversely, it can greatly expand its sales without anything approaching a proportionate increase in costs.

The high ratio of fixed costs to total costs need not occasion any difficulty so long as demand remains constant. But from 1877 to 1893 demand for most products was subject to sharp drops during recessions and to random drops as competitors from neighboring areas bit into your market. When demand fell, a firm's receipts fell much more than its costs. It fought back by striving to capture a larger share of a shrinking market, and the usual technique was to cut prices. Just here did the high ratio of fixed costs to total costs become crucial. To make a profit, a firm's receipts must more than cover its total costs. But if a company with high fixed costs is losing money, it can minimize its losses by selling at any price that covers variable costs and leaves a margin, however small, to apply against fixed costs. In this situation the selling of goods at a price that did not cover total costs became so common as to give rise to the term "cut-throat competition."

A firm with large fixed costs simply must keep its plants in operation; otherwise, it goes into bankruptcy. Thus a premium attaches to stability and certainty, and the integration movement arose as an effort to eliminate uncertainty. A company reached backward to control its suppliers so that it could have a dependable supply of raw materials at predictable prices. It reached forward to control its distribution outlets so that it could promote sales and dispose of the ceaseless flow of goods from its factories. It fought all efforts to establish trade unions because it could not afford to lose control over its labor costs. It opposed government regulation of business because the impact would be unpredictable and beyond its control.

No company became so big that it could feel safe from others, not even Standard Oil. In the late 1880's output of crude oil in the Pennsylvania oil region began to decline, and the Lima-Indiana fields came into production. What if somebody else seized control of the new fields? What if the producers of crude oil combined to raise prices? Standard Oil, to ensure a steady supply of crude oil at its refineries, embarked on aggression for purposes of defense. For the first time it went directly into the production of crude by swooping into the Lima-Indiana fields to buy properties. It also set up committees and staff units to coordinate a more efficient flow of oil from the wells all the way to the customer.

Thus integration, especially vertical integration that reached backward or forward to other stages of production, could result in genuine economies. A manufacturer of steel wire knew exactly the kind of steel that his firm needed; if his firm merged with a manufacturer of ingot steel, his knowledge became available to both firms. Also sales costs were reduced, the quality of the steel became more certain, the production schedules of steel mill and wire mill could be coordinated with resultant savings in inventory costs and reduction in number of shutdowns. Integrated plants in the steel industry brought huge savings in fuel costs because the material could be moved without cooling from blast furnace to Bessemer converter to rolling mill. In other companies the integration of sales outlets with the factory meant goods that were better aimed at the market, lower inventory costs, availability of specialized knowledge to all the retail outlets, preparation of point-of-sale displays on a mass basis, and so on.

Thus vertical integration often looked toward the creation of a firm that could compete more effectively because it increased efficiency by reducing costs. But an increase in efficiency was far less likely to result from horizontal integration; that is, creation of a multi-plant firm from the combination of several companies at the same stage of production and competing more or less directly with each other.

In 1887 the Distillers' and Cattle Feeders' Trust was formed by several Midwestern firms with more than 80 small plants. Some rationalization of production was effected, and by 1895 only 21 plants were being operated. But the company was also careful to keep the price of whiskey from falling. Unfortunately for it, the cost of starting a distillery was low; entry into the industry was too easy. The Trust's answer to new competitors was to buy some out and to cut prices of whiskey in order to put pressure on the others. This strategy proved fatal. Unable to survive the depression that began in 1893, the firm went into bankruptcy in 1896. Thus mergers between erstwhile competing firms were a substitute for cartels or other agreements among independent firms to divide the market and fix prices. After 1890, when cartels and other combinations "in restraint of trade" were made subject to legal prosecution by the Sherman Act, the merger of competing firms became even more attractive as an alternative means to the same end. Such mergers aimed at increasing profits, not by reducing costs, but chiefly by maintaining prices at a level that would more than cover total costs. Would-be monopolists often burdened themselves with useless plants; useless plants were even built for sale to them as a form of industrial blackmail. So horizontal integration often meant the creation of a giant firm that was less efficient than smaller firms that had been merged into it.

The creation of a giant corporation brought with it serious legal and organizational problems, and Standard Oil pioneered in devising solutions in both areas. Under its charter from the state of Ohio, it could not own plants in other states nor could it own stock in other companies. So when another company was acquired secretly, its stock was turned over to an officer of Standard Oil acting as trustee for the stockholders of Standard Oil. This arrangement could lead to difficulties if an important trustee died, and it left open the possibility that a trustee could embark on an aberrant course. The answer found was the Standard Oil Trust Agreement, signed in 1882, under which nine trustees had control over all the properties associated with Standard Oil of Ohio.

An even more important legal innovation than this first trust was the amendment by New Jersey in 1889 of its general incorporation law to permit one corporation to buy stock in another. Some railroads and other utilities had done so earlier, but usually their action was authorized by their individual charters. The laws of some states specifically forbade intercorporate stock purchases. Now New Jersey had provided a general legalization of the holding company, and in 1899 the Standard Oil Company (New Jersey) became the parent over the entire Rockefeller combination.

Every company that grew substantially in size also met with problems of internal organization. The usual solution was to set up an administrative hierarchy, which, to be workable, had to give a proper balance of coordination and flexibility, of centralization and decentralization. As messages flowed upward toward the chief executives from salesmen on the road or foremen in the plant, some were cut out of the flow at every stage of the hierarchy, decisions were made, and orders given. The remaining messages continued upward, sometimes in their original form, sometimes condensed into reports. In addition to creating such a hierarchy, the company had to fill each job with a suitable person —an incredible task considering that most of these administrative jobs were new in character, that nobody had experience in them, and that professional training of administrators was unknown.

Changes in technology helped this organizational revolution along. Railroads carried company officials from one city to another, and the telegraph carried messages back and forth. In 1884 the Bell telephone system began to make intercompany connections, but really long-distance use of the telephone came only after the turn of the century. In local communication, however, the change occurred earlier; in 1893 more than 300,000 telephones were in use, and typewriters were in the front offices of most corporations.

Other and equally vital inventions were administrative ones. The top executives of most manufacturing concerns had been accustomed to supervising production by walking through their plants to see what was going on. When firms became so large and were scattered over so many cities that this technique was physically impossible, statistics and cost accounting developed as a substitute for direct observation. The intra-firm memo and the weekly report replaced conversation as a technique of information and discussion. But these devices did not dictate any particular structure for the company, and the early big firms suffered long periods of trial and error. At first several tried to apply rigidly the notion of hierarchical delegation of powers. This structure proved to have three main disadvantages: it delayed or distorted information, it inclined subordinates toward conventionalized rather than imaginative actions, and it failed to make full use of the advantages of specialization.

Some firms then turned to a functional delegation of powers. In the marketing apparatus of General Electric in the 1890's the vice-president in charge of sales supervised four or five product sales managers, each the boss over a sales force handling a particular line of product such as lighting equipment or street railway equipment. The product sales managers were all at the home office in Schenectady, but each product sales force had its separate local sales offices and local salesmen. Such functional specialization could also have its drawbacks: the inflation of expenses due to duplication of personnel, or a splitting of command so that a person might get conflicting orders from his various superiors.

Most companies ultimately arrived at what is known as the line-and-staff system of delegating power. In the line organization—the men actually engaged in buying raw materials or processing them or selling the output—the principle of hierarchical delegation was preserved. But staff specialists were given the job of collecting data, analyzing them, advising the line officers, and checking up on the operations of the firm. At the top of the company, the tasks of making general policy and of coordinating the enterprise were likely to be discharged by committees rather than by an all-purpose executive. Already by 1886 a "galaxy of committees" shone in the heavens above Standard Oil.

True, much remained to be done by later administrative experts: Alfred D. Chandler has argued that at Standard Oil "the lines of authority and communication were particularly unclear and confused." But much had been achieved. Several huge firms had devised structures that, if sloppy, were not fatally so. To that extent they provided models for other men to follow in other industries. But they also made it vastly more difficult for others to follow in their own industries. A new oil company, for instance, would need years to build up a workable organization, and during that period it would have to compete against Standard Oil which had built its organization and filled each job with a suitable person. The advantages of being a going concern were added to those of being a large company, and it happened with Standard Oil, as with other giants, that the rich got richer.

Capitalist: ANDREW CARNEGIE

He was built like a fire hydrant: short, chunky, his pathway as fixed as steel rails, high-grade vanadium. In his early years he benefited from the patronage of a high official in the Pennsylvania Railroad, but still he qualifies as a self-made man. His career might serve as the prototype for the fiction of Horatio Alger. Unlike real fire plugs, he did not leak water into the streets or the securities exchanges; since he always owned most of the stock in his companies, each share stood for solid equity.

Carnegie (1835–1919) emigrated from Scotland to Pittsburgh at age 12 with impoverished parents. By 30 he was an established railroad executive. He quit to go into steel making. His recipe for an empire became clear early. Unlike the general entrepreneurs of earlier times who would invest in any venture that promised a profit, Carnegie advised his juniors to put all their eggs in one basket and watch the basket. By and large, he followed his own maxim. He watched costs of production instead of profits. He was a canny tiger fighting the railroads over freight charges. He paid low salaries to administrators, rewarding them with small shares of ownership. He plowed profits back into the mills; an almost new machine might be scrapped if an alternative promised to do the work cheaper. Although he finally got into coal mining, railroads, and iron ore, he seemed almost deaf to the allure of vertical integration.

Specialization brought him gigantic rewards. When he sold Carnegie

Steel as the main constituent in the formation of U.S. Steel in 1901, he personally owned 58.5 per cent of the shares in his firm. He was paid $225,639,000 in 5 per cent first-mortgage bonds in the new corporation. Although the industrialist was also a pacifist, he benefited greatly from opportunities spawned by the Spanish-American War. The profits of Carnegie Steel approximately quadrupled in the two years after 1898. That rise in net earnings was precisely reflected in the price that Carnegie could wangle when J. P. Morgan was conceiving his billion-dollar baby called U.S. Steel.

CHAPTER 4

The Restless, and Their Discontents

But even the successful had their anxieties. At the core of the economic worries of many businessmen was the problem of over-production; that is, the inability of the American market to grow fast enough to absorb at profitable prices all that American producers could turn out. At times the overproduction was latent, in the form of excess capacity that was kept idle; at other times it was actual, in the form of cut-throat prices. Doubtless the falling level of prices for three decades was due partly to mechanization and the resultant lower costs, and partly to Federal fiscal and monetary policies. But it was also due partly to the failure of demand to increase as rapidly as productive capacity. Doubtless too, excess capacity from time to time in specific portions of an economy is a necessary price of economic progress, an indication that equipment becomes obsolescent under conditions of rapid technological advance. But from 1873 to 1898, excess capacity in the American economy was chronic and it afflicted virtually every industry (in marked contrast to the years from, say, 1843 to 1861). The sole important exception that I have found was raw wool, the price of which rose through this period. A major reason seemingly was the inability of sheepmen in many countries to muster enough political power to win government favors: in Germany, where the woolen manufacturers blocked an import duty on raw wool, the number of sheep fell from 25 million in 1873 to 5,800,000 in 1912; and in the United States the sheepmen were repeatedly out-maneuvered by cattle ranchers who won grazing rights on the public domain. But sheep interests, as compensation for their other sufferings, benefited in terms of price for their output.

Not so with growers of two great staples, wheat and cotton, whose dismay at the collapse of prices for their crops set off a succession of political rebellions. Not so with railroads, whose vicious rate wars inspired a series of combinations or "pools" aimed at restoring remunerative rates. Not so with steamship companies who found the Pacific trade "definitely over-tonnaged" by 1878 and who sent the rate on wheat from New York to Liverpool tumbling so far that in 1882 it was only 39 per cent of what it had been in 1873.

In oil refining only about 75 per cent of rated capacity was typically in operation, and more than 60 per cent of the refineries in operation were selling their products in markets abroad. Although Rockefeller and his associates were accumulating huge fortunes, they were not finding it easy. "All the fortune I have made has not compensated for the anxiety of that period," Rockefeller said later. "Work by day and worry by night, week in and week out, month after month. If I had foreseen the future I doubt whether I would have had the courage to go on." The efforts of Standard Oil to solve its problem are only an illustration of similar efforts by many other companies. They also show how excess capacity was the major element in a context that shaped many other developments of the period. The drive of American firms for foreign markets became increasingly important in shaping the foreign policy of the Federal government, as in Standard Oil's efforts to expand its sales in Brazil, China, and elsewhere. Prominent among new constitutional doctrines was the Rule of Reason advanced in the Standard Oil Case of 1911, which guaranteed that the Sherman Anti-Trust Act would not prohibit all efforts to combine to maintain profitable prices. Of these matters, much more will be said later.

Taken all in all, overproduction was so pervasive as to justify labeling the entire period as an "Age of Excess." The Distillers' and Cattle Feeders' Trust was motivated by the fact that stills usually operated at only 40 per cent of capacity. Five years of "overabundant plantings" in the California wine industry led to depression in 1886 followed by a decade of low prices. After competition among some 40 firms drove the margin between the price of raw sugar and the price of refined down to seven-tenths of a cent, the Havemeyers built their American Sugar Refining

Company into the Sugar Trust to control prices and to lobby in Washington.

There was excess capacity to mill flour, to make watches, to manufacture stoves. A large textile-machinery builder expanded to service a boom market from 1880 to 1884 and then found that "much of this capacity could not be utilized and was an unwelcome burden until the turn of the century." American farmers were expected to buy a mere 65,000 binders in 1883, but manufacturers expressed their wish to turn out 105,000. Substantial numbers of sewing machines and saws were being sold abroad. Coal mining was supposedly on a six-day week, but seldom did the typical miner work more than 200 days in a year. The *Bulletin* of the Iron and Steel Association commented in 1884 that it was exceptional "for half the works in condition to make iron to be in operation simultaneously." In 1892 *Iron Age* reported of the pig-iron industry "that the question is often asked, Will consumption ever catch up to anything like the production?" The Carnegie Steel Company, as will be seen, responded by using a diplomatic crisis to seek larger orders from the United States navy. Carnegie himself, while rejoicing at the age of 33 that his income had reached $50,000 a year, resolved to retire at 35: "To continue much longer overwhelmed by business cares and with most of my thoughts wholly upon the way to make more money in the shortest time, must degrade me beyond hope of recovery."

Although Carnegie long remained in close touch with his business, he did partially carry out his resolve and spent much time in Europe. But few wage earners could look forward to voluntary retirement at any age. In a population of about 50 million in 1880, the labor force was more than 17 million. Perhaps 4.5 million were industrial workers—wage earners in construction, in manufacturing, on trains, streetcars, ships. Most lived hard lives: a work week that might total 72 or more hours if you were employed, an exhausting pace of work, brutalizing conditions on the job, low pay for all but the skilled workers, the recurrent threat of layoffs or wage cuts during slack times. By 1877 general opinion in Cleveland held that the wages paid to employed workers were "scarcely adequate for the support of the laborer and his family," and yet Cleveland was one of the quietest cities in the Northeast during the great railroad strikes that summer.

On the morning of July 16, in the junction town of Martinsburg, West Virginia, firemen began deserting their freight trains in protest against a 10 per cent wage cut by the Baltimore & Ohio. Strikebreakers that the company had on hand quickly took their places. Brakemen and a few of the highly paid engineers joined the strike. They stopped trains by force. They fired on members of the state militia who arrived to protect the strikebreakers. The governor telegraphed President Hayes that he could not maintain order. Federal troops were dispatched to Martinsburg.

A train was stopped at Cumberland, Maryland. The governor ordered state militia to go there from Baltimore, but as they were about to entrain at the depot they were stoned and fired upon by a hostile mob. Civil war raged through Baltimore's streets. At the request of the governor, the President sent in the United States army.

At Pittsburgh the division superintendent of the Pennsy decreed a change in the working rules. Strikers refused to let trains leave the yards. They demanded that the company restore the old working rules and that it rescind a 10 per cent pay cut put through in June. Strikes broke out against the B. & O. in Ohio, against the Erie in New York. In Pittsburgh the militia fired on a mob and killed at least ten men. The city went insane. Strike sympathizers looted weapons from gun stores and besieged the militia in the Pennsy roundhouse. Other rioters derailed freight cars. Oil cars were set afire. Looting began. Mobs controlled the city. The Union Depot was burned down. Two miles of Pennsy track was littered with smoking ruins: 104 locomotives, 2,152 railroad cars of all kinds. A member of the militia reported: "I talked to all the strikers I could get my hands on, and I could find but one spirit and one purpose among them: that they were justified in resorting to any means to break down the power of the corporations."

The great strike was on. It hit all four of the Eastern trunklines. It broke out in Reading, in Buffalo, and swept westward across Ohio. Riots occurred in Chicago and St. Louis. Although the strike was slackening by July 25 and thereafter receded rapidly, it brought benefits to many railroaders. It stopped the downward drift of wage rates. Some roads rescinded wage cuts that had previously been imposed. The reason was clearly put by Robert Harris, president of the Burlington: "We have seen that a reduction of pay to employees may be as expensive to the Co. as an increase of the pay." Harris also proposed other reforms, including the cessation of Sunday freight service except for goods in transit because endless toil was "brutalizing our trainmen."

The President of the country wrote in his diary on August 5: "The strikes have been put down by force; but now for the real remedy. Can't something be done by education of the strikers, by judicious control of the capitalists, by wise general policy to end or diminish the evil?" A mass meeting called during the strikes by the New York Amalgamated Trades and Labor Union advocated another solution: it called on all workers to "organize in trade unions and to aid in the establishment of a national federation of trades, so that combined capital can be successfully resisted and overcome."

Even after the return of prosperity in 1879, wage earners were slow to follow this advice. In 1884 the predecessor of the American Federation of Labor spoke up for a concerted campaign to win a working day of only 8 hours by 1 May 1886. A mere five months before the deadline it suggested, the federation had only 7 national unions affiliated with it; its annual income was less than $800.

But labor resistance was stiffening. The Brotherhood of Locomotive Firemen, founded chiefly as a mutual insurance organization, repealed its no-strike rule in 1885, and thereafter it and other Brotherhoods put up an increasingly militant fight against the railroads. Even more impressive was the Knights of Labor, which won great strike victories over Jay Gould's Southwestern railroad system and other employers. The 8-hour movement made headway, with the burden of agitation and organization being borne by local unions and labor editors. The national unions whose members took an active part in the 8-hour campaign showed substantial gains in membership: the Cigarmakers grew from 12,000 to 24,672; the Carpenters from fewer than 6,000 to more than 21,000.

Nowhere was the struggle for the 8-hour day more aggressive than in Chicago, where prominent roles in the movement were played by a young Southerner, Albert R. Parsons, and other convinced anarchists. Just as Chicago was the railroad center of the United States, so was it a center of heavy industry, and no plant in town was more important than the giant McCormick reaper works. In February 1886, the company locked out its workers to break the union, and the next month it reopened with nonunion labor. The locked-out unionists continued a boisterous picket line around the plant.

Respectable Chicago was jittery about the labor situation. The anarchists' voices were loud and their language was unrestrained in its violence. The commercial newspapers replied in kind. Strikes were many. An estimated 100,000 workers were involved in the 8-hour movement, one of every 8 residents of the city. As the May 1 deadline approached, all reserve police were mobilized, but the day passed without incident. On May 3 a prominent anarchist was addressing a crowd of striking lumber shovers near the McCormick plant, when a battle erupted between the picketing unionists and nonunion workers. The police came and before they left, 2 unionists were shot to death and several others were wounded.

A meeting was called for the evening of May 4 to protest against police brutality. The site chosen was the Haymarket, a plaza of sorts near downtown Chicago which would hold 20,000 people. Mayor Carter Harrison went to the meeting, but when he saw the audience was orderly he went home. Then a police inspector at the nearby station formed 176 of his men in ranks and marched them on the meeting. As they reached the meeting a bomb was thrown. It exploded near the front ranks. The police began to shoot into the crowd. Nobody knows how many citizens were shot. The toll of police was 7 dead, 67 wounded.

The police rounded up every anarchist they could find, and many unionists who were not anarchists. Eight men were brought to trial for the bombing. All were convicted. Eighteen months after the bombing, on 11 November 1887, Albert Parsons and three others were hanged. One defendant committed suicide just before his scheduled execution. The three others were imprisoned.

When employers sought to blame all trade unions for the Haymarket bomb in order to discredit their economic demands, labor turned to politics in self-defense, and the most successful labor party in Chicago's history was formed in 1886. That autumn it elected 8 members of the state legislature, 5 judges, and came within 64 votes of electing a Congressman.

Even more notable were the political activities of labor in the mayoralty campaign of 1886 in New York City. In April, although New York had a reform Democratic administration under the shipping magnate William R. Grace, all but two of its aldermen were indicted for bribery in connection with a streetcar franchise for lower Broadway. With this evidence of corporate wrongdoing before them, workers reacted with even more anger than usual in May when a streetcar strike was broken with police help. The sense of outrage was aggravated on July 2 when a judge sent five leaders of the Central Labor Union to Sing Sing for extortion. These grievances against the municipal authorities reinforced the mood attendant on the 8-hour campaign and the hysterical newspaper reaction to the Haymarket bombing.

The Central Labor Union called for a united-front effort to capture the city's offices. The man they tapped to run for mayor was Henry George, who had become a world figure since the publication in 1879 of his classic *Progress and Poverty*. George had no desire to be mayor, but he did want to agitate the land question in practical politics. When he was presented with 34,640 signed pledges to work for his candidacy, he accepted the nomination.

The threat to the Democrats was grave: they had come to count on the votes of most wage earners. And for five years they had been split into warring factions, chief among them Tammany Hall on the one hand; on the other, the "reform" County Democracy led by prominent businessmen who allegedly believed in good government. But leaders of both factions died during the summer, and the possibility of a reconciliation emerged. The extent to which principle had figured in the earlier conflicts became apparent when Tammany named for mayor its most frequent bolter, a leader of the County Democracy, the iron manufacturer Abram S. Hewitt. There can be no doubt that the nomination resulted from a deal: Tammany and its supposed enemies later divided the Congressional nominations 50-50. Of such realism was politics made, and the reformers were politicians too.

With two candidates in the field whose fiscal probity was beyond question, the Republicans had to put up a third. Theodore Roosevelt was a blustery young man, 27 years old, who had served in the New York legislature from 1882 to 1884. In the latter year his wife died, and he moved to his ranch in the Bad Lands of Dakota. But he was restless; writing to his friend Henry Cabot Lodge on 10 August 1886, he indulged in a remarkable piece of self-assessment: ". . . as my chance of doing anything in the future worth doing seems to grow continually smaller I intend to grasp at every opportunity that comes up." In this spirit he agreed to be the Republican candidate for mayor, even though he knew that the party would have picked another if it had not felt it would lose.

Besides the evidence it furnished of just how shallow the ditch was between the machine politicians and the upper-class "reformers" such as Hewitt and Roosevelt and Grover Cleveland, the campaign demonstrated two other significant relations. First, that the Roman Catholic Church could be counted on by the Democrats of New York: the archbishop and his lieutenants threw their full weight against Henry George and for Tammany. Second, that labor would be accommodated in American politics, not by means of independent labor parties, but by incorporation of labor demands into the platform of a major party whenever the pressure rose high enough. The squeaky wheel got the grease.

When the brief but vigorous canvass ended, the official tally showed 90,552 votes for Hewitt, 68,110 for George, 60,435 for Roosevelt. After a careful assessment of the available evidence, Charles A. Barker in 1955 suggested that very possibly George received a majority of the legal votes, but was counted out by Tammany Hall. If so, the campaign is also significant as a precursor of the methods by which the dominant groups would keep power when confronted by Populist revolt.

But, for the moment, the political effort of labor had ended. George was roundly beaten in his race for state office on the United Labor ticket in 1887, and the party dissolved after a poor showing in the Presidential election the following year. In Chicago the labor party was strong enough to force a fusion of Republicans and Democrats in the mayoralty race in April 1887; then it fell apart. When labor next penetrated the consciousness of respectable elements, it did so by several spectacular and violent strikes.

During the Haymarket frenzy, Theodore Roosevelt had written from his ranch that he would have shot down the rioters. In the summer of 1887, while the case was on appeal, he said in a speech that all Americans would benefit if the "Chicago dynamiters" were hung. Probably few ranchers or farmers in the West felt so much concern about the subject. They had problems of their own.

Of the 7,700,000 farmers and farm laborers in the United States in 1880, about a million lived in the newly opened regions west of the Mississippi and east of the Rockies: in Minnesota, Iowa, Missouri, Kansas, Nebraska, the Dakotas. It was there, and in the South, that the farm revolt reached its highest pitch. Farmers suffered severely at times from natural hazards—drought, grasshoppers, blizzards. Even more serious were the falling prices of their chief cash crops. Cotton sold for 16.5 cents a pound in 1869; for 4.6 cents in 1894. Wheat sold for $2.06 a bushel in 1866; for 48.9 cents in 1894. Corn brought 65.7 cents a bushel in 1866; only 21.4 cents in 1896.

The general price level was falling, too, through those years. But some prices did not fall. Farmers were most conscious of the burden, fixed in dollar terms and therefore growing in terms of their effort, of paying the interest and principal on their debts. Once a man signed a mortgage, he was stuck. If he borrowed $500 for five years at 10 per cent in 1877, when wheat was selling for $1.08 a bushel, he was borrowing in effect about 500 bushels of wheat. But if the price of his wheat crop fell 50 per cent, he had to sell 100 bushels every year to pay $50 interest, and he had to sell 1,000 bushels in 1882 to pay off his $500 principal. For twice as much work, he got no more.

So farmers roared with agony and rage, because most of them were debtors. Why did they borrow? To buy land, many of them. Supposedly anybody could get 160 acres of public land without charge under the Homestead Act of 1862. Later Federal laws, including the Timber Culture Act of 1873, the Desert Land Act of 1877, and the Timber and Stone Act of 1878, offered an equal or greater quantity of land free to any person meeting certain conditions. But these laws did not work out as the land reformers and poor farmers had hoped. Much of the public domain was obtained illegally by speculators and monopolists. Settlers often found it advantageous to pay a railroad or a state for land that was better or that was closer to transportation than the available Federal land.

The total land in farms more than doubled from 1860 to 1900 —itself a major cause of the plummeting prices of farm products. But Fred A. Shannon has concluded that at most about a sixth of the new acreage was "land that came as a gift from the government." The price of raw land was often $3 or more an acre, so that even 80 acres of unbroken land would cost $240. And that size was the bare minimum for farming on the prairies, where the aridity dictated an extensive mode of cultivation. The advantages of being a big farmer were further increased by the mechanization of agriculture that was going on: large-scale methods were most economical for the cultivation of corn, and even more so of wheat.

The "cash capital costs" of settling a farm were probably higher on the plains of western Kansas or Nebraska than they had been on the prairies of eastern Kansas or Illinois. Yields per acre were lower, the chance of crop failure was greater—a farmer was virtually forced to farm more land less intensively by using large horse-drawn machinery. The editor of the *Prairie Farmer* estimated in 1885 that $500 would buy "a good span of working horses, first rate farm wagon, plows, harness, seeder etc. almost anywhere in the West," and that the cost of the building first erected on government land was usually $250 or less. The cash cost of breaking sod through the 1880's ran from $1.50 an acre up. In 1879 a farmer spent some $200 to run two strands of Glidden barbed wire around a quarter section in Kansas. A well cost some $2.00 a foot, and the average well in the state might be 40 feet deep.

Thus the farmer who got 160 acres of free land in Kansas, put buildings on it, bought horses and machinery, fenced his farm, drove a well for water, and hired somebody to break a mere 40 acres of sod (a job that took more than one team on the plains), incurred cash outlays of more than $1,000. In addition, he had to support his family for at least a year. So—he often borrowed.

The resulting problems and conflicts have been clarified by Allan G. Bogue, whose researches in business manuscripts have yielded far more reliable evidence than was previously available. Most commonly the farmer turned for funds to a broker of land mortgages—essentially a middleman between Western farmers and Eastern or English investors. Such a firm was J. B. Watkins and Company, founded at Lawrence, Kansas, in 1873. The ensuing depression proved favorable to Watkins, for it destroyed the confidence of persons of means in other forms of investment. Railroad stocks and bonds shrank in value; frequent failures of insurance companies aroused distrust; savings banks ended up in trouble. The steady decline in long-term rates of interest in the following years caused investors to look favorably to the promise of higher yields in the West, backed by the most tangible and meritorious security of all—the soil.

Meanwhile investment funds were accumulating rapidly in the Northeast. Big fortunes were being made. Even more important to Watkins, modest competences were piling up in the hands of thrifty farmers like Joseph Cook's father, of merchants who could not profitably use all their funds in their own firms, of lawyers and doctors and ministers. Watkins advertised his mortgages in the New York *Weekly Tribune* and the Springfield *Republican*, but from the start he relied chiefly on the Protestant religious press. To manage his branch office in New York he hired an expatriate Englishman who was a Quaker. Another Friend in Ferrisburg, Vermont, handled mortgages for Watkins. With many Quaker contacts in the Northeast and in Britain, he began advertising in Quaker papers in London and Glasgow. In 1878 he opened a London office, also with a Friend in charge.

Watkins was only one of many mortgage companies located in the West, selling their paper chiefly in the East or abroad. By 1880, when some 40 major companies were operating in Kansas, the biggest of them was the Corbin Banking Company of New York and New Hampshire. The Hartford insurance companies put millions of dollars a year into farm mortgages in the plains states—certainly more than the $8–12 million a year that the investors of Massachusetts were putting into Western mortgages in the period around 1885. The shortage of alternative chances for investment that seemed promising was yet another reflection of pervasive excess capacity: by driving interest rates down and making loans readily available to farmers, it enabled many of them to venture into unsound situations and helped set the stage for the farm revolt.

The advertising of the mortgage companies brought a swelling flood of funds into the region, and by 1881 Watkins' chief problem was to find enough sound applicants to fill orders from Eastern investors. In the arid regions, such as western Kansas, drought and bad crops tempted many farmers to take a mortgage and then leave their land, in effect selling it to the Eastern investor. The Eastern investor did not want the land, nor did Watkins. The former wanted interest on his loan; Watkins wanted his commissions for arranging the transaction. But Watkins found himself forced to foreclose on increasing quantities of land, especially in the bad years after 1887. Those were exactly the years in which he could not resell the land at a profitable price; often not at any price. The problem helped to swamp him. In 1894 his company went into receivership, following the road to disaster taken by most of his competitors in the business. By that time Watkins' firm had helped to arrange loans of some $17 million against farm land in the West.

Other troubles of Eastern investors can be seen in the experience of John and Ira Davenport, two brothers in a small town of western New York who controlled the use of several hundred thousand dollars a year and put much of it into Western mortgages. Interest rates were falling, and debtors wanted to pay off mortgages before they came due so the loan could be refinanced at lower interest. Local agents in the West, who made and supervised the loans, often proved dishonest or unreliable; indeed these sharpies of the plains states may have been the chief beneficiaries of the system. Land titles sometimes proved bad, due to fraud or other cause. Funds lay idle for months in Western banks, drawing no interest until they were loaned. This last was a serious problem for mortgage brokers. The flow of loanable funds into their hands tended to be fairly steady over the year, but Kansas farmers did most of their long-term borrowing from September to December, after the harvest was in, when they could compute their need for money.

But the farmers had legitimate grievances. Their efforts to control the cost of loans by setting a legal maximum rate of interest proved largely ineffective. The legal maximums themselves were high: 12 per cent in Kansas; 12 per cent in Nebraska, lowered to 10 per cent in 1879; 10 per cent in Illinois, lowered to 8 per cent in 1879. But the legal maximums meant little, because the borrower usually paid several other charges when he got the loan: (a) commission to the mortgage company; (b) commission to the company's local agent; (c) an examination fee; (d) clerk's fees for drawing the mortgage papers; (e) cost of the abstract; (f) recording fees. In 1874 these service charges could total 15 per cent of the face value of the loan in Kansas, where interest was 12 per cent. Loans at the time were usually made for three years, so the farmer in effect was paying 17 per cent to borrow money.

If farmers got little relief from the usury laws, they did benefit from competition among the lenders. By 1878 loans at 12 per cent had ceased to be the rule in Kansas, and Ira Davenport began pulling his funds out of the state and investing them in Michigan timberland or in Wall Street. That year an investors' agent at Cedar Rapids wrote that in Iowa "There are plenty of funds offered at eight per cent and coms of three to five per cent." By

1880 Watkins was lending money in Missouri at a straight 10 per cent and absorbing the commissions. He decided the time had come to form a combination among lending agencies to maintain rates, but his efforts met with no success. Total charges trended downward to as little as 8 per cent in central Kansas by 1886 and 1887.

But that was just when the years of disastrous crops began, and, in spite of the reluctance of most lenders to foreclose, more and more farmers lost their land. Of the mortgages taken in one township in central Kansas in those two years, nearly half ended in failure. A company official estimated that 9 out of 10 mortgages in the western part of the state were foreclosed. The fact that Watkins went into bankruptcy was no consolation to the farmers who tried in vain to pay off their debts so they could keep their land.

The career in Kansas of P. P. Elder shows the road that others trod from the Republican party to the Populists. While a young man he migrated from Vermont before the Civil War, was an active Republican in the hectic pre-war days, served in the Union army. After the war he served several terms in the legislature, and in 1870 he was Republican lieutenant governor of the state. In the next two years he organized two banks in Ottawa, but sold them out, and in the process he accepted a good bit of real estate rather than force his debtors into bankruptcy. Now he became a debtor, borrowing $10,000 from the Davenports to carry the property. He launched a feeder stock operation, fattening livestock for market; to build it up to optimum scale he borrowed further from the Davenports. He also supervised the management of their real estate in Franklin County, and his relations with them were close.

Hearing in 1881 that the Davenports were investing in Wall Street, he wrote to John: "I understand the whole develtree there —Banks cannot rule this government much longer—no more than slavery did—The end is foreshadowed as sure as there is a 'God in Israel.'" The next year, although the interest rate on his debt had been cut to 8 per cent, the debt was agreed to total $16,000. That November an Ottawa banker wrote to John about Elder: "I am mighty sorry he is going to the Legislature this winter—He will make war on *interest*." And so he did, over the years, proposing several amendments to the collection laws of Kansas.

Five years later he still owed the Davenports $16,000, and

wrote: "It now takes 2 steer & 2 hogs to pay the same sum as one did in 1883 or 84." A year after that, in May 1888, Elder explained to John Davenport: "I had as live deed that land at once to Ira as to try to meet 8 pr ct. This would perhaps be the best way—But I do not feel right in abandoning the land and you men after you have been so kind to me in the past. . . . Some of my neighbors . . . have lost from 2 to 5000. . . . The devilish dressed beef men is the cause."

Not until the depression of the 1890's ended was P. P. Elder able to get out of debt; even then he had to sacrifice most of his security. In spite of his sentiments about the kindness of his own creditors, he had no love for money lenders in general or for the dressed beef men like Gustavus Swift. In 1891, P. P. Elder, former banker, former Republican, was Populist speaker of the state House of Representatives.

That year J. B. Watkins wrote his London agent that the Farmers' Alliance, along with the harm it was causing, was doing good in urging farmers to pay off their mortgages. The president of a Nebraska loan company wrote privately about a rival: "If the truth was known, it was conceived in fraud." Watkins thought that many mortgage companies were "robbing both East and West and should be shown up."

Also robbing the South, so many Southerners thought. For every farmer in the North in 1880 between the Mississippi and the Mountain states, there were nearly four in the South—3,750,000 of them. The Civil War had hit agriculture in the region with devastating impact: every third horse or mule was destroyed, nearly half of the farming machinery. Recovery was slow. The valuation of Southern farm equipment in 1900 was less than half what it had been in 1860. Meanwhile farmers turned increasingly to a single cash crop, cotton, and they saw the price of that crop swing disastrously against them. Cotton output in 1894 broke all records— but as a reward for planting nearly 2½ times as many acres in cotton as in the panic year 1873, farmers were credited with fewer dollars when they sold their crop.

And what they were credited with, they often did not get, for they had already spent it. By 1880 one farmer out of three in the South was a sharecropper or tenant; in South Carolina and Georgia, one out of two. In the next ten years, the percentages rose.

A farmer on the Western plains could mortgage his land if he wanted to borrow. But in many areas of the South land was almost impossible to mortgage because, in the words of a Mississippi merchant, land would "be an incumbrance to own." Nobody wanted it, except Negroes and whites who could not even get a bare subsistence from any other occupation. Hence arose the crop-lien system; that is, the practice of mortgaging a crop when it was planted in order to get credit from the crossroads supply merchant for seed, for sowbelly and corn meal and molasses, for overalls and maybe a little tea or coffee. The farmer drew his pittance at the store, and paid exorbitant prices for it, and he sweated and strained through the hot summer, and when he harvested his crop he might owe more than the crop was worth. "The basest fraud on earth is agriculture," wrote a farmer in Mississippi. "No wonder Cain killed his brother. He was a tiller of the ground."

Merchant and planter often became the same man. If a man prospered in farming, he opened a store; if he prospered as a storekeeper, he took over land at bargain prices. But the local storekeeper did not keep all he squeezed from the farmer. He in turn paid high prices and high rates of interest to the factors and wholesalers who supplied him on credit. The factors and wholesalers in turn split what they got with manufactures and bankers, usually in the Northeast or in Europe. In his *Origins of the New South*, C. Vann Woodward concludes: "The merchant was only a bucket on an endless chain by which the agricultural well of a tributary region was drained of its flow." Six decades earlier a Populist orator in Kansas, Mrs. Mary Ellen Lease, had shouted: "The great common people of this country are slaves, and monopoly is the master. The West and South are bound and prostrate before the manufacturing East."

Industrialization had occurred in the South—true. Coal mines and steel mills opened in Alabama and Tennessee. Textile mills were built in Georgia and the Carolinas. Yet as late as 1900, 69 per cent of the labor force of South Carolina was in agriculture, less than 4 per cent in manufactures. At that time fewer than one person in 25 in North Carolina lived in a town with 2,500 or more inhabitants. These were states that had led the South in industrialization.

In industry as well as agriculture, men in the South often worked for the benefit of men in the Northeast or in England. When an act of Congress opened to unrestricted cash entry the

Federal lands of the five public-land states in the South, Northern capitalists poured into Alabama, Arkansas, Florida, Louisiana, and Mississippi. By 1888 they controlled the best stands of yellow pine and cypress in the South. When a railroad pushed into a region, Northern lumber syndicates were riding the rails before the spikes had cooled. They cut wide swaths through the South. The value of Louisiana's lumber output rose 10 times from 1880 to 1900; in the five Gulf states together the increase was more than 5 times. And in 1900 a United States forestry expert looked back and saw "probably the most rapid and reckless destruction of forests known to history." But some men got rich, and they did not live in the South anyway. By 1900 they could invest safely in Cuban sugar plantations.

State lands went the same way as Federal lands. Twelve railroads got free from Texas more than 32 million acres—their own Indiana. Florida in 1881 sold 4 million acres to a syndicate headed by Hamilton Disston of Philadelphia, at two bits an acre; the same year Disston resold half the land to an English syndicate. Another English firm bought a big tract in the Yazoo Delta of Mississippi; two others bought land in Texas. Most important of all the English firms in the New South was the North American Land and Timber Co., Ltd., which J. B. Watkins promoted among his English investors. The firm, and Watkins personally, bought 1.5 million acres of unsettled land along the Louisiana coast between Vermilion Bay and the Texas border. Much of it was swampland recently granted to the state by the Federal government, and the firm got it for 12½ to 75 cents an acre.

Watkins hired his brother-in-law, Professor Alexander Thomson, and President Seaman A. Knapp, both of the Iowa State Agricultural College, to show that farming was feasible on his Louisiana holdings. They opened lands for sugar and rice cultivation. By using wheat machinery on the upland prairies they revolutionized methods of rice production; yield per man went up 10 to 20 times, and in 5 years Louisiana was the leading rice state in the country. The company started in 1882, the same year that the Southern Pacific linked New Orleans to San Francisco; railroad and syndicate together boomed the area. Watkins planned his own railway—with the marvelous name of the Kansas City, Watkins, and Gulf—and after 1890 he built a section of it in Louisiana. He sent a railroad car filled with Louisiana products on tour of the North Central states. Midwestern settlers came to the Gulf coast; land values boomed. But Watkins had overextended his resources, and the venture did not pay off as quickly as he had hoped; it contributed to his bankruptcy in 1894.

The president of the National Cotton Planters' Association contended in 1881 that fewer than a third of the cotton plantations in the Mississippi Valley were still held by the men who had owned them in 1865, and that others were passing daily "into the hands of the commission merchants." Behind many if not most commission merchants stood Northern capitalists. Behind Milton H. Smith, president of the Louisville and Nashville Railroad, stood the New York financiers Jay Gould, Thomas Fortune Ryan, Jacob Schiff, and August Belmont, all members of its board of directors. Behind the directors stood English investors, reached through the House of Rothschild, which was represented in the United States by Belmont. The rival Alabama and Chattanooga Railroad had among *its* investors other New York financiers, Russell Sage and Henry Clews. It had also had William D. Kelley, Congressman from Pennsylvania. Kelley was called "Pig Iron" because of his staunch service to the cause of high tariffs.

The lines of control led to New York and Boston and London and even to Lawrence, Kansas, and the South remained predominantly an agricultural section, and agriculture was losing out. Farmers had gotten nearly 31 per cent of the national income in 1859; less than 16 per cent in 1889. Nearly 40 per cent of the national wealth was in agriculture in 1860; only 20.5 per cent in 1890.

In 1880 the average wealth per person in the states outside the South was $1,086. In the South, it was $376.

It was hard to be a farmer, harder yet to be a farmer in the South, still harder to be a Negro farmer in the South. And of the 6,575,000 Negroes in the United States in 1880, nine out of ten were dependent on farming or personal and domestic service in the South. They had few white allies, in this country or abroad. Leopold II of Belgium organized his International Association for the Exploration and Civilization of Central Africa in 1876, and soon Belgium, Britain, and France were out to take over Africa. Germany and Italy jumped in. By 1900 all Africa except Abyssinia and Liberia was under European rule. A decade earlier, all Asia except China had met a similar fate. Nowhere in the industrial world was there a body of respectable opinion to challenge American treatment of Negroes.

During the Presidential canvass of 1876 the Democrats campaigned strongly for the withdrawal of the United States army from support of Reconstruction governments in the South. And the day after the election it seemed that the Democrats had beaten the Republican nominee, Rutherford B. Hayes, and Hayes wrote in his diary: "I don't care for myself; and the party, yes, and the country, too, can stand it; but I do care for the poor colored men of the South. . . . The result will be that the southern people will practically treat the constitutional amendments as nullities, and then the colored man's fate will be worse than when he was in slavery."

Then Northern politicians and businessmen worked out an arrangement with Southern politicians and businessmen—having previously made many business arrangements with them that looked toward a joint search for profits in the development of Southern resources. The disputed election of 1876 was given to the Republican party. Hayes became President by the margin of one electoral vote, even though he had fallen 250,000 votes behind the Democrat in the popular vote. The new Chief Executive pulled Federal troops out of the statehouses in Louisiana and South Carolina, and the last Reconstruction governments collapsed. In the "Redeemed" South, treatment of Negroes was more or less as Hayes had predicted. But in his first annual message to Congress he claimed, in blatant neglect of the facts, that the former slaves were "now advanced to full and equal citizenship." He said that he would maintain their legal rights.

But he did not, and they despaired. The Great Exodus began; by 1879 some 30,000 Negroes had left Louisiana and Mississippi, most of them going to Kansas. At first they were welcomed there, but as the number of refugees grew, they were met with hostility. Messages were sent from Kansas to the South advising Negroes not to migrate.

Frederick Douglass, the great agitator against slavery and the foremost Negro in the country in 1879, also opposed the Exodus. He claimed that the South would perforce continue dependent on Negro labor in the fields and would therefore be compelled to treat Negroes fairly; he also claimed that Negroes could exercise more political power in the South, where in some areas they were a majority, than they could hope to do in the North. Douglass, a devoted Republican, had just been named United States marshal of the District of Columbia, and he put great faith in the President's recent assertion of the need to maintain the public peace in all parts of the Union. To make migration from the South into a general policy at such a time, Douglass said, would be cravenly to abandon the principle that the civil rights of all men should be upheld everywhere.

Negroes were making gains in some parts of the South: in Louisiana, according to Douglass, Negroes were paying taxes on at least $40 million worth of property; in Georgia, on $6 million. Negroes could vote in many areas, largely because the upper-class whites now back in control of Southern politics could use Negro votes to beat back the opposition of lower-class whites. But the number of Negroes in public office fell drastically. In South Carolina, 39 Negroes served in the legislature in 1877–1878, only 5 in 1888–1889.

From the Federal government Negroes now got nothing but promises, and sometimes not even promises. After Chester A. Arthur became President in 1881, he chose to use his power and patronage in the South to seek support among whites who were opposed to the Democratic machine, prompting a Negro editor to declare bitterly: "The Republican party has eliminated the black man from politics. . . . It has left the black man to fight his own battles." The Supreme Court too cast Negroes back on their private resources in the Civil Rights Cases (1883). These five cases arose under the Civil Rights Act enacted by Congress in 1875, declaring that nobody could be discriminated against by inns, public conveyances, or places of public amusement because of his race or color or previous condition of servitude.

Inquiring whether the 13th or 14th Amendments gave Congress the power to enact such a law, the Court decided that the 13th Amendment had to do only with slavery or involuntary servitude and that: "Mere discriminations on account of race or color were not regarded as badges of slavery." The former slave can no longer be "the special favorite of the laws" but must take on the "rank of a mere citizen. . . ." Therefore the 13th Amendment does not confer on Congress the required power. The 14th Amendment was intended to prohibit "State action of a particular character . . . Individual invasion of individual rights is not the subject-matter of the amendment." The civil rights guaranteed by the Constitution cannot be "impaired by the wrongful acts of individuals, unsupported by State authority. . . ." Therefore the pertinent sections of the law are unconstitutional, as beyond the powers of Congress. The sole dissenter against this line of reasoning was a Kentuckian, Justice John Marshall Harlan, who protested that it was "entirely too narrow and artificial" and that Congress possessed the powers it had exercised.

Other Federal agencies chipped away at the status of Negroes. In four cases from 1882 to 1888, lower courts upheld the doctrine of "separate but equal": an Ohio case involving segregated schools, and three cases involving segregation on public carriers. Administrative agencies joined the procession after the establishment of the Interstate Commerce Commission in 1887; three rulings by it in that year, 1888, and 1889 approved the "separate but equal" principle.

In two areas a majority of the Supreme Court allowed Congress to use its power to protect Negro rights. The Court upheld a section of the Civil Rights Act providing that no citizen could be disqualified from service on a grand or petit jury solely because of "race, color, or previous condition of servitude. . . ." And in *Ex parte Yarbrough* (1884) it held that Congress could legislate against violence to voters in an election that involved Federal offices. But would Congress pass legislation that would make effective the potential G.O.P. support among Southern Negroes?

Republican leaders had good reason to be irritated about the matter. Themselves the authors of political rights for Negroes, they had been forced since the end of Reconstruction to watch their beneficences work to the advantage of the rival party. Before the Civil War each slave had been counted as three-fifths of a person in apportioning seats in the House of Representatives and in the Electoral College. But after the Reconstruction Amendments each Negro voter counted as a whole person. The result was to give the South 37 additional votes in the Electoral College. In 1880, in 1884, in 1888, all 37 of these votes were cast for the Democratic candidate.

Repeatedly Republicans had sought to solidify their ranks among white voters in key Northern states by waving the bloody shirt, by refighting the Civil War, by branding the Democrats as the party of treason. Related to this tactic, but far from identical with it, was the problem of building up the G.O.P. in the South. Here Republican leaders were sharply divided, and fluctuated back and forth between two contradictory approaches. After Hayes' policy of conciliating Southern whites "made a wreck of the Republican party," as his Secretary of State put it, Republican campaigners in 1880 splashed more blood on the shirt and demanded protection for Negro voters. The two policies were not entirely consistent: many ordinary Northern whites were far from enthusiastic about Negro suffrage.

An alternative policy—building a lily-white high-tariff Republican organization among the growing class of Southern industrialists—appealed to three key groups in the North. James G. Blaine won the Republican nomination for the Presidency in 1884 by joining the faction of Republican politicians and Eastern manufacturers who embraced this tactic. It was also attractive to Northern merchants with Southern customers. Finally, several prominent editors of national periodicals spearheaded by E. L. Godkin of the *Nation* and Richard Watson Gilder of the *Century* had long been advocating a sectional reconciliation including acceptance of anti-Negro sentiment. Mainly Liberal Republicans of the 1872 variety, these men sought to purify politics by means of civil-service reform, and they were convinced that Negro suffrage was a potent source of corruption. Gilder put it thus in 1883: ". . . the negroes constitute a peasantry wholly untrained in, and ignorant of, those ideas of constitutional liberty and progress which are the birthright of every white voter; . . . they are gregarious and emotional rather than intelligent, and are easily led in any direction by white men of energy and determination."

The lily-white strategy was tried for a while in 1881–1882. Benjamin Harrison followed it in the campaign of 1888, and in the election he secured more Southern votes than any Republican nominee for the Presidency since the end of Reconstruction. But after the policy suffered crushing defeats the next year in Louisiana and Virginia, President Harrison abandoned it. He now believed that elaborate schemes to recruit Southern whites were not the answer, that the answer was the use of Federal power to insure that Republican votes in the South were registered at the polls. Several bills to that end were advanced, but the struggle came to center on the measure introduced on 26 June 1890 by Representative Henry Cabot Lodge and sponsored in the Senate by George

Frisbie Hoar. Although Lodge and Hoar, both of Massachusetts, were aware of the party advantages of the measure, it seems clear that they also thought the disfranchisement of Negroes was undemocratic and immoral. The core of their rather complicated bill was this: In a Federal election if a specified number of voters in any election district petitioned Federal authorities, Federal supervisors from both major parties were to be appointed, with power to pass on the qualifications of any voter challenged and to place in the ballot box any ballot wrongly refused by local officials.

A week before Lodge introduced his bill, the *Nation* predicted that it would pass the House, and explained why: "The only question as to any Republican measure proposed in the House of Representatives is whether Speaker Reed wants it to pass." Reed, who saw nearly all questions primarily in terms of his party's interests, had decided that a Federal Election Law was needed. With him in the chair on the afternoon of July 2 as the Lodge Bill was being read for the third time, an opponent protested that a quorum was not present. Reed ignored him. The dissident then said: "I appeal from the decision which the Chair declines to make." The ensuing laughter did not prevent passage by a vote of 155 to 149, with 24 abstentions.

While the Democratic party denounced the "Force Bill" as antidemocratic and a violation of state rights, white supremacists in Mississippi moved to guarantee that Federal intervention in elections there could not possibly be effective. A state constitutional convention that met on August 12 drew up a document that included the "Mississippi Plan" for restricting suffrage. It imposed residence requirements. It required the voter to pay his poll tax eight months before an election—and to keep the receipt (eight months before November was just the time of year when a poor farmer was least likely to have any money). It required him to read a portion of the state constitution, or, if he was illiterate, to understand it when read to him and to interpret it reasonably. Hostility to the new constitution was so widespread that the convention did not present it for popular ratification at all but simply declared it to be the fundamental law of the state. It proved effective: by 1892, the size of the potential electorate had been reduced from 257,000 to 77,000. Negro suffrage had virtually disappeared. Many poor whites had been disfranchised.

Opposition to the Lodge Bill, even apart from Democratic

partisanship, was substantial in the North. Few white Americans dissented vigorously from the notion that this was "a white man's country." On the negative side, the chief source of hostility to sectionalism had been described in the *North American Review* in November 1888: "The manufacturing sections of the North are as much interested in the peace, content and development of the Southern States as the Southern States themselves can be. Each desires a market for its respective products; and the more contented each is, and the more intimate the relations of both are, not only will the product be larger but the means of purchase will be increased." Thus Negro unrest over disfranchisement came in conflict with business unrest over limited markets. Wealthy merchants in New York and flour millers in St. Louis fought the Lodge Bill. The Republican national chairman, Senator Matthew S. Quay of Pennsylvania, was repeatedly warned by Hamilton Disston that the bill would upset business and reduce property values in the South. Quay also explained publicly that the president of the Philadelphia Manufacturers' Club had raised $300,000 for the G.O.P. campaign in 1888 in the expectation that its success would result in higher duties on imports.

Now the Republicans had to keep the bargain, and the McKinley Tariff Bill had already passed the House. As early as July the Baltimore *Sun* charged that the Republicans were pushing the Election Bill in order to weaken free-trade sentiment in the South, that they would finally offer to kill the Lodge-Hoar measure if Southern Senators would not filibuster against the McKinley Bill. Soon after, Quay introduced a resolution that had the effect of sidetracking the Election Bill to get a final vote on the tariff. The deal prompted Senator Orville H. Platt (Republican of Connecticut) to remark: "It will probably give us a Tariff bill—but acquired at what a sacrifice!" But moral queasiness proved weaker than the dictates of politics, and in early October the McKinley Tariff Act was signed into law.

Although the Republican party a month later was trounced in the Congressional elections, it kept control of the Senate as well as the White House. But could its leaders hold the members in line on the Election Bill? Time after time in these years the votes in Congress revealed that, while party solidarity was usually maintained on minor issues, it was likely to break on crucial ones. On a major issue the way a Congressman voted was influenced more by the section of the country he came from than by the party he belonged to. And ironically the growth of the West, even as it built up Republican strength in the Senate, also helped to split that strength and finally to bury the Lodge-Hoar Bill. In two years from February 1889 to January 1891 six new states— Washington, South Dakota, North Dakota, Montana, Wyoming, and Idaho—sent members to the Senate. All twelve men were Republicans. But they also came from silver-producing states, and they desperately wanted to secure free coinage of silver. Some of them were indifferent or hostile to Negro suffrage. By the end of the 51st Congress in 1891, there were 51 Republicans in the Senate to only 37 Democrats, but Negro unrest over disfranchisement conflicted with silverites' unrest over excess capacity. On 5 January 1891 the Senate again pushed aside the Federal Election Bill, by a vote of 34 to 29, to permit debate on a bill providing for free coinage of silver. Of the six Republicans who split with their party to join the majority, two were from Nevada and two from Idaho, and one, Leland Stanford, was from California.

Racist feelings were probably as intense in the West as in the South. When a Missouri editor wrote, "No simian-souled, sooty-skinned, kink-curled, blubber-lipped, prehensile-heeled, Ethiopian gorilla shall pollute the ballot box with his leprous vote," a Democratic paper in San Francisco quoted the statement approvingly. The fact that the West Coast had few Negroes was no barrier to hating dark-skinned persons, and California was inflamed against its residents from Asia.

During the hard times of 1877 a meeting of unemployed men on the sand lots near the new city hall in San Francisco ended in a two-day riot against the Chinese. The Sand Lot Movement produced a Workingmen's Party of California with a platform that called for getting rid of "cheap Chinese labor as soon as possible," an end to "land monopoly," destruction of "the great money power of the rich by a system of taxation that will make great wealth impossible. . . ." Led by an immigrant Irish drayman named Denis Kearney, the party in 1878 elected about a third of the delegates to a state constitutional convention. There they united with farmers to put through a clause prohibiting corporations from employing any Chinese. The constitution was adopted by the voters, and in 1880 the legislature passed a law to enforce the anti-Chinese provision. Some large corporations fired quite a few

Chinese, even though the law was declared invalid in *In re Tiburcio Parrott* (1880). By that time the Sand Lot Movement, torn by personal ambitions and factionalism, harassed by the repeated imprisonment of its leaders for their violent language, had ceased to be an effective force.

But anti-Chinese agitation persisted. The Burlingame Treaty of 1868, which had granted "most favored nation" status to Chinese subjects in the United States, was revised in 1880 to allow the Federal government to "regulate, limit, or suspend" Chinese immigration but not to "absolutely prohibit it." Anticipating new barriers under the new treaty, 18,000 Chinese entered the United States in 1880–1881 and more than 39,000 in 1882. The protests of the weak trade unions were reinforced by complaints from white manufacturers in some Western industries, such as boots and shoes, who resented the competition of Chinese employers using Chinese labor. West and South united in Congress to put through a bill, over Eastern opposition, to suspend Chinese immigration for 20 years.

The bill was vetoed by President Arthur, and one paragraph in his message deserves special notice: "Experience has shown that the trade of the East is the key to national wealth and influence. . . . It needs no argument to show that the policy which we now propose to adopt must have a direct tendency to repel Oriental nations from us and to drive their trade and commerce into more friendly lands. It may be that the great and paramount interest of protecting our labor from Asiatic competition may justify us in a permanent adoption of this policy; but it is wiser in the first place to make a shorter experiment. . . ." Confronted with this reminder of current economic realities, Congress reduced the term of the suspension to 10 years. Now Arthur did not block the bill. Suspension was later extended until it became permanent. Thus the United States adopted its first immigration law that was frankly discriminatory on the basis of national origin.

The restriction was symptomatic of the growing animosity aroused by the nationality of many immigrants. Increasingly after 1880 they came from southern or eastern Europe; the so-called New Immigrants were Russians and Poles, Bohemians and Jews, Italians and Greeks. Unlike the Old Immigrants who had often headed for the Midwest and even for farms, the new arrivals tended to cluster in Northeastern cities. Few were Protestants. Many could not read

Frederick Douglass. (Original etching by Suzanne Hodes.)

or write. Most were dark-skinned. They lived in filthy slums. They worked for miserable wages. Italian immigrants, the majority of them illiterate, most of them former peasants who now toiled at the most menial jobs as ditch diggers or ragpickers, were regarded by many Americans as the most depraved nationality among the New Immigrants. When a construction boss in the West was asked, "You don't call . . . an Italian a white man?", he replied: "No, sir, an Italian is a Dago." Two decades later President Theodore Roosevelt, concerned over the deportment of Latin American nations, declared his intention to "show those Dagos that they will have to behave decently."

In Russia the pogroms of 1881 created an emigration spirit among the 3 million Jews, and they began to move toward the Land of Promise. By 1890 New York City had 80,000, Chicago 20,000, Philadelphia 10,000. The next year the Russian government without warning expelled thousands of formerly privileged Jews from Moscow, St. Petersburg, and Kiev, and the tempo of emigration quickened. In the Old Country most of the migrants had been artisans—tailors, butchers, carpenters, bakers. A few started farming colonies in the United States, but most found jobs in sweatshops in the garment districts. However promising the future, conditions in the present were terribly degraded for most,

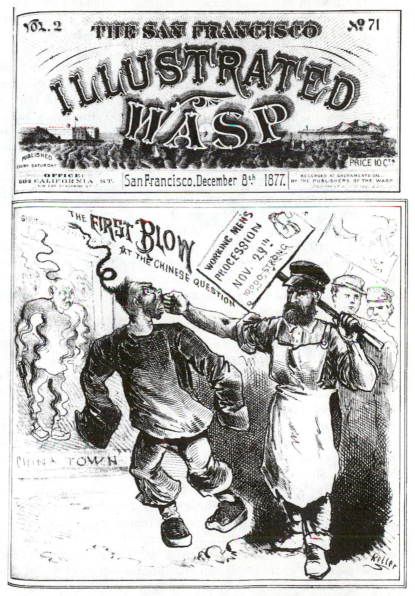

Anti-Chinese cartoon. (Courtesy The Bancroft Library.)

and the rare early efforts to improve them by joint action were likely to meet with police brutality. During a Philadelphia cloak-makers' strike in 1890, a leader tried to rally his fellows by saying, "I have six children, and sooner than give in I would kill them one by one and eat them to keep me alive." He was arrested for having threatened to kill his children.

Patterns of acceptance and rejection were complex. On the one hand, financier Joseph Seligman, perhaps the most eminent German Jew in the United States, was denied accommodations at the leading resort hotel in Saratoga Springs in 1877. On the other hand, German Jews, although often generous in their philanthropies to new Jewish arrivals from eastern Europe, would not embrace them wholeheartedly. At Mount Sinai Hospital in New York, 90 per cent of the patients in the 1880's were treated free, nearly all of them being Jews from eastern Europe. But Jewish physicians from that area were not admitted to the hospital's staff. In 1894 the *Yiddishe Gazetten* complained: "In the philanthropic institutions of our aristocratic German Jews you see beautiful offices, desks, all decorated, but strict and angry faces. Every poor man is questioned like a criminal, is looked down upon; every unfortunate suffers self-degradation and shivers like a leaf, just as if he were standing before a Russian official."

Old immigrants themselves frequently faced discrimination. A Danish farming settlement in northeastern Nebraska was the birth-place in 1874 of Alvin Johnson. Native-born Protestants in the area, antagonistic as they were to the papist Irish, were even more hostile to the Danish. The Danes allegedly were taking over the country. They ate food that pigs wouldn't touch. They used disgusting language: Didn't they persist in using the word "bull" to refer to gentleman cows? Alvin Johnson, when he was 4 years old, was taken by his sisters to visit the school. A girl named Hattie took him in charge. She was 10 years old, tall, and beautiful. Then up marched a big girl and shrieked, "Hattie! Take your hand away from that nasty little Dane." Johnson, even after he had become an elderly man and a famous scholar, still remembered.

Among these groups, then, were most of the disinherited. Industrial wage earners—more than 4 million of them in 1880. Farmers—more than 7.5 million. Southerners—16.5 million. Negroes—6.5 million. Immigrants—6.5 million. If a man was an immigrant and an unskilled worker, or a Negro and a Southern farmer, he had it doubly hard, or triply so. Even the last statement may oversimplify. In a thorough and thoughtful study, Alexander Saxton points out that even a Henry George could be polluted by prejudice in talking about the stance of white labor toward Chinese immigrants. George's arguments displayed both "the rational economic argument which would focus on importation under servile contract and the emotional hostility toward Chinese themselves . . ."

Tailor: Conrad Carl

When Carl testified in 1883 to the Senate Committee upon the Relations between Capital and Labor, he had spent three decades as a tailor in New York City. When he took up the trade, a tailor did piecework at home with his wife and children. About 1854 the sewing machine was introduced: "it stitched very nicely, nicer than the tailor could do . . ." An ancient laboriously acquired skill, one which had gnarled his fingers, bent his back, and dimmed his eyes, had been rendered obsolete by technology. Bosses insisted that each tailor buy a machine out of his own pocket; although it enabled him to work faster, earnings did not rise, so the investment was lost. Also it caused trouble in the tenement. "The machine makes too much noise in the place, and the neighbors want to sleep, and we have to stop sewing earlier; so we have to work faster. We work now in excitement—in a hurry." Nobody could stop working to eat lunch.

> Q. As a class, then, the workers save nothing?
> A. No.

Senator Henry W. Blair asked for the names of bosses who were regarded as likely to punish a worker for testifying before the Committee.

> A. Now, sir, if I lose my work who can give me another work? I am an old man now, you know, and the young ones, they get the work and they say, "He is an old man; what can he do?"

But on certain topics, Carl did not hesitate to speak. Like many of his peers, he was an ideologue:

So long as legislation is unjust to the poor, to tax the poor who have nothing but their daily earnings, to tax them by indirect taxes, there is no way to better the condition of the workingman. The foundation of all society is based upon injustice, to make the rich richer and the poor poorer. The rich receive donations from the state by legislation; from the laboring men will be taken the last cent, by high rents and high-priced provisions. . . . The dangerous classes are not to be found in the tenement houses and filthy districts, but in mansions and villas. To make rich people as we have today, means to make them superior to their fellow citizens; to give them power to dictate to their fellow citizens their own will. . . .

CHAPTER 5

Onward (Mainly to Cities) and Upward

With businessmen weighted down by excess capacity, with industrial workers sometimes so provoked that they engaged in tumultuous disturbances, with farmers losing their land, with Negroes and immigrants meeting discrimination daily, the years after 1877 might seem to be a time when widespread discontent would have generated pressure upon politicians to rectify the situation. But national politics until 1890 do not reflect such pressure; the Federal government was the epitome of lethargy. It was astoundingly idle. This paradox—grave problems seemingly affecting millions of persons on one hand, an elected government seemingly indifferent to their fate on the other—needs to be confronted before we enter into a description of national politics from 1877 to 1893.

Of course we might exaggerate either the amount or the nature of the discontent that existed. Those who seem underprivileged to us did not necessarily seem so to themselves. Their standards of expectation were not ours. A man who grew up on a Southern farm and then took a job in one of the new mill towns in the Piedmont did not think it cruel that his sons had to work as bobbin boys; he regarded child labor as part of the order of nature. An immigrant living in a tenement and working in a sweatshop yet knew that for the first time in his life he was wearing shoes seven days a week. He was also aware that he was no longer threatened by compulsory conscription into the Russian army for a term of six years.

Even more pacifying for man after man was the knowledge

that his children need not live out their lives exactly as he had lived out his. No group in American society was so downtrodden that some individuals from it did not get ahead—by toil, by thrift, by crucial bits of luck. Perhaps the progress that a Negro farmer in the South could make in a decade was painfully slow, but he could realize every moment that he was moving upward and that the ascent from generation to generation might be enormous. Consider, for instance, the faith needed to power the achievements of such men as Zack Hubert. When the Civil War ended he was a slave child in Georgia. Until he was 21 he worked with his father who rented a farm. Then Zack Hubert rented for himself a while. About 1885, when he was perhaps 27, he and two brothers bought 165 acres in Hancock County, Georgia. Agreeing to pay $1,650 in three equal annual payments, they set to felling trees and clearing land. They built a log cabin. Then they built a brush arbor and called in the neighbors for Baptist services. Paying off the land as scheduled, they split it equally. Although Zack Hubert himself never went to school, all twelve of his children had graduated from college by 1924. One daughter was married to a physician in Atlanta. The oldest son, who had done graduate work at the University of Chicago, was principal of a Negro high school with 2,000 students in Savannah. Another son was director of agriculture at Tuskegee Institute in Alabama. There he had as a colleague another former slave, the famous chemist George Washington Carver.

American politics until 1892 was acted out against this background of upward mobility. The chances to save money and to get ahead may have been slender in rural areas, but they were not absent. While Mexican sheepherders on the Southwestern range were being paid only $30 a month plus food, an expert at shearing could make as much as $10 a day. Fortunes could be made on the range, even by boys who had been reared in modest circumstances. Charles Goodnight proved that. In 1877 he set up the JA Ranch in the Texas Panhandle as a partnership with John George Adair, a British broker who had emigrated to Denver. Adair was to provide the capital, Goodnight the management. They built up a ranch 35 miles square on which they grazed thousands of cattle. In five years Adair had gotten back his entire investment, plus 10 per cent interest, and the partnership was showing a clear profit of $512,000.

Goodnight withdrew from the JA in 1887. During the ten years he had managed it, it had earned 72 per cent a year on its capital.

Outside the sections devoted to wheat and cotton, agriculture could furnish many success stories. This was especially true east of the Mississippi and north of the Ohio. Connecticut had fewer acres of farm land in 1900 than in 1860, but the farmers who remained were better off than ever before. A good herd of dairy cows by 1893 was yielding twice as many pounds of butter per cow a year as in Civil War days. H. C. Downer, who operated a diversified corn-hog farm 60 miles from Chicago, felt prosperous enough in the depression year 1893 to make more than one trip to the city during the Columbian Exposition.

Profits were often made speculating in farm land. From 1881 to 1887 in a block of six counties in southeastern Nebraska—counties which were not particularly involved in the contemporary land boom—the price of land doubled to reach about $17.50 an acre. But speculators in farm land were well advised to focus on the environs of towns and cities. A farm near Abilene, Kansas, sold for $6.25 an acre in 1867. Twenty years later it brought $270 an acre. A quarter section near Clifton, Kansas, earlier thought to be worthless, sold for $6,000.

Such facts are symbolic. The rapidly growing towns and cities were the centers of opportunity. Historian Fred A. Shannon has estimated that for every industrial worker who moved to the country and succeeded at farming, twenty farm boys became urbanites. Shannon's conclusion was that "the rise of the city in the nineteenth century was a safety valve for rural discontent." While the population of rural areas rose less than five million in the decade after 1880, the population of urban areas rose eight million. And under the census definition, hundreds of thousands of industrial wage earners—miners, timber workers, railroad employees—were rural inhabitants. Most mining towns, for instance, had fewer than 2,500 residents, but they were certainly centers of industrial opportunity. And if we use for the moment another standard of "urbanization" than simply counting heads—namely, that the place of work is not identical with the homes of the workers —they were urban.

These mining towns, in a booming industry, held important opportunities to get ahead. Quite a few of the men in middle management in the big anthracite companies in 1900 had begun working in the mines before they were ten years old. Seniority counted for a great deal. For that matter, so did survival. If we assume a representative group of 200 anthracite miners, each age 20, at the end of the Civil War, half of them were dead of natural causes by 1900. Another 15 were dead of occupational injuries. Fifty or so had left the industry. They had opened saloons or other small stores. They had taken jobs in expanding steel mills in nearby towns. They had become lawyers, or politicians, or both. They were union officials. Three had become foremen in the mines. The remainder, perhaps three dozen, were still miners, but they were getting the more lucrative jobs and each had several helpers working for him.

The existence of natural resources such as anthracite which could be rapidly and profitably exploited was in itself very important in sustaining high rates of upward mobility in the United States. But more important, anthracite mining was unusual among the extractive industries in this country in being limited to a single concentrated area in northeastern Pennsylvania. Bituminous coal in contrast existed in many states in veins that could be worked economically: a belt from Virginia to Illinois, Alabama, Kansas, Utah. Other minerals were widespread. So was lumber. Some kind or kinds of farming could be conducted profitably in most regions. Summed up, many of the undeveloped areas in 1877 held a *variety* of openings for business ventures which would yield high returns to different types of capital goods and labor. It has been suggested that this happy occurrence was so unusual that it may have made the American frontier unique among the frontiers of the world.

The process of opening up virgin territory in the United States has been aptly termed "sequential growth." The first venture in an area might be copper mining. Lumbering begins to provide timber for the mine shafts. A town springs up with smelters to process the ore. The region, any new region, offers quite a few chances for "once-and-for-all" investment: railroads, construction of roads and public buildings, residential subdivisions. There are openings in law, in banking, in politics. Then, perhaps only then, do farmers invade the county to provide food for the growing urban market. Next, the town grows to service the farmers. Real-estate values surge upward, and the resulting profits provide the capital for other commercial and manufacturing enterprises. After the population of the city reaches a certain point—perhaps in 1880 the crucial figure was 50,000 or 75,000—growth becomes almost self-sustaining. However, as Jane Jacobs has wisely said, a city that does not repeatedly generate new exports can languish.

Thus, although it is broadly true that farms on the frontier did little directly to drain off industrial wage earners from Eastern cities, it does not follow that the process of settling the Western frontier did little to alleviate Eastern discontent. New farms in the West absorbed vast quantities of products from Eastern factories. Western railroads were built with Eastern iron. Also, and not least, the West from the beginning contained cities as well as farms. In the late 19th century, urbanization west of the Mississippi River was nearly as rapid as for the nation as a whole.

This result obtained in part because the relatively slow rate of urbanization of the South dragged down the national average. In that section the cities that grew rapidly from 1880 to 1890 were those such as Atlanta, Birmingham, and Nashville which developed substantial manufacturing; long established commercial cities showed population gains of less than 25 per cent: New Orleans, Richmond, Louisville. The major Eastern cities recorded gains in the same decade that were important but not spectacular:

	1880	1890
New York (Manhattan only)	1,911,692	2,507,414
Philadelphia	847,170	1,046,964

Fully 39 of the fifty largest cities in the United States in 1890 were located east of the Mississippi and north of the Ohio.

But the Midwest was the scene of the startling gains in the decade:

Chicago	503,125	1,099,850
Minneapolis	46,887	164,738
St. Paul	41,473	133,156
Kansas City	55,781	132,710
Denver	35,029	106,773

With American cities growing with such breathtaking speed, the typical urban resident was getting ahead. This was true even of men who began life in very modest circumstances. Consider the son of a German peasant couple who migrated to Ohio in 1847 when he was three months old. Although his family was poor, the boy managed to go to high school for a while. He served in the Civil War, did menial labor on a railroad, worked as a farmhand, taught school. Then he read law, and practiced for a few years in Missouri. In 1875 he moved to Chicago. He knew nobody there. For two years he slept in his office until he was earning enough to rent another room. But in 1879 he made his first $500 investment in real estate. By 1890 his property was valued at $500,000, and his supplementary career in politics had made him a judge in Cook County. Two years later John Peter Altgeld was chosen governor of Illinois.

Jean Daniel Debs was penniless when he arrived in New York from Alsace in 1849. He ended up in Terre Haute, where he supported his wife and growing family by a series of unskilled jobs. He worked in a packing house. He too served time on a railroad section gang. At last he was able to invest $40 in a stock of groceries and open a small store in the front room of his house. In 1890 he was the moderately well-to-do proprietor of a neighborhood grocery. He was happy. He had reared six children. His oldest son, Eugene, was only 34 years old, but already he had served as city clerk of Terre Haute and as a member of the state legislature. Now he was secretary-treasurer of a thriving national trade union. He had built a lavish home in one of the wealthy sections of the city; the lot alone cost $4,000, and the mantles were San Domingo mahogany.

There can be no doubt that immigrants were badly exploited when they first arrived in the United States. The huge armies of men who built railroads during the decade were recruited through labor exchanges in the big cities. One exchange in New York claimed to have a contract to supply 5,000 men to a single firm in the summer of 1885; another bureau sent 11,000 men to the West Shore Railroad, and so on. Wages could be extremely low: the Italian Labor Bureau in New York offered men at 50 or 60 cents a day. Often these gangs worked under some variation of the padrone system. The labor exchange would advance to each man his passage money to the site of the job, and keep his baggage as security for the loan. It also sent a boss-interpreter along with the gang. The immigrant's earnings were paid to the boss, and he commonly did not pass them all along to the man.

But immigrants were quick to adjust their material expectations to American standards. A British consul observed in 1880 that English textile operatives in Philadelphia were living very comfortably for workingmen. Back in Staffordshire, it was charged, a potter was content to wear "a flannel shirt and a handkerchief around his neck from one week's end to another," but soon after he arrived in this country he bought "a white shirt and a white collar and nice necktie and a pair of patent-leather shoes." A mill owner in the silk-manufacturing center of Paterson, N.J., grumbled about English immigrants there: "They can make at least one half as much again here as in England, but they do not live in the same penurious manner. They come here to enjoy rich food, and want meat three times a day, whereas in England they would be satisfied with cheese and porridge."

Even casual laborers, at least those who were employed and who had no families, could live well by their standards. One man without a definite craft arrived in Chicago while the grounds for the Columbian Exposition were being prepared. He worked there a while building roads. Then he got a job as a hand truckman in a factory on the West Side. His pay was $1.50 a day. But he got board and room nearby for $4.25 a week. In his words:

> In the tenement house in Chicago we breakfasted at half past six in the morning, had a porridge, meat, a vegetable, we had all the coffee we wanted for breakfast, and excellent bread—all . . . very well prepared. For our midday meal at each man's place was a steaming bowl of soup. It was replaced with a plate containing a slice of roast of some sort, and two or three vegetables, and an abundance of bread, and after that would come dessert, usually pie—or sometimes a pudding. In the evening, after our day's work was done, we had a simpler meal, some cold meat and a hot vegetable, with an abundance of bread, and we finished up with a fruit.

Similarly a young Jewish girl who emigrated from Poland to New York got work in a sweatshop making underskirts. Her pay was only $4.50 a week, but she and her roommate lived on $2.00 a week each. "Of course," she testified, "we could have lived cheaper, but we are both fond of good things and felt that we could afford them."

Immigrants and urban wage earners sometimes accumulated property with what was, by European standards, unbelievable speed. Chicago contained the third largest Bohemian city in the world, with 60,000 or 70,000 of them by 1893. The flood tide of immigration from Bohemia came in 1884–1885, but the migration had begun more than three decades before. Early arrivals in Chicago, although most of them knew crafts or even professions, had to take menial jobs as streetsweepers or cigarmakers; it was reported that graduates of the University of Prague worked for $2.50 per week. But the many Bohemian buildings-trades craftsmen benefited from the city's enormous population growth after 1880, and even when their wages were low they saved a bit toward buying a house. Having reached that goal, they enlarged the house with a second story which they rented out. "When more was saved, the house was pushed in the rear, the garden sacrificed, and in its place an imposing brick or stone building was erected, containing frequently a store, or more rooms for tenants. The landlord, who had till then lived in some unpleasant rear rooms, moved into the best part of the house; the bare but well-scrubbed floors were covered with Brussels carpets, the wooden chairs replaced by unholstered ones, and the best room received the luxury of a piano or violin." The flow of savings into home mortgages was institutionalized in some forty Bohemian building and loan associations, which from 1885 to 1893 paid out an estimated $4 million or more.

By 1893 individuals among the early Bohemian settlers were worth as much as $200,000, and young Anton J. Cermak had begun his Chicago career in business and politics that would make him president of a bank, head of a real-estate company, and, in 1931, mayor of Chicago. Cermak was representative of the sizable group of immigrants, of many nationalities, to whom politics was itself a business, one of the roads most available to poor boys to rise toward the top in money and power. Political office could yield income in many ways: Cermak as a young legislator introduced a bill attacking the trust companies so that they would pay him to withdraw it. Streetcar companies and other public-utility firms would pay for franchises. Stores would reward inspectors who failed to enforce building regulations and fire laws. Liquor interests were grateful for immunity from sumptuary legislation. And there was always "honest graft": an alderman who had advance secret knowledge of a streetcar extension could do well by dealing in real estate along the intended route.

When all this has been said, it remains true that ward bosses and political machines helped to make life easier for millions of new arrivals in the cities, whether the migrant had come from a Russian ghetto or from a Vermont farm. The boss passed out Thanksgiving turkeys and buckets of coal. He set up free lunches in the saloon he owned. He tempered justice with mercy, and was often willing to fix a minor offense against the laws by a confused immigrant who did not know either the law or the English language. Most crucial of all, the boss could provide jobs. The leaders of Tammany Hall after 1880 controlled an annual city payroll of $12 million; with 12,000 municipal jobs to fill, they were a bigger employer than Carnegie Steel. Politicians also had influence with the employment offices of private companies that depended on favors from government. Twenty per cent of all voters in one Chicago ward, said an informed observer, had jobs "dependent on the good will of the alderman." If the alderman thus got votes, yet the voters got their pay.

This estimate was made by Jane Addams, who helped found another, a new, type of agency to make life more tolerable for the urban poor. Hull-House opened its doors in 1890. Almost at once it was providing a bewildering array of services to residents of the surrounding sweatshop district. It provided hot lunches to factory workers. It sponsored courses on cooking and home management. It had a University Extension program. The twenty residents at the settlement campaigned for safety inspection of factories, for a ban on child labor, for compulsory school attendance. They got the city council to build a new public bathhouse. Hull-House had a gymnasium. It sponsored concerts (Beethoven) and lectures (John Dewey on "Epictetus"). Far from being condescending to immigrants, Hull-House saw the respects in which they were superior to Americans. One resident, saying that she had never seen in the home of a native-born urbanite any decoration "which he had himself designed and wrought for pleasure in it," went on to describe the home of a former Italian peasant where "I have seen wall and ceiling decorations of his own design, and done by his own hand in colors. The designs were very rude, the colors coarse; but there was nothing of the vulgar in it, and there was something of hope."

This esthetic sense could be fed not only by art shows at Hull-House and other settlements but also by the public museums being established: the Metropolitan Museum of Art originated in New York in 1870; the Corcoran Galley in Washington opened four years later; the Chicago Art Institute was built in 1893. Public libraries were being expanded rapidly. Public schools provided evening classes for adults and also taught many more elementary and secondary pupils: 9.9 million in 1880, 12.7 million in 1890. As enrollments increased, the public schools in cities also, inevitably but not always wisely, took on such functions as instruction in personal hygiene.

Another agency that sometimes protected the poor immigrants in cities was the trade union. Such unions as the Locomotive Engineers seem to have thrived partly at the expense of unorganized workers during a period when the supply of unskilled labor was growing rapidly; that is, railroads compensated for the concessions made to their engineers by forcing down the conditions of their unskilled employees. But other unions of skilled workers brought benefits even to unskilled workers in the plant who were not members of the organization. The McCormick Harvesting Machine plant in Chicago offers an illustration of this phenomenon. Except for a brief period when the Knights of Labor penetrated the McCormick factory, the only union there was among the skilled molders who numbered about 10 per cent of the labor force. But this small band of men with irreplaceable skill repeatedly won gains in their own conditions—and their improved wage patterns tended to spread quickly to all employees. In 1886, just before the Haymarket bombing, a strike in the McCormick works was smashed and the molders' union was destroyed. Ironically, the skilled workers, whose efforts had done so much to help their fellows, were then replaced by common labor operating automatic molding machines, while the conditions of unskilled workers in the plant continued to improve. The hourly rate of common laborers (apart from pieceworkers) remained steady at 15 cents for the entire decade from 1886 to 1896; even the onset of severe depression in 1893 did not bring a pay cut for common laborers. Meanwhile the cost of living was falling. The index of real hourly earnings of day-rate employees (1860 equals 100) rose from 160 in 1879 to 220 in 1896; the rate of increase was quite rapid from 1879 to 1886 and slow thereafter.

What explains this result, in view of great immigration into the United States, falling prices of consumer goods, and a lower wage rate for casual laborers in the general labor market of Chicago? Seemingly there were two causes. The widow of the company's founder was fearful by 1886 that the recurrent labor troubles in the McCormick plant had harmed her family's "good name" in the community, and she more than once urged the firm's executives to avoid any action that might provoke further unrest. Second, the executives themselves feared that wage cuts might prompt a revival of unionism.

Thus urban workers, even casual laborers, were far from helpless. A visible sign of their rising standard of living was the growth of a cluster of lower-middle-class communities around most of the large cities. In Boston, for instance, before the Civil War, all but the very wealthy (who maintained country houses in addition to their downtown mansions) had to live within walking distance of their jobs in the downtown area; that is, within a radius of three miles of City Hall. After the War, the downtown slums still existed, and were growing more congested than ever. But thousands of families were escaping from them into the new "streetcar suburbs." The index of residential construction (1875 equals 100) tells the story. The national index rose from about 60 in 1880 to a peak of nearly 200 in 1890. But the index for three streetcar suburbs of Boston—Dorchester, Roxbury, West Roxbury —soared after 1880 and was five times as high in 1890 as it had been at the beginning of the decade. The three neighborhoods together held 95,691 persons in 1880; 144,927 by 1890. If life in the area provided little or no sense of community, if it lacked the color sometimes provided by life in the slums, if the streets were drab and monotonous, yet all of the residents were sure that they had bettered themselves by fleeing from tenements to homes of their own with small patches of lawn.

From 1880 to 1890 more than 6,000 dwellings were built in Roxbury, West Roxbury, or Dorchester. The implications of this boom are clear for the building-trades craftsmen who would themselves inhabit some of the new homes. If semiskilled workers were rising, many skilled workers were attaining to true comfort. In the Homestead plant of Carnegie Steel in 1892 the hourly rate for common labor was only 14 cents but a few workers in the mill made as much as $14 a day. That same year the New York *Times* reported on a "sober and thrifty" Welsh immigrant in Homestead who lived with his family in "a large, handsome cottage in the Queen Anne style, gaily painted," with electric lights, heavy carpets, upholstered furniture—and a parlor organ.

To keep track of and co-ordinate ever larger organizations (the work force in the McCormick factory in Chicago went from 393 in 1877 to 1,394 in 1887), corporations needed more clerks in the front office. They also provided more openings in lower and middle management, and Carnegie Steel was only one of many companies that preferred to promote its supervisors from its own ranks. Few of the chemists and metallurgists hired from technical schools were able to reach major decision-making positions in the firm. The typical Carnegie superintendent had been hired as a boy with only a public-school education. He had risen very rapidly into the top group. Upon arriving there he was permitted to buy stock in the company, and Carnegie Steel had fewer than three dozen stockholders. A superintendent got a good salary, and he could reasonably expect to retire with a fortune by the time he was 45 years old.

Although men who reached the pinnacle of American business had risen far, available evidence indicates that they had started fairly high. A study of 190 men at the top in 1900 shows that, while 45.6 per cent of the American population had at least one foreign-born parent, only 19 per cent of the executives did so. Most of the business leaders were members of old American families, and nearly four of every five were of British descent. These men were born about 1850, when 83 per cent of the American population lived in rural areas, but only 40 per cent of the executives were born and reared in rural settings. In this sample of the business elite, 86 per cent were sons of business or professional men.

The crux of the matter is that, in most American cities from 1877 to 1893, the *entire social structure* was moving upward rapidly. Even the very bottom, occupied mainly by immigrants in slums, was yet higher than the environments left behind in Europe. Similarly the top was moving upward. Commodore Vanderbilt was worth $100 million at his death in 1877. His eldest son and chief heir, William, left a fortune of $200 million a mere eight years later—during times of general deflation.

The same phenomenon can be seen at slightly less exalted levels. A liberal estimate of the number of American millionaires on the eve of the Civil War would be 300 or 400, and many of those were slaveholders who lost their fortunes. But by 1892 the New York *Tribune Monthly* could list by name 4,047 alleged millionaires. Chicago alone had 280. Substantial parts of one in every four of those 280 fortunes were reportedly made by dealing in real estate, and that estimate is surely too low.

Government officials in Washington breathed in an atmosphere of land speculation. Demand for residential and business properties swelled incredibly. The typical Federal employee had considerably more purchasing power than did a common laborer or a clerk in other cities: since 1853 the lowest salary of any Federal clerk had been $920 a year, and some earned as much as $2,000. The number of Federal employees in Washington rose from 7,800 in 1880 to 23,000 in 1890. This rapid growth of a high-income population boomed the price of some plats which sold for only 8 cents a square foot in 1882 to 48 cents in 1887. A reporter told in 1882 of a Negro woman on F Street who sold for $80,000 a house that had been worth $5,000; a boardinghouse keeper was offered $64,000 for a house that she had purchased twenty years earlier for $5,000. Small wonder that the speculative fever invaded all classes: in 1883 a lady newly appointed to a $900 clerkship in the Federal Land Office urged upon her sister the view that a great deal of money could still be made in Washington "on very small real estate investments. . . ."

In Washington as in nearly all cities, men were preoccupied with their personal affairs. Opportunities for gain were great, but other men also were trying to seize them. He who did not rise might fall fast and far. The situation demanded constant attention to the main chance. As a result the tone of the cities was not likely to produce sustained action aimed at social reform. What urbanites wanted of government was personal favoritism. This man wanted a franchise for a gas company. That one wanted a liquor license. A third wanted higher import duties on foreign goods that might compete with his products.

The Federal government responded with laws and other policies that further promoted urban prosperity at the expense of rural areas. The protective tariff could do nothing to help staple-crop farmers who sold a major portion of their output abroad.

On the contrary, it harmed them by tending to stabilize at high levels the prices of commodities that farmers bought. Since most of those commodities were manufactured in cities, the tariff helped to increase the profits of urban companies. Nor did these benefits accrue only to the owners of factories; a profitable concern need not pay higher wages to its workers, but it can, and in many instances it did. Just as the protective tariff served to siphon income and wealth out of farm districts into cities, so did the fiscal and monetary policies of the Federal government. Their general effect was to reduce the price level, and, as has been seen, such deflation tends to harm debtors and to benefit creditors. Countless urbanites were in debt, including businessmen who borrowed much of their working capital, but the cities on balance were undoubtedly creditors. Farm regions on the other hand were on balance debtors. And, again as with the tariff, the gains from deflation derived by the cities were spread fairly widely among their social groups. In addition to bankers, who were nearly all urbanites and who were invariably opposed to inflation, deflation benefited everybody whose income was relatively fixed: government employees, surviving war veterans who continued to get Federal pensions, beneficiaries of insurance policies. It also benefited factory employees, such as the common laborers in the McCormick plant, whose wages fell less rapidly than the cost of living. The consequent conflict of interest between farmers and industrial wage earners was to be a major obstacle to efforts to forge them into an alliance after 1890 behind the demand for free coinage of silver.

In the cities, then, a massive complacency permeated all classes. Few men were satisfied with their own stations in life, but they were content with the structure of society. The aim was to rise in it rapidly, not to force the government to alter it. This general complacency in urban areas had a disproportionately great effect on the Federal government for a simple reason: American cities produced a disproportionately high number of political leaders. In politics, as in business, the able and ambitious men flocked to cities. Even those Congressmen of 1890 who had been reared on farms had nearly all been living in cities for decades; insofar as they had a first-hand understanding of rural problems, what they knew was the rural problems of the preceding generation.

Urban domination of the Federal government can be detected in its policies; the same domination was reflected in personnel. In the House of Representatives elected in 1892, the membership of the two most powerful committees—Rules; Ways and Means—was composed of twenty-one men. Sixteen of them lived in urban areas. Two others lived in towns with more than 2,000 but fewer than 2,500 residents. In comparison, only one third of all Americans lived in urban areas in 1890. Cities, then, furnished most political leadership.

Other features of the structure of politics and government also helped to make Federal officials sit on their hands for a decade after 1880, while the emergence of grave social and economic problems was virtually ignored. Democracy was far from perfect, and many of those who were suffering the most cruelly were excluded from politics altogether. In large regions of the South in 1890 a Negro had neither a vote nor a voice. Countless immigrants, with no tradition of suffrage in the Old Country, never qualified to vote in the new. The plight of these Negroes and immigrants could safely be neglected by politicians.

The division of powers prescribed by the Constitution was not calculated to stimulate decisive action on important issues, and this factor was especially stifling during a period when the two major parties were evenly balanced nationally. Such a condition pertained from 1875 to 1889; during those years there was never a time when the same party controlled the Presidency and both branches of Congress. Even the party that had a working majority in the United States Senate was often unable to get its program passed because party discipline was woefully weak. Worse, the issues on which Congressmen were most likely to bolt their party were crucial ones, not minor ones. Democrats might hold firm behind their leaders when confronted by a private pension bill to give relief to a specific individual, but Senators from Louisiana and Maryland were sure to desert the ranks when a bill to reduce import duties was under consideration. On major pieces of legislation, Congressmen tended to vote with their section rather than with their party. Democrats and Republicans from the Northeast opposed inflation, which was urged by most Western Congressmen of all parties.

A notable monograph gives this example. Senators from the "antispeculator tier"—the Dakotas, Nebraska, Kansas, Oklahoma, Texas—were prone to support any measure aimed at curbing the activities of the professionals on the stock and commodity exchanges. In 1893 the Hatch bill would have taxed at 10 per cent any trading in futures (that is, an agreement to buy or sell so much wheat or cotton now for delivery at a specified price at some future time) unless the seller already owned the commodity being traded. This measure drew solid support from the forenamed states, as did comparable bills in 1909 and 1913. Party ties did not matter much.

As the country expanded geographically, as it diversified socially and economically, and as eight new states were admitted to the Union from 1876 to 1896, the variety of sectional interests and attitudes represented in Congress became immense. The task of putting together a majority for an important bill in either branch of Congress was terribly difficult even for such a master negotiator and strategist as William McKinley.

Under these circumstances, any discussion of politics in terms of "national parties" is questionable. Presidential elections offer a seeming exception, but even that exception disappeared in 1896 when Gold Democrats and Silver Republicans deserted their parties. It is certain that Democrats who united every four years in efforts to put their man in the White House could not agree on legislation to solve a single one of the major issues of the times. Even at state and local levels, party solidarity sometimes meant little. Tammany Hall had friends as well as enemies in Republican ranks. Democratic ward bosses in Chicago made deals with the Republican machine that dominated county government. Kansas, until the Populist revolt, was safely Republican, but the state was not governed by the party. It was run by factional combinations that shifted to some extent for each election, and politicians often crossed party lines secretly when they dared not do so openly.

Finally, the great problems of Federal policy—monetary legislation, the tariff, fiscal matters, pensions for veterans, national defense, civil rights for Negroes, and so on—were not the sole issues that determined who became governor or Senator or President. Often they were not even the chief issues to determine elections. Each aspirant to state office in New York, for instance, confronted the bitter animosity between New York City (Catholic, many Irish and German immigrants) and the rest of the state (rural, Protestant). The animosity produced repeated rural efforts to force temperance or prohibition and election reform upon New York City. A Democrat seeking to become governor could not yield to those efforts without losing Tammany, but to win he also needed rural votes. The Democrats who succeeded—David B. Hill was one—had managed to straddle the problems of clean elections and temperance.

Speaking broadly, the United States in 1890 was two nations. One centered in the region east of the Mississippi and north of the Ohio. Its cities were growing rapidly, and their inhabitants had few demands that the Federal government did not fulfill. Farmers in the region were producing diversified crops for sale to the burgeoning cities, and were in general satisfied. Allied to this region were cities and towns west of the Mississippi. But in rural areas elsewhere in the country discontent was growing. It centered in the sections that relied on cotton, wheat, or silver. A complex of institutional factors prevented this discontent from having any substantial impact on national politics until 1890. Unrest would swell rapidly after a severe depression began in 1893. Within a year its manifestations would generate fears that a cataclysm was at hand. America, said many of its citizens, was on the eve of social revolution.

This foreboding, common in 1894, would have seemed lunatic a decade earlier.

Social Worker: ALZINA P. STEVENS

Alzina Parsons Stevens (1849–1900) was born in Maine, where poverty forced her into a textile factory at age 13. She lost her right index finger in an industrial accident. Her early marriage ended in divorce and she never talked about it. Having learned typesetting, she was in Chicago in 1872. There she worked as a compositor and organized a women's trade union. In Toledo from 1882 to 1891, she began as compositor and ended as editor on the *Toledo Bee*. During these years she became prominent in the Knights of Labor—now past its salad days.

Back in Chicago she was for a time co-proprietor of a reform newspaper, and helped to organize several unions. But her major contributions began when she moved into Hull-House. Governor John Peter Altgeld in 1893 named her assistant factory inspector for Illinois. Concentrating on nearby sweatshops where badly paid women finished garments in their living quarters, she found in a smallpox-infested tenement some bales of cheap coats and jackets bearing the Marshall Field label. She ordered the clothing burned, but not before removing the labels. She, well armed, confronted the department-store magnate. He was not abashed. On the contrary, he called Mrs. Stevens "no lady," an "unsexed woman," a "termagant." Then she really got sarcastic.

She had no respect for those who tried to apologize for crooked trade unionists or for boodlers in public office. She flared out at another resident of Hull-House: "That is the worst kind of snobbishness to assume that you must not have the same standards of honor for working people as you have for the well-to-do." She was a leader in a persisting effort by the women of Hull-House (all disfranchised) to topple the Democratic ward boss of the surrounding district. The ladies did not succeed.

Mrs. Stevens' greatest achievements probably were gained in behalf of the young. She was a steadfast crusader for advanced rules on the employment of children in factories and mines. When Cook County (Chicago) in 1899 established the first Juvenile Court in the nation, the former mill girl from Maine became its first probation officer. The court was right across the street from Hull-House.

CHAPTER 6

The Politics of Complacency

While more and more farmers in the South and West called for relief, other groups of owners fought each other for influence with various governments. The basic objective of each group was to seize hold of state power and use it to effect a redistribution of the national income, to fatten the calf of profits, interest, and rents, and to slice off for itself a bigger slab of golden flesh.

Control of the monetary and banking system rested in Washington, and there financial interests dug in to resist any changes that would reduce the value of interest-bearing mortgages and bonds. But sometimes Congress gave ground to the inflationary demands of debtor groups. In November 1877, Representative "Silver Dick" Bland of Missouri introduced a bill calling for "free and unlimited coinage of silver" at a parity of 16 to 1 with gold. The measure swept through the House by an overwhelming bipartisan vote. A canvass of Congress showed enough support in both houses to pass the bill even if President Hayes should veto it. But in the Senate William Allison from the farming state of Iowa came forward with amendments to provide for coinage each month of not less than $2 million nor more than $4 million in silver bullion. Secretary of the Treasury John Sherman observed that the amendments "completely revolutionized that measure"; that is, largely derevolutionized it. Hayes noted in his diary: "Belmont, the agent of the Rothschilds, fears the effect of a veto—prefers the bill should be approved, *bad* as he thinks it is." The Bland-Allison Act became law, as amended.

Sherman meanwhile was buying gold, looking forward to 1 January 1879, when the government would resume specie payments on paper money presented to it for redemption. Farmers and other debtors were infuriated at this deflationary outlook; as one said, "Inflate the currency and you raise the price of my steers. . . . Resumption means falling prices and shrinkage of wages." The Greenback party in 1876 had won fewer than 100,000 votes; in 1878 their popular vote passed 1,000,000 and they sent 14 men to the House of Representatives. But by the end of the year the Treasury had accumulated nearly $200 million in gold, and, since it clearly could pay gold, resumption went off smoothly. And in 1879 the price of wheat went from 78 cents to $1.11 a bushel, due chiefly to crop failures in Europe, while the harvest in the United States was 28 million bushels larger than in 1878. Wheat farmers prospered, and in the North the Greenback party collapsed.

Just as the greenback issue was inherited from the war and early post-war years, so was the problem of railroad debt to the Federal government. The Pacific railroads had failed to pay current interest and in 1877 their indebtedness to the United States was estimated at $65 million. Senator Allen G. Thurman introduced a bill to set up a schedule for retirement of the mortgage bonds of the railroads which the government held. The struggle against the measure by Jay Gould of the Union Pacific and Collis P. Huntington of the Central Pacific was aided by Republican Senator James G. Blaine of Maine. Another Republican Senator wrote privately: "It is my opinion that Mr. Blaine acts as the attorney of Jay Gould. Whenever Mr. Thurman and I have settled upon legislation to bring the Pacific railroads to terms of equity with the government, up has jumped James G. Blaine, musket in hand, from behind the breastworks of Gould's lobby, to fire in our backs."

Blaine was pioneering a more stable relation between politicians and businessmen. Old-style spoilsmen in politics, such as Republican Senator Roscoe Conkling of New York, regarded politicians as an independent army. They would of course give a corporation a helping hand, for a price, but they would form no permanent alliances. In that sense, they were isolationists. They liked their independence. They financed their machine by levying assessments on office-holders in city and state government and in the New York Customhouse. They might also charge a merchant for the favor of appraising his imports at less than the true valuation. They might even set up their own warehouse, send to it all imports that were not picked up immediately at the Customhouse, and then charge the importer exorbitant storage charges to get his goods back. They might sell a franchise to operate street-cars on Lower Broadway.

Such anarchy was troublesome to businessmen at a time when they sought stability and predictability above all benefactions. So Blaine offered his services in the Senate on a more reliable basis. He would watch out for their interests, day in and day out. They in turn would let him in on a few stock deals and would finance his campaigns for re-election. To Conkling and his kind, the Blaines had sold out. The Conklings were the Stalwarts of the Republican party; the Blaines were Half-Breeds.

Civil war broke out between the two factions soon after Hayes entered the White House. A committee that investigated the New York Customhouse turned in a report to the President that confirmed charges of bribery, political assessments, and underappraisals of imports. It was more than a respectable middle-class Ohioan could stand, and Hayes wrote his fellow Ohioan Secretary Sherman that "the collection of the revenues should be free from partisan control, and organized on a strictly business basis. . . ." A month later he issued an executive order forbidding political assessments on office-holders and banning all appointive officials from the management of party affairs.

More was involved than Hayes' ethical views. Once again, intercity competition was at work. An intimate friend who was collector of the customs in Chicago complained to the President that, due to the illegal favoritism that officials in the New York Customhouse showed to merchants there, Western merchants could not compete with them. Hayes replied that he had gotten similar protests from Boston and other cities. Also, Conkling had opposed Hayes' nomination; he had sat out the campaign; and the Democrats had won New York in 1876. Finally, Conkling was not the most corrupt of the spoilsmen, but he was the most powerful.

Hayes' challenge to the Republican machine in New York was accepted. It had just lost the state offices to the Democrats, and it had no choice but to fight for Federal patronage. The two top officials at the Customhouse, Alonzo Cornell and Chester A. Arthur, were prominent participants in a special state Republican convention at Rochester in September 1877. But Conkling, who referred to the merit system in public offices as "snivel service," held the stage. In a slashing attack he shouted: "Some of these worthies masquerade as reformers. . . . Their real object is office and plunder. When Dr. Johnson defined patriotism as the last refuge of a scoundrel, he was unconscious of the then undeveloped capabilities and uses of the word 'Reform!' " The convention voted a Conkling slate.

The President retaliated by trying to remove Arthur and Cornell from their posts. The Senate, holding to the traditional "Senatorial courtesy" which gave Conkling a veto power over Federal job-holders in New York, refused to let him do so. Not until 1879 did Hayes get his nominees into the Customhouse, and then he did so only with Democratic support.

But the shrewder men were beginning to see that the way of Blaine was the way to win. Such a man was Representative James A. Garfield of Ohio. In 1870 he had complained privately about the iron manufacturers in the Mahoning valley that they "want a representative that they can own and carry around in their pantaloons pocket." But he calmed down a good deal, and in 1878 he proved his reliability by voting against Bland's free-silver bill. He was the only Representative from Ohio to do so. In 1880 he was the Republican candidate for President, with the Stalwart Chester Arthur as his running mate.

Two months before the election Garfield wrote to a Cleve-lander named Amos Townsend asking how that other Cleve-lander "Rockafeller" felt about him: "Is it such that I might safely invite him for consultation . . . ?" At once Townsend warned: "It would not do for him to visit you, as it would be reported and *cut* like a *knife* in Pennsylvania. He is however, *all right* and will do what he can for your success." The candidate then wrote that the Republican bosses in Indiana would be very grateful if Standard Oil's 500 selling agents in the state would lend a hand in the campaign. Garfield did not get "cut" in Pennsylvania by any public association with Rockefeller, and he carried that state. He carried Indiana, by a margin of 6,625 in a vote of nearly half a million. He carried New York, by a margin of 21,000 in a vote of well over a million. He became President, with a plurality over the Democrat of only 7,368 votes. In a close election, a big campaign fund and the help of corporation employees could make the difference.

Garfield made Blaine his Secretary of State, and the two of them resumed the war over patronage with Conkling and his junior associate from New York, Senator Tom Platt. In a dramatic gesture that Conkling doubtless loved, he and Platt resigned their seats in the Senate, then hurried off to the state capitol in Albany where they expected the legislature to re-elect them in triumph to their former jobs. Not so—for six weeks a coalition of Half-Breeds and Democrats thwarted their hopes. Then, one night, a group of Half-Breeds carried a step ladder into a hotel in Albany and used it to peer through the transom into Platt's room. They found him locked in the embrace of "an unspeakable female." In order not to hurt the chances of his political bedfellow, Conkling, Platt withdrew from the Senate race on 2 July 1881.

That same day President Garfield was standing in the railroad station in Washington waiting for a train and listening to Secretary Blaine harangue him on the glorious prospects for expanding exports to Latin America. Suddenly Garfield was shot in the back by a madman who shouted, "I am a Stalwart and Arthur is President now." But 1881 was a year when many hopes were frustrated, and Garfield stayed alive through the summer. While charges that a group of government officials had benefited from fraudulent Star Route mail contracts in the West were feeding the demands to halt corruption, the civil-service reform movement leaped ahead. As early as May 1881 local groups had been formed or were being formed in 30 cities from coast to coast. On 11 August 1881 the National Civil Service Reform League was founded. The campaign to institute the merit system had been led from the beginning chiefly by professional men, especially editors Godkin and Curtis, and lawyers, ministers, professors. They tended to be Protestants, of established family and inherited wealth, college men who thought of themselves as aristocrats and disliked the new barons of business as well as the spoilsmen of politics. Even in 1881, although business support of the movement increased, it usually came from financial or mercantile circles rather than from manufacturers. And significantly, most of the reformers were dissident Republicans who might bolt their party over the issue.

Garfield died on September 19, and did more for the civil-service cause dead than he had done while alive. Now he was made into a crusader for the cause and a martyr to it. Moreover, after Chester Arthur entered the White House he seemed a new man, hardly a Stalwart at all. That too, by the laws of American politics, was almost predictable. Federal patronage had always been dispensed really by local bosses who stood behind and controlled most Congressmen. As a result, parties were decentralized, sectionalized, irresponsible. Abolition of spoils would enhance the power of the Chief Executive in a more centralized party. Thus, while Congress has normally opposed reform, Presidents have normally favored it.

Now, legislators were subjected to mounting pressure: petitions, letters, mass meetings, editorials. Although a Star Route trial ended in a hung jury, many citizens remained convinced that the defendants were guilty. Some Republicans foolishly refused to bend to this wave of sentiment. In May 1882 the chairman of the Republican Congressional Campaign Committee, Jay A. Hubbell, sent out to office-holders the traditional assessment letter asking for "voluntary contributions." The consequences were persuasive. Hubbell had hoped to move up to the Senate, but he failed even to win renomination to the House from Michigan. The election saw the Republicans lose ground in Pennsylvania, Indiana, Connecticut, New Jersey, even Massachusetts. Most impressive of all, Grover Cleveland, with a reputation as a reformer, was elected governor of New York over an alleged spoilsman, and he won by the largest majority ever gained up to that time in the state.

The effect on many Congressmen was electric. Their attitudes toward "snivel service" did not change, but their behavior did. The lame-duck session of Congress passed the Pendleton Act to reform the executive branches of the government. On the final vote in Senate, there were 38 Ayes and only 5 Nays. Not one Republican opposed the bill. In the House where the vote was 155 to 47, nearly all the opponents were Democrats from the South or the Old Northwest. But the bill that Arthur signed into law on 16 January 1883 was as weak as Congress had dared to make it. Aside from offices in Washington, the new Civil Service Commission got jurisdiction only over customhouses plus the postoffices in large cities. The great majority of the 100,000 Federal jobs remained outside the merit regulations. Another indication that the main purpose of the law had been to divert public wrath was the fact that examinations applied only to new applicants for Federal positions, not to incumbents. After the final vote in the Senate, Joseph E. Brown caused his brothers to laugh by suggesting that the Pendleton measure be called "a bill to perpetuate in office the Republicans who now control the patronage of the Government." That is how it worked out. Arthur extended the merit system to some 14,000 positions. In the years that followed, with the White House changing party every four years, each outgoing President extended the merit system to more jobs in order to protect his partisans against replacement by his successor.

The Republicans had also been struggling with the Southern problem. One of their chief strategists, Secretary of the Navy William E. Chandler, thought that the 1882 elections were vital, because if they did not leave the G.O.P. in control of both houses of Congress it could not hope to win the Presidency in 1884. Chandler's hope was to pick Congressmen elected by independent factions that had bolted the Democratic party in several Southern states. The regular Democrats, chiefly upper-class whites allied to business interests in the North, were men who believed in sound money and in the sanctity of public credit. Seeking above all to pay interest on the state debts, they cut other public expenses such as school appropriations, and they leased out convicts to private corporations. Their opponents, the bolters, were mainly cheap-money men. They also wanted to repudiate or scale down the state debts contracted during Reconstruction or after. Supposedly these views were anathema to Chandler, but conflicts of principle did not faze him.

In Alabama the Republicans endorsed the Greenbacker-independent slate. Chandler was counting on new, lily-white forces in the South. What they were was stated clearly in a letter to him from a "northern immigrant" at Talladega who wrote of factories springing up around Birmingham, *all controlled by Northern men* who will cooperate if the proper influences are brought to bear." In Virginia, Chandler swept hundreds of regular Republicans out of Federal jobs so that he could give them to an independent party to which he looked for support in the next House of Representatives. The strategy failed. After conservative Democrats had carried the state, one of them rejoiced: "We have Virginia once more in our possession, and we will keep her this time, be sure of that." The victors changed the election laws so that they could stuff ballot boxes with abandon.

Throughout the South the 1882 election saw corruption and violence. In Mississippi, third-party men were beaten, murdered, run out of their counties; ballot boxes were stuffed. South Carolina reported four political murders and a lynching. The insurgent forces were exhorted to fight back. "Greenback men, you must learn to shoot," exclaimed an independent paper in Texas. "You must make up your minds to kill." But most of the votes were counted for the other side, and the Democrats carried the election.

In 1883 the Republicans still controlled the Senate by 3 votes, but in the House they were greatly outnumbered by their rivals. The self-proclaimed low-tariff party set up a hubbub about the import duties, which were still at the record levels imposed in 1864 while the war was still on—1,450 dutiable commodities had been burdened with an average tariff of 47 per cent of their value. But the Republicans had shrewdly taken insurance in 1882 by authorizing the President to appoint a Tariff Commission. He had. Nelson Aldrich, a staunch Republican elected to the Senate from Rhode Island in 1882, explained "there was a representative of the wool growers on the commission; there was a representative of the iron interest on the commission; and those interests were very carefully looked out for." And when the hubbub in Congress died, when the last back had been scratched, when the last log had been rolled, the Tariff Act of 1883 reduced rates by an average of 5 per cent. Carnegie would survive. And he knew it.

For the Republican ticket in 1884 was headed by a man who was safe, James G. Blaine. The Democratic ticket was headed by another safe man, Grover Cleveland. As governor of New York, Cleveland had been faced with a bill that had been passed by wide margins by both houses of the legislature. The maximum fare on the elevateds of New York City had been 5 cents during rush hours; now the limit was extended to a 24-hour basis. Although the elevateds were controlled by Jay Gould and his partner Cyrus Field, who had watered the stock without mercy and needed high rates to pay dividends on the inflated capitalization, many Wall Street firms urged Cleveland to veto the bill as a violation of "the chartered rights of the corporations of this state." So he did, with a veto message that virtually flew back to the doctrine of the Dartmouth College Case (1819) that the constitutional ban on impairment of contracts barred a state from altering the charter of a private corporation.

The New York *Times,* although normally Republican, had backed Cleveland in 1882, but its Albany correspondent now explained the veto by writing that "the history of the politics of the last few years is to create the impression that moneyed concerns are the ones to patronize, because of the financial support which they can render in a hotly contested campaign." He added that some Democratic leaders thought they could regain national dominance by "currying the favor of men of Gould's stripe." James Gordon Bennett's *Herald* added: "Monopolies of all kinds. . . . have many political theories in common . . . , and it is quite touching to witness a hopeful Presidential candidate choose his side in the coming struggle between them and the people for the control of the powers of government." But Cleveland held to his course: when a bill came before him fixing a maximum work-day of 12 hours for streetcar conductors, he vetoed it on the ground that it violated freedom of contract.

In 1884 Samuel J. Tilden, the Wall Street lawyer who had himself run for President 8 years earlier, assured president Hill of the Great Northern that Cleveland was "all right." Hill contributed $5,000 and wired his underlings in the West to "get busy" for Cleveland. The New Jersey iron masters Peter Cooper and Abram Hewitt chipped in about $75,000; Levi Leiter, Marshall Field's old partner, $10,000; Isidor Straus, head of Macy's, $5,000. The party needed it all; a manager of the Democratic campaign in Illinois later recalled: "The most trouble I had was to keep the Democratic ward heelers of Chicago under control. They were demanding more money than it was possible to give them."

The campaign was mighty dirty. Blaine's soiled public morality was matched against the soiled private morality of his opponent, who did not deny that he was the father of an illegitimate child. But Cleveland's indiscretion had occurred long ago, whereas a Protestant clergyman supporting Blaine committed one in the last days of the campaign. The minister, one of a group interviewing Blaine in New York City, called the Democrats the party of "rum, Romanism, and rebellion." The final epithet hardly troubled the candidate, who was himself waving the bloody shirt at the time. But Blaine's failure to repudiate the assault on Catholics and wets probably cost him crucial votes in New York.

A reporter in Washington noted intense apprehension among the 60,000 Negroes there. The invalidation of the Civil Rights Act the preceding year had caused the more ignorant of them to fear a return of the branding iron and the whipping post. Now they were terrified that a Democratic victory might bring back slavery. One Democrat shouted in a restaurant that he would bet a thousand dollars that Cleveland would win, and added that the situation looked so favorable that he had already bought ten Negroes. "Many a former slave," wrote the reporter, "has spent the past three nights on his knees."

Grover Cleveland won New York, by a statewide margin of only a thousand votes. He barely won Indiana and Connecticut. His national plurality was 68,299. But he was President-elect.

He received a wire from Jay Gould expressing confidence "that the vast business interests of the country will be entirely safe in your hands." A farm leader sourly agreed: "Cleveland is elected . . . yet I do not look for much relief for the masses, for the same monopolies that run the Republican run the Democratic party." Another agrarian spokesman complained about Minnesota, "The millers ring runs the Republican party and the railroad ring runs the Democratic party." Railroad influence was greater in the Democratic machines of Nebraska and Iowa than among the Republicans. The chief agent in Wisconsin of the Chicago and Northwestern Railroad became the new Postmaster General. Melville W. Fuller, a wealthy railroad lawyer whom Cleveland would soon name Chief Justice of the United States, was his chief adviser in Chicago on policy and patronage.

"The day broke, clear and sunny . . . ," wrote a correspondent of the inauguration. "No President has ever had a finer day for his coming in than Cleveland has; no President has ever had so many onlookers and so cold a reception. . . . The Democrats have come here to look over the man they have elected, rather than to honor him. They are not yet proud of him, and they are afraid of how he may conduct himself, for the charge that they have elected a Republican is current among their leaders." But Cleveland proved to be a Democrat so far as public offices were concerned. Of 120,000 Federal employees, two out of three were replaced by 1889. All 85 internal-revenue collectors were replaced, as were 100 of the 111 heads of customhouses. But the size of the classified civil service was also doubled, to cover about 29,000 jobs by 1889.

However friendly to railroads many Democrats were, the party had to do something about the railroad problem. In the early 1870's states of the Old Northwest, pressed by irate farmers and merchants, had passed the so-called Granger laws to regulate railroads and grain elevators. But in November 1874, the Baltimore & Ohio entered Chicago—the fifth trunkline tying that city to the Eastern seaboard. The ensuing rate wars among the five railroads brought through rates to the East and Europe toppling down. In the next decade the growth of cities in the Midwest afforded farmers a nearby market for much of their output, and the centers of anti-railroad agitation shifted elsewhere.

Eastward. The New York Central granted lower rates to certain wholesalers in upstate New York than to local merchants there. To the Vanderbilts, the policy seemed sound, but wholesalers in New York City complained because it benefited their upstate competitors at their expense. They also saw themselves losing more and more of the overseas trade to rivals in Boston and Baltimore and Philadelphia who enjoyed lower rates to Chicago and the hinterland. In 1876 rates from Boston inland were only about half those from New York City, and an irate group of merchants from the Chamber of Commerce went to see William Vanderbilt. He agreed to cut his charges. His act set off the rate war of 1876, the most bitter of them all.

It could not last; in March 1877, Vanderbilt commented: "five great railroads to New York, with only business enough for two." Rates were ruinous. To save himself, he agreed to sacrifice the merchants of New York City. Omitting the Grand Trunk, which ran westward from Boston and Portland across Canada to Chicago, the trunklines got together in April and set differential rates on westbound traffic from the various cities. They also agreed that, effective in July, they would divide the westbound tonnage from New York City: the Central and the Erie to have 33 per cent each, the Pennsy 25 per cent, the B & O 9 per cent. Thus was born the Trunk Line Pool, which was extended in 1879 to cover eastbound traffic.

New York merchants rebelled, and they were joined by many Eastern farmers who were losing out to the new farms in the West. In New England from 1860 to 1900, wheat output fell 85 per cent; corn production fell 25 per cent; the number of beeves and sheep declined; the quantity of improved land decreased a third. The countryside was deserted; only in dairying was agriculture on the upgrade in New England. In western New York, cattle and wheat farmers leaned on their fences and watched products from the prairies hurtle past them. They put much of the blame on the long-haul short-haul differentials in railroad rates. On competitive runs, such as Chicago to New York, the railroads charged much less per mile than on noncompetitive runs; it cost more to ship freight of the same quantity and kind from Rochester to New York than from Chicago to New York. Farmers bled in upstate New York. One man in Monroe County owned 800 acres of top farm land, worth in the middle 1870's at least $100 an acre. In 1879 he estimated that land values had fallen 25 per cent because the rate policy of railroads was favoring the Western farmers. Thus his own loss was $20,000. With good cause and good wit the unofficial organ of the state Grange charged that the railroads "load our farms on their freight cars and carry them a thousand miles farther from our markets without the consent of the owners."

Urged on by farmers and merchants, the New York legislature set up the Hepburn Committee in 1879 to inquire into railroad practices, including the allegation that railroads gave special rates to favored shippers. In a joint letter to the committee, Vanderbilt and the president of the Erie stated that all shippers on their lines paid the same, publicly announced, rates. But when the committee subpoenaed the Central's books, they found it had granted 6,000 special contracts in six months. Its freight agent conceded that half of the local traffic was carried at special rates. Revelations about stock watering led to various estimates, but all agreed that the Central and the Erie together had issued at least $100 million in stock above the actual cost of their properties. The public was even more shocked by the testimony about rebates and other favoritism to Standard Oil. As interpreted by a leader of the regulatory movement, "The railway charge is so important an element in the price of every commodity that is carried from a distance in the United States and intended for export, that it is within the power of railway magnates to become partners in every special line of occupation, and it is this power to destroy and build up which no community can allow to roam and to exercise itself unchecked. . . ."

Vanderbilt found himself in a terribly exposed position. He had been quoted as saying that he owned 87 per cent of the Central's stock, and the road was paying annual dividends of $7 million, so his income from that source alone was nearly $17,000 a day. Through the banking firm of J. P. Morgan he arranged the sale of 250,000 shares of his stock; he received $30 million for it.

But soon he was being squeezed from two directions. New

York merchants early in 1881 set up the National Anti-Monopoly League, with a program devoted almost entirely to railroad reform. In its first year the League sent millions of pieces of propaganda to every state in the country. The National Grange helped circulate its petition for Federal regulation of railroads; in the winter of 1881–1882 the standard League document poured in on Congress from at least 35 states. Miraculously the Nebraska Farmers' Alliance endorsed the League position that railroad rates should be based on "cost and risk of service," even though the *Railroad Gazette* pointed out that application of the principle would so increase freight rates from Nebraska to the East that the state could not ship its products and the value of its farm land would fall to less than 50 cents an acre. Repeatedly the League pointed to the fortunes of Vanderbilt, Gould, and others, and asked: "How Did They Get It?" At the same time it made clear its basically conservative program, its concern for good government, the substantial fortunes of its own leaders, by saying: "The Anti-Monopolists are trying to lift the safety valve and prevent an explosion which will surely come, if the great financial free booters of the country are allowed to go on corrupting our elections, controlling legislation, debauching our courts, and riding roughshod over public rights. Capitalists who honestly earned their accumulations are as much interested in the success of anti-monopoly as any other class."

The other group squeezing Vanderbilt were financial freebooters. The Lake Shore was built to parallel a section of his road, started a rate war, and offered to sell out to the Central at a blackmail price. The West Shore was built parallel to his road along the Hudson, and did the same thing; its promoters included John Jacob Astor and George M. Pullman. The Seney crowd on Wall Street built the Nickel Plate parallel to his road from Buffalo to Chicago, and did the same thing. Everybody wanted some of Vanderbilt's fat.

And he had little sense. By 1879 he had commented to the press on the possible railroad commission in New York, ". . . the commission must either own the railroads or the railroads own it. . . ." In 1882 he was worse. The Lake Shore was completed in the autumn, and Vanderbilt arrived in Chicago on October 8 to ponder the dismal situation. In a press interview he blurted out a phrase he had used many times in the past, "The public be damned." When asked what he thought of the anti-monopoly movement, he replied, "It is a movement inspired by a set of fools and black-mailers. . . . When I want to buy up any politician, I always find the Anti-Monopolists the most purchasable. They don't come so high."

New York merchants did not take kindly to such talk. They carried their battle into the National Board of Trade, and gradually they pushed that body toward advocacy of Federal regulation of railroads. Bill after bill was introduced into the House of Representatives—more than 30 of them from 1874 to 1885. Some actually passed, but they were killed in the Senate. As early as 1882 the *Commercial and Financial Chronicle* was wailing that "the tendencies of the times seem to be slowly carrying us towards federal intervention of some sort, whether we will or not. The fact is that the railroad has revolutionized everything." Vanderbilt was wailing too. And on 8 May 1883, his vice president and political fixer, Chauncey M. Depew, spoke at a banquet of the New York Chamber of Commerce and offered a deal. He proposed "a national tribunal" to do two things. It should give "impartial justice" to railroads and shippers. In return it should protect the existing railroads "against being pirated, by being unnecessarily harassed and paralleled." Thus more than one railroad executive came to see how government regulation, in the right hands, could be used to restrain competition.

There were other converts to regulation. While the Central was being harassed, Vanderbilt himself had joined with Carnegie and Rockefeller to build the South Pennsylvania, a parallel road aimed at smashing the Pennsy. J. P. Morgan did not like it: it was bad for investors and for bankers. Besides his involvement with Vanderbilt, Morgan handled the Pennsy's financial affairs. He concluded that "something should be done to bring more harmony among the trunk lines." His efforts included sale of the West Shore to the Central.

In January 1885, the Reagan bill passed the House, and the Cullom bill passed the Senate. Both provided for railroad regulation, but the former was to be enforced by the Federal courts, the latter by an independent commission. Then the two branches squabbled over their differences until October 1886, when the Supreme Court helped to end the bickering by its decision in the *Wabash Case*, denying to the states any power over interstate commerce.

The Interstate Commerce Act became law on 4 February 1887. It set up a five-member Interstate Commerce Commission with investigatory powers. The ICC could also issue cease and desist orders, but if a railroad chose to ignore an order, the Commission had to rely for enforcement on the injunctive powers of the Federal circuit courts. The Act fell back on the common-law principle in requiring that all railroad charges in interstate commerce must be "reasonable and just." Rates had to be public, and no shipper could be granted any "unreasonable preference." Pools were outlawed. So were certain long-haul short-haul discriminations, but with a power of appeal to the ICC.

So Congress did something in 1887 for Vanderbilt and the merchants of New York. But other needy groups—what did they get?

Consumers? Since 1880 the Federal government had collected each year in taxes an amount greatly in excess of its expenditures; the surplus in most years was greater than $100 million. The time seemed propitious to reduce tariff rates, and just before 1887 ended, the President sent Congress a ringing message on the subject. Pointing out that more than 4,000 items were subject to import duties, he said: ". . . while comparatively a few use the imported articles, millions of our people, who never used and never saw any of the foreign products, purchase and use things of the same kind made in this country, and pay therefor nearly or quite the same enhanced price which the duty adds to the imported articles." But the Republicans had a majority in the Senate, and Congress also contained some high-tariff Democrats, and so nothing happened.

Investors? Perhaps most investors were not needy, but President Cleveland did something for them. Since 1879 the Federal debt had been reduced about a third, and the country had learned, as England had learned after the Napoleonic wars, that a surplus in the government accounts may result in a falling price level, which in itself had benefited investors. But in 1887 the President went further. The outstanding Federal bonds were all immature; they had not reached their due dates. To induce investors to voluntarily turn in their 4 per cent noncallable Federal bonds, the President offered a premium for each bond of $28 or so above the face value of $100. By 1890 some $45 million—collected from consumers in the form of tariff duties or internal revenue taxes—had been paid to investors in premiums.

Potential homesteaders? The President helped them too. The grants to the Pacific railroads had provided that they should get 10 square miles of public lands for each mile of track built in a state, and 20 in the territories. To make sure that they got their land, huge areas had for many years been closed to settlement. Cleveland now threw these tracts open to settlers.

Farmers?—that is, homesteaders who had already set up shop—what did they get in 1887? The Hatch Act established under the control of the land-grant college in each state an agricultural experiment station and pledged $15,000 a year of Federal funds to support it. Congress also took note that serious drought had left many Texans in need of seed grain, and appropriated $10,000 to help them out. The President vetoed the bill as unconstitutional, declaring that the Federal government had limited powers and that "though the people support the Government the Government should not support the people."

Indians? Most of the 120,000 Indians lived on reservations, and Congress passed the Dawes Act for them. Land on the reservations was allotted in severalty to the Indians located there: a quarter section to each head of family, an eighth section to each single person over 18 and to each orphan under 18. The land was to be held in trust for 25 years "for the sole use and benefit of the Indian to whom such allotment shall have been made." Then each tract would be conveyed to the individual Indian or his heirs. Not what a white man could get under the Federal land laws, but something.

Wage earners? They got congratulated on being Americans, because "life and fire" typified the views of Americans and in consequence the United States had a depression every 10 or 15 years whereas Englishmen had to wait 20 and the Dutch a full century. Thus spoke the Reverend Henry Ward Beecher in the depression winter of 1877. The Reverend Joseph Cook in one of his Boston Monday Noon-Hour Lectures condemned "secret socialistic societies." Declaring them to consist chiefly of infidels and foreigners, he warned: "We shall keep order roughly here, if necessary; for all Americans are capitalists, or expect to be."

In the great strikes of 1877 order was kept roughly—by the army. Mark Twain exclaimed to a friend: "Pittsburgh & the riots neither surprised nor greatly disturbed me; for where the government is a sham, one must expect such things." James Ford Rhodes, a business executive in Cleveland before he turned to writing his history of the United States, drew another lesson. Recalling how the strikes had set off discussions in respectable parlors of the possibilities of revolution, he concluded his account of the episode by saying: "It was seen that the federal government with a resolute President at its head was a tower of strength in the event of a social uprising." So far as wage earners were concerned, the job of the government was to keep order, not to alleviate their problems. In 1877 Tom Scott of the Pennsy urged the need of adequate Federal forces, and Cyrus McCormick bought equipment for the Illinois militia. Eight years later, publisher Joseph Medill of the Chicago *Tribune* said that workers were poor because of their "improvidence and misdirected efforts." He said they wasted their money on liquor, cigars, and amusements. In 1892 the Texas legislature passed a law saying that, when a man left the payroll of a railroad, he had to be paid all wages due him within fifteen days. A court held the law unconstitutional, saying: "Unquestionably, so long as men must earn a living for their families and themselves by labor, there must be . . . oppression of the working classes."

Although such an extreme viewpoint was seldom expressed so candidly, both major parties in 1888 leaned toward similar sentiments. Businessmen had not led the fight for Federal civil-service reform, but many of them benefited from it. The extension of the Federal merit system meant that politicians had fewer jobs to sell or bargain away, and increasingly they turned to big corporations as another way to finance the political machines. The old talk of patronage was giving way to the new talk of "frying the fat" out of favored companies. But this basic change in the structure of politics did not mean that politicians were any less eager to get and hold office. A politician consistently whipped at the polls is no good to anybody, and even those most friendly to business would make concessions to antithetical groups if they were needed to win a campaign. Thus pro-business Republicans like Chandler and Senators John C. Spooner (Wisconsin) and Joseph B. Foraker (Ohio) repeatedly waved the bloody shirt to achieve victory even though they knew the practice was repugnant to many businessmen. They had to balance the desires of business with the interests of their party and with their own lust for office.

A concise picture of a state boss was given by his sometime

aide, later Tammany mayor of New York. Here is the portrait of David B. Hill, Democratic governor of New York and later United States Senator, as painted by George B. McClellan, Jr.: "Hill was a thinking machine with neither likes nor dislikes that he could not easily overcome when necessary. He was absolutely cold-blooded and would sacrifice a supporter or favor an opponent with equal facility if it was to his interest to do so. He was unscrupulous in politics and absolutely money honest. Money meant nothing to him, except as a lubricant to the political machine. He had devoted supporters, but no real friends. The only human being I ever heard him speak of with affection was his mother." Even a monomaniac like Hill could not reach the pinnacle of power. Most politicians were warmer-hearted than he, but his gravest handicap was that the better element suspected him of involvement in too many shady deals. The coming men in politics were those like Grover Cleveland who called for governmental honesty, efficiency, and economy.

With the President running for re-election in 1888, the Republicans put up a former Union general, Benjamin Harrison, who had the added virtue of living in Indiana. The campaign methods used in that state were lavish. The state boss, who was also treasurer of the national committee, sent out instructions: "Divide the floaters into blocks of five and put a trusted man with the necessary funds in charge of these five and make him responsible that none get away and that all vote our ticket." Formerly votes in Indiana had cost $2 to $5; the price in 1888 was $15 to $20. Those corporate contributions came in handy.

Although Harrison lost nationally by more than 90,000 popular votes, he won 233 electoral votes to 168. He won Indiana by 2,300 votes. He won New York by a mere 14,000, while David Hill was re-elected governor by 19,000 votes. It was widely charged that Hill had betrayed Cleveland to the Republicans, and according to George McClellan's memoirs Hill had as much as admitted the charge. McClellan recorded that years after the event he had queried Hill about it, and had gotten this reply: "No, I never sold out Cleveland. When our fellows came to me and asked, 'What do you want us to do?' I answered, 'Don't kill yourselves working for Cleveland.' That's all there was to the charge." But Hill's recent biographer, Herbert J. Bass, has written a persuasive reply to the allegation. Not only did Hill campaign vigorously in his own state, he also spoke for the President in other key areas. Cleveland himself later wrote that whereas the Presidential contest had turned almost entirely on the tariff issue, the state race in New York involved local issues—ballot reform and liquor regulation chiefly. Moreover, since Hill hoped for the Presidential nomination in 1892, it was clearly in his interests to have Cleveland re-elected in 1888 and thus made unavailable for a third nomination in 1892.

With Harrison the incoming President, Matt Quay went to Indianapolis to congratulate him. Harrison, a Presbyterian deacon, said to the national chairman: "Providence has given us the victory." Quay later commented to a friend: "Think of the man. He ought to know that Providence hadn't a damn thing to do with it." Quay added that probably Harrison "would never know how close a number of men were compelled to approach the gates of the penitentiary to make him President."

The G.O.P. victory was complete: for the first time since 1875 the same party controlled the White House and both branches of Congress. As already mentioned, the most pressing Republican debt was to enact even higher protection for American industry, but the tariff problem got tangled up with other matters. Some of the complications arose from American foreign policy. Could American business expect to get a tariff so high that it could monopolize the American markets while simultaneously selling more abroad? For more than a decade our diplomats had designed to expand foreign markets for American goods. As early as 1878 American consuls abroad were informed by Secretary of State William M. Evarts: "The question which now peremptorily challenges all thinking minds is how to create a foreign demand for those manufactures which are left after supplying our home demands." Requests from businessmen for more frequent publication of commercial reports from our consuls prompted Evarts in 1880 to begin issuing them on a monthly basis. They were distributed free to chambers of commerce and to firms engaged in foreign trade. These groups, seeking more efficiency in the promotion of American exports, increasingly (but for years, vainly) urged that the consular service be put under the merit system.

Volumes of special consular reports were also issued periodically. Nearly all of these diplomatic messages were content to cite statistics, make optimistic predictions, deliver pep talks to American exporters. But as early as 1880 Henry J. Winser, American representative at Sonneberg, Germany, was writing of "a feeling of ill-concealed jealousy and amazed regret in Germany that the great Republic of the West is now able not only to supply other countries with the raw materials of commerce, but, having served her apprenticeship honorably in almost all the branches of skilled labor, has become a competitor in foreign markets with the time-honored manufacturing establishments of Europe." Winser's next statement was ominous for the future: "This is looked upon, to some extent, as an encroachment upon vested rights. . . ."

James G. Blaine, who again became Secretary of State in 1889, had long been especially concerned to build American sales in Latin American. He was convinced that mutual concessions were needed. Counselled by William R. Grace, shipping magnate and former Democratic reform mayor of New York, Blaine organized the Pan-American Congress of 1889 in the hope of getting agreement there on reciprocal reduction of import duties. But his scheme ran afoul of the McKinley Tariff Bill being considered in the House, which would impose new duties on imports of hides. An irate Blaine protested to William McKinley that these duties were "a slap in the face to the South Americans with whom we are trying to enlarge our trade." Blaine also wanted to offer cuts in our duties on raw sugar in exchange for reductions on other products by sugar-producing countries. But the Bill was about to put raw sugar on the free list, leaving Blaine with nothing to bargain about. The sugar provisions in the Tariff Act as finally passed were most instructive. Refined sugar got a duty of a penny a pound, to the benefit of Henry O. Havemeyer and the Sugar Trust. Raw sugar went on the free list, also to Havemeyer's benefit. And, to gain support for the Bill by Congressmen from such states as Louisiana, American growers of raw sugar got a bounty of 2 cents a pound.

While preparing thus to enrich Havemeyer and his kind, Congress felt that it simply had to do something about the trust problem. When Senator John Sherman got his Anti-Trust Bill into final form, it declared illegal any combination to restrain interstate or foreign commerce. But what did that mean? During the Senate debates, on 27 March 1890, Orville Platt keenly forecast how the courts might make it mean very little. Many historians have quoted a part of this speech in which Platt stated that the aim of Congress was less to suppress monopolies than to divert the voters, that "the whole effort has been to get some bill headed, 'A Bill to Punish Trusts' with which to go to the country." But so far as I know, nobody has noted how brilliantly Platt predicted the judical history of the law. Yet never was there a more striking demonstration that Platt, among several able Republican leaders, was the one who could best combine their business-minded philosophy with a long view and a sweeping strategy.

The Bill, said Platt, was intolerably broad: "You can scarcely find an article of commerce, an article of merchandise in any State which does not compete with similar articles which are the growth, production, or manufacture of another State. So then, this bill sweeps in all business." What remained of state rights, of the Federal system? By asserting that the "one constitutional provision" of the Bill was a proposed amendment limiting its action to persons engaged in interstate "transportation," Platt anticipated an interpretation by the Supreme Court. In *United States* v. *E. C. Knight Co.* (1895), the Court ruled that manufacturing and commerce are distinct entities, that sugar refining is not part of interstate commerce and is therefore outside the regulatory powers of Congress. This doctrine, as will be seen, evoked rage in many circles, and the Court abandoned it for a more palatable interpretation.

Platt outlined that too. Reminding his colleagues that the Interstate Commerce Act had been passed "to prevent ruinous rate wars between railroads," Platt suggested that excess capacity was ubiquitous by citing the experience of "eight representative woolen establishments" in Connecticut. The eight firms, employing among them some 2,000 men, had suffered an aggregate loss of nearly $50,000 in the prosperous year 1887, "not taking into account the matter of loss by bad debts. . . ." Platt continued: "They are running their business at a loss; they are making articles to which this bill refers; and this bill says that if those eight men should combine to get a fair, living profit upon their manufacture, that contract, that agreement is against public policy, unlawful and void." The theory of the Bill was "utterly untenable" and "immoral." Only in 1911 would the Supreme Court, in the Standard Oil Case and the American Tobacco Case, fully enunciate the Rule of Reason by which only "unreasonable" combinations in restraint of trade were held to violate the Anti-Trust Act. But even before the act was passed, Senator Platt used the same reasoning:

Whenever the price of anything is below what it costs to produce it, it ought to be raised, and any combination for the purpose of raising it to a point where the price is fair and reasonable ought not to be condemned; it ought to be encouraged.

No amount of logic could prevent passage of the law. Just as Congress felt compelled to placate anti-monopoly voters, so it had to yield something to inflationist sentiment and the Silver bloc. The latter, wanting the United States mint to be a big customer, was dissatisfied with the Bland-Allison Act; in 1878 the price of silver had been $1.15 an ounce, but now it was below 94 cents. Congress gave ground by passing the Sherman Silver Purchase Act of 1890, which promised to more than double purchases of silver by the Treasury. In practice it would have some other effects too, and in three years they would create a crisis. But the Silver Act helped clear the road for the McKinley Tariff Act.

Titled "An Act to Reduce the Revenue," the measure achieved that goal in several ways. Removing all duties on raw sugar and molasses cut the Treasury's income perhaps $50 million a year. Coffee and hides stayed on the free list, which also included acorns, beeswax, and dandelion roots. Rates on other items were raised to prohibitive levels, which likewise served to cut Federal income. The internal revenue tax on tabacco was lowered, making it possible for American Tobacco to sell more cigarettes. And of course expenses were raised: the bounty to American sugar planters cost at least $6 million a year. Taken all in all, the average rates were some 50 per cent of the value of imports—the highest level in history. Removal of all duties from three big imports from Latin America seemed to endanger Blaine's program for reciprocity, which at the time was in effect only with Hawaii. But the Senate wrote into the Act a negative provision by which the President was empowered to raise duties against any country unjustly taxing imports from the United States.

With the tariff law, and the act to punish trusts, and the Silver Purchase Act, and a more generous Pension Act for veterans, the Republicans took to the hustings in November 1890. They were decisively beaten. Two of their three foremost Representatives, McKinley and Joseph G. Cannon of Illinois, were defeated. The new House held fewer Republicans than at any time since the Civil War; the Democrats had a margin of nearly 3 to 1. But the Senate continued Republican, and the politics of stalemate lasted until 1893.

President Harrison could do some things without Congress. During his first year in office more than 30,000 postmasters were swept out of their jobs and replaced by Republicans. But with the White House changing hands every four years, the pressure was strong on a President to protect the officeholders of his own party before he left office. Harrison extended the civil service list to another 14,000 jobs; it covered some 43,000 employees when he left office.

As he did, in 1893. The campaign in 1892 of former President Cleveland was well financed. The interlude from public office he had spent in a New York law firm headed by Francis Lynde Stetson, Morgan's lawyer. He got money from Henry Villard, who controlled the Northern Pacific and was agent for large Berlin and Frankfurt banks which had invested heavily in American securities. From Oscar Straus of Macy's. From Charles S. Fairchild, formerly his Secretary of the Treasury, now a big New York banker. From Henry B. Payne, a Standard Oil man who had persuaded (bribed, some said) the legislature to make him a United States Senator in 1886. From Payne's son-in-law William C. Whitney, who had been busily setting up monopolies in streetcar lines, whiskey, and tobacco. Whitney reportedly got the heads of the Sugar Trust to ante up $100,000; two years later Henry Havemeyer told a Senate committee: "We receive a good deal of protection for our money." The Republicans had trouble raising money. Henry Frick of the Carnegie Steel Company had put in $50,000 in 1888; now he paid only half that. Even this, he told a friend, was "a waste of money." After Frick made the contribution, he got a letter from Andrew Carnegie, enjoying himself in Europe, saying he should give only $10,000. On election day former President Hayes noted in his diary that the struggle was not arousing much interest, and that Cleveland would probably win. He added complacently: "The country can stand it."

Cleveland had by far the widest margin of any President in 20 years. Not only did he win New York and Indiana, he also won Illinois and Wisconsin. Frick wrote Carnegie: "I am very sorry for President Harrison, but I cannot see that our interests are going to be affected one way or the other by the change in administration." Carnegie wrote back: "Cleveland! Landslide! Well we have nothing to fear and perhaps it is best. People will now think the Protected Manfrs. are attended to and quit agitating. Cleveland is a pretty good fellow. Off for Venice tomorrow."

The Interstate Commerce Act may well have seemed the most effective measure that had been devised since 1877 to curb any American corporations. But even that—what did it really amount to, and what kind of men were supposed to enforce it? In December 1892 Charles E. Perkins sought the aid of Richard Olney in persuading the incoming administration to abolish the Interstate Commerce Commission. Olney wrote that such an effort would not be wise "looking at the matter from a railroad point of view exclusively. . . ." He explained: "The Commission, as its functions have now been limited by the courts, is, or can be made, of great use to the railroads. It satisfies the popular clamor for a government supervision of railroads, at the same time that that supervision is almost entirely nominal. . . . The part of wisdom is not to destroy the Commission, but to utilize it." Olney, a Boston corporation lawyer, was a director of Perkins' road and its corporation counsel. He was also a director of the Boston & Maine and of the Santa Fe. And in February 1893, when President-elect Cleveland offered to appoint him Attorney-General of the United States, Olney wrote again to Perkins inquiring if it would be "to the true interest" of the Burlington for him to accept. He took the job.

Perkins fretted about the Interstate Commerce Act, with its prohibition of pooling, but he had benefited from some of its other provisions. In January 1888 the Burlington was confronted by the Engineers and the Firemen with various demands including payment on a straight mileage basis. The company insisted on its right to pay more to experienced men and to pay more for runs on the main lines than on branch lines. On February 27 a strike began —the two strongest Brotherhoods against one of the major railways in the West, with 6,000 miles of track from St. Paul to Chicago to St. Louis to Denver. Some 2,000 men, 95 per cent of the enginemen on the road, walked out quietly. The quiet soon ended, as the company hired some 600 Pinkerton detectives and used the agency to advertise for strikebreakers in cities from New York to Denver. At first the strikers tried to buy the new men off, but the policy proved too expensive. On March 14, Perkins claimed that 70 per cent of the strikers had been replaced. A company official wrote on March

20: "The result has demonstrated the fact that an abundance of labor will break up any strike, no matter how strong the striking party may be. We can easily get two thousand engineers if we need them."

Faced with defeat, the striking Brotherhoods instituted a boycott against Burlington cars and Burlington-originated freight on the connecting railroads. Now the company found the Interstate Commerce Act handy. It got injunctions from Federal circuit courts in Omaha, in Chicago, and elsewhere against the boycott, alleging that the Act required other roads to handle its cars and freight without discrimination. Although several court orders had been issued in the Gould Southwest strikes of 1886, the labor injunctions in the Burlington strike were the first to attract widespread notice. The device proved attractive to employers, and the next few years saw "government by injunction" become a bitter grievance of labor.

The two Brotherhoods sought to save their strike by inducing the switchmen and brakemen in Chicago to strike against the Burlington. The members of those crafts did strike, on March 26, only to see engineers scab on them. They went back to work on April 4. As the railroad returned to almost normal operations, some strikers began to think about sabotage, and a few were arrested in July for participation in an alleged dynamite plot. In December three men were convicted in an Illinois court and sent to prison; two others, who had turned state's evidence, got nominal sentences. On 8 January 1889, more than ten months after it started, the strike was officially ended. Fewer than 10 per cent of the strikers were re-employed by the Burlington; the two leading Brotherhoods had been virtually eliminated from its lines. The result had been accomplished by the availability of strikebreakers, by Federal injunctions, by Pinkerton spies (one Pinkerton served as secretary to the chairman of the strike committee), by the superior resources of the company and its superior access to the newspapers—and by factionalism in the ranks of labor.

Directly out of the Burlington strike came an effort to achieve unity of action among all the Brotherhoods. Leader in the campaign was Eugene Debs, secretary-treasurer of the Firemen and editor of its journal, whose views had changed considerably since he expressed his horror at the railroad strikes of 1877. Now he wrote: "The strike is the weapon of the oppressed, of men capable of appreciating justice and having the courage to resist wrong and contend for principle." His union endorsed the idea of a federation of the Brotherhoods, and in June 1889 its three top officers met in Chicago with the top officials of the Brakemen and of the Switchmen to form the Supreme Council of the United Orders of Railway Employees.

In the next year the federation won some victories; new organizations of railroaders were founded in several crafts; Debs worked unceasingly to bring the Engineers into the new Supreme Council. Then the Brakemen changed their name to the Brotherhood of Railroad Trainmen and began to organize switchmen. A heated jurisdictional dispute began with the existing union in that craft. Both contesting organizations were members of the Supreme Council. The clash died down. The Conductors joined the Supreme Council. Debs was jubilant.

Then what began as a petty dispute between two men ended in general ruin. The culmination came when the Trainmen entered into a neat conspiracy with the Northwestern railroad. The road fired all members of the Switchmen—500 of them. The Trainmen supplied replacements. This episode disrupted and dissolved the Supreme Council. Then Eugene Debs, convinced that unity of all railroaders could not be achieved within the organizational forms provided by the craft Brotherhoods, led in the formation of the American Railway Union—a move that culminated in the turbulent Pullman Boycott.

Railroads had learned how to break unions; so had steel firms. Early in 1892 the Amalgamated Association of Iron and Steel Workers was one of the strongest unions in the country, with skilled workers constituting a good part of its more than 20,000 members. In 1889 it had signed a 3-year contract covering the 4,000 workers in the Carnegie plant at Homestead, about 10 miles from Pittsburgh. Before the expiration date of the contract, 30 June 1892, a board fence topped by barbed wire encircled the plant. At regular intervals in the fence, three-inch holes were cut.

On June 28 Henry Frick locked out 800 men. The next day the entire labor force went on strike. Frick had already arranged with the Pinkerton agency to furnish 300 armed guards on July 6, when he planned to reopen the mill. Meanwhile the workers, although most of them were foreign-born and many could not speak English, were showing what solidarity meant. They set up a 24-hour watch to guard against strikebreakers. The Pinkertons arrived at Homestead at 4 A.M. on July 6, having come up the Mahoning River from Youngstown. They were met by armed strikers along the shore. After an all-day battle, the Pinkertons surrendered and were escorted out of town. Three Pinkertons and ten strikers were dead.

The governor of Pennsylvania sent 8,000 state troops into Homestead, but Frick still had trouble getting his mill in operation because of a shortage of skilled workers. The strike dragged on through the summer, with unionists all over the country sending financial aid to the strikers. But by mid-October some 2,000 men were at work, only about 400 of them former employees. The union was dead at Homestead, and the great majority of the strikers were out of a job.

The same day the militia arrived at Homestead, July 11, a battle was fought a half continent away. Silver miners at Coeur d'Alene, Idaho, had struck against a wage cut and lockout. They drove out the strikebreakers and seized the mine. The governor declared martial law and requested Federal troops from the President. The army arrested every union man it could find and imprisoned several hundred of them for months in a bull pen made of barbed wire. It even prohibited the mines from hiring unionists.

Many wage earners by 1892 were convinced that their pockets were being picked by giant corporations and their lackeys in government, with a callousness and contempt matched only by a sporting woman rolling a drunk. Lots of farmers felt the same way.

In 1890, in the five states of Minnesota, Kansas, Nebraska, and the Dakotas, the number of farm mortgages equaled the number of farm families. "The great middle class, including the farmer, is gradually being undermined and destroyed," declared the *Farmers' Alliance* of Lincoln, Nebraska. "To this end legislation, both state and national, has directly tended . . ." But the first major expression of the farmers' remedies came, not from the West, but from the South. In December 1890 the Southern Farmers' Alliance, the Farmers' Mutual Benefit Association, and—most ominous of all for the major parties—the Colored Farmers' Alliance issued a set of demands from a joint meeting in Ocala, Florida.

They wanted national banks abolished. A system of government subtreasuries to lend money at 1 per cent against the security of "non-perishable farm products"—wheat, corn, cotton. A circulating medium of $50 per person. They wanted unlimited coinage of silver. Removal of the heavy tariff on necessities. A graduated income tax. Government control of transportation and communication and, if that proved ineffective, government ownership. Reservation of all land to actual users.

In 1891 the Farmers' Alliance in the South was said to have 35,000 lecturers in the field, all preaching the Ocala Demands. Local lodges held semimonthly meetings. County conventions, district conventions, state conventions—they met and argued and sang and swore at the bankers on Wall Street and in London. They were out to change things. They sought to ally South to West, farmer to wage earner, white to Negro.

At the end of 1891 the editor of the *Southern Alliance Farmer* claimed that "the farmer has about reached the end of his row." From Burke County, Georgia, came a letter that Representative Tom Watson read into the *Congressional Record:* "Our county is in a terrible, terrible condition. Out of fifteen hundred customers at one store only fourteen paid out; five hundred paid less than 50 cents on the dollar." Watson, sent to Congress as an Alliance candidate in 1890, was advocating formation of a third party by 1892, and in it he proposed to bring together the white farmer and the Negro farmer. He told them both: "You are made to hate each other because upon that hatred is rested the keystone of this arch of financial despotism which enslaves you both."

When the new People's party met in national convention in Omaha in 1892, Southern delegates were there in force, and had the satisfaction of seeing the Ocala Demands written into the platform. In some respects the new document was more advanced: it made a flat demand for government ownership and operation of railroads, telephone, telegraph. The accompanying "Expression of Sentiments" sought labor support by calling for shorter hours, the 8-hour day on government contracts, and condemned "the maintenance of a large standing army of mercenaries, known as the Pinkerton system. . . ." The platform was adopted on the Fourth of July. The delegates then nominated a national ticket of General James B. Weaver of Iowa, veteran of many agrarian campaigns who had been the Greenback-Labor nominee for President in 1880, and a former Confederate officer, James G. Field of Virginia.

But in the election in November, when the Populist ticket ran up a national vote of more than a million, only some 362,000 votes were recorded for the party in the South. Of these, nearly 30 per cent were in Texas. In Georgia, the Populist candidate for governor had been beaten by only a 2-to-1 margin in the state election in October 1892. But a month later, Weaver got a mere 42,000 votes in the state, ran third behind the Republican, and had less than 20 per cent of the total vote.

How was this result accomplished? And why? In the South the Democrats had their backs to the wall. Not only were local and state offices at stake, but the Democrats felt they could not win the Presidency in 1892 without the Southern vote. They were willing to let Iowa and Kansas and other Western states go: if they tried to win support there by advocating free coinage of silver, they might drive away the independents they needed to give them New England and New York. But they had to have the South as well as the East to win.

So their violence against the Populists was unrestrained. The Democratic press of Georgia claimed that mobbing was too good for "the atheistic, anarchistic, communistic editor of the *People's Party Paper*." An estimated 15 Negroes were killed by Democrats in the state campaign. The Democratic governor was heard to say that "Watson ought to be killed and it ought to have been done long ago." The Democratic chairman in Wilkes County sent a circular to planters that said: "It is absolutely necessary that you should bring to bear the power which your situation gives over tenants, laborers and croppers." Negro field hands were hauled to the polls in wagonloads and voted by squads. Augusta polls were filled with Negro imports who had been brought across the Savannah River from South Carolina; at wagon yards in that city the voters were paid in cash and whiskey was dispensed by the barrel. The vote recorded in Augusta, in Watson's congressional district, was roughly twice the number of legal voters. By such methods was Watson licked. The Democracy was saved. But was democracy saved? Was it worth saving?

City Boss: GEORGE B. COX

Cox (1853–1916) was born in Cincinnati to a recent British immigrant. He lived there all his life, and said he was a Republican because his father was. He wasn't a man to flit around. The father died when George was eight; the son worked as bootblack, newsboy, lookout for a gambling joint, deliveryman for a grocery, tobacco salesman, bartender. Then he got his own saloon. He served two terms on the city council starting in 1879. It was the only elective office he ever held.

The *Dictionary of American Biography* presents Cox as an austere man with no intimates. Unlikely on its face, this portrait is contradicted by solid evidence. Lincoln Steffens liked him, with his "great hulk" and "his hoarse, throaty voice." True, Cox was taciturn—what successful executive isn't? He liked good cigars and good stories. With friends he bought the Cincinnati baseball team from its Indianapolis owner, and was a power in pro baseball's hierarchy. He became head of the American Bowling Congress. Perhaps not as convivial as some of his lieutenants, he won lasting loyalties. The abilities that he carried to the sporting world were those that made him the kingfish at home: "great executive talent and political sagacity," as explained by his fellow-townsman William Howard Taft.

By patience and imaginative effort that reached into every ward and into most precincts, amid a maelstorm of treachery and shifting alliances and frequent setbacks, George Cox perfected a machine that dominated the city for two decades. Many of his techniques were traditional: a 2 or 2½ per cent levy on the salaries of all Republican office-holders, with higher officials paying more (Cox would always fight over patronage), kickbacks from contractors who got business from the city or county, backscratching arrangements with newspapers, influence in the state and Federal governments. But in Cincinnati all this was done more systematically and persistently than in other municipalities. Moreover, Cox had a flair. He won the establishment of a "bipartisan" (three Republicans, two Democrats) board of administration. This appointed body had sole control of any extension of a franchise held by a public-utilities corporation. Not surprisingly, the head of the Cincinnati Gas, Light and Coke Company noted in his diary in 1891 that he had "concluded arrangement with Geo. B. Cox for services at $3500 per year quarterly to last for 3 years." The boss claimed that he had never gotten a dishonest dollar. He also said, probably with considerable truth, that he had never broken a promise.

Since Cox needed to know everything happening in his city, his spies and ferrets were an informal ancestor of the FBI; the journalist Steffens, in town to study the machine, found himself being followed everywhere. The result of efficient organization was described by another writer as "more compact and closely knit than any of the political machines which have dominated New York, Philadelphia, Chicago, St. Louis or San Francisco."

In 1905 a cartoonist for the Scripps press depicted Secretary of War Taft and Governor Myron Herrick as bootblacks shining the shoes of the ex-bootblack George B. Cox.

CHAPTER 7

Understanding It All

Henry Adams thought that democracy was hardly worth saving. (No, no, not the Henry Adams from Louisiana; the one from Massachusetts.) When he brought out his novel *Democracy* in 1880, he did so anonymously. The book was an instant success, and its satire about Washington was widely copied.

The young widow Madeleine Lee is bored by New York Society: "What was it all worth, this wilderness of men and women as monotonous as the brown-stone houses they lived in?" Nor is Boston better; there too everybody is "six inches high." So in December 1876 she sets out for Washington "bent upon getting to the heart of the great American mystery of Democracy and government." The first evening reception of the new President, "the Hoosier Quarryman," seems to her devoid of dignity and terrifying in its banality:

> They took their places in the line of citizens and were at last able to enter the reception-room. There Madeleine found herself before two seemingly mechanical figures, which might be wood or wax, for any sign they showed of life. These two figures were the President and his wife; they stood stiff and awkward by the door, both their faces stripped of every sign of intelligence, while the right hands of both extended themselves to the column of visitors with the mechanical action of toy dolls.

Madeleine, so precious in her sensibilities that she can only be the alter ego to Henry Adams, is sure that nobody shares her reaction. All the thousands present "thought it a democratic institution, this aping of monarchial forms."

The government is suited to the country. Senator Silas P. Ratcliffe of Illinois defends the lack of principle in politics by contending that "no representative government can long be much better or much worse than the society it represents." As for the society, says a cynical Bulgarian baron, it is the worst he has seen: "The children in the street are corrupt, and know how to cheat me. . . . Everywhere men betray trusts both public and private, steal money, run away with public funds."

This outburst upsets even Ratcliffe, but soon he is telling Madeleine (in the presence of John Carrington, his potential rival for her hand) about an episode that happened during the Civil War when he was governor of Illinois. It seemed that the "peace party" would carry an election in the state. This might mean the loss of the next Presidential election and thus the destruction of the Union. He instructed the Republican counties in the northern part of the state to hold back their returns until all votes from the southern counties had been reported. Then he wired the northern counties what votes they should report to insure a Republican victory. He concludes: "I am not proud of the transaction, but I would do it again, and worse than that, if I thought it would save this country from disunion. But of course I did not expect Mr. Carrington to approve it. I believe he was then carrying out his reform principles by bearing arms against the government."

A reader might think that Ratcliffe hardly has the worse of this joust so far as ethics are concerned; he poses, at the least, a neat problem. But thereafter the author steadily contrasts the immorality of Ratcliffe and other products of the free North with the virtue of Carrington, a product of the slave South. At last Carrington, lacking any other means of blocking Madeleine's marriage to Ratcliffe, tells of the efforts of the Inter-Oceanic Mail Steamship Company to get a subsidy from Congress. Ratcliffe had been chairman of the Senate committee considering the bill. At first he opposed it. He switched his vote in exchange for $100,000 for his party's campaign fund.

Madeleine confronts Ratcliffe with the story. He admits that much of it is true, and urges that the campaign contribution had hurt nobody except that perhaps the stockholders had gotten a dollar less in dividends. Now Madeleine sees him as "a moral lunatic." She and her younger sister Sybil Ross return to New York, with Madeleine saying that she wants to go to Egypt. "Democracy has shaken my nerves to pieces."

Long before that, Henry Adams has shaken *Democracy* to pieces. The book does raise important questions about morality in politics; Madeleine Lee asks: "Where did the public good enter at all into this maze of personal intrigue, this wilderness of stunted natures where no straight road was to be found, but only the tortuous and aimless tracks of beasts and things that crawl?" But Madeleine, too, was a stunted nature, and so was the author. His ancestors had carried their principles with them into the complexities of civic affairs; he saw no choice but to carry his away from public life, to sit on the sidelines, a disengaged observer, virginal perhaps, but hardly superior.

How can a writer act superior when he slides into such phrases as "a serious disaster?" The good American novelists of the period were alert to dialect, but Adams' best efforts are a couple of pathetic attempts to render foreign accents. ("Mees Ross" or "what for is my conclusion good?" What for, indeed?) At times—as when he describes a young Representative as "rather wealthy, rather clever, rather well-educated, rather honest, and rather vulgar"—Adams can be rather witty. But even this passage shows an essential failing in a novelist: Adams is seldom content to let his characters discover and reveal their character by their behavior. He stands aloof, commenting on them in a looking-down-the-nose mode. He was far too self-indulgent to amount to much as a novelist, and his book is interesting chiefly as an index to the collapse of one of the most honorable American strains of political leadership.

That Adams' novel was inferior as fiction would have seemed only natural to Lord Bryce, for his generation the most eminent foreign commentator on the United States. Bryce catalogued several reasons why this country was not more creative in art, literature, science. Life was so restless and held so many distractions that it did not afford those "hours of comparative tranquility" in which great creations usually germinate. Most of the nation's ability went into subjugating nature and progressing materially. These interests monopolized even men's thoughts and conversations, to the detriment of literature and art. Men of leisure, feeling out of place, were "wont either to make amusement into a business or to transfer themselves to the ease of France or Italy." The cultured people who remained in the United States were strewn about in tiny pockets rather than being gathered in a capital city or about a university. Far from ascribing the plight of culture solely to the influence of democracy, Bryce held that the "prevalence of evangelical Protestantism" had influenced American thought as much as had the form of government.

Bad taste and pecksniff morality were both apparent in the one New York production of Sophocles in the last half of the 19th century. "Oedipus" was staged in 1882 with a score by a Harvard professor which made no effort to be faithful to the playwright's time; it required a large orchestra and a chorus of 60 voices. The costumes followed the style of Periclean Greece, as more colorful than those of Sophocles' day. The actor playing Oedipus spoke in Greek; the rest of the cast used English. The New York *Herald* found the play an affront to the American belief in individualism and optimism; the *Times* thought its subject "highly immoral"; a theatrical weekly said a modern play with similar themes would probably be shut down as a violation of the city's ordinances.

Wholesomeness was stressed in large measure because the bulk of the audience for any form of art consisted of women, most men being too busy and too earnest to bother with such frivolities. And yet, said Bryce, things had been worse: Puritan sentiment was declining and "the theatre is now extremely popular, perhaps more popular than in any part of Europe." Traveling companies played in nearly every settlement in the country—not always with pleasure. The actor Edmund Kean complained that one New England audience was so cold that it would "put out Vesuvius," and he refused to appear for the next scene unless he heard some applause.

The theater, like so much of American society, had been revolutionized by the railroads. As long as travel was slow and costly, a star actor had traveled alone, playing with a resident company in each town. The public became less and less willing to patronize a show without a big name, and the big names were paid more and more. So local managers cut costs in the only way left to them: they slashed the salaries of the resident companies. The competence of supporting casts fell steadily. To meet this situation stars like Dion Boucicault and Joe Jefferson founded traveling combination companies after 1860. Thirty years later the star on a solo tour had disappeared, and the traveling companies, which had been repertory, tended increasingly to do a single play for the entire season, or for several seasons.

Thus the theater, like other businesses, was reshaped by technology and by its pecuniary motives. For a few actors the financial results were happy. For the 1876–1877 season, playing six large cities from Boston to San Francisco, Edwin Booth received $121,353. The cost of such earnings was clear—catering to the biases of a mass audience. When Booth played "Hamlet" in London in 1880, it did not draw well enough. After two weeks he switched to Bulwer-Lytton's "Richelieu," which ran for more than a month.

City newspapers too, observed Bryce, "think first of the mass and are controlled by its taste, which they have themselves done so much to create." Book publishers tended to reject books that they regarded as atheistic or immoral, but they also were sensitive to the pressures of the market. In 1880 Charles Scribner wrote to his London partner: "You write that you do not know what I want in books to reprint. I can only say I want anything that *will sell*." The emphasis was his.

Some Indians continued to stand outside the demands of the callous cash nexus and went right on thinking, for reasons often not clear to the environing white savages, that one of man's purposes on earth is to create useless beauty. In Dakota a Sioux baby, perhaps a descendant of Crazy Horse, wore a hooded bunting of beaded cloth and leather. As was customary with Sioux bead-work, the background was tiny white beads set one against another, ornamented with geometric nonrepresentational designs of similar beads in royal blue and a rich medium blue, mustard yellow and olive green. The front was closed by five leather ties. It, and the opening for the face, were adorned by little brass bells. Hanging down the back of the hood was a beaded leather flap, with its own tassels and bells. For design and sense of color, the garment is a delight.

As the Plains Indians became horsemen in the 19th century, they began to design more ornate clothing that would give especially pleasing effects trailing out in the breeze behind a galloping pony, such as the long feathered headdresses of the braves. An Arapaho woman in Colorado made a dress of beaded and painted leather. The shoulders and upper breast were covered with tiny azure blue beads, relieved by perfectly placed triangles of royal blue, deep red, and mustard. Below that came another irregular horizontal band, extending to slightly above the waist, painted a vivid mustard. The remainder of the dress was natural leather, light beige. Also banding the dress were three rows, about a foot apart, of bright blue beads a quarter inch in diameter, from each of which hung two leather fringes; other long fringes hung from the bottom of the dress, the sides, and the bottoms of the sleeves, which came about to the elbows, were very deep, and were not sewn under the arms. Again, the eye of the maker was superb.

But no better than the eye of an American whose creations were less traditional, more individual. Winslow Homer said that his aim was simply to paint what he saw as truly as possible. "If a man wants to be an artist he must never look at pictures," he warned (and did not abide strictly by his own maxim). Born in Boston in 1836, he was an illustrator for *Harper's Weekly* during the Civil War and for a decade thereafter. Then he took up watercolor, and from then on it was as important to him as oil. Incapable of learning from others, forced to work everything out for himself, he grew slowly but steadily, seeking to capture the wildness and beauty to be found outdoors: light, wind, the sea, mountains, hunting, fish, the men who have built their own characters by coping with the elements and not with other men. Unsociable, testy, he moved in 1883 to a rocky peninsula on the Maine coast, ten miles south of Portland. There he lived for 27 years, seldom seeing anybody, trying to subdue with eye and brush the mysteries of nature. "The sun shall not rise or set, without my notice, and thanks." The years of schooling his powers to see, the struggle to master his craft—they show in his painting of 1886, "Eight Bells." The scene is stripped bare, and caught, in muted deep tones. Waves, clouds, twin masts, the railing of the ship. Two bearded sailors stand in oilskins, with a quadrant. They are quiet, lost in their work, indestructible as the ocean.

Homer despised men who weren't lost in their work. Once at a dealer's he was told that another painter, also present in the store, wanted to be introduced to him. Knowing that the man had found a formula and was using it endlessly, for the money, Homer replied: "Tell Mr. G——to go to Hell." Although he never earned more than a comfortable living, Homer had his rewards: a lifelong fascination with the world outside, a mastery of watercolor that is matched by few in the history of art, recognition by those of his own time best able to judge. Thomas Eakins, asked who was the greatest American painter of his generation, singled out Homer.

Eakins got less money and, during his lifetime, less fame. Six years younger than Homer, he reached maturity as an artist sooner.

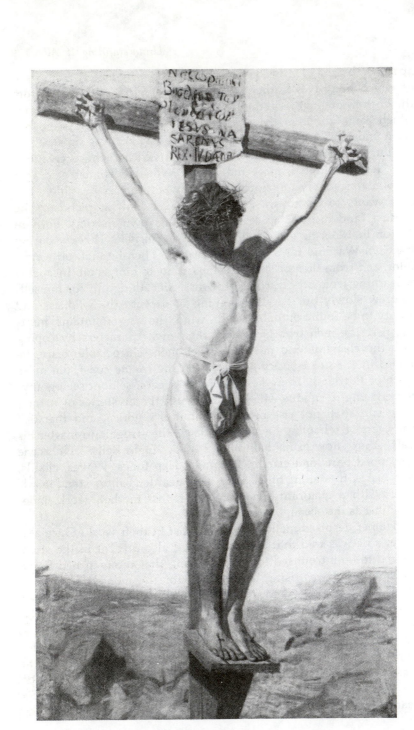

Already in 1880 he finished a treatment of one of the enduring themes of Christendom, the Crucifixion. Objecting that he had never seen a painting in which the dying Christ seemed to be in the open air or to be actually hanging from the cross, Eakins found ways to remedy both defects. It is a lonely landscape, low mountains and barren plains, in gunmetal grays and dull browns. Nature is not hostile, just indifferent. To the death of the central figure there are no human witnesses, and no divine ones. He is alone, on the cross. The only color is the blood oozing from his hands and feet; even the blood seems dusty. The anguish that his face might have shown is lost in shadow. His head has sagged, against his shoulder and breast.

[OPPOSITE] "The Crucifixion" *by Thomas Eakins. Oil on canvas, 1880.* (Philadelphia Museum of Art: Given by Mrs. Thomas Eakins and Miss Marry A. Williams. Photograph by A. J. Wyatt, staff photographer.)

"Eight Bells" by Winslow Homer. (Courtesy of Addison Gallery of American Art, Phillips Academy, Andover, Massachusetts.)

And, in one of those touches, simple yet stunning in impact, that mark the greatest artists, Eakins has him standing on a small wooden platform. His knees have collapsed. The thigh muscles are slack. His full weight hangs from the nails through his hands. He rips his own flesh. Not only is it a staggering portrayal of human suffering, Eakins seems too to imply that sometimes we aggravate our own agonies when our strength gives out.

Eakins' best work was in portraits. Quiet domesticity in a picture of Mrs. Eakins with a red setter at her feet. Rollicking Walt Whitman in his last years. The decisive command of Dr. Agnew at an operation. Oarsmen in their shells and sculls. Musicians. A boxer waving to the raucous crowd in the arena. Catholic priests in their robes. Middle-aged women who carry each day of their toil-worn lives in their faces and eyes. ("How beautiful an old woman's skin is!" he said. "All those wrinkles!" He had Rembrandt's sure sense of the greenish tones in human skin.) A young woman singer straining for the proper note. A young woman whose eyes tell of her loneliness. The world out there, and the worlds inside the people out there, gave to Eakins an infinity of subjects.

To Albert Pinkham Ryder, there was only one subject: his own soul and the furies it held. He projected those furies onto the outside world, and thus transformed it. He studied nature of course, closely, but in later life he never painted from it or from sketches of it. At his hands it became eerie, almost haunted. Many of his themes came from the unworldly subjects of the Bible, of Shakespeare, of Wagner. Ryder himself told the origins of his canvas, "The Race Track." A waiter at his brother's hotel lost his savings betting on the horses. He committed suicide. Ryder could not get the incident out of his mind. Years later it emerged onto canvas. The Grim Reaper, scythe upraised, spurs his horse at breakneck speed around an otherwise deserted track, under an ominous orange sky.

Caring little for money, or comfort, or even food, Ryder lived in solitude, in filth. "The artist needs but a roof, a crust of bread, and his easel, and all the rest God gives him in abundance," he said. "He must live to paint and not paint to live. He cannot be a good fellow; he is rarely a wealthy man, and upon the potboiler is inscribed the epitaph of his art."

Henry Hobson Richardson showed that good fees and good work need not be incompatible. Born in Louisiana in 1838, Richardson spent the Civil War years in Paris studying architecture. Then to New York, where he began a persistent attempt to adapt Late Gothic and Romanesque forms to a strong and robust personal style. He did not always succeed. Many buildings were dull and drab, unintegrated and chaotic; efforts to achieve polychromy by using different kinds of stone often seemed arbitrary and garish. But Richardson, the leading architect in the country after his design for Boston's Trinity Church in 1877, achieved some memorable work. The large Stoughton House near Harvard was an admirable town house in New England shingles. The Ames Gardeners' Cottage at North Easton was a model suburban dwelling.

He did nothing better than the wholesale store in Chicago which Marshall Field commissioned in 1885. Seven stories, it had massive supporting walls of red granite and sandstone. Although much of the wall space was given to recessed windows, the structure seemed to embody the store's claim of permanence and solidity. The windows, rectangular or arched, were grouped into exciting rhythms. At each corner a huge pier rose unbroken to a heavy cornice.

Had Marshall Field known it, he could have found in Chicago itself an architect who could have put an equally beautiful building, with just as many square feet of floor space, on a smaller plot of ground. Rising land values in the cities were creating financial pressures for the construction of taller buildings. Improvements in the elevator in the preceding thirty years made it possible to move goods and men to unprecedented heights. Structural steel held the promise of walls that did not have to support weight, but would be merely a thin external shield against the elements. Louis Sullivan accepted the esthetic challenge in these possibilities. Fresh from the triumph of the Chicago Auditorium (containing what Frank Lloyd Wright continued to call "the finest room for opera in the world"), Sullivan did the Wainwright Building in St. Louis. Around its base swept a band of giant windows two stories high, broken by corner piers from sidewalk to cornice nine stories up. Horizontal panels and the frieze of terra cotta, all bearing Sullivan's flowing designs, tied the vertical pillars in place. The elements of this shell seemed almost to sing together, like some grand chorus.

As with great painters, great architects in the United States faced terrible problems. Richardson became too popular, and he was enticed into more projects than any man could handle prop-

erly. Sullivan outran the taste of his clients, and the time came
when he got no commissions at all. Yet in the decade after 1880
five Americans did artistic work that would grace any country in
any age. Lord Bryce's conclusion about the inferiority of the creative intelligence in this country was wrong. It followed, not from
any close acquaintance with his subject, not from his logical
analysis, not from his often perceptive remarks on the difficulties
of the arts in a new country, but from the patronizing air toward
New World imaginations which has been adopted by many
Europeans—and by many Americans.

Similarly in fiction. In 1885 three novels were being serialized
simultaneously in *Century Magazine*. They were: *The Bostonians*,
by Henry James, *The Rise of Silas Lapham*, by William Dean
Howells, *The Adventures of Huckleberry Finn*, by Mark Twain.
Such juicy plants do not grow in profusion in a desert. And yet,
it is symptomatic, only Howells of these three men could come to
a wholehearted liking of the two others. To James, Twain hardly
existed, and Howells was clearly not a great novelist. In 1885,
while reading Howells' *Indian Summer*, Twain wrote the author
admiringly: "I am restricted to you; I wouldn't give a damn for the
rest." He brushed aside *The Bostonians* with a single comment: "I
would rather be damned to John Bunyan's heaven than read that."

Twain's fondness for *Indian Summer* is easily understood: the
book is a charming comedy of manners about three Americans in
Italy. A vacationing newspaper editor from the Midwest, who,
though retired from his trade, is just entering his middle years,
becomes involved in an emotional triangle with a widow his own
age and with her attractive and newly eligible ward. *The Bostonians*,
on the other hand, is too long; it is often diffuse and chatty; James
indulged in too many extended commentaries. But his characters,
while just as inane as those in *Indian Summer*, are seen far more
deeply. The suspicion arises that Twain, who had taken to wearing
white linen suits and observing (publicly, at least) all the proprieties
that were dear to his Hartford wife, rejected *The Bostonians* partly
because it was the first American novel which could be subtitled
"Varieties of Sexual Attraction." It is in large measure an effort
to depict mutations on the masculine and feminine, corruptions of
each, the threatened atrophy of each in favor of an epicene breed.

Selah Tarrant, mesmeric healer, self-seeking fraud, former in-
habitant of a colony which was irregular in its sexual ties, has

remained a libertine after his marriage. Toward his delicate and desirable, if unformed and virtually unconscious, daughter Verena, he is a potential agent of incest. The amoral reporter Matthew Pardon explains how Verena's father entrances her into her inspirational talks: "She has to have her father to start her up. It seems to pass into her." In preparing Verena to speak at an evening seance at Miss Birdseye's, Dr. Tarrant "stroked and soothed his daughter." Basil Ransom, a displaced Southerner, is angered by "Tarrant's grotesque manipulations" which seem "a dishonor to the passive maiden." Ransom does not catch the deep implications, for he later wonders "whether even a carpetbagger hadn't the right to do what he pleased with his daughter." Before Ransom can deliver the maiden from her father's clutches, she has another savior, Olive Chancellor.

The name betrays. To be a chancellor is to be a judge, and Olive passes self-righteous judgments on whatever she meets. Her older sister Mrs. Luna says of her: "She would reform the solar system if she could get hold of it." Her great crusade is "equality" for women. To be a chancellor is also a male role, and Olive was born for it. A wealthy young woman who affects great culture, she dresses without ornament; her body is shapeless; her eyes have the "glitter of green ice." When introduced to a gentleman she offers him her hand, "at once cold and limp." She smiles perpetually—like "a thin ray of moonlight resting upon the wall of a prison"—but never laughs. "Exhilaration, if it ever visited her, was dumb." She was "unmarried by every implication of her being. She was a spinster as Shelley was a lyric poet, or as the month of August is sultry." The epithet "unwomanly" she hated "almost as much as she hated its opposite."

With amazing success James is flippant and amusing in setting forth a series of perversions. Olive feels on meeting Verena that she has found "what she had been looking for so long—a friend of her own sex with whom she might have a union of soul." Verena, coming under her spell, swallows her views whole. Verena has no views of her own, and Olive's are simple: "She considered men in general as so much in the debt of the opposite sex that any individual woman had an unlimited credit with them; she could not possibly overdraw the general feminine account." Verena says to Olive, "You are my conscience," and Olive replies by stating her male impulses, "I should like to be able to say that you are my

form—my envelope." Thus did James plunge into the interplay of
public and private morality, of political creeds with pubic itches.

Verena soon moves into Olive's home on Charles Street, osten-
sibly so that Olive can groom the younger woman for a great career
as a lecturer for women's rights. To insure that Dr. and Mrs.
Tarrant will not interfere, Olive presents them with a large check
on her bank. Thus Selah Tarrant escapes the temptation to incest—
by becoming his daughter's pimp—for the benefit of a woman who
is, however haltingly, sailing to Lesbos.

Olive is early "haunted, in a word, with the fear that Verena
would marry." Mrs. Luna, a coquette who regards men as objects
for women to manipulate, predicts that her sister will not be able
to keep Verena: "She will run off with some lion-tamer; she will
marry a circus-man!" Olive fends off all threats until Basil Ransom
appears as a contender. Olive and Ransom both want to dominate
Verena, and as this duel progresses through the last half of the
novel, Verena slips increasingly into the man's orbit. On one
occasion she complains that Olive does not trust her: "You didn't,
from the first, with gentlemen." Moved by these protests of
fidelity, Olive "came to her slowly, took her in her arms and held
her long—giving her a silent kiss."

James, avoiding the blunder that Henry Adams had made in
Democracy, does not try to make his Southerner a moral hero.
Basil Ransom is part a silly survival from the Middle Ages, part
an unscrupulous man on the make. He would do whatever might
contribute to success at the bar, but he is too "unpractical" to
succeed. He fails as a lawyer, deservedly. Yet he suspects that his
failure is due to "a prejudice against his Southern complexion."
He is hostile to democracy, and admires Carlyle's views on heroes.
Admitting that he wants to keep women out of public life, he tells
Verena: "My plan is to keep you at home and have a better time
with you there than ever."

What might that better time consist in? James hints broadly at
the answer. The book closes as Ransom snatches Verena out of
her dressing room at the Boston Colosseum just before she is to
step on stage and give a triumphant performance for the emancipation of her sex. Ransom "by muscular force, wrenched her away,"
and hurried her out of the building. On the sidewalk, she bursts
into tears. "It is to be feared with the union, so far from brilliant,
into which she was about to enter, these were not the last she was

destined to shed." Thus the last sentence in the novel plays back against James' early remark: "Ransom's conception of vice was purely as a series of special cases, of explicable accidents." Here, one gathers, is a man whose notion of love might sometimes verge on rape.

Even these mutations on evil seem often more human than the sexless women who populate the world of reform in Boston. Miss Birdseye, nearing her dotage after a half century of agitation for feminism and abolition and short skirts and European revolutions, is "a confused, entangled, inconsequent, discursive old woman, whose charity began at home and ended nowhere, whose credulity kept pace with it. . . ." Mrs. Farrinder, a famous lecturer for women's rights and temperance, maintains even in intimate conversation the air that she is just about to be introduced "by a few remarks." Doctor Prance, the woman who is most sympathetically portrayed, is yet "spare, dry, hard, without a curve, an inflection, or a grace. . . . It was true that if she had been a boy she would have borne some relation to a girl, whereas Doctor Prance appeared to bear none whatever." James seems to be saying that feminism, however generous and warm-hearted it may have been in the years when it was allied with abolition, had after the Civil War become ridiculous if not downright destructive.

The Rise of Silas Lapham, while seeing the problem in far different contexts, also copes with the definition of masculine and feminine. Lapham as the story opens is saying that his wife is unusual in not being one of the "silly little girls grown up to *look* like women." He is ironically mistaken, and much of the book describes how Mrs. Lapham, a middle-aged woman with two eligible daughters, grows toward maturity. And at the end of the novel Howells says of her husband: "Adversity had so far been his friend that it had taken from him all hope of the social success for which people crawl and truckle, and restored him, through failure and doubt and heartache, the manhood which his prosperity had so nearly stolen from him." What has happened?

Lapham is a self-made man, a poor boy off a Vermont farm who has grown wealthy in the manufacture of mineral paint. He is proud that he makes a good product; he is also proud that he has defaced the Vermont countryside with advertisements for it. Although he is vulgar and ignorant, he is puffed up with his achievements. A reporter who writes a tongue-in-cheek eulogy of him is sure that Lapham will never see that he is being laughed at. Driven by pretensions, by the desire to occupy the place in Boston society to which their riches should entitle them, the Laphams begin to build a mansion on the Back Bay. But they deceive themselves into thinking that they are doing it for the girls, Penelope and Irene. They also deceive themselves into thinking that Irene may marry Tom Corey, a product of aristocratic Boston. Tom, in fact, is enamored of Penelope. When he at last makes his true intentions known, Mrs. Lapham at first responds like a sentimental "silly little girl": if Tom will not marry Irene, Penelope will have nothing to do with him. After much needless anguish for Penelope, her parents are straightened out by a minister who insists that it is better for one person to suffer than for three to do so. He tells them: "It's the economy of pain which naturally suggests itself, and which would insist upon itself, if we were not all perverted by traditions which are the figment of the shallowest sentimentality."

Some critics have taken this subplot as farce, and have gone on to blame Howells for allegedly letting his main plot become too serious, thus losing the integrity of tone. But the subplot can be taken quite differently, since the mix-up seems credible. What is farcical, if only from an Olympian perspective, is the sex morals of Boston gentility, which lure the blameless into tragedy. What are we to say of a code for courtship in which all the permissible signs of affection are so ambiguous that two sisters can remain uncertain who is being courted?

Mrs. Lapham's sentimentality, and her husband's willful vanity, also set the main plot in action. Lapham at one time had a partner, Milton K. Rogers, whom he bought out. Rogers is both dishonest and incompetent, but Mrs. Lapham like a "silly little girl" worries that perhaps he has been mistreated by her husband. To please her, Lapham lends Rogers money. In hope of recovering what he has loaned, he lends more. Rogers lures him into margin speculation of stocks. Thus exposed financially, Lapham is confronted by a glutted market for his paint. A new manufacturer of mineral paint appears in West Virginia, able to turn out a comparable product at far less cost.

Lapham flails around, trying this expedient and that. He is forced to close his factory, for the first time since it began operation. He resolves to sell the new mansion, now near completion, but he accidentally burns it down after the insurance has lapsed. Now he has only one hope to save his business. Rogers has unloaded onto him some lumber and grist mills in Iowa. If he can sell them, he might survive. But there is a hitch. The mills are located on a little railroad, against which he has been able to bargain successfully about freight rates. But the little road has just been leased to a Western trunkline, the Great Lacustrine & Polar. The G. L. & P. plans to build car-works right next to Lapham's mills, and it may want them, at a price that it could dictate. Having this inside knowledge, could he morally dump the mills onto some unsuspecting buyer before calamity struck?

Rogers, hoping for a commission, brings in the potential victims, two English agents for principals in Britain who are eager to start a utopian colony in the American West. Their discussion with Lapham is masterfully done. They treat his refusal to sell as a mere bargaining tactic. They assure him that they are representing rich philanthropists who could afford to take any loss, thus appealing—successfully, too—to the feeling in Lapham "which regards common property as common prey." But of course they don't think there will be any loss. They say they won't haggle over the price, thus suggesting that they want him to bilk their principals and share his gains with them. Lapham, even confronted with this treachery, asks the night to think it over. The next morning, before he has decided, a letter arrives from the G. L. & P. making an offer for his mills. The last chance for a sale is gone.

Lapham, in saving his manhood, loses most of his fortune. This is the fate, Howells implies, of the old-school businessman, still living by standards he had learned before the Civil War. The new men are less scrupulous. But if Lapham does not fall to the level of his successors, neither has he risen far, and Howells' title is partly ironic. Lapham is not particularly more ethical, or wiser, at the end of the book than at the beginning; it is only that the loss of his fortune has limited the scope within which he can indulge his folly. Similarly Mrs. Lapham consents to a sensible resolution of her daughter's love affair, not because she has gained an independence of public opinion, but because the minister's attitude shows that she was mistaken in her judgment of what public opinion demanded.

As Howells wrote of the results of vanity, of sentimentality, of false notions of guilt, so *The Adventures of Huckleberry Finn* studies the consequences of false codes of honor. The first code we meet seems gentle burlesque, as 13-year-old Huck and Tom Sawyer and their buddies work up a "real beautiful oath" for their robber gang. They agree that if anybody gives away their secrets, he—and his family—should be killed. Then they argue about whether it would be "fair and square for the others" to admit Huck because he doesn't have a family, leastways nobody but Pap, who "used to lay drunk with the hogs in the tanyard," but who hasn't been seen for a year.

Questions of honor begin to have serious overtones when Pap appears. He is offended because Huck has broken the family tradition of illiteracy. He is outraged on hearing that a free, educated Negro can vote in Ohio, and vows that he will have no truck with such a government. A new judge in town tries to win Pap for temperance, out of the sentimental belief that "what a man wanted that was down was sympathy." Pap takes the pledge, then gets drunk, falls off the porch roof, and breaks his arm.

Twain scoffs at the sentimentalists; as Huck thinks, when he is trapped on the wrecked steamboat with real robbers, "it warn't no time to be sentimentering." He tries to rescue the robbers from death by drowning in order to save them for death by hanging, and is confident that his guardian the Widow Douglas would approve, "because rapscallions and dead-beats is the kind the widow and good people takes the most interest in." After Mrs. Judith Loftus has unveiled Huck in his masquerade as a girl, she promptly deceives herself by inventing the story that he is a runaway apprentice whose master was cruel to him. The dead Emmeline Grangerford did countless pictures in crayon which sentimentalized death: a girl cries as she holds a dead bird in her. hand, and the caption reads, "I Shall Never Hear Thy Sweet Chirrup More Alas." All this, and much more, in a tone of chuckling. The chief agents of sentimentality, and its chief victims, are women.

They are also agents of cruelty. Whereas the depiction of women in *The Bostonians* is satiric, and that in *Silas Lapham* is ironic, that in *Huck Finn* is, simply, savage. The mode is sometimes farce, sometimes satire, or irony, even realism, and the total effect is savage. Huck has a companion in his travels, the runaway slave Jim, because Jim was about to be sold away from Missouri to the Deep South, away from his wife and children; the pious Miss Watson just could not resist an offering price of $800. Huck and

Jim have to leave their sanctuary on Jackson's Island because Mrs. Loftus sends her husband and another man to try to capture Jim— for the reward. The hilarious account of dead Emmeline and her crayons and her poetry erupts into the Grangerford-Shepherdson feud, and two Grangerford women dash about the countryside rounding up the clan to kill Harney Shepherdson—who is the lover of their daughter and sister (The Grangerfords are "aristocracy" of the slaveholding sort, and must protect their honor. So the father and his three sons are killed). When Huck tells Mary Jane that the King and the Duke are not her English uncles at all but confidence men, she exclaims, "Come, don't waste a minute—not a *second*— we'll have them tarred and feathered, and flung in the river!" Huck later sees them in that condition, in another town, and in spite of their many offenses against him, he thinks: "Well, it made me sick to see it; and I was sorry for them poor miserable rascals, it seemed like I couldn't ever feel any hardness against them any more in the world. It was a dreadful thing to see. Human beings *can* be awful cruel to one another." But Mary Jane was a very sentimental young lady. Thus, says Twain, sentimentality and cruelty go together, like hedonism and puritanism. And behind the psychological linkage was the chivalry, and the slavery, of the South.

At the Phelps plantation in Louisiana, where Jim is captured and locked up in a hut, Huck makes up a story for his supposed Aunt Sally about his pretended steamboat trip down the Mississippi. He says:

"We blowed out a cylinder-head."

"Good gracious! anybody hurt?"

"No'm. Killed a nigger."

"Well, it's lucky; because sometimes people do get hurt."

Out of slavery came cruelty. The surface of life is placid, even amusing, but it is a thin veneer that might crack open at any moment and unleash volcanoes of violence in man. A harmless old drunk shows up in an Arkansas town and begins cussing out the most prominent merchant, Colonel Sherburn; Sherburn shoots him dead in the street for no reason except that honor demanded that he enforce an ultimatum he had delivered. Then Sherburn disperses the lynch mob that comes for him by calling them cowards and facing them with a shotgun. No Southern jury would convict a man of murder, he says, because the jurors fear that the man's friends would shoot them at night, from the shadows, in the back.

(While Twain was writing *Huck Finn*, the number of lynchings went up, and up: 114 in 1882, and in 1885, the year the book was published, 211. The whole South was desperately short of equipment to work with, but in 1881 the state auditor in Alabama reported that the value of tools and farm implements in the state was less than the value of guns and dirks. They were not used just for hunting possums and skinning rabbits.)

In back of the violence lay, too, boredom, the need for amusement that could be appreciated by ignorant people in Southern backwaters. The Arkansas town where Sherburn lived had streets of black mud where hogs wandered up and down. There was a man loafing against each awning-post in front of the stores, whittling, chewing tobacco, waiting for some excitement. Such as a pack of dogs chasing a hog. "There couldn't anything wake them up all over, and make them happy all over, like a dog-fight—unless it might be putting turpentine on a stray dog and setting fire to to him, or tying a tin pan to his tail and see him run himself to death."

The quality that most separates Huck and Jim from the rest of the human race is that they don't need the excitements of cruelty and violence. They don't get bored. They have in plenty what Ahab called "the low enjoying power." They like to watch a summer storm from the comfort of their cave, and to lazy in the sun and watch the boats go by on the river, and to fish, and eat what they caught, and smoke their corncob pipes, or seegars if they got 'em, and swim from their raft in the cool of the night. They especially like each other's company. The world for them is a good world.

Except for the people in it. Huck and Jim repeatedly flee from society back to their cave, back to their raft. But why, then, do they ever leave these sanctuaries? Well, sometimes they are driven out, as by Mrs. Loftus' husband, or by the steamboat that crashes into their raft, and sometimes the sanctuary is invaded, as by the King and the Duke. Sometimes Huck is lured out by his urge to follow Tom's code rather than his own, as when he goes onto the wreck where the robbers are: "I says to myself, Tom Sawyer wouldn't back out now, and so I won't either."

Huck says of Jim, "he had an uncommon level head for a

nigger," and usually this is true of Huck too. But something other than Tom Sawyer's code of honor keeps luring Huck into society. He gets lonesome. At night in his room at Widow Douglas's, "I felt so lonesome I most wished I was dead." Locked by Pap into the cabin, "It was dreadful lonesome." After he escapes from Pap. Out in the fog when he is separated from Jim. After Jim has been caught again. But in the central section bounded by Chapter 16 and 31, in both of which Huck wrestles with his conscience about whether to turn Jim in, he is with Jim, and doesn't get lonely once.

The last section of the novel, when Huck and Tom Sawyer are trying to rescue Jim from his hut, has been much criticized, perhaps from a failure to see how it parallels the first section. Having begun with childish make-believe, and then journeyed among the horrors created by adult conceptions of duty and honor and conscience, Twain now makes us see adolescent behavior in a macabre light. The final chapters have the same incredible balance of comedy and tragedy, the same instant glide from one to the other. Tom's antics are often hilarious, but they are no longer harmless. He keeps the now legally free Jim locked in a hut, breaks his teeth with bits of brass candlestick baked into cornpone, subjects him to snakes and spiders and rats, and exposes him to the risk of being shot, all in order to satisfy his own desire for mystery and adventure. He is a moral idiot, fully deserving the bullet in the leg that he gets.

Now recognized as a masterpiece, *Huck Finn* was criticized in its day for its lapses from gentility. A Massachusetts library excluded it as "trash and suitable only for the slums"; the Boston *Advertiser* charged it with a "spirit of irreverence" and called it a failure. Far different was the verdict of Howells, twelve years later: "the Southwest lives in that book, as it lives nowhere else, with its narrow and rude conditions, its half-savage heroisms, its vague and dim aspirations, its feuds and its fights, its violence, its squalor, its self-devotion, all in the shadow of that horrible cloud of slavery darkening both the souls and the minds of men."

Huck Finn was a book of the frontier, and it might have been an epitaph. Already Henry George in *Progress and Poverty* (1879) had tried to show how the virtual disappearance of good unoccupied land posed for the United States a stark alternative: retrogression, or reform. Free land had meant high wages, and high wages had stimulated technical advance. But amid growing riches, poverty had persisted and even increased: "amid the greatest accumulation of wealth, men die of starvation, and puny infants suckle dry breasts; while everywhere the greed of gain, the worship of wealth, shows the force of the fear of want."

George carefully demolishes theories by which classical political economy had sought to show that poverty was dictated by the laws of nature: the "iron law of wages," which held that the general level of wages depended on the ratio between the amount of capital available to pay wages and the number of workers seeking jobs; and the companion Malthusian theory that population constantly tends to outrun the means of subsistence. But his own effort to formulate the laws of income distribution is the worst part of his book—in large part because he accepted some assumptions of his classical predecessors. He bases his analysis "upon the fundamental principle, which is to political economy what the attraction of gravitation is to physics—that men will seek to gratify their desires with the least exertion." (Later he makes contrary assumptions about human psychology, and even asks if Michelangelo had painted "for board and clothes?") He also accepts the exploded Say's Law, which held that general overproduction is not possible because the production of each supply will produce an equivalent demand, and he even argues that land speculation is the chief cause of the business cycle.

But these flaws do not erase his insights. The growth of population and technical progress will both increase the productivity of labor. But simultaneously they will increase the demand for land (meaning any natural resource that is available gratis, without human effort). Land values and rents will rise. More and more of the national product will go to landowners, less and less to labor and capital. "Poverty deepens as wealth increases, and wages are forced down while productive power grows, because land, which is the source of all wealth and the field of all labor, is monopolized." The only remedy is to confiscate in taxes all the rents on land. All other taxes would be abolished in favor of the "single tax." George's objections to other kinds of taxes are keen; his argument for the tax on land is persuasive. It would not discourage production. It would be easy and cheap to collect. It could not be shifted from the landowners to others. It would be equitable.

Most important of all, it would do away with those inequities between individuals which stifled all past civilizations. If society is to progress, men must be equal, and they must associate together in co-operative endeavors. "Political economy and social science cannot teach any lessons that are not embraced in the simple truths that were taught to poor fishermen and Jewish peasants by One who eighteen hundred years ago was crucified." A Christian who believed in human immortality, George was also an intense individualist who held that a man's liberty should be bounded only by equal liberty for others. In seeking to justify individual ownership he held that the full product of a man's labor must belong to him because "each man is a definite, coherent, independent whole. . . ."

Even as Henry George wrote the assumption down, the most important American in the history of psychology was beginning his major work, and some of its phrases could be construed into a similar assumption. William James, brother of novelist Henry, was trained as a physician, and he started at Harvard the first course in the United States on physiological psychology. In 1878 he began writing a textbook for it; *Principles of Psychology* appeared twelve years later, two massive volumes. Still a rich mine of data and hypothesis on perception and emotions and imagination and will, no part of the book was more influential than the chapter on "The Stream of Consciousness." And there James says that the breaches between the thoughts of two men are "the most absolute breaches in nature."

But James was also well aware of "the social Me," and others of his day were quick to assert that each man is partial; that no individual is definite, or coherent, or independent, or a whole. One devastating critique of George's postulate is contained later in *Progress and Poverty* itself: "Change Lady Vere de Vere in her cradle with an infant of the slums, and will the blood of a hundred earls give you a refined and cultured woman?" Another came in 1887 in a novel which rejected the whole idea of individual ownership of the means of production, Edward Bellamy's *Looking Backward, 2000–1887*. Arguing that nobody is capable of self-support and that each person, including the lame and the halt and the blind, is entitled by right to an equal share in the national product, the spokesman for the future American Utopia asks:

How happened it that your workers were able to produce more than so many savages would have done? Was it not wholly on account of the heritage of the past knowledge and achievements of the

race . . . ? How did you come to be possessors of this knowledge
and this machinery, which represent nine parts to one contributed
by yourself in the value of your product? You inherited it, did you
not? And were not these others, these unfortunate and crippled
brothers whom you cast out, joint inheritors, co-heirs with you?
What did you do with their share?

The book is charming in its depiction of a society founded on
Christian and equalitarian principles. Gone are wasteful competition and business warfare. Gone is the moral squalor at which
Henry George had raged so eloquently ("The higgling of the
market takes the place of every other sentiment."). Bellamy
wrote some memorable passages to point the defects of the society he lived in. The monetary system was "an imperfect device
to remedy an unnecessary defect, the clumsy crutch of a self-
made cripple." On the high cost of distributing goods: "If people
eat with a spoon that leaks half its contents between bowl and lip,
are they not likely to go hungry?" Here, thought Mark Twain,
was "the latest and best of all the Bibles."

Progress and Poverty had been an immediate success; *Looking
Backward* was an unbelievable one. Within two years of publication it sold 300,000 copies, a record matched only by *Uncle
Tom's Cabin*. In contrast, although Henry James' *Daisy Miller*
was his most popular novel, he reported to Howells in June 1879
that his total earnings from its American sales were $200. Not
only were most Americans too bemused by business, or by politics, to read books, but many of the books they did read were not
written by Americans.

The United States had never adhered to the international
copyright code, with the result that all foreign books were in the
public domain in this country. No sooner did a new novel by a
popular writer hit the bookstalls in London than an American
printer or publisher would pirate it and bring out an edition over
here, without paying its author a penny in royalties. Why pay
Henry James when you can get Trollope for nothing? Why buy
Daisy Miller when *Barchester Towers* is cheaper? As Henry
George wrote in outrage: "How difficult it is to get over the idea
that it is not theft to steal from a foreigner, the difficulty in
procuring an international copyright act will show." And it was
difficult. In 1883 Richard Watson Gilder and two other authors

formed an organization to lobby for the purpose. Bills were introduced, but they failed of passage. The agitation went on. Some newspapers took it up. Wider circles of the public became sympathetic. It was a matter of national honor. In 1891, at last, the bill was passed. Gilder exulted, "Never despair of America!"

None had better cause to despair than Charles Sanders Peirce. Son of a Harvard professor, reared in proper Boston, intimate of William James and the younger Oliver Wendell Holmes, yet he was cast out when he dared to divorce his wife. Chemist, mathematician, physicist, philosopher, he never had a decent job in a university. For thirty years he worked for the United States Coast Survey, while also writing for encyclopedias and magazines.

Fortunately the better magazines were still printing serious articles, more serious than publishers a generation later would have thought suitable for general readers. Peirce's "How to Make Our Ideas Clear," a closely reasoned foray into science and logic, ran in the *Popular Science Monthly* in 1878. While others were trying to puzzle out the relations of the individual to society, Peirce tried to puzzle out the relations of subjective ideas to objective things. The result was perhaps the most important work in philosophy ever written by an American.

Thinking, said Peirce, begins with doubt, and its purpose is to produce Belief. Belief involves establishing in our nature a course of action, a habit. Thus "what a thing means is simply what habits it involves." From this point he works out the meaning of such ideas as "hard," as "weight," as "force." And finally he comes to explore the meaning of "the real" and "the true," bringing to bear his knowledge of the history and methods of science.

A thing is real if its qualities are independent of what any specific person thinks them to be. They are even independent of what everybody, at a given time, thinks them to be. But the qualities that make a thing real are not independent of human beings, for the only way we have of knowing what is real is that it causes Belief. The question is: How can we distinguish true Belief from false Belief?

> . . . the ideas of truth and falsehood, in their full development, appertain exclusively to the scientific method of settling opinion . . . all the followers of science are fully persuaded that the processes of investigation, if only pushed far enough, will give one

certain solution to every question to which they can be applied. One man may investigate the velocity of light by studying the transits of Venus and the aberration of the stars; another by the opposition of Mars and the eclipses of Jupiter's satellites; . . . a sixth, a seventh, an eighth, and a ninth, may follow the different methods of comparing the measures of statical and dynamical electricity. They may at first obtain different results, but as each perfects his method and his processes, the results will move steadily together toward a destined center. So with all scientific research. Different minds may set out with the most antagonistic views, but the progress of investigation carries them by a force outside of themselves to one and the same conclusion. This activity of thought by which we are carried, not where we wish, but to a fore-ordained goal, is like the operation of destiny. No modification of the point of view taken, no selection of other facts for study, no natural bent of mind even, can enable a man to escape the predestinate opinion. This great law is embodied in the conception of truth and reality. The opinion which is fated to be ultimately agreed to by all who investigate, is what we mean by the truth, and the object represented in this opinion is the real. That is the way I would explain reality.

The investigation may take centuries, or aeons, it may even be completed by successor races to man, but if it is continued long enough, at last all the investigators will agree on the qualities of reality.

In a letter to William James in 1907 Peirce put it bluntly: "Truth is public."

*   *   *

To embrace, or to flee? Thoughtful men of the time were ambivalent about their country. Henry Adams and Henry James fled to Europe. Bellamy and George fled the present, to embrace the future. Ryder fled the real, and embraced his visions. Homer fled society, to the Maine coast. Huck and Jim found sanctuary only in their cave, on their raft. Hovering in the age was the dichotomy from *Moby-Dick:* You can be safe and happy so long as you cling to your domestic hearth, to your "green, gentle, and most docile earth," but all around you in society is "the universal cannibalism of the sea. . . . For as this appalling ocean surrounds the verdant land, so in the soul of man there lies one insular Tahiti, full of peace and joy, but encompassed by all the horrors of the half known life. God keep thee! Push not off from that isle, thou canst never return!''

Indian Spokesman: Susette La Flesche

Both of her parents were métis, one grandfather being French, the other English. Her father, Joseph La Flesche, also known as Iron Eye, was the chief of the Omaha from 1853 to 1864 and continued thereafter as a leader until his death. He became a Christian, and urged that the Indian must accommodate himself to the ways of the whites. He must trade the buffalo for the plow, and accept the white man's God or die under the white man's guns. While not rejoicing in these changes, Iron Eye believed that they were inevitable—and he thought it more useful to cooperate with the inevitable than to languish in proud but futile resistance. Educated in the white man's schools, four of his children became luminaries in white occupations.

Susette La Flesche (1854–1903), because of her lecture tours on behalf of Indian rights, was better known in the white world than were her siblings. She grew up on a reserve in eastern Nebraska, attending there a Presbyterian mission school and than a girls' seminary in New Jersey. Her prominence began in 1879 when she publicly protested the forced removal of the Poncas from their home in Nebraska to the Indian Territory. An Omaha newspaperman, Thomas Henry Tibbles, described her appearance on the platform at a large local church: ''There stood the little figure, trembling, and gazing at the crowd with eyes which afterwards thrilled many audiences. They were wonderful eyes. They could smile, command, flash, plead, mourn, and play all sorts of tricks with anyone they lingered on.''

When Tibbles went East to rally support, she went with him. Wearing Indian garb and using her name Inshta Theumba (''Bright Eyes''), she galvanized an audience in Boston that included Helen Hunt Jackson and Senator Henry L. Dawes. The experience helped move Mrs. Jackson to write the best-known pro-Indian tracts of the period: *A Century of Dishonor* (1881) and *Ramona* (1884). Dawes was inspired to sponsor the Severalty Act of 1887, which permitted the division of a reservation among individual Indians who could gain the rights of citizenship. Although this act, sponsored by humanitarians and relished by incipient thieves, probably did more to threaten the survival of Indians than all the crooked Indian agents who ever lived, Bright Eyes, faithful to her father's tenets of assimilation, was among its most ardent advocates.

Remaining on the lecture circuit after her marriage to Tibbles in 1881, she also became a writer and artist. She presented a paper on Indian women to the Association for the Advancement of Women. She wrote stories for the famous children's magazine, *St. Nicolas.* She illustrated *Omaha City* (1898) by Fannie Reed Giffen. Although outside the circle of tribal life, she never lost her dedication to the cause of her people.

PART TWO

1893–1898

Wherein Some Questions Are Answered; Others, Evaded

CHAPTER
8

Crisis at Home

The convulsions that wrenched so much of American society between 1893 and 1898 had been long in the making. In the twenty years after 1873 the ferocious battles for markets were a strong stimulus for each company to reduce its costs of production so that it could undersell its competitors. A common route to this goal was the recurrent addition of new and more efficient machinery. McCormick Harvester, for example, by introducing automatic molding machines and other improvements, reduced its labor cost per machine produced from $14.82 in 1879 to only $5.19 in 1893. The company was so successful that it showed a profit in every year from 1873 to 1897; in 1884, a recession year for the economy generally, McCormick set its record by earning an estimated 71 per cent on its invested capital. Meanwhile it was discharging many of its best paid workmen. Similar developments occurred in many other firms. The result was a very unequal distribution of income in the United States. Purchasing power in the hands of consumers grew less rapidly than did the productive capacity of the economy.

This contradiction between soaring production and restricted markets was alleviated for a time by two policies followed by many industrialists. To illustrate once more by McCormick's actions, it accepted a constantly falling profit per machine produced in order to build its sales volume. While the company manufactured nine times as many machines in 1893 as in 1879, its profits only increased three times. Second, if the unequal distribution of income enabled many persons and companies to achieve a very high rate of saving, manufacturers also maintained very high rates of investment. Carnegie Steel reportedly replaced all of its productive facilities every three years. It was always willing to junk existing plant and replace it with better so long as it thought the new expenditures would yield a return. A corollary was that it could produce more and more steel with fewer and fewer workers. "The place," reported an Englishwoman who visited the Carnegie works, "seemed almost deserted by human beings."

But with existing equipment in many industries idle, businessmen increasingly doubted that further investment could yield a profit. At last the basic unbalance in the economy made itself felt. A financial panic in 1893 sagged into the worst depression in the country's history. Unemployment rose steadily. Suffering, long common in large segments of agriculture, came to plague the cities. Unrest by 1894 was so acute that it burst forth in a series of turbulent strikes involving hundreds of thousands of men. Troops were called out in many states. Blind hatred flared up between the defenders of the gold standard and advocates of free coinage of silver.

Then Cassandras seemed to spring from the ground; historian James C. Malin has recently remarked how many men in those years were predicting "a day of judgment. . . ." They foresaw a cataclysm, doom. They were in dead earnest. They were alarmed, even terrified. From every hand came bleatings, roars, ravings, expostulations, theories. "We are on the eve of a very dark night," Francis Lynde Stetson warned the President in 1894, "unless a return of commercial prosperity relieves popular discontent." Senator William Frye of Maine declared that "we shall have revolution" if we did not capture the markets of China. Another conservative Republican Senator, J. Donald Cameron of Pennsylvania, went so far as to advocate free coinage of silver, and he voiced his suggestion with a militant nationalistic tongue that became increasingly popular. The "bankers of London," said Cameron, had coerced us from our true interest: "England holds us to the single gold standard by the force of her capital alone, more despotically than she could hold us to her empire in 1776." Frederick Jackson Turner bleakly pointed out that American democracy had always depended on the frontier, but now the frontier was gone. Brooks Adams extended the implied apprehension about the future of democracy into a demand that the United States acquire new frontiers—overseas.

The popularity of foreign expansion grew quickly during the depression. Producers of cotton and wheat had always been conscious that they needed markets abroad to be prosperous, and after 1873 industrialists increasingly sought a similar solution to their own problems. Manufacturers, less than 10 per cent of American exporters in 1880, constituted more than 15 per cent of the total a decade later. And accomplishments were less telling than hopes. Some companies aspired to a vast expansion of trade with Latin America. Others reasoned that the great prize was the supposedly limitless market in China. A canal across Nicaragua or Panama was needed to shorten the route to the Far East from our Atlantic Coast. Coaling stations and naval bases—Hawaii, the Philippines—were required as stepping stones on the way. That is not true, replied the oppositon; the expansion of American exports is not dependent upon our having foreign colonies. But prominent among the alleged opponents of imperialism were men who sapped their position by agreeing that the economic problems of the United States could not be solved without a massive surplus of exports over imports.

This schematic review of twenty-five years of complicated history needs to be supplemented by an account in some detail of the complexities of five years.

In 1891 America's opportunity came from Europe's misery. Crop failures there led to a rise of $150 million in exports from this country, chiefly of breadstuffs. The rise in exports caused gold to flow in. But business was hurting. Output was high in 1892, but men were more aware that profits were low in many industries. The great growth in demand for pig iron up to 1890 had helped obsolescent plants to survive, but now the pressure on them was increasingly severe. From February to September, output of pig iron fell a sixth. The same with railroads. Competition among them forced improvements such as reducing grades and building stations and bridges; although not many miles of new track were laid by the standards of earlier years, gross investment by railroads probably reached its peak in 1892. But competition also forced reductions in freight rates. The finances of many lines were strained. Early in 1893 the Philadelphia & Reading borrowed to pay interest on its bonds. On February 26, with liquid assets of about $100,000 and short-term debts of $18,500,000, it went into bankruptcy. From January to April, 28 banks suspended payment. In May another 54 did the same, and the prominent National Cordage Company went under. In June, 128 banks failed.

Foreigners began selling American securities and pulling their capital home. A stream of gold flowed out of the country. Much of it came from the United States Treasury, which also had to redeem in gold large quantities of silver certificates issued under the Silver Purchase Act of 1890. In April the Treasury's gold reserve fell below the $100 million regarded as essential to defend the gold standard. The President announced that it would be defended to the limit, but he was widely disbelieved, and gold exports went on. In June he called a special session of Congress for August to repeal the 1890 statute which was exposing the gold standard to such peril.

From his St. Paul headquarters, James J. Hill on June 25 wrote the President that a survey along 500 miles of the Great Northern had revealed that "very few of the farmers have any money, and the local banks are unable to aid them." The banks themselves, including many "which have been considered entirely strong," were terribly pinched. Hill said that business organizations throughout the West "feel the great difficulty now is want of confidence," and he seemed to favor repeal of the Silver Purchase Act. But three weeks later, questioning whether repeal would be enough, he suggested to the President that the Federal government might issue bonds to raise the funds needed to pay a large pension appropriation. Under the National Banking Act, the banks could then issue additional National Bank Notes up to 90 per cent of the value of the bonds they held.

The Act empowered banks in the South and West to hold part of their legal reserves as deposits in New York banks. Now, faced by runs themselves, they began to pull their reserves home. This aggravated the panic in New York, and values on Wall Street tumbled. In the South, savings banks required 60 days notice before they would give money to depositors, and some commercial banks suspended the honoring of checks. Textile factories shut down. Men who had grown up on farms now found themselves out of work and out of money in cities. All over the country jobless men shuffled aimlessly down roads or stole rides on freights. States and cities were passing "panicky" laws to control the tramps.

India closed its mints to private stocks of silver, and American silver mines and smelters closed down; Colorado had 30,000 unemployed. As banks suspended payments, other firms could not raise cash to meet their payrolls. The depression brought a drop of 100,000 in immigration, and that hurt the construction of houses. Misery was spreading. Mothers poked through garbage cans seeking something for their children to eat.

No city in the country was so prosperous that dread summer as Chicago, which on May 1 had opened its mammoth Columbian Exposition. Visitors could see prize livestock, or a long-distance telephone to New York, or the "high-tension currents" of Nikolá Tesla, or a Krupp cannon weighing 130 tons, or a map of the United States made of pickles. School teachers spent their savings to see such marvels. An old man at the Exposition was heard saying to his wife, "Well, Susan, it paid, even if it did take all the burial money." The young writer Hamlin Garland wrote to his parents on their Dakota farm: "Sell the cook stove if necessary and come. You *must* see this fair."

When the Exposition closed on October 30 it had drawn over 27 million visitors—more than any preceding world's fair. They were not even deterred by the widespread belief that the governor of Illinois was not a Democrat at all, as he claimed, but an anarchist. John Peter Altgeld on June 26 pardoned the three Haymarket survivors. Since the bombing and trial in 1886, hundreds of citizens had circulated petitions asking that amnesty be extended to the prisoners in Joliet prison—usually on the ground that they had been punished enough. Altgeld did not take that ground. He pardoned the men because, he wrote, they had been unjustly convicted, and he justified his act in a state paper vibrant with anger at the conduct of the trial. The jury had been deliberately packed. Its members were biased. The conviction was had on an absurd rule of law. The evidence had not proved guilt. The judge was prejudiced. It had been hatred and fear, not justice, that claimed the lives of Albert Parsons and his fellow defendants.

A question had emerged in the years since 1877: Are all Americans, regardless of opinion and social position, equal in the eyes of the law? In the Haymarket trial, said Altgeld, the answer was no.

Although during the summer the Columbian Exposition was a dike guarding Chicago against the depression, a deeper flood of deprivation swept in when the dike was removed. Thousands of common laborers drawn to Chicago by the fair were unemployed. The mayor estimated that the city held 200,000 jobless. The floors and stairways of City Hall and the police stations were

covered each night by homeless men. And the poor were dependent almost wholly on private charity: the saloonkeepers were said
to be giving free lunches to 60,000 men a day. The state, Altgeld
himself, had no program for positive action. Municipal relief was
woefully inadequate. Other cities and states did no more. The
counsel of public officials to the destitute was to keep smiling
and bear it like men. The passivity of government at last goaded
the liberal editor of the *Arena* to write that, although such worthy
projects as the construction of roads and Mississippi levees might
relieve unemployment, "gold is more precious in the eyes of our
legislators than independent, self-respecting citizenship."

To the President, the gold standard was indeed precious. It was
the soul of honor. How could an honest man go off gold, and let
inflation come, and pay off his debts in dollars less valuable than
those he had borrowed? British investors tended to see the problem almost solely in terms of economics. In 1893 they owned an
estimated $4 billion in American securities, chiefly bonds. Both
interest and principal would suffer greatly in value if the United
States went off the gold standard and allowed its currency to
depreciate. Likewise to some American politicians and corporate
executives the problem was mainly a matter of business; their
concern was that some types of American enterprise still relied
on foreign financing. "As a nation," declared a Representative
from Wisconsin, "we must have a form of money that will cancel
our obligations held in other countries—our bonds must be paid
in the money that represents to holders a standard of value the
world over." But for other Americans, especially among influential ones along the Eastern seaboard, less tangible forces were at
work. A rising tide of sentiment pushed them to seek identification with Western Civilization, and they saw Great Britain as the
mother of that culture. They wanted respectability in English
eyes (and, ironically, as a conduit to carry this influence through
the country, many Westerners who thought of themselves as anti-
British wanted respectability in Eastern eyes). These feelings were
reflected in the growing desire of art collectors for Old Masters,
in the neglect of American writers for English ones, in the passion
of eligible daughters to marry European titles. They would help
to work major changes in foreign relations. And they fed into the
movement to maintain the gold standard.

When the special session of Congress met, Rep. William L.

Wilson for the administration introduced a measure to repeal the Silver Purchase Act. Richard Bland countered with an amendment providing for free coinage of silver. In the bitter and sometimes brilliant debate, the eloquent William Jennings Bryan of Nebraska declaimed:

> The poor man is called a socialist if he believes that the wealth of the rich should be divided among the poor, but the rich man is called a financier if he devises a plan by which the pittance of the poor can be converted to his use.
>
> The poor man who takes property by force is called a thief, but the creditor who can by legislation make a debtor pay a dollar twice as large as he borrowed is lauded as the friend of sound currency. The man who wants the people to destroy the Government is an anarchist but the man who wants the Government to destroy the people is a patriot.

John Dalzell of Pennsylvania in a telling reply pointed out that the free-silver forces were not committed to altruism: "Why, Mr. Speaker, I have been amused here listening to the self-styled champions of the poor man, advocates of the millionaire mine-owners of the West, denouncing millionaires; in one breath denouncing all moneyed institutions, . . . and in the next demanding a market for the products of the Western mines and for the surplus silver of the world."

The divisions in Congress showed again that party discipline could not hold against inflamed sectional feelings. The nine seaboard states from Maine to Pennsylvania had 99 Representatives: 54 Republicans to 45 Democrats. But in the vote on Bland's amendment there were 98 Nays to a single Aye. Conversely the eight states from Colorado to the Pacific had 17 Representatives: 9 Republicans, 7 Democrats, and a Populist. They voted 13 to 4 for Bland's amendment. The President at last managed to have the Silver Purchase Act revoked, but chiefly by means of Republican votes, while his own party split up the middle.

Before repeal, on September 25, Grover Cleveland wrote to the free-silver governor of Georgia: "I want a currency that is stable and safe in the hands of our people. I will not knowingly be implicated in a condition that will make me in the least degree answerable to any laborer or farmer in the United States for a shrinkage in the purchasing power of the dollar. . . ." The position, if not dishonest, was stupid. The total stock of money in the United States had suffered a prolonged decline in 1892–1893. Prices of farm products had collapsed. The value of money based on gold, so far from being "stable and safe," had risen steadily. Other things than money have purchasing power, or exchange value, which comes to the same thing; and the farmer who sought to pay his debts had watched the purchasing power of his cotton go down and down.

Prices received for American harvests in 1893 were very low, and the gold outflow continued. By December more than 600 banks and other financial institutions had gone bankrupt during the year. So had some 32 iron and steel companies. So had one railroad of every six in the nation. After the failure of the Richmond Terminal Company, not one large railroad on the South Atlantic seaboard was solvent. In January came another gold crisis. To increase its gold reserve, the Treasury issued $50 million in 10-year bonds, to yield 3 per cent. The bankers bought the bonds—with gold they had obtained by redeeming legal tender at the Subtreasury in New York. Members of the City Council of Chicago were also getting along, for, said the Chicago *Record*, they had received recently as much as $5,000 each for votes in favor of one franchise ordinance.

But many workers were not getting along, and their resentment brought giant strikes in the spring of 1894. The president of the United Mine Workers told his national convention on April 10 that "thousands" of miners had been flocking to the union because of "oppression, low wages and hunger. . . ." The convention, demanding that pay scales be restored to the level of May 1893, called a strike effective April 21 in the bituminous fields from western Pennsylvania to Illinois. At the time the union had only 13,000 paid-up members, but 125,000 miners answered the strike call. By May 14, 180,000 men were out. On June 12 the strikers compromised and called off their strike. Most of the modest gains proved illusory. The great majority of the strikers had not joined the union, and they soon learned that an agreed-on pay scale meant little unless the union was strong enough in each locality to enforce it. In 1897, the membership of the United Mine Workers was less than 10,000, and pay scales were far below those of early 1893. The previous year, 1896, annual earnings of Ohio miners ranged from $213 to $319. But in 1894 miners had shown that they could check the economy. They had virtually shut down the bituminous industry. They had cut production of pig iron in half. They had made it hard for railroads to move trains. And the railroads were having other troubles in moving trains.

Total membership of the various Railroad Brotherhoods was only about 90,000, and their conservatism combined with the prevailing hard times to make them docile. But not so with the American Railway Union. It organized its first local union in August 1893 at Fort Madison, Iowa. With only Eugene Debs and two other paid organizers in the field, it signed up 200–400 men a day in the months that followed. At year's end the Santa Fe, the Denver & Rio Grande, the Union Pacific, and several other railroads were organized from end to end. On the Southern Pacific there were 40 ARU lodges; on the Northern Pacific, 22. Most of the members were unskilled or semiskilled—section hands, roundhouse workers, switchmen, brakemen—but quite a few were firemen and engineers.

The first big test came on the Great Northern. James J. Hill had cautiously but steadily pushed his road west, laboring hard as he went to fill up each area with farming, mining, or industry. A railroad can't make money without freight. And it can't make money if wages are too high. The Great Northern cut its pay scales in August 1893, in January 1894, again in March. On April 13 its workers struck. The walk-out was amazingly solid. Hill instructed his lieutenants to fire anybody known to be sympathetic to the ARU. Huge signs were posted the length of the line, from Minneapolis to Puget Sound, displaying a warning by the Assistant Attorney General that interference with the United States mails could be punished by two years in prison and a $10,000 fine. But the railroad's 9,000 employees would not work. Mail trains were moving on Deb's orders. But nothing else was.

Hill offered to arbitrate if the panel contained men from the Brotherhoods, all of which had either denounced the strike or enjoined their members to neutrality. Debs scornfully rejected the condition. Soon he was summoned to the office of the governor of Minnesota, who began to berate him for "stirring up strife among peaceful and contented workingmen." Debs, listening to the words emerge from the livid face above the chin whiskers, became furious and exclaimed, "You can't bluff me. I can see clear

through you and your game. You wear Jim Hill's collar. I don't."
He refused to ask the men to go back to work. The next maneuver was to have Debs invited to address the Chamber of Commerce of St. Paul. Hill thought the strike leader would antagonize
his business audience and unite them against the strike, but Debs'
talk had the opposite effect. After he explained what it was like
to rear a family on a dollar a day, his audience called for arbitration. The Great Northern could not refuse. The arbitration board,
headed by flour milling executive Charles Pillsbury, gave the
strikers 97½ per cent of their demands—an aggregate pay raise
of $146,000 a month. But ironically, this strike victory over a big
railroad led the union to its own destruction.

When 400 delegates met in Chicago on June 12 for the first
national convention of the ARU, they felt swaggering. They had
whipped Jim Hill. In less than a year of life their organization
had brought in 150,000 men. They cheered a fighting speech by
their president, who called on all of labor to unify in a great
army instead of splitting up into craft unions. Debs insisted that
if workingmen would "march together, vote together and fight
together" they would get their rights. No corporation would
dare to fight them. Strikes would be unnecessary. "An era of
good will and peace would dawn."

To these cocky unionists came a delegation from the Chicago
suburb of Pullman, Illinois. Its members told bleak stories of
working for the Pullman Palace Car Company, which dominated
not only its own shops but everything about life in the "model
factory town" built by the autocratic George M. Pullman. Although the firm continued to make a profit after the onset of
depression, it ruthlessly squeezed its workers. The number of
employees fell from 5,500 in July 1893 to 3,300 in May 1894. The
persons still working found their daily wages cut at least 25 per
cent, and they did not work every day. But rents were not reduced on the company-owned houses in Pullman. As early as
December 1893 the firm had to deny publicly that extreme distress existed among its workers. When spring came, on May 11,
the workers struck. A month later they were desperate, and needed
help.

The sentimental delegates were impressed when a minister told
them that Pullman residents were about to starve. But they were
overwhelmed when a pinched and tired seamstress told her story.

Her father, she said, had worked 13 years at Pullman. He died, owing the company $60 in back rent. The sum had been taken out of her pay. Some delegates instantly proposed that the American Railway Union should boycott Pullman cars until the company settled the dispute. Instead Debs suggested that a committee from the convention should call on the firm's executives and ask for arbitration. This was done. The committee was told that there was "nothing to arbitrate." The boycott was called, to take effect on June 26. Although Debs now worked brilliantly to win the struggle, he had tried to avoid it, knowing the dangers in leading his raw organization against so powerful an opponent as the Pullman Company.

Very quickly, Pullman seemed minor among the opponents. When union members began sidetracking all sleeping cars, they were told that the railroads' contracts with Pullman were inviolable. Now the ARU faced the General Managers Association, which represented the 24 railroads terminating or centering in Chicago. The leaders of the Brotherhoods were also hostile to the boycott. The railroads began to hire strikebreakers, and the depression helped their efforts. Even so, the union seemed to be winning. By June 29, 125,000 men were supporting the boycott. The men would not move trains with Pullman cars, and the railroads would not move trains without them, so one road after another was tied up.

The press was violent in its reaction, and nowhere more so than in Chicago. The *Herald* declared that the railroads had to defeat the boycott: "If they yield one point it will show fatal weakness." The *Tribune* began a story: "Through the reckless acts of Dictator Debs' strikers the lives of thousands of Chicago citizens were endangered yesterday." Day after day the newspapers charged that Debs was profiting personally from the strike, that he had called it without consulting his membership, that he was a dictator, that he was a drunkard. Never had there been such a strike in this country. From Chicago to San Francisco, only the Great Northern was coming close to maintaining its schedules. On July 1, so Debs said later, he thought the railroads were beaten: "Their immediate resources were exhausted, their properties were paralyzed, and they were unable to operate their trains." He claimed that there was "no sign of violence or disorder."

Then the Federal government stepped in. Attorney General

Olney, appointing as special Federal attorney in Chicago for the strike situation a man who was also attorney for a railroad that belonged to the General Managers Association, wired his appointee: "I feel that the true way of dealing with the matter is by a force which is overwhelming and prevents any attempt at resistance." Olney was determined to break the boycott. He was helped by Federal agents in Chicago, who misstated the amount of violence there in telegrams to Washington. He was helped by two Federal judges in Chicago, who granted an injunction against any act or speech aimed at helping the boycott. And, the crucial help, by the President, who ordered Federal troops into Chicago. Governor Altgeld hotly protested that the Constitution gives the President power only to send the army into a state "on application of the Legislature, or of the Executive (when the Legislature cannot be convened)" to protect the state "against domestic Violence." No Illinois official had asked for Federal troops. Illinois was competent to suppress any violence within its borders. He had not been asked by anybody in Chicago for aid. Grover Cleveland replied that the mails were being obstructed, that the injunctions had to be enforced, and that interstate commerce was being obstructed. On any of these grounds he could send the army to Chicago. The President had his way, and the troops stayed. But Altgeld would soon get revenge.

Violence, which had been slight, became spectacular after the troops arrived on July 4. Two days later, railroad property valued at $340,000 was destroyed. A chain of railroad cars along the lake front became a monstrous balefire in the night sky. The New York *Sun* told its readers: "Wild Riot in Chicago." In Chicago the *Evening Post* shrieked: "Frenzied Mob Still Bent on Death and Destruction." The militia were under arms in 20 states. Union members were being arrested everywhere.

Federal intervention broke the boycott. Debs and other national leaders of the union were picked up on July 10 for conspiracy, but were released in a few hours on $10,000 bail. They were arrested again on July 17 for violation of the July 2 injunction. Two days later the United States army left Chicago. The boycott was over. The disorganized and uninformed strikers straggled back to work. Most of their leaders were placed on a nationwide blacklist by the railroads. The largest trade union in American history had been destroyed.

In the years since 1877 a question had emerged: In labor disputes, will the government be impartial between the contestants? In the Pullman boycott, the answer was no. And a middle class brought close to hysteria by the social unrest endorsed the bias on the theory that, as the *Nation* put it, the boycott had been "a rebellion." The usually liberal senior editor of the *American Law Review* applauded the railroads for having "entered upon a struggle with an unknown and appalling force, which threatened to revolutionize the very foundations of society and to reverse all the processes by which our splendid industrial system has been built up."

That Federal policy toward the boycott was left so largely to the Attorney General was due chiefly to the President's involvement in a tariff battle with the Senate. In November 1893 the Ways and Means Committee of the House had made public its proposed bill. Although the measure put major raw materials on the free list, the reductions on most manufactured items were moderate. It aimed to reduce the average duty from the prevailing 49 per cent ad valorem, under the McKinley Act of 1890, to about 30 per cent; the New York *Journal of Commerce* pointed out that the new measure would still leave the tariff "more highly protective than that of any other country." The bill, ably managed by William L. Wilson, passed the House in February 1894 by a vote of 204 to 140. The Republicans, solid against it, were joined by 18 Democrats.

In the closely divided Senate, the defection of eight Democrats proved fatal. While the lobbies and nearby hotels swarmed with agents of Standard Oil and the National Lead Trust and coal interests and the Sugar Trust, the Senate voted more than 600 amendments to the Wilson bill. Rates on iron, glass, chemicals, woolen and cotton goods—all were raised above the House proposals. Raw sugar got a 40 per cent duty: the tariff on refined sugar was raised an eighth of a cent per pound.

But farmers were sacrificed. They had hoped that the reciprocity provisions of the McKinley Act would help them to get additional markets abroad for their staples; those provisions were dropped. Raw wool was put on the free list. So was lumber. But the Senate knocked wire fencing off the free list. In the entire bill farmers could take satisfaction in only one provision, which had been added in the House at Western insistence. An income tax—

all of 2 per cent on incomes over $4,000 per year—was imposed on both individuals and corporations.

The bill was passed by the Senate on July 3, as the Pullman boycott neared its crisis, and went to a conference committee—which deadlocked. Six weeks later the House surrendered, and accepted the Senate version. As the final vote in the House approached, Republican leader Tom Reed taunted the Democrats, "You are going to enact a bill which you believe not to be an honest bill, and you are going to accompany it with a parade, which you also know is not honest." On August 28 the Wilson-Gorman Act became law without the signature of the President, who declared that "the livery of Democratic tariff reform has been stolen and worn in the service of Republican protection. . . ." Duties were reduced somewhat, but many of them were higher in 1894 than they had been under the law of 1883. A shabby outcome indeed for the crusade for tariff reduction which had been demanded in 1887 by Grover Cleveland.

By August 1894 the gold crisis was with him again. The Treasury's gold reserve fell to $52 million, and in the emergency it got $14 million in gold from the bankers. In November another $50 million in bonds were issued, through a Morgan-Belmont syndicate, to raise gold. A loan of that amount in January 1894 had held things together for ten months; now it sufficed only for ten weeks. From November 1894 to January 1895, $69 million in gold was drawn out of the Treasury. Only $29 million of the sum went abroad; the rest went into hoards in this country.

In January 1895 gold flows out of the Treasury totalled a record $43 million, and Cleveland had to act or watch the gold standard perish. He asked Congress on January 28 for power to retire all paper money that could not be redeemed in gold and to replace it with National Bank Notes secured by gold bonds. He wanted authority to issue long-term bonds payable only in gold. While Congress debated, the Treasury opened negotiations with a banking syndicate headed by Morgan. Thinking the syndicate's terms were too high, the Treasury prepared to offer its bonds directly to the public, but Morgan, working chiefly through Secretary of War Daniel Lamont, blocked the public issue. The House rejected Cleveland's proposals.

Cleveland was trapped. He accepted terms dictated by the bankers. For $62 million in 30-year bonds, the syndicate agreed to furnish 3.5 million ounces of gold. Having bought the bonds at 104½, the syndicate offered them to the public at 112½. The loan was oversubscribed in 20 minutes. Morgan and the 60 other members of the American syndicate made more than $1½ million. It was one of the most humiliating episodes in the history of the Presidency. But Cleveland, for the moment, had saved the "safe and stable" gold standard. A few days later the President wrote piteously to his Ambassador to England, "Think of it, not a man in the Senate with whom I can be on terms of absolute confidence."

"It is probably safe to say," observed *Railway Age*, "that in no civilized country in this century, not actually in the throes of war or open insurrection, has society been so disorganized as it was in the United States during the first half of 1894; never was human life held so cheap; never did the constituted authorities appear so incompetent to enforce respect for the law." This baleful disorganization had alarmed the judges of the country, and they had been trying for a decade to build judicial ramparts against the popular and legislative threats to private property. Their efforts were intensified amid the tumults of depression, and came to a climax in 1895.

Richard Olney did not approve of the Anti-Trust Act of 1890, and no prosecutions were instituted under it while he was Attorney General. But he did instruct his subordinates to expedite a hearing in the Supreme Court on a prosecution initiated in 1892 of the American Sugar Refining Company. Ironically, this firm had been formed by a previous loose combination of companies in order to escape challenge under the Sherman Act, so the law had actually prompted a tighter monopoly. The Wilson-Gorman Act was a stunning display of the power in Congress of Havemeyer's company. By that time it controlled about 90 per cent of the sugar refining capacity of the country. *United States* v. *E. C. Knight Co.* involved the Sugar Trust's acquisition, by stock purchase, of four Philadelphia firms having among them some 10 per cent of the refining industry's capacity.

In the Supreme Court the prosecution did not offer any evidence that the Trust exercised interstate control of prices, and the omission opened the door to the decision by Chief Justice Fuller, a Cleveland appointee. "Commerce succeeds to manufacture," he wrote, "and is not a part of it." (Does it follow that manufacture is not a part of commerce?) The Constitution gives

Congress power only over interstate commerce. The Sugar Trust was engaged in manufacture, not in commerce, and was not subject to Federal control. The decision conceded that a monopoly in manufacturing might restrain interstate commerce, but, making some remarkable distinctions, it held that such restraint would be only secondary or indirect or incidental and was therefore beyond the power of Congress. Only one Justice, John M. Harlan, dissented. Frequently citing John Marshall's decision in *Gibbons* v. *Ogden* (1824) on the unrestrained power of Congress over interstate commerce, Harlan insisted the Constitution did not force the Federal government to "fold its arms and remain inactive" while great combinations of capital dictated the price of "the necessaries of life."

Could the national government check the growth of monopoly to insure competition and equality of opportunity? Not if the monopoly was an industrial one.

Even before the *Knight* decision was announced on January 20, 1895, the Justice Department had agreed to a hearing in the Supreme Court on March 7 of *Pollock* v. *Farmers' Loan and Trust Company*. At issue was the constitutionality of the income tax imposed by the Wilson-Gorman Act. Olney had just quarreled bitterly with the official who would normally have argued the government case, the Solicitor General, whose resignation left the matter to Olney. He had only about five weeks to get ready. Of his prepared argument he wrote: "I am not proud of it, but it will have to do." By February 24 he was working on his argument for the coming *In re Debs;* he thought it more important to uphold an injunction than an income tax. But he had no doubt the tax was constitutional, and that the Court would so decide. An income tax, imposed during the Civil War and continued in various forms until 1872, had been unanimously sustained in *Springer* v. *United States* (1881).

Argument was had before a packed courtroom. An array of expensive lawyers for the plaintiff argued that an income tax violated the constitutional requirement that "direct taxes" must be apportioned among the states according to their populations. It violated the requirement that "all duties, imposts, and excises shall be uniform throughout the United States." These legal arguments probably had less impact on the Court than did appeals to it to resist the leveling tendencies of legislative majorities. Ex-Senator

George F. Edmunds urged that the tax was "intentionally and tyrannically and monstrously unequal" and violated the due-process clause and the equal-protection clause of the 14th Amendment. He predicted that validation of the law would be followed by even greater abuses until we would get "finally a provision that only the twenty people who have the greatest estates should bear the whole taxation, and after that communism, anarchy, and then, the ever following despotism." Joseph H. Choate, widely regarded as the finest legal orator of the time, hammered away: "Now, if you approve this law, with this iniquitous exemption of $4,000, and this communistic march goes on. . . ."

In reply Olney and his associates contended that it had been decided since 1796 that the term "direct taxes" applied only to head taxes and to taxes on land. The requirement of uniformity for "duties, imposts, and excises" was intended only to prevent discrimination against some section of the country. Moreover, the distinction between incomes over $4,000 and those under that sum was a reasonable exercise of Congress's power to classify. Olney declared that the plaintiff's case was "nothing but a call upon the judicial department of the government to supplant the political in the exercise of the taxing power. . . ."

The decision came down in just a month, on April 8. Chief Justice Fuller delivered a decision, for six members of the Court, which accepted two of plaintiff's contentions. A tax on rents was equivalent to a tax on land, and therefore a direct tax, and must be apportioned among the states by population. A tax on income from state and municipal bonds was invalid as an infringement of state sovereignty. Justice White dissented, joined by Harlan. They insisted that in defining "direct taxes" to include income from rents, the majority without admitting it was overturning a century of precedents.

Opponents of the income tax were far from satisfied, because on the remaining issues before the Court it had divided 4 to 4. The tax on income from personal property, for instance, still stood. The *Albany Law Journal*, the chief weekly law review in the East, wanted the Court to administer "a crushing defeat of the pet schemes of the scum of Europe. . . ." In Chicago the *Legal Adviser* asserted: "Never since civilized man first planted foot on this continent has any legislative body enacted a statute more threatening to human liberty than the income tax of the late

Congress." Plaintiff petitioned for a rehearing; Olney insisted that it deal with all issues in the case rather than solely with the undecided ones; the ill Justice Jackson who had missed the first hearing was summoned from his home in Tennessee; and the re-argument was set for May 6.

Although he had never approved of the income tax, Olney now determined to restore the tax on rents—thus increasing the chance that the Court would void all of the income tax provisions. Writing to his private secretary on April 18 he said, "You will see that if the landlords are exempt I want myself and others exempted also." The rehearing found Choate arguing that the income tax had been aimed at great wealth, especially landlords. With the tax on rents voided, he claimed, the income tax now would fall chiefly on "thousands of widows and orphans" whose income came from investments in corporations. To avoid violating the intent of Congress in passing it, the Court should throw out the whole act: "The biggest fish have got out through the rent [a pun?] your Honors have made in the meshes of the law. Will you allow the little fish to be alone the victims?"

The majority would not. Supported by four Justices, the Chief Justice could on May 20 discern no difference between rents and income from personal property such as stocks and bonds. A tax on any such income was a direct tax. Then, having excluded from the law so many sources of income, the Court invalidated all of the income tax clauses. The four dissenters were, each in his own way, caustic. Harlan asked of the majority why they had not invalidated the whole Wilson-Gorman Act, since Congress would never have passed it without the income tax clauses.

A question had emerged: Would the burden of supporting the government be imposed equitably on those who benefited from it? The Supreme Court and Congress had let stand the tariff on consumers, while the Court struck down a modest tax on the well-to-do. Wrote dissenting Justice Henry B. Brown: "The decision involves nothing less than a surrender of the taxing power to the moneyed class."

The day after the decision Olney wrote his secretary: "If the Court should follow up the work by deciding against me in the Debs business, I should regret I ever came to Washington. . . . I take comfort in thinking I have saved the $——or $——of my own personal tax." On the Debs business, at least, the Court was safe.

In re Debs involved a petition for habeas corpus by the union leaders. In December 1894 they had been sentenced to jail for violation of the injunction by one of the judges who had issued it. The procedure, they held, deprived them of due process of law and particularly of trial by jury. A strike or boycott was legal. Therefore, if they had erred at all, they must have committed a criminal act. They should be indicted and tried properly. The procedure that had been followed made any judge a virtual dictator over other Americans.

On May 27 Justice Brewer for a unanimous Court praised the government for having resorted to equity for an injunction. The lower court had based the injunction in part on the Sherman Anti-Trust Act, but the decision now did not even mention that statute. Saying that the Federal government had "all the attributes of sovereignty" in its proper sphere, Brewer sustained the writ with a sweeping gesture: "The entire strength of the nation may be used to enforce in any part of the land the full and free exercise of all national powers and the security of all rights entrusted by the Constitution to its care. The strong arm of the national government may be put forth to brush away all obstructions to the freedom of interstate commerce or the transportation of the mails."

The issues of the 1896 campaign were complete, with the election 17 months in the future. Government by injunction. Arbitration of labor disputes. State's rights. Anti-monopoly. Income tax. Judicial intervention. Above all, free coinage of silver.

It was Altgeld who led the Democratic insurgents against the President. In June 1895 a special convention of the party in Illinois declared for free silver, and for the next year Altgeld worked throughout the Ohio valley to rally the silver Democrats. He thought the issue a good one politically. He believed that justice demanded an increase in the money supply and inflation of the price level. Yet beyond free silver he sought to gain a broad spectrum of reforms.

Other forces were at work to narrow the reform program to the single demand: free silver. The simple economics of a new book called *Coin's Financial School* was convincing many farmers that silver coinage was a cure-all. The same message was being

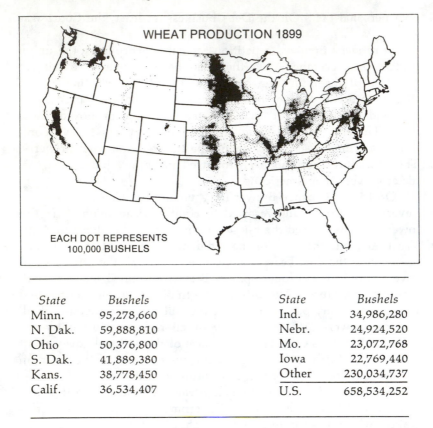

WHEAT PRODUCTION 1899

EACH DOT REPRESENTS
100,000 BUSHELS

State	Bushels	State	Bushels
Minn.	95,278,660	Ind.	34,986,280
N. Dak.	59,888,810	Nebr.	24,924,520
Ohio	50,376,800	Mo.	23,072,768
S. Dak.	41,889,380	Iowa	22,769,440
Kans.	38,778,450	Other	230,034,737
Calif.	36,534,407	U.S.	658,534,252

spread by ex-Representative William Jennings Bryan, lecturer for the American Bimetallic League. And here a sinister influence played among the revolting Democrats and Populists. The mining areas of the West were badly stricken. Free coinage of silver, however it might affect the prices of other commodities, would surely raise the price of silver. So Marcus Daly, the Montana mine owner, subsidized the Bimetallic League. Other magnates gave funds to a movement that might help them to capture the Federal mint as a great customer for the output of their mines. But they cared little or nothing about social justice.

Ironically, the farmers' efforts to increase the money stock caused it to decline in 1895–1896. The major part of the nation's "money" was not gold, or silver, or National Bank Notes, but

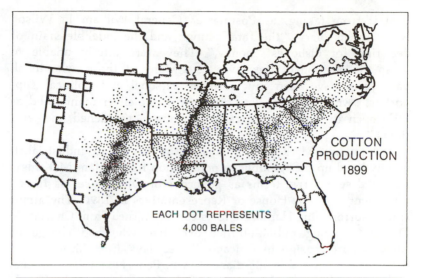

COTTON
PRODUCTION
1899

EACH DOT REPRESENTS
4,000 BALES

Cotton Production, 1899, in 500-Pound Bales

Tex.	2,584,810	N. C.	433,014	Ky.	1,371
Miss.	1,286,680	Tenn.	235,008	Kans.	70
Ga.	1,232,684	Ind. T.	155,729	Nev.	18
Ala.	1,093,697	Okla.	72,012	Ariz.	15
S. C.	843,725	Fla.	53,994	Utah	5
Ark.	705,928	Mo.	25,732	U. S.	9,434,345
La.	699,521	Va.	10,332		

bank deposits. The menace of free silver made bankers alarmed
about the security of their investments. As they reduced loans,
the volume of bank deposits shrank. Everybody wanted to be
safe. The gold crisis returned. And the President was almost
powerless in domestic affairs. The 1894 elections had turned
Democratic majorities in Congress into Republican ones: slight in
the Senate, overwhelming in the House. In December 1895 Cleveland asked for legislation to build up the gold reserve. The Ways
and Means Committee answered with a bill to increase the tariff.
As the year ended, the Treasury's gold reserve was down to $63
million. And once more gold bonds were issued. The gold Democrats fought desperately to keep control of their party and pre-

vent it from taking, as Postmaster General William L. Wilson wrote in his diary, "the fatal plunge and the indelible stain of declaring for dishonest money." They were utterly unable to grasp the position of the silverites. "Many of those, who in all past years have been my warmest personal and political supporters," wrote Wilson, "are bitten with the silver mania, and as little open to reason or to facts as animals maddened and irrational."

Meanwhile Mark Hanna, a wealthy Cleveland industrialist, quietly lined up the Republican nomination for William McKinley, who had served two terms as governor of Ohio since his forced retirement from the House of Representatives in 1890. The atmosphere surrounding Hanna's efforts can be learned from Charles G. Dawes, a young public-utilities executive who had charge of McKinley's campaign in Chicago. Three days after Christmas in 1895 Dawes entered in his diary: "Wm. Penn Nixon sent for me, and proposed to give the support of the Inter-Ocean to McKinley if a loan of $25,000 could be secured for his paper. As I did not have that amount of change with me I postponed decision." Hanna got pledges from convention delegates in the South, then in the West. When the Republicans convened in St. Louis in June 1896, McKinley was named on the first ballot. "There is no life in it," reported William Allen White to his Kansas newspaper. "The applause is hollow; the enthusiasm dreary and the delegates sit like hogs in a car and know nothing about anything."

The Democratic convention was tense, bitter, eloquent, and, at last, ecstatic. Altgeld, leading the Illinois delegation and in his own city of Chicago, was the chief draftsman of the platform. A comprehensive program for reform, it had the effect of reading the President out of his own party. While it was being debated, the young Bryan gave the most famous convention speech in American history in posing the issues of silver against gold, of cities against farms:

> You come to us and tell us that the great cities are in favor of the gold standard; we reply that the great cities rest upon our broad and fertile prairies. Burn down your cities and leave our farms, and your cities will spring up again as if by magic; but destroy our farms and the grass will grow in the streets of every city in the country.

The platform was adopted by a vote of more than 2 to 1, and Bryan was nominated for President.

The Populists met two weeks later, with a wing of radical delegates who wanted to maintain the party's independence by naming its own candidates. A movement to nominate Debs was frustrated when he withdrew his name. The free-silver craze had gone too far. The party endorsed Bryan, and virtually merged with the Democrats.

An alarmed Mark Hanna abandoned his plan for a cruise along the New England coast and settled into the campaign. His demands for money were insatiable. James J. Hill helped him raise campaign funds in New York, and they were seen in a carriage day after day going from Wall Street to the offices of the Pennsylvania Railroad to the New York Central. Hanna repeatedly tapped the (Democratic) president of New York Life. The head of Equitable gave company funds. Standard Oil gave $250,000; J. P. Morgan the same. The four big meat packers in Chicago gave altogether some $400,000. By frying the fat out of men who feared that free silver would lead to depreciation of their investments, Hanna collected at least $3,500,000. Mrs. Henry Cabot Lodge set the figure at twice that sum. Most of the campaign fund was raised in the East, and used to convert the West. Expenditures of the Chicago headquarters were nearly $2 million, of which more than 75 per cent had come from New York. Now, at last, the "usury states" were giving something back.

The Republicans distributed more than 100 million tracts and pamphlets—at least five for every voter. At one time they had 18,000 speakers going for them. A flood of words told the farmers that they were suffering from foreign competition, that prices depended on supply and demand, that there was domestic "overproduction" of farm staples; thus during the campaign the farm surplus was often prominent. When Bryan told New York farmers in August that "the law of supply and demand reaches and controls all sorts of property," the New York *Times* asked how a man who believes that can blame declining farm prices on the gold standard?

The Democrats, with a campaign fund hardly greater than what Standard Oil alone had given to the Republicans, could not publish so many pamphlets or field so many speakers. Bryan tried to compensate by a tireless campaign in which he traveled 18,000 miles and spoke to some 5 million people. Meanwhile McKinley stayed at home in Canton, addressing a stream of delegations sent by Republican organizations. (Railroads kindly provided reduced rates.) In September he told a labor group that the price of wheat was set by the "eternal" law of supply and demand. Gold had not opened the wheat lands of Russia and India and Argentina; gold did not make "high prices or low prices." He also stressed that high tariffs, by protecting American industry, would raise the home demand for farm products and thus raise their prices.

The Republicans did not depend solely on abstract argument. In mid-August the chairman of the state central committee in Iowa thought the situation "really looked threatening." Private polls in early September showed that Bryan would win the state. Eastern insurance companies which had been lending on farm mortgages sent their agents in Iowa to see farmers and assure them of extensions of their loans—if McKinley were chosen. By mid-October, a poll showed Iowa was saved. A contract with a shipyard in Wilmington, Delaware, provided for cancellation if Bryan was elected. Reported the local *News:* "If the boat is built here $160,000 of its cost would be paid to Wilmington workmen for wages." Factories said they would close if the Democrats won.

Mark Hanna tried to leave nothing to chance, but chance helped him anyway. When the campaign opened, the price of wheat at Chicago was about 60 cents a bushel. Then reports of wheat shortages in India, Russia, and Australia sent the price moving upward, until on October 19 it reached 80 cents. A front-page story in the Chicago *Tribune* announced that this price rise "has done more than all the campaign documents to convert the farmers." The election was not until November 3, but on October 28 Hanna returned a check sent to the campaign fund: "It is all over. Reports are satisfactory just where we wanted them most."

In a total of nearly 14 million, McKinley's plurality topped 700,000. He won every state in the Northeast. He won Minnesota, Wisconsin, and Iowa. He won North Dakota. He won California and Oregon. Bryan won the South, and the silver states, and most of the plains states. That was all.

Were the voters convinced by the Republicans, or coerced by them, or were many of the elections stolen? Altgeld, who lost Illinois, claimed that 100,000 fraudulent votes had made the difference. Once more the truth discovered by Grover Cleveland and

James G. Blaine and others had been demonstrated: In a close election, it pays to have the big money on your side.

To the question: Can farmers and wage earners and reformers unite to win control of the Federal government?, the answer was no.

The 1896 election signaled the emergence of the Republicans as the party with a permanent national majority. They won every county in New England. They lost only three in Wisconsin. Immigrants from Germany and Scandinavia who had flooded into the Midwest usually voted a straight Republican ticket. The days of 50–50 politics had ended. True, Woodrow Wilson was twice elected to the White House, but both times in peculiar circumstances: as a minority President in 1912 when the Bull Moose secession split his opponents, as a "peace" President in 1916 when war was an imminent threat. Not until 1932—after massive shifts of population from rural areas to cities had occurred; after the worst depression in our history had struck in 1929—could the Democrats again win in the North. And not until long after that could Negroes again vote in the South. The Lodge bill of 1890 was the last strong Republican effort to secure Negro suffrage. Able to win after 1896 as a sectional party, they had no need of Southern supporters.

Events after 1896 also gave additional proof that Populism in the Midwest had consisted of two distinct wings, joined for a time by a body of excruciating economic pains. The return of prosperity beginning in 1897 saw most Midwestern Populists return to the Republican party; thereafter they sought to gain narrowly economic ends by pressure politics, and the Farm Bloc in Congress became their true symbol. But a sizeable minority, mainly from the "Middle of the Road" Populists who opposed fusion with the Democrats in 1896, were interested not just in higher prices but also in social reconstruction. Thousands of these voters moved leftward toward socialism. From reading the *Farmers' Alliance* they went to reading the *Appeal to Reason*.

In the South, the aftermath of Populist collapse was far more tragic than in the Midwest. The well-to-do leaders of the Democratic party had demonstrated that they would do anything to keep control. White and Negro farmers had been shown that, even if they ignored slander and braved violence to vote for the People's party, they would be counted out at the polls. Despairing at the realization that they would never be allowed to take power, stung into hatred by their frustration, seeking at least the psychological sop of white supremacy, former Populist rednecks turned against their erstwhile black allies and helped conservative Democrats drive the Negro out of politics. Thus a one-party system that was unprecedented in its rigor came to dominate almost all of the suffering South.

Labor Leader: Eugene V. Debs

Debs' contemporaries, especially intellectuals, labelled him a splendid human being who could not think straight. They were wrong. If scientific psychology has anything to tell us, it is that we must be concerned with the whole man. That was Eugene V. Debs (1855–1926). But it is hard for Americans, living in a society where equality of opportunity is reserved strictly for the individual, to comprehend a man who would not rise from the working class, but with it. He must be crazy. Can't be done. Wild-eyed idealist. "While there is a soul in prison I am not free." Could he possibly mean that? Yes.

Born to recent Alsatian immigrants in Terre Haute, Indiana, Debs had his residence there until he died. But he was never at home. Apart from two sojourns in jail, he hurled himself like a perpetual-motion machine back and forth across the nation, agitating for social justice. He was nearly always among the first to anticipate the next great moral crisis that was about to confront the nation. He protested bitterly against war, both the Spanish-American conflict and World War I. He made the welkin throb with his indignation against class justice in the courts. He hurled himself into the unions' cause in thousands of strikes and other struggles. For thirty-five years he was the country's foremost advocate of the organization of trade unions by industry rather than by craft.

Five times the Socialist Party's candidate for President, this tall, spare man in banker's dress had a platform presence that few of his rivals could match. His wit, finely honed, could pop the fat bubbles of complacency, or, wielded like a bludgeon, he could use it to smash the stupidities of self-deceit, "Many of you think you are competing. Against whom? Against Rockefeller? About as I would if I had a wheelbarrow and competed with the Santa Fe from here to Kansas City," He had no competitors in his ability to fuse a variety of Marxism with the American tradition of antimonopoly that reached back to Thomas Jefferson. Insofar as a bias toward humanism persisted in the country's political contests, it stemmed from Debs more than from anybody else.

Like us all, he had illusions. The worst was his failure to foresee the depths of the corruption through which his culture was doomed to pass. He believed the republic would vote itself into socialism—soon. But Socialists in droves deserted the party's antiwar stand in 1917, and Debs went to prison for violating the Sedition Act. He ruefully reflected, "The people can have anything they want. The trouble is they do not want anything." At his death, the party of his faith barely existed. Now he was convinced that society could be reconstructed only in "its own tragically slow and painful way."

CHAPTER
9

Empire

Nobody can be sure, but we may doubt that free coinage of silver would have helped farmers and other debtors. It might have prompted such a reduction in gold and bank deposits that the total circulating medium would have declined. Even if the money stock had increased, a large part of it might simply have disappeared into hoards, with the result that the dollar demand for goods would not have increased and the price level would not have risen. As a heartsick Henry Lloyd declared after the Populists virtually fused with the Democrats in 1896, "The Free Silver movement is a fake. Free silver is the cow-bird of the reform movement. It waited till the nest had been built by the sacrifices and labor of others, and then it laid its eggs in it, pushing out the others which it smashed on the ground."

The insurgents would have done better to protest against control of credit by private bankers, under a National Banking Act whose provisions worked to turn any monetary stringency into financial collapse. Firmer ground yet would have been a protest against the fiscal policies of the Federal government. Year after year it sucked out of the economy by taxes far more than it pumped back in by spending. The falling price level was due in considerable part to these Federal surpluses, which had averaged over $100 million annually, or 1 per cent of the gross national product, from 1881 to 1890. The deflationary impact was aggravated by the fact that Federal taxes—the tariff and excise taxes—were regressive; that is, they fell most heavily on low-income groups who spent currently for consumer goods the major part of their incomes. Real-estate taxes, which provided almost all of state and local revenues, were also regressive and furthered the deflation. The Federal surpluses posed a hard problem for politicians. For years they were used chiefly to retire Federal debt, but sometimes not enough debt came due. In 1887 Grover Cleveland paid a handsome premium to induce investors to cash in Federal bonds before maturity, and his annual message dealt with one question only: the surplus. The dilemma arose, of course, because the chief Federal taxes were not imposed primarily for purposes of revenue, but for protection. Not only was this true of the tariff, but the Whiskey Trust supported a higher excise tax on its product in order to discourage competition.

To counter demands for a lower tariff it was wise to keep the surplus down by spending more money. Civil War pensions were a godsend. The same Congress that voted the McKinley Tariff Act, merrily titled "An Act to Reduce the Revenue," used this other way to reduce the surplus. As a result Civil War pensions, which had cost $75 million in 1887, used up $142 million in 1894, with a million beneficiaries on the rolls. Twenty-nine years after the end of the Civil War! By 1908 Union veterans had received in pensions more than $3,533,000,000. And the 1890 Congress took cognizance of a third way to reduce the surplus—build battleships.

The Arthur administration after 1881 made fumbling efforts to improve the navy, but its real revival dates from the tenure of William C. Whitney as Secretary of the Navy in the first Cleveland administration. The United States at the time had no steel mills equipped to make gun forgings or roll armor plate, but Whitney offered Bethlehem Steel large enough contracts that they started putting up a special mill which would be, he boasted, "second to none in the world." Thus the government helped to create a powerful lobby with an interest in maximizing the construction of war vessels, and the Navy Department appropriation more than doubled from 1885 to 1892. But Cleveland was never an advocate of an offensive navy.

In that he differed from Captain Alfred Thayer Mahan, head of the Naval War College at Newport from 1886 to 1889. In 1890 Mahan published his *The Influence of Sea Power upon History, 1660–1783*, which argued that no country could be prosperous or strong without an expanding foreign trade. The "foreign" was crucial. To succeed in the worldwide struggle for markets, a nation needed a strong merchant marine. These vessels needed safe ports abroad, and they needed protection on the seas. The first required colonies overseas; the second, a strong navy. Mahan's doctrine won powerful friends: The steel industry, plagued by excess capacity. Shipping firms, glad for any argument that would induce Congress to raise the mail subsidies. The navy. Henry Cabot Lodge, second-ranking member of the Naval Affairs Committee in the House, and soon to be elevated to the Senate. Voters who were titillated by feeling that, as Lord Bryce wrote, "it is a fine thing for a great country to have vast territories, and to see marked as her own, on the map of the world, dominions beyond her natural borders." An increasingly yellow press in the cities, eager for copy that might give vicarious zest to their readers.

European observers thought the Big Navy idea was absurd. Wrote Bryce: ". . . the power of the United States to protect her citizens abroad is not to be measured by the number of vessels or guns she possesses, but by the fact that there is no power in the world which will not lose far more than it can possibly gain by quarreling with a nation which could, in case of war, so vast are its resources, not only create an armoured fleet but speedily equip swift vessels to attack the commerce of its antagonist. The possession of powerful armaments is apt to inspire a wish to use them." The words were prophetic.

A Policy Board of six naval officers in 1890 brought forth a report calling for the construction of more than 200 modern warships; it pointed to indications that this country was entering a period of "commercial competition." Even the pro-navy New York *Herald* felt obliged to call the report "naval fanaticism." But Congress that year voted funds to build three battleships, and two years later it added a fourth. In 1893 the new President put into the Navy Department an enthusiast for capital ships, Hilary A. Herbert of Alabama (Senator John T. Morgan of Alabama had long been calling for a canal across Nicaragua to open up for South-eastern products the markets of the Pacific). But the depression cut down imports, a condition that was reinforced by the high tariff rates; the customary Federal surplus became a deficit of $60 million in 1894; and the program of naval expansion was checked.

Just as the McKinley Act helped to slow naval construction, so did it help to precipitate a major problem of foreign policy. Under a treaty of 1875 the United States and Hawaii each admitted duty-free the chief products of the other. From then until 1890 the sugar planters in the islands, most of them American by birth or extraction, enjoyed fantastic prosperity. More than 99 per cent of the exports of Hawaii went to the United States. But under the law of 1890, sugar from any country was admitted here without duty. The price of sugar in Honolulu fell from $100 a ton to $60. Hopes of setting up an independent government, securing annexation to the United States, and getting the bounty of 2 cents a pound paid on American-grown sugar—this strategy helped set off a revolt against the queen of Hawaii. The rebels, with the connivance of the United States Navy, succeeded. They quickly negotiated a treaty of annexation, which the Harrison administration submitted to the Senate.

Sentiment for expansion overseas was growing in the United States. As early as 1889 the *Commercial and Financial Chronicle* had declared that only by the conquest of foreign markets could the American economy avoid collapse. Now many advocates of Hawaiian annexation saw it as merely part of a broad program of expansion. The *Journal of Finance* urged that "the political change would certainly make a greater opening for American manufactures." The New York *Tribune* and the San Francisco *Evening Bulletin* hit similar notes. But Grover Cleveland was not convinced. The treaty had not yet been ratified when he became President, and he withdrew it. "The mission of our nation," he said later in a public statement, "is to build up and make a greater country out of what we have, instead of annexing islands." After an investigation he went so far as to propose that Hawaii should return to the political situation that had prevailed before the revolt. The new rulers in Honolulu ignored the suggestion.

The signs are good that the Harrison administration, had it been continued in power, would have made an aggressive foreign policy the chief feature of its second term. Even Grover Cleveland approved a law passed just before he took office which broke more than a century of precedent. Although the State Department had long since given diplomatic pre-eminence to ambassadors on the grounds that they were the personal representatives of sovereigns, the United States had never given this title to any of its agents because it was thought to be identified with monarchy. A law of 1 March 1893 authorized the undemocratic nomenclature, and Great Britain, France, Italy, and Germany quickly made their men in Washington ambassadors. President Cleveland not only responded in kind but declared in his first annual message: "This step fittingly comports with the position the United States hold in the family of nations."

Others were determined that colonies too were needed for a proper stature. During new Congressional debates on Hawaii, the chief speech in the House favoring annexation was given by W. F. Draper of Massachusetts, who was also head of a big textile-machinery manufacturer. He demanded the acquisition of several bases, not just Hawaii but also Samoa, an isthmian canal with a base at its mouth, another at the Straits of Magellan. "With these bases, a properly organized fleet, of sufficient size to keep the communications open between them, will hold the Pacific as an American ocean, dominated by American commercial enterprise for all time." Opposition to the policy was staunch, especially among the Democratic majorities in 1894. The House announced itself as opposed to annexation, while the Senate resolved by 55 to 0 (with 30 abstentions) that neither this country nor any other foreign power should intervene in Hawaii.

But enthusiasm for foreign aggrandizement persisted, and much of it fed on religious impulses. Way back in 1881 the American Board of Foreign Missions had declared: "That which is good for communities in America is good for the Armenians and Greeks and Mohammedans of Turkey." Similar notions had been spread by the Congregationalist minister and writer Josiah Strong. In 1885, when he was secretary of the American Home Missionary Society in Ohio, he brought out a little book called *Our Country*. Anglo-Saxons above all other races were champions of "a pure *spiritual* Christianity," wrote Strong, and Anglo-Saxons in the United States were superior to those in Great Britain. They were, in fact, superior to all other races. Latching onto the ancient rhetoric about the manifest destiny of the United States, Strong proclaimed that they had a mission. In past times it had been the mission of the soldier. Now barbarism was dying out, and the new mission was to carry "the arts of peace." The Anglo-Saxon was being schooled for "*the final competition of races*," during which he would spread his civilization all over the world. "Is there room for reasonable doubt that this race, unless devitalized by alcohol and tobacco, is destined to dispossess many weaker races, assimilate others, and mold the remainder, until, in a very true and important sense, it has Anglo-Saxonized mankind?"

The qualifying phrase, the word of warning, was no accident. Much of *Our Country* was an attack on the "perils" that had created "the present crisis": immigration, the Roman Catholic Church, the Mormon despotism, liquor, tobacco, socialism, cities, materialist appetites. Such forebodings found a ready audience. Strong's book sold well over 100,000 copies; he followed it with others; he lectured and preached. But while the spread-eagle Americanism in his work tempered the ominous note, others served it up raw. Dr. Richard Jordan Gatling, inventor of a new gun that would fire as many as 250 shots a minute, was asked if he thought that war would ever become obsolete. "I do not think so," he answered. "Human nature is the same in all ages, and the strong will continue to oppress and rule over the weak as long as time shall last. . . . In this world the weakest must always go to the wall."

Allegedly isolationist Kansas had extremely militant doctrines dinned into its ears and minds over a long period of time. Influential politicians demanded policies that would drive all European goods out of North America. Aggressive continentalism was the keynote of Senator John J. Ingalls' program in 1890. Although he said that we had "no need for costly armaments" because there would be no war with England or any other power, Ingalls urged action to unify America from the North Pole to a new isthmian canal. The man who served as chairman of the Republican state convention in 1892 declared in a public address in October 1893: "As Napoleon turned to the east for military fame and glory, so we must turn to those countries for commercial conquests and financial success . . . to provide business and employment for the millions who come after us. . . ." Another Kansan tirelessly exalted war. Summarizing the lessons taught in "Mundane University" he proclaimed: "We are taught that war is not the great evil that it is painted. That nations require war to break up the vicissitudes of luck and disastrous periods of peace during which the air becomes oppressive and superheated with avarice." He loved his own phrases, saying nine years later: "I am one who believes in war as an educator, as part of our public school system. . . . In nations where war is too long delayed the people forget; patriotism becomes a reminiscence and the atmosphere becomes superheated with avarice." This was not some crackpot talking to himself on a street corner; it was Eugene F. Ware, who has been described as "the unofficial poet laureate of Kansas." The first statement quoted is from his speech to the alumni banquet of the University of Kansas in 1886; the second is from his address at a flag-raising ceremony at the Topeka High School in 1895. Ware's rhetoric may sound anti-business, but we may marvel that he received such invitations if the businessmen of Kansas were united in hostility to his attitude. The suspicion is heightened by another statement made in Kansas in October 1895, this one by the *Linn County Republic:* "While it might be putting it too strong to say that war is needed in this country, now, yet who is there who does not believe, and in fact know, that such a thing would clear the atmosphere and stamp out the growth of socialism and anarchy, discontent and sectional prejudice that is gaining a foothold in this nation." Small-town newspapers are not noted for their independence of business sentiment.

Very soon after Eugene Ware sounded his bugle call it seemed that he might get what he wanted. The occasion was a dispute with Great Britain, which in 1814 had taken over part of Guiana from the Dutch. The boundary line between British Guiana and Venezuela had never been settled. Since 1887 the United States had discussed the problem with the British Foreign Office, but no agreement had been reached. Through the early months of 1895 the President tried to induce Britain to arbitrate. Failing, he became exasperated (and he surely realized that the contemporary growth of pro-British sentiment did not obliterate the anglophobia of millions of voters, not just those of Irish or German descent but also radical Democrats such as Altgeld and Darrow who loved to orate about the Declaration of Independence).

The Secretary of State, Walter Q. Gresham, died on May 28, and Richard Olney moved up to the office. Agents of Venezuela were intriguing, with marked success, to draw the United States into the dispute on their side. Senator Lodge charged in June in the *North American Review* that British "aggression" in Venezuela was aimed at getting control of "the Orinoco . . . and also of the rich mining district of the Yuruari." British policy, Lodge argued, violated the Monroe Doctrine.

The new ministry of Lord Salisbury was treated to Olney's dispatch of 20 July 1895. This brash and often inaccurate document was approved by the President, who called it "the best thing of the kind that I have ever read. . . ." It demanded that Britain agree to arbitrate all of the territory in dispute. Referring to South America, Olney wrote:

> Today the United States is practically sovereign on this continent, and its fiat is law upon the subjects to which it confines its interposition. Why? It is not because of the pure friendship or good will felt for it. It is not simply by reason of its high character as a civilized state, nor because wisdom, justice, and equity are the invariable characteristics of the dealings of the United States. It is because, in addition to all other grounds, its infinite resources combined with its isolated position render it master of the situation, and practically invulnerable as against any or all other powers.

The Monroe Doctrine had existed for more than 70 years, and nobody had said that it implied compulsory arbitration of a boundary dispute in Latin America involving a European power. Yet Olney made the claim.

While for months the United States vainly pressed for a reply, American journals shrilly agitated the point. A former Texas Congressman wrote the Secretary of State that his policy was "a 'winner'," especially if one considered "the country's internal ills." He thought that "one cannon shot across the bow of a British boat" would do wonders in curing "the anarchistic, socialistic, and populistic boil" in our politics. The President in his annual message to Congress in early December prejudged the controversy by protesting against "the enlargement of the area of British Guiana in derogation of the rights and against the will of Venezuela." A few days later Lord Salisbury's note of November 26 reached Washington. Not by cable. By mail. The Prime Minister emphasized Britain's ties to Canada and to Latin American countries in rebuking Olney's contention that "any permanent political union between a European and an American state" was rendered "unnatural and inexpedient" by the intervening ocean. In tones now pompous, now supercilious, Salisbury said that the Monroe Doctrine was not international law, nor was it pertinent to the present conflict. He rejected arbitration.

Grover Cleveland was tired of temporizing. On December 17 he sent a message to Congress asking for funds to pay the expenses of a commission, which he would appoint, to determine the disputed boundary. The United States should then use "every means in its power" to stop Britain from transgressing the line. Congress in three days unanimously provided a million dollars for the commission.

The threat of war prompted British investors to pull their capital out of this country. On December 20 their selling on Wall Street touched off a slump of stock prices that led to losses of $170 million. The bankers of New York were heated in denouncing the President's belligerence. Chauncey Depew, now president of the New York Central, dined with several of them on Saturday evening, and reported that men like Morgan and the president of the New York Stock Exchange all thought "that the frightened English investor and European holders of our securities would be tumbling them across the Atlantic at a rate which would take out all the gold from the Treasury to pay for them; that they would find no market here capable of buying them, and so they would sell for nothing; that they would cramp the banks; that the loans would all be called in, and no new ones made; that everybody owing money would fail in business, and that we were on the eve of a financial cataclysm the like of which had never been witnessed."

The slump lasted less than a day. Investors in Cincinnati, elsewhere in the Midwest, in New York, showed that they had money to spend when they saw bargains, and their buying stabilized stock prices. Industrialists, merchants, even bankers except in New York and Chicago, applauded the President's message. A Boston banker thought the Monroe Doctrine was "well worth going to war to maintain." War on the issue might be a "blessing" for it would "prove once for all that the country is united." The president of the Massachusetts State Board of Trade said that Cleveland was trying to protect American commerce, "and we should demand, in justice to our mercantile interests, that respect to which we are entitled." In large cities of the Midwest, commercial bodies endorsed the President. So did Marshall Field and Philip D. Armour. Lamentations came from trade journals in industries dependent on English investors—railroads, mining—but in Pittsburgh the *American Manufacturer* contended that Britain would not arbitrate because the "markets of the world are being wrested from her" so she "seeks to extend her commercial influence in South America." The United States had to resist, even if it led to " 'blood and iron'."

Symbolic of the state of mind of many American businessmen is the first program of the National Association of Manufacturers, which was formed in 1895. Over half of the document was devoted to the problem of increasing our markets abroad, specifically favoring reciprocity treaties as a means to that end. Also symbolic was Andrew Carnegie's perspective on the Venezuela crisis; he wrote to John G. A. Leishman, president of Carnegie Steel, suggesting that the international tension afforded a chance to get a large order from the United States navy. This vigilance for sales was natural in the circumstances. Since 1893, American steel-ingot capacity had leaped upward; the rate of increase was about 1,100,000 gross tons a year. Production had not risen with anything like equal speed. As early as January 1894 a Democratic Representative charged in Congress that the Carnegie Company had joined two other big manufacturers of steel rails in offering to pay the Pennsylvania Steel Company $400,000 as its estimated profits for the year if it would close and keep closed for 12 months its mills at Sparrows Point, Maryland, even though the closing would turn 4,000 men out on the streets. In 1896, steel-ingot production would actually fall; capacity that year was 12 million tons, while output was less than half that.

The Cleveland administration's harsh words had the desired effect on the Salisbury cabinet. Britain at the time found herself without a single important ally anywhere in the world. In Africa her conflict with France was so sharp that the two nations would come to the verge of war in 1898. In no position to fight the United States, she initiated friendly discussions, and eventually the Venezuela boundary was arbitrated. (This was only the first in a series of diplomatic concessions by Britain that did much to promote her friendship with the United States and laid a groundwork for the American entry into World War I.) Meanwhile the strident assertions by Cleveland and Olney served to stimulate sentiment for an enlarged American role overseas.

The Venezuela affair points up how very lopsided is any characterization of American diplomacy as "isolationist." Traditional policy had been to avoid political involvement and especially to avoid political commitments in Europe. But it had also been to intervene in the Far East unilaterally or with other powers, and it emphatically had been to intervene unilaterally in the Americas. In the words of Senator Roger Q. Mills (Democrat of Texas) on 24 March 1896: "It has been stated . . . that Mr. Canning was the author of the Monroe Doctrine. The Monroe Doctrine is as old as humanity. God is the author of the Monroe Doctrine." Already, as the dispute with Britain was being resolved, the problem of Cuba was taking its place.

Back in 1868 the Cubans had revolted against Spanish rule, and President Grant had wished to take action that would probably have resulted in a Spanish-American War. That crisis had been passed in peace, but almost immediately Germany adopted policies that would help to provoke another Cuban rebellion. By paying what amounted to a bounty on exports of beet sugar, the Imperial Government enabled Germans to capture much of the British market, which had always been the chief vent of Caribbean cane sugar. The price in London of unrefined cane sugar was 21.09 shillings a hundredweight in 1881, only 10.85 shillings in 1896. The impact on Cuba became acute in 1894, when sugar fell from 14 shillings to 12. It fell another two shillings the next year, and revolution in Cuba began in February 1895.

The Junta at the head of the revolt angled zealously for American support. Senator Wilkinson Call of Florida got his son named its agent to sell Cuban bonds in England. Call also put the Junta's man in Washington in touch with ex-Representative Benjamin Le Fevre, an influential lobbyist. Le Fevre advised the Junta to make "arrangements for mutual benefit" with Standard Oil and the Nicaragua Canal Company. Senator Lodge and other jingoes made passionate speeches against Spanish "butcheries" in Cuba. They denounced the Spanish army for herding Cubans together in concentration camps. An independent Cuba, said Lodge, "would mean a great market to the United States; it would mean an opportunity for American capital." On 28 February 1896 the Senate passed a resolution favoring recognition of the Cuban rebels as belligerents.

The next month an anonymous correspondent in Atlanta wrote to the President that if he would act "strong and courageous in the defense of Cuba, you will have a solid South at your call. . . . Strengthen the Army and Navy of this country & in this way give employment to the thousands of idle men who need it." Even John Peter Altgeld was bellicose. Although he suspected that Cleveland's trumpeting of the Monroe Doctrine was an effort to divert voters from the domestic crisis, he supported it anyway. And in March 1896 he wrote about Cuba for the New York *Journal*, organ of the Democratic jingo William Randolph Hearst. Comparing the Cuban struggle with the American Revolution, he made a strong plea for intervention: "The nations of the earth recognize the right to interfere in foreign affairs in cases where the moral sense of the civilized world is shocked as in cases of cannibalism and the slave-trade. But these are innocent amusements compared with the atrocities which the Spaniards have practised for over a century in Cuba."

"The jingoism in the air is a curious thing, and unaccountable," wrote William L. Wilson in his diary, "except on account of the unrest of our people, and the willingness to turn from domestic to foreign affairs, always making greatest allowance for political maneuvering, and the ridiculousness of conducting foreign affairs by such town meetings as the Senate and House have become." Although Cuban independence clearly had great appeal, Grover Cleveland would not be stampeded. The House of Representatives on April 6 concurred in the resolution favoring belligerent status for the rebels, but the administration made clear that it would not take such action. Still many conservative newspapers as well as the "yellow press" continued to whoop up sympathy for Cuba.

Cleveland and Olney calculated that American investments in the island were worth at least $30 million, and both men asserted publicly that a continuation of fighting would make Cuba commercially useless. Soon after William Jennings Bryan became a candidate for the White House, the repudiated President got a fascinating letter from Fitzhugh Lee, whom he had named consul general in Havana. Lee urged Cleveland to form a party of gold Democrats, have it demand Cuban independence, and then intervene in Cuba: ". . . successful war . . . might do much towards directing the minds of the people away from imaginary ills, the relief of which is erroneously supposed to be reached by 'Free Silver.' "

During the campaign the monetary issues pushed foreign policy into the shade, but the Republican platform did call for "continued enlargement of the Navy," and the triumphant party did contain most of the vociferous expansionists in the country. Also it brought in as Chief Executive a man who had few ideas, read no books, never publicly disputed the word of any American except for a few jibes at Democrats, and could be easily pushed. William McKinley and Mark Hanna in 1894 went to their first football game: Yale vs. Princeton. There Hanna overheard a question about his companion: "Who is that distinguished-looking man—the one that looks like Napoleon?" Perhaps never were appearances more misleading.

Joseph Cannon once remarked that McKinley kept his ear so close to the ground that he got it full of grasshoppers.

But the overheard question does point to a significant craze of the depression years—a Napoleon revival. Publication of books about his personality spurted amazingly. Leading magazines competed in running serial essays and picture biographies. Major responsibility for playing up militarism must go to the Century Company and its magazine, which were preoccupied first with military aspects of the Civil War and then with Napoleon. Seemingly some Americans, overwhelmed by depression and by the futility of government, longed for a man on horseback to guide them out of the wilderness. As ex-Senator Ingalls put it in April 1896, "A man will come."

The hoped-for Hero was soon installed, at the urging of Senator Lodge, as Assistant Secretary of the Navy. Theodore Roosevelt at various times had lusted for war against Mexico, Chile, Britain, Spain, Germany, and any European country with a colony in the Americas. During the Venezuela crisis he wrote to Lodge: "Let the fight come if it must. I don't care whether our sea coast cities are bombarded or not; we would take Canada." Early in 1897 he told the Naval War College: "All the great masterful races have been fighting races. . . ." He rather deprecated success in commerce or finance; the warlike virtues were "higher things . . . than the soft and easy enjoyment of material comfort." As his mentor Roosevelt had taken Captain Mahan, whose "Preparedness for Naval War" appeared in *Harper's New Monthly Magazine* in March 1897.

McKinley's mind at the time was on the tariff; his first act as President was to call a special session of Congress to revise it. For him the problem was closely tied to Cuba. The Sugar Trust, an important source of campaign funds, was forced to pay $3 to $4 more per ton for raw sugar from other sources as imports from Cuba fell 75 per cent. The Trust had powerful friends in Congress who might put forward their own Cuba policy. Also McKinley hoped to get lower duties on raw sugar in order to strengthen the argument for raising rates on other items.

The new Dingley Bill passed the House in less than two weeks simply because Thomas B. Reed favored it. The Speaker's powers at the time were almost incredible. He named all members of all committees and their chairmen. He, two other Republicans, and two Democrats were the Committee on Rules which determined the scope of all other committees and apportioned the bills among them. The other majority members on the Rules Committee owed their jobs to Reed, and the minority members in practice were hardly on the committee. Joseph W. Bailey, the Democratic leader in the House, complained that the Ways and Means Committee had not really considered the Dingley Bill at all. The Republicans wrote the complicated measure, and then gave the Democrats on the committee just 24 hours to look it over before reporting it to the House.

The bill ran into more trouble in the Senate, but by July 24 the President had his new law. It set a level of rates in general even higher than those of the 1890 Act. The reciprocity provisions of the McKinley Act, until repealed in 1894, had opened foreign markets to American goods to a degree that nobody had foreseen. Now the President got power to bargain about tariff concessions with other nations; the new duties on raw sugar, wool, and hides were high enough that he had something to bargain about. In October, speaking to the Commercial Club of Cincinnati, McKinley declared: "It should be our settled purpose to open trade wherever we can, making our ships and our commerce messengers of peace and amity." In agreement was the president of the N.A.M., who said: "Many of our manufacturers have outgrown or are outgrowing their home markets, and the expansion of our foreign trade is our only promise of relief." The Pan American Society and the American Asiatic Association were trying to promote economic penetration of specific areas. American businessmen, reported the *Journal of Commerce*, were thinking of "the industrial supremacy of the world."

The economy was finally jolted out of stagnation in the early summer of 1897. The cause was an expected rise in exports as it became clear that crops would be good here and poor overseas. "Wheat sold at one dollar per bushel today—the highest price since 1891. Prosperity seems to be dawning at last," noted Charles Dawes on August 21. The *Literary Digest* that month reported that the Trans-Mississippi Congress, presided over by William Jennings Bryan, had demanded independence for Cuba, annexation of Hawaii, and construction of a Nicaraguan Canal by the United States alone. With farmers as well as manufacturers suspecting a correlation between sales abroad and good times at home, the administration became more conscious of foreign affairs.

McKinley had not even mentioned Cuba in his inaugural address. As for the Philippines, Senator Foraker reported the President's response to his request for a consular post for one O. F. Williams. McKinley hesitated to offer the one place available. It was called Manila, "somewhere away around on the other side of the world; he did not know where exactly, for he had not had time to look it up." But in May prominent businessmen, including August Belmont who was floating bond issues for the Cuban rebels, began going to McKinley urging intervention. As Spanish efforts to put down the revolt seemed to be succeeding during the summer, American sentiment for intervention grew. An American ultimatum to Spain was predicted by the German ambassador in Madrid, prompting Kaiser Wilhelm to note on the margin of the dispatch: "I believe it is now high time that we other monarchs . . . agree *jointly* to offer our help to the Queen in case the American-British Society for International Theft and Warmongering looks as if it seriously intends to snatch Cuba from Spain." The Kaiser's proposal was blocked by his Foreign Minister, who argued that unanimity of the powers would be impossible to achieve. In Spain the absolutist premier was assassinated, and in October a Liberal ministry took office. It soon recalled the most offensive Spanish general from Cuba, released all prisoners there who were United States citizens, and directed the new governor general to conduct the war by Christian methods. The Liberals were committed to seeking a negotiated peace that would give Cuba some autonomy, maybe even dominion status similar to Canada's.

Agitation continued in the United States. Eugene F. Ware urged that the Federal government raise a public loan of $250 million. The proceeds would be used to hire tramps to build warships.

> And when we have our navy completed there is but one more step to prosperity. Get us a war with some of these pestering nations we have on the face of the globe, lick the socks off them, and then compel the payment of an indemnity of 2 billion dollars.

The indemnity, even after retiring the public loan, would leave a good profit. Theodore Roosevelt wrote a friend: "In strict confidence, . . . I should welcome almost any war, for I think this country needs one." But his chief by December could profess to be cheered about Cuba. Devoting most of his annual message to the subject, McKinley said that Spain should be given a chance to carry out her proposed reforms. Forcible annexation of Cuba to the United States would be, he said, "criminal aggression." The administration also moved to halt navalism. Secretary John D. Long made clear his view that the United States was safe, so ships would be "gradually taken out of commission and put into reserve" to cut expenses.

If the President did not want militarism, yet he clearly did want to expand American exports. An Executive Order of 1 January 1898 ordered the daily publication of all consular reports currently of value. At this time the *Wall Street Journal* could detect only two "blue spots" in the economy: New York City which was being upset by rate cutting of the railroads, and Boston which was suffering from poor demand for cotton textiles. Rising prosperity and expanding exports encouraged some businessmen to hope that they could conquer foreign markets by strictly business methods, by underselling their competitors. But two ominous developments suddenly suggested that equal competition might become impossible in much of the world. The Foreign Minister of Austria-Hungary called for European unity against the "destructive competition with transoceanic countries. . . ." (The Kaiser had frequently urged upon Russia an economic union against the United States.) Even more threatening was the scramble to divide up China. On 14 November 1897 Germany grabbed Tsingtao. A week later Russia took Port Arthur. Germany on 5 January 1898 extracted a 99-year lease of Kiaochow. Britain and France quickly seized compensating benefits.

The common American reaction was alarm. Several sizeable fortunes were based on the China trade of a century earlier. The United States had applied the Open Door Policy, insisting on equal access to commercial opportunities for its citizens, to China as early as 1842. Desire for ports en route to China had triggered the American thrust to Puget Sound and the Golden Gate in 1846. After the Civil War the markets of China were important to Standard Oil and to textile manufacturers. Other firms for whom the actuality was nothing yet maintained hopes of capturing the 400 million customers in China.

The mixed atmosphere of late 1897 was smashed early in 1898. Soon after McKinley's annual message to Congress, the Spanish minister at Washington set down his opinion of it in a private letter which declared that the President was "weak and a bidder for the admiration of the crowd." The letter, stolen by a postal clerk in Havana, was printed in Hearst's New York *Journal* on February 9. Six days later came a worse disaster. In January a riot had broken out in Havana, and McKinley had sent the battleship *Maine* there. An explosion sank it in Havana harbor on February 15, and 250 men were killed. Nobody knows what caused the explosion, but newspapers at such moments are not overscrupulous. The *Journal* told its readers that "the Maine was destroyed by treachery." The Kansas City *Star* flared the headline: "HE SAW THE TORPEDO . . . A MAIMED SEAMAN'S STORY." While an American court of inquiry investigated the sinking, the President continued his efforts to negotiate a peaceful settlement of the Cuba question.

On St. Patrick's Day the Senate heard a speech by Redfield Proctor of Vermont. He had just returned from Cuba, and was the first member of the Congressional tour of inspection to report on their observations. His straightforward account of alleged Spanish crimes was widely publicized because it was rumored that he had made the trip as McKinley's observer and that the President had cleared his speech. The impact on the public and Congress was great (although Tom Reed, an opponent of the war drive, took advantage of the fact that Proctor had made a fortune as head of the world's biggest producer of marble to comment: "A war will make a large market for gravestones."). Four days later Senator Lodge warned the President that the voters of Massachusetts were almost unanimous and that political disaster lay ahead; if the war in Cuba lasted through the summer "we shall go down in the greatest defeat ever known." But the business community of Boston was opposed to war by the United States. As a correspondent wrote Lodge: "I have not met a man . . . in the aristocratic upper crust in which you & I are imbedded, who considers that we have any justifiable cause for war. Below that crust . . . the wish for war is *almost* universal." Lodge's son-in-law disgustedly made a similar report.

In New York the picture was different. An executive of New York Life who was engaged in the crucial task of assessing war sentiment among businessmen found a division of opinion. Steel man John W. Gates, traction magnate Thomas Fortune Ryan, William Rockefeller, all were war-minded. John Jacob Astor wore a boutonniere of red, white, and blue. James J. Hill was fighting for peace, but he was the only big railroad man of that viewpoint. The executive, reporting "Nothing but war talk," concluded that the war drive could not be halted from New York and he predicted that even the opposition of Mark Hanna would fail to halt it in the Senate.

Roosevelt exaggerated when he wrote to Morgan partner Robert Bacon: "We here in Washington have grown to feel that almost every man connected with the big business interests of the country is anxious to court any infamy if only peace can be obtained and the business situation be not disturbed." An exaggeration in the other direction is a confidential note to McKinley from the city editor of the New York *Herald:* "Big corporations here now believe we will have war. Believe all would welcome it as a relief to suspense." It seems likely that many businessmen, including some who were most eager to expand their exports, had not concluded that colonies were essential to that purpose. Many of them certainly had not concluded that war was essential, or even desirable. War brings risks, which businessmen abhor. It disrupts stability, which they love—and especially do they love it when they seem to be emerging from 25 years of relative stagnation and from four years of acute depression.

An indication of the disruptive impact occurs in the correspondence of Henry Lee Higginson, a Boston banker who opposed the war. The episode is also amusing in retrospect for what it shows of the irrational worries about Spanish naval power. William W. Davis, a member of the state senate, had been negotiating to buy a resort hotel on the coast. The threat of hostilities stifled the purchase. Informing Higginson that hotel owners were "receiving letters daily cancelling rooms engaged at close of last season," Davis wrote that "the Western patrons will not come East."

The court of inquiry to investigate the *Maine* reported on March 28, and the result was to reinforce the belief that Spanish agents were guilty. Three days later the French ambassador in Washington wrote home: "A sort of bellicose fury has seized the American nation." Influential and once pacific newspapers had begun to beat the drum. The peace camp had splintered. McKinley at last feared there might be no alternative to an ultimatum to Spain. Then he wrote a message to Congress asking for authority to use American military power to restore peace and stable government in Cuba. But the message did not ask for recognition of Cuban independence, and the President withheld it pending steps to withdraw Americans in Cuba from the danger zone.

Already the Pope had asked Spain to accede to an armistice, and on the morning of April 9 the six European ambassadors in Madrid requested that Spain agree to the Vatican's petition. Before night fell, Spain had consented. Archbishop John Ireland of St. Paul broke the news to McKinley; Ireland reported later that the President was "delighted." But joy expired soon. One of McKinley's essential conditions (which ironically he dared not state explicitly, fearing that it might leak out and knowing that it would alienate conservative Republicans in the Senate) was independence for Cuba. This Spain would not grant. All chance of an armistice was gone.

McKinley sent his message to Congress on April 11. By then it was obvious that he was not in control of Capitol Hill. Bryan had come out for independence; the Democrats in Congress were solid for it; Lodge and Foraker and Cushman K. Davis of Minnesota and other leading Republican Senators were hot for war. In the Senate an amendment was voted recognizing the independence of Cuba. But party discipline had been restored in the House; it failed to follow suit; and the conference committee struck out the independence clause. As passed on April 19, the resolution said that the sole American purpose was to force the Spanish to withdraw from Cuba, and the Teller Amendment added that the United States had no intention of exercising sovereignty there. Two days later Spain ruptured diplomatic relations, and on April 25 Congress voted a war resolution. A week later Senator John C. Spooner, conservative Republican from Wisconsin, wrote a friend: "I think . . . possibly the President could have worked the business out without a war, but the current was too strong, the demagogues too numerous, and the fall elections too near."

The previous December political influence, especially the activities of Theodore Roosevelt, had gained the appointment of Commodore George Dewey as commander of the Asiatic Squadron of the navy, stationed at Hong Kong. Now Secretary Long cabled to Dewey that war had started: "Proceed at once to the Philippine Islands. Commence operations at once, particularly against Spanish fleet. You must capture vessels or destroy. Use utmost endeavors." Dewey steamed away from Hong Kong on April 27 with a fleet in which the largest vessels were four cruisers. On April 30 they sighted Luzon. The Spanish admiral was anxious to avoid bombardment of Manila, and he arrayed his vessels in almost unprotected waters at Cavite. The Asiatic Squadron on May 1 blew the moribund Spanish fleet out of the water. Ten ships were destroyed; 400 men were killed. Not a single American life was lost, and no American vessel was seriously damaged.

News of this ideal victory gave quite a fillip to patriotism in the United States, and Dewey became the first hero of the war. But his success did not prevent panic at the thought that the Spanish fleet in the Atlantic might bombard cities along the coast of the United States. Instead of concentrating all possible vessels under the command of Admiral William T. Sampson in the Caribbean, the Navy Department yielded to public hysteria and put many of the best American ships into a Flying Squadron at Hampton Roads to guard against naval raids. For a month the jitters spread, as nobody knew where to find the Spanish fleet of Admiral Cervera. At last it was located and blockaded on May 29 in Santiago harbor on the southern coast of Cuba.

Now the expeditionary force was free to move. Free, but not ready. The President had issued a call on April 23 for 125,000 volunteers, and the response had been even greater than the contemporary rush to the Klondike gold fields in Alaska. Once enlisted, the men could not be equipped. Many were dressed in blue woolens for a summer campaign in Cuba. Efforts to assemble the invasion force at Tampa were obstructed because only a single-track railroad led to the wharf. In the absence of regular troop transports, the government chartered a motley array of private vessels. Admirals quarreled with admirals; the army and navy did not cooperate at all. But on June 14 the largest expeditionary army in American history, nearly 17,000 men, put out to sea. It arrived off Santiago six days later.

The commanding general was William R. Shafter, a veteran of the Indian wars. Goutish, immensely fat, with a belly that hung down, Shafter was even more defective in mind than in body. First he landed his men at Daiquiri beachhead, where he had to anchor his vessels in an open roadstead and send his men ashore through heavy surf. Fortunately the Spanish did not defend the beach. A few days later a Spanish commander again lent a helping hand by evacuating strong positions at Las Guasimas after a skirmish in which the Americans lost 16 dead and 52 wounded. Then on July 1 the Spanish showed they could fight.

At El Caney the American casualties were 81 dead and 360

wounded. The American artillery did a job there; a Spanish fort was "simply punched to pieces" and the garrison was practically all killed. At nearby San Juan Hill, although the artillery was a failure, the Rough Riders with Theodore Roosevelt at their head were immensely helped in their successful charge by Gatling machine guns. "It was terrible when your guns opened—always," said a Spanish officer. "They went b-r-r-r, like a lawn mower cutting the grass over our trenches. We could not stick a finger up when you fired without getting it cut off." Shafter's forces suffered over a thousand casualties.

"We are within measurable distance of a terrible military disaster," Colonel Roosevelt wrote. On July 3, as the American army settled down to besiege Santiago, Roosevelt sent off an urgent plea to Senator Lodge: "Tell the President for Heaven's sake to send us every regiment and above all every battery possible. We have won so far at a heavy cost, but the Spaniards fight very hard and charging these intrenchments against modern rifles is terrible. . . . We *must* have help—thousands of men, batteries, and *food* and ammunition."

That same day the war was won—at sea. Admiral Cervera, having been bottled up in Santiago harbor for five weeks, tried to run the blockade and escape. He did not make it. The Americans had six heavy ships to four; they had far heavier guns. The Spaniards were short of ammunition. They were terrible marksmen. Their fleet was destroyed. The American casualties were one dead, one seriously wounded. Although Santiago was surrendered on July 17, the Spanish were not conquered on land. But the loss of fleets in both the Pacific and the Caribbean left them hopelessly incompetent to defend their colonies. Already by July 27 John Hay could write to Roosevelt: "It has been a splendid little war. . . ."

Glorious, but not severe. Perhaps it was that combination of qualities that commended it to so many. The only religious denominations to oppose it seriously were the Quakers and the Unitarians. Observers in all parts of the country reported its giddy popularity.

Jewish immigrants on the Lower East Side saw Spain as the country of the Inquisition, Cubans as oppressed people, and the war was an opportunity to prove their devotion to their new country. Thirteen-year-old Sinclair Lewis ran away from his home in

Minnesota and walked the ten miles to Melrose. He intended there to catch a train to Minneapolis to enlist as a drummer boy and help free the Cubans, but his father caught him and took him home. The President called up four companies of troops from Colorado, but Governor Alva Adams wanted to send twelve even though the fiscal condition of the states was so bad that he had to borrow the money from his friends to meet the expenses of raising the men: "all the best youths of the State are volunteering, . . . young fellows throwing up places worth $10,000 a year." Scholarly Beatrice Webb, visiting from England, went to the Fourth of July exercises in a crowded hall in San Francisco: "The note of the whole thing was the unique character of American Institutions—the Americans being the chosen people who had, by their own greatness of soul, *discovered freedom,* and who were now to carry it to other races (notably to the Cubans)."

By the time the preliminary peace was signed on August 12, the factional line-up in the United States had changed markedly. Businessmen who early in 1898 had opposed war now wanted to keep all colonies as markets in themselves, as sources of raw materials, and as stepping stones to the great markets of China. Early in the war Albert J. Beveridge, racing for a Senate seat from Indiana, warned: "American factories are making more than the American people can use; American soil is producing more than they can consume. Fate has written our policy for us; the trade of the world must and shall be ours." Conversely many who had favored intervention to free Cuba came to oppose American action to obtain colonies. Thus, before war came, Marshall Field & Co. had joined six other leading Chicago firms in informing McKinley that they would "deprecate war with Spain except as a last resort." But during the war the great merchant smilingly congratulated an expansionist speaker on his address to the Literary Club of Chicago. Now Henry Lloyd wrote scornfully: "Our business men are all poll-parrotting the cry that American production has outrun American consumption and we must seek markets for the surplus abroad." But on May 4 Lloyd had written a friend that "a nation should be a gentleman" and that "no gentleman would stand by while a Spanish brute was kicking the life out of a Cuban baby."

In the *Democratic Magazine* for July, John Peter Altgeld warmly supported the war effort and claimed that credit for it belonged to his party. He wanted a strong navy; he also wanted the expansion of foreign trade on the basis of reciprocity. He thought the United States should take the Spanish colony of Puerto Rico, and that Cuba, Haiti and Santo Domingo should be annexed if their peoples desired it. He wanted assurances of permanent American access to "a number of the best harbors of the Philippines. . . ." But he insisted that those islands should be left to govern themselves. On that point he differed from Roosevelt, who on June 12 wrote Lodge that peace should not be made without guarantees that "we get Porto Rico and the Philippines as well as secure the independence of Cuba."

What did the President want? He had jotted down: "While we are conducting the war and until its conclusion, we must keep all we get; when the war is over we must keep what we want." But was he even sure he wanted Hawaii? In the spring of 1897, alarmed at signs of Japanese interest there, he had negotiated with the Hawaiian government a treaty of annexation. But the two-thirds majority in the Senate needed to ratify it could not be mustered. In March 1898 the Republicans abandoned the treaty and determined to annex Hawaii by vote of Congress, which would require only a simple majority in each House. This effort ran into the barrier of Tom Reed. After war started, Lodge thought that McKinley might just annex the islands by proclamation as a war measure. Such a step seemed dangerously bold. But by early June annexationists in the House knew they could get the 219 votes needed to override the Speaker and bring the resolution before the House. At last McKinley knew his own mind, and it was announced on June 4 that he favored annexation. "We need Hawaii just as much and a good deal more than we did California," he told his secretary. "It is manifest destiny." The joint resolution passed 209 to 91 in the House, 42 to 21 in the Senate. Hawaii became a territory.

As for Cuba, at least nominal independence was almost sure to be her final fate. But for the moment the American army reigned. The President had directed the occupation to be "as free from severity as possible," but the controls thought necessary proved to be strict; Cubans after all were not white men. No armed Cuban could enter Santiago. The ringing of church bells was banned in Havana. The occupation decreed stringent rules on observance of the Sabbath. It prohibited gambling.

McKinley insisted that Spain by the peace treaty should cede

Puerto Rico to the United States. Plus an island in the Ladrones with a harbor for a coaling station. Plus a port in the Philippines. To help American trade he wanted Manila as a foothold in the Far East, but he also had denounced "greed of conquest." Save for Manila, he was inclined in early June of 1898 to leave the Philippines under Spanish control. Such a policy might have been satisfactory even to Lodge, who wrote Roosevelt that Manila was "the great prize, and the thing which will give us the Eastern trade." But Senator Platt wrote McKinley after a tour of Connecticut that nine tenths of the people there wanted to keep the Philippines and would consider Spain's retention of any part of the archipelago as our failure "to discharge the greatest moral obligation which could be conceived." The *Baptist Union* spoke for widespread missionary feelings: "A still higher obligation rests upon us. . . . The conquest by force of arms must be followed up by conquest for Christ."

Other governments made themselves heard. In July Britain indicated that she would regard American retention of the Philippines with favor. Japan declared that to preserve peace in the Far East she would be willing either to see the United States alone keep the archipelago or that she herself would join us in a three-power protectorate. The conclusive obstacle to leaving part of the Philippines in the hands of Spain was provided by Filipino insurgent armies under Emilio Aguinaldo: it became clear that Spain could not keep control. For a time it seemed that Aguinaldo might even take Manila before American forces could occupy it. McKinley became convinced that an American naval station at Manila would be secure only if the United States controlled all of Luzon. In mid-September he instructed the five commissioners who were in Paris negotiating the terms of peace to demand all of Luzon and an Open Door throughout the Philippines.

Two weeks later the general who had commanded the second Philippine expedition arrived back in Washington. In a memorandum to the President he set forth the commercial potential of the Philippines and the great extension of their trade that could result if her resources were "explored with American energy." But this happy outcome could not occur if the islands were split up. By October McKinley was persuaded. Speaking in Iowa during the Congressional campaign he declared: "We have good money, we have ample revenues, we have unquestioned national credit, but what we want is new markets, and as trade follows the flag it looks very much as if we were going to have new markets." On October 26 he sent word to Paris: "The cession must be of the whole archipelago or none. The latter is wholly inadmissible, and the former must therefore be required."

More than a year after he concluded to keep the Philippines, President McKinley one morning received the General Missionary Committee of the Methodist Episcopal Church, one of the more active expansionist groups. He had not wanted, he told them, to keep the archipelago. But there were insuperable obstacles to any means of getting rid of them.

> I walked the floor of the White House night after night until midnight; and I am not ashamed to tell you, gentlemen, that I went down on my knees and prayed Almighty God for light and guidance more than one night. And one night it came to me late this way— I don't know how it was, but it came . . . that there was nothing left for us to do but to take them all, and to educate the Filipinos, and uplift and civilize and Christianize them, and by God's grace do the very best we could for them, as our fellow-men for whom Christ also died.

Then he went to bed and slept soundly.

Questions had emerged: Could Americans set their domestic economy in order so that the marvelous new powers of production could be used to reduce need? They evaded the question by seeking to sell their surpluses in foreign markets or to Federal, state, and local governments. Were Americans fit to govern themselves? They evaded the question by shouting that Filipinos and Negroes were not. The new empire was to provide both bread and circuses.

Some sort of revolution had obviously occurred in the relations of the United States to other nations, but historians have been far from unanimous in defining its nature. Recent books by both Ernest R. May and Howard K. Beale have included in their titles the notion that the turn of the century was the time of "the rise of America to world power." This interpretation seems untenable. Revising slightly a formulation by Thomas A. Bailey, it seems more in line with the facts to say that the United States was a power from the Declaration of Independence forward, a world power after the War of 1812, and a great power by the time of the Civil War. What happened in 1898 was that we acquired for the first time noncontiguous colonies with substantial populations. Probably even more important was the changed tone of our diplomacy and of popular American demands upon it. In the words of Norman A. Graebner, the "newly acquired sense of moral obligation" prompted the United States to abandon "those principles of statecraft which had guided it through its first century of independence." It is not easy to see McKinley as having a stronger "sense of moral obligation" than, say, John Quincy Adams. But the rest of Graebner's argument is true and profound. John Quincy Adams was a moral man; he also had a laudable desire to mind his own business and a keen grasp of reality. Traditional American policy had been limited to what American power could hope to achieve. Although the leaders of the United States repeatedly applauded the struggles of other peoples for independence and democracy, they also made clear that we would not lift a finger to help them. They would have to liberate themselves. Our duty was to set a good example, not to free the world. This realism gave birth to the tradition of recognizing any government that actually ruled a country. It also produced the Monroe Doctrine, a great policy exactly because we could in general enforce it. The new American objectives, neither so precise nor so limited, proved endlessly dangerous. And they were symptomatic, as will be seen later, of a growing self-delusion that touched many spheres of American life and thought.

Senator: WILKINSON CALL

Florida before the Civil War was settled only in spots. Barring Spanish settlements, it was frontier, rich in resources, poor in men and capital to exploit them. It offered rich soil for a young man of good family and sufficient ambition to flourish in.

Wilkinson Call (1834–1910), born in Kentucky, was taken to Florida as a boy. He served the Everglade State as an officer for the Confederate States of America. In Jacksonville after Appomattox, he watched his town grow to become, for a time, the largest in the state. Florida land booms were not invented in the twentieth century; like all speculative frenzies, the Jacksonville boom provided fine opportunities for clever local operators to grow with the community. Call grew. Practicing law and maneuvering in politics, he won election to the United States Senate in 1879. He was so likable and accommodating that a grateful legislature sent him back in 1885 and 1891, despite (or because of?) the fact that his first two terms had been quite unremarkable. Then, with much shilly-shally, he found a cause. He drifted into imperialism.

None of his colleagues believed that Call had thought through the problem. John T. Morgan of Alabama, for instance, had clear visions of what overseas expansion might mean for an impoverished South, especially if it were linked to the construction of a Panama Canal. But Call seemed for a while not to know whether he was for or against new colonies; indeed, he seemed unable to distinguish one part of the Pacific from another. When Grover Cleveland was holding out against the annexation of Hawaii, Call explained that the President was duty-bound to defend the Hawaiian monarchy because it was guaranteed by the Berlin Treaty of 1889. His false reference was to a tripartite treaty on Samoa. But the tide of imperialism swelled for many reasons, some of them implausible: Populists could favor war against Spain in the hope that the administration would have to coin silver to meet the costs of conflict. Call established ties with the Junta that was leading the revolt in Cuba and sought ways for his family to profit from the situation. Profit they did, from many situations. A son was named to be a United States district judge in 1913, after the former Senator had died. Although Wilkinson Call did not succeed in founding a dynasty like the Bankheads in Alabama or the Byrds in Virginia, his vision, usually cloudy on matters of State, was always sharp when the main chance lay before him.

PART THREE

1898–1914
Wherein Americans Go
to Live in the Clouds

CHAPTER 10

Success

George W. Perkins never achieved his ambition to unite three great life insurance companies, but in 1901 he had reason to be proud. Only 39 years old, he was drawing $50,000 a year as a vice-president of New York Life Insurance. On a visit to Washington on March 2, he was pondering a decision so important that he sat up until 1 a.m. discussing it with Charles G. Dawes. J. P. Morgan had offered to take Perkins as a full partner, with a guarantee of $300,000 per year profit. "Perkins is not avaricious of money, but seeks power," Dawes noted. Perkins took the offer, and got the power. By August he was chairman of the finance committee of the new International Harvester Company which Morgan had helped to create. In November he was negotiating the Northern Securities deal, intended to eliminate competition among the Western railroad empires of James J. Hill and Edward H. Harriman. Perkins, wrote Dawes, had a "rare combination of two qualities so seldom found together—great energy and untiring and unfailing patience." Even while "scaling the cliffs of the business world" Perkins kept his "natural, hearty and unaffected methods. . . ."

Perkins' senior associate was cold, hard, domineering. J. P. Morgan was more powerful than the President of the United States, and knew it. It had been Morgan, not the Treasury, who saved the gold standard. And it was Morgan who reorganized much of the nation's railroad network. As far back as 1888 Charles Francis Adams, president of the Union Pacific, had predicted the creation of giant systems with 20,000 miles of track each. It had happened.

As late as 1895 many regions still had independent railroads competing against each other. But the depression after 1893 put a third of the trackage in the country in the hands of receivers; Francis Lynde Stetson said that consolidation was made necessary by "the inability of the corporations to meet their fixed charges, an inability which had been due largely to the ruinous reduction of railroad rates, partly through legislation and partly through ruinous competition." Then Morgan moved into the Southeast. In 1894 he picked up the bankrupt Richmond Terminal Company and created the Southern—7,500 miles. In 1900 he formed the Seaboard Air Line running south from Washington along the coast—2,600 miles. He got the Plant System, from Charleston to Tampa, and bought stock control of the Louisville & Nashville. Combined in 1902 as the Atlantic Coast Line, the system criss-crossed the whole Southeast—10,000 miles.

The freight traffic on Southern rivers declined drastically, but the ocean ports were favored by low railroad rates. They also benefited from Federal expenditures to improve rivers and har-bors: $8 million for New Orleans, nearly as much for Galveston, $3 million for Mobile. Western products began to flow south over the shortest and best route to the seaboard. Ten times as much flour was shipped from the South in 1901 as in 1880. Nearly twice as much cotton. Much more lumber, coal, pig iron, tobacco, oil. Exports from the Gulf ports nearly quadrupled in the two decades after 1892: New Orleans was second only to New York, and Galveston was third.

Morgan's operations did not always end happily. He had three rules in reorganizing railroads. J. P. Morgan and Company must dominate the board of directors. Competition must be minimized. Fixed charges must be reduced to a figure that can always be met. But his methods of achieving the third goal contradicted them-selves. To compensate bondholders for lower interest rates he gave them stock. But then the road could not issue stock to raise working capital, so it had to issue more bonds. The greater quan-tity of bonds outstanding could offset the reduction in interest rates. In 1903 Morgan began trying to build a transportation monopoly in New England, including trolley systems and coastal shipping. As a basis he used the New Haven Railroad. The road's capitalization in 1903 was $93 million; ten years later, $417 mil-lion. Only some $20 million went into improving the properties. In pursuit of monopoly the New Haven had paid exorbitant prices for unprofitable lines. It paid, for instance, more than $36 million for the New York, Westchester and Boston Railway. That sounds fair enough. But the word "Boston" in the firm's name was honorific only. The line ran from upper New York City to Mt. Vernon and White Plains; it was 18 miles long. Two million dollars per mile was a lot to pay for a railroad that was losing $1,250,000 per year.

The National Biscuit Company had already learned that an effort to drive out or buy out competitiors can be disastrous. Formed by merger in 1898, the company originally sought to control competition, but within four years it had determined to buy out no competitors. Now its focus was on cutting costs and improving sales techniques. It bought its raw materials as cheaply as possible in huge quantities. It centralized its manufacturing, especially in the New York and Chicago plants near big markets. It improved plant layout and production processes. It stopped selling in bulk to wholesalers, and began selling small packages under brand names directly to retailers. And it launched a big advertising program to build demand for its "Uneeda Biscuit" brands. By 1909 National Biscuit was one of the biggest industrial firms in the country, catering mainly to urban customers. But it seemed a pigmy compared to the railroad organizations.

The country by 1906 had been divided among seven systems. Morgan controlled the Southeast, and he had also helped to reorganize the Erie, the Philadelphia & Reading, the Lehigh Valley, and the Northern Pacific. Controlling the latter as well as the Great Northern, James J. Hill held the Northwest. Hill for many purposes was allied to Morgan. So were the Vanderbilt interests, with 22,500 miles from New York to the Midwest. So were the Pennsylvania interests, with over 20,000 miles running west from Pennsylvania and Maryland. So, for a brief time, were the railroads of Edward H. Harriman, who emerged as the sole dangerous rival to Morgan in matters of railroad finance by his conquest of the reorganized Union Pacific in 1898.

Harriman was just as cold as Morgan, just as ruthless. And he was not above looting a railroad if he felt like it. He and president James Stillman of the National City Bank headed a syndicate about 1898 which bought up the stock of the Chicago & Alton. The road had been prosperous, paying a steady 8 per cent on its common stock. The new management nearly trebled its capitalization—an additional $75 million in securities, while spending only $18 million for improvements. Offering 3 per cent bonds to other buyers, including New York Life Insurance, at 90, they sold the same bonds to themselves at 65. By such deals the insiders took a profit of over $23 million.

But Harriman also knew how to run a railroad. Backed financially by Jacob Schiff of Kuhn, Loeb, who had strong connections in Hamburg and Berlin, Harriman acquired strong stock interests in the New York Central, the Chicago & Northwestern, and the Baltimore & Ohio. By alliances he affected the operations of another 16,000 miles of track. And he directly controlled 25,000 miles including the Union Pacific, the Central Pacific, and the Southern Pacific, on which more than 70,000 men were employed. He made great physical improvements in his properties. On the Oregon Short Line, right-of-way was regraded so that no grade was more than 44 feet to the mile; track was reballasted; carrying capacity was increased 75 per cent. In the Rocky Mountains, other railroads needed two locomotives to move 15 or 20 freight cars up their steep grades. But on the mountain division of the Union Pacific, a single locomotive could handle 35 to 45 cars; east of Cheyenne, one locomotive could move 50 to 75 loaded cars. Commented General Grenville M. Dodge, who had built the original line, "This shows where the great net earnings of the Union Pacific come from."

Scarcely less sweeping were Harriman's administrative reforms. Any proposal for investment, even a minor one, had to be approved by Harriman himself. Julius Kruttschnitt, director of operation and maintenance with offices in Chicago, investigated and supervised the whole system. Actual operations were in the hands of the vice-president in charge of each of the seven railroads. Thus the system got seven independent solutions to many problems, and could choose the best one. Each railroad in turn was cut up into semiautonomous divisions on a geographical basis. A so-called unit system was introduced by which all of the division officers were located at the office of the division superintendent. As a result, correspondence was reduced by some 30 to 50 per cent—an estimated saving of 500,000 letters a year. Many routine reports were dispensed with. But statistics and accounting were used in ways unknown to smaller organizations. Ton-mile and passenger-mile figures were watched carefully, and from them a host of other computations were made. All of the 75,000 freight cars on the system were pooled. The Chicago office got, each day, reports of the loaded and empty cars at each point, cars in transit, orders for loading, cars interchanged with other railroads, cars out of order for repairs. Within two years, the movement of empty freight cars on the system had been reduced by 54 million car-miles.

Harriman was by no means content to have achieved this empire within the United States. Connecting up with his railroads on the Pacific Coast he operated 35,000 miles of steamship lines to the Far East. In 1905 he got the idea of reaching farther yet. He began efforts to buy the Southern Manchuria Railway from Russia and to secure transit rights on the Trans-Siberia Railroad. Having thus reached the Atlantic, presumably he would have put another fleet on that ocean and bought a railroad or two east of the Mississippi. This scheme was frustrated in 1905 by the currents of Japanese politics. Then it got caught in complicated international maneuvers which found Great Britain hesitant to offend Japan or Russia because of her fears of Germany in Europe. Harriman died in 1910 without having realized his plan for a round-the-world transportation system.

Combinations of the railroads were motivated by the ambitions of such grandiose men. Or they came from the desire of investment bankers to earn promoters' profits and commissions from the issue of securities. Or they were forced by the need for a revised capital structure which would make possible an escape from bankruptcy. Or they were forced by the need to eliminate competition in order to keep rates up. Ironically, the Interstate Commerce Act, by its prohibition of the pooling of traffic, stimulated actual merger of railroads. The Supreme Court contributed to the same effect by holding in *U.S.* v. *Trans-Missouri Freight Association* (1897) that a combination to fix railroad rates violated the Sherman Anti-Trust Act.

In manufacturing, most combinations heretofore had been of companies producing consumer goods. But the great combination movement at the turn of the century took place among firms that produced for sale to other firms; that is, in the producers' goods industries. Also, whereas earlier combinations had usually originated with and been financed by the industrialists themselves, now the initiative and capital often came from outsiders, especially from Wall Street. In 1890 an industrial firm with a capital of $10 million was a rarity, but by 1905 most major industries had a company ten times that size, and in United States Steel the country got its first billion-dollar corporation.

As with National Biscuit, the desire to control production and prices was crucial to the formation of United States Rubber. Charles A. Flint, a large rubber importer, promoted the merger of four companies, and by 1898 the new organization produced 75 per cent of the country's rubber boots, shoes, and gloves. But already the company was emphasizing internal reforms and cost reduction. It consolidated purchasing so that it could buy in large quantities at low prices, and it set up a central sales office in New York with branches elsewhere. It instituted uniform cost accounting so that headquarters would get some information on profit and loss. It reduced the number of brands it made, shut down the unprofitable plants, and centralized manufacturing in the most efficient ones.

Carnegie Steel showed what efficiency meant. The firm led the United States to a position where in 1914 its production of steel was greater than that of Great Britain, Germany, and France combined. The device used was technology. Great advances in labor saving occurred in the decade preceding 1898, chiefly in the use of electricity to drive automatic machinery. In that year Henry Frick said that although the firm's output had risen threefold in the last few years, the number of men needed had decreased by 400. To visitors the mills seemed almost devoid of men. (There were costs, but many of them were not paid by the company. Pittsburgh was dirty, smoky, and smelly; its politics and those of Pennsylvania were so "abjectly corrupt that state and city have become bye-words, even among American politicians." But the company executives took no civic responsibility and devoted themselves solely to business, with the intention of retiring at 45 and hying off to New York or Europe in the fashion of their mentors Carnegie and Frick.)

When Carnegie Steel in 1901 became part of the newly formed U.S. Steel, several motives were at work. The first moves were defensive. By 1896 the rich iron of the Mesabi Range was owned by three companies: Rockefeller's Consolidated Iron Mines, the Minnesota Mining Company, and the Oliver Mining Company. Iron and steel mills feared that they might be blocked off from their raw material. Carnegie joined with Henry Oliver to buy

Rockefeller's holdings. In 1898 Judge Elbert H. Gary merged Minnesota Mining with Chicago's Illinois Steel and with Lorain Steel to form Federal Steel—with capital provided by J. P. Morgan. Then Republic Steel was formed by merger, as was National Steel. Steel fabricators became frightened by the growing size of their suppliers, and they began to unite. American Wire & Steel was formed. National Tube. These new giants set up their own blast furnaces and rolling mills, and began to cancel their contracts with Carnegie for steel ingots. In return he began to consider turning out finished products.

At the famous Simmons dinner on 12 December 1900, J. P. Morgan learned that the outlook for steel was good, and he scented handsome commissions from public sale of steel securities. Andrew Carnegie, eager to retire from business and turn to philanthropy, had the problem of liquidating his enormous sunk investment in his steel company. When he announced his willingness to accept payment in bonds in a new firm, thus reducing the size of the public issue that Morgan would have to underwrite, the deal was set. The great quantity of bonds that Carnegie demanded meant that only an enormous capitalization could give the new firm a balanced capital structure. So Morgan brought together Carnegie, Federal, National, six giant fabricating firms, which continued as semi-autonomous operating companies while U.S. Steel became the holding company with financial control of all of them.

Carnegie in effect had already set this pattern. When he acquired the Frick Coke Company in 1889, it continued as an independent firm, and sold its output to the steel firm by contract. The same rule held as ore mining companies and Great Lakes shipping firms were picked up; relatively little was done to coordinate mining, shipping, and manufacturing. But this lack of systematic integration was rare among the new giants being formed, and U.S. Steel was virtually unique in being a holding company only. In coal mining, in paper making, in explosives, combination was quickly followed by efforts to integrate the acquisition of raw materials with manufacturing and marketing.

Accompanying and making possible the merger movement was the development of a device for the easy transfer of ownership in manufacturing firms—a public market for industrial securities. Most manufacturing firms had been small, and little known, and owned by a family or a small circle of partners who worked in the business. Many were not even corporations in 1893. Trading on Wall Street was confined to government and railroad securities. Henry Varnum Poor had long been publishing his yearly manual on railroad securities, but about 1895 he rejected the idea of adding to it an industrial supplement. He saw no future in industrials. The prognosis was wrecked by two influences: increasing issue of preferred stock, and experience during the depression. As attorney for the Sugar Trust, John R. Dos Passos had noted that the value of a firm's securities could be increased if it replaced an all-purpose issue with a variety of securities. Because their sales volume fluctuated widely, most industrialists had a horror of issuing bonds—the type of security that investment bankers were accustomed to. But a manufacturing company could issue preferred stock, thought to represent safe year-to-year earnings and usually backed by physical assets, to appeal to persons seeking sound investment value. Most preferreds specified a 7 or 8 per cent dividend, usually cumulative. For speculators who would accept more risk if a chance for growth value went with it, a firm could issue common stock.

In 1893 some thirty industrial concerns had the prices of their securities quoted in the financial journals. The next four years showed that railroad securities were not so safe after all. Of the two most actively traded railroad preferreds, the Wabash paid no dividends, and the preferred of the Northern Pacific was scaled down in a reorganization. Meanwhile the industrial preferred issues of more than $10 million did very well. General Electric paid no dividends—but only because it was conserving its cash. American Tobacco and U.S. Rubber paid dividends regularly. By 1897 more than 200 industrials were being quoted.

J. P. Morgan and Company confirmed the point in 1898 when it organized a syndicate to form the Federal Steel Company. In the next four years Morgan was the only one of the large investment banks to play a leading role in the merger movement; most of the new combinations were set up by independent promoters like Dos Passos. By 1902 there was widespread interest in the market quotations of new firms such as U.S. Steel, International Harvester, American Can, United Fruit, American Smelting & Refining. In manufacturing, as in railroads, the separation of ownership from management had begun.

The mergers around 1900 were a culmination of the business opportunities created by the railroads and expanding urban markets. In metal fabricating and in the processing of farm products, the firms developed internal organizations and types of market relations that would remain basically the same for the next half-century. The era of administered prices had arrived. No longer would prices be set by competition. In industries dominated by one or a few large firms, the executives of a company would henceforth compute their costs of production, add on the margin of profit they deemed desirable, and announce the sum as their price.

After 1900 the most sweeping economic changes would come in the great clusters of industries that exploited three new technical inventions—electricity, the internal-combustion engine, and industrial chemistry. The first to have a major impact was electricity. Dynamos were produced in 1895 for a giant hydroelectric installation at Niagara Falls. In city after city, generating stations were built. Transmission lines were strung. By World War I, electric trolleys were running over 40,000 miles of track. Western Union, a monopoly since 1866, had 76,000 miles of wire then; 827,000 in 1896; twice that in 1914. The country in 1896 had one telephone for every 175 people; in 1914, one for 10. The jump in per capita use of electric devices was reinforced by a jump in population: from 67 million in 1893 to 99 million in 1914.

The rise in population helped to keep the construction of buildings in its wonted place as the chief single outlet for investment. Railroads until 1915 continued to be the second most important consumers of capital. But the iron and steel industry found itself only in fourth place as it was passed by the electric-utilities industry.

The burgeoning demand for copper wire led Henry H. Rogers of Standard Oil to join Marcus Daly in setting up the Amalgamated Copper Company. While J. P. Morgan was reorganizing railroads and several major industries, the stupendous profits from Standard Oil—although only partially divided among the few owners—flowed out in all directions to grasp other giant companies. The Rockefellers invested in iron ore in the Mesabi Range and controlled the Colorado Fuel and Iron Company. Henry Payne invested in a seat in the Senate. Henry M. Flagler, who had negotiated with railroads for Standard Oil and arranged those fat rebates, took his money to Florida where he built railroads and luxury hotels and opened up Key West. Standard Oil men got together with William C. Whitney and forced Buck Duke to let them into American Tobacco.

Of all the pioneers in electrical applications, none was so versatile as Thomas Alva Edison. Witty, self-educated, Edison worked twenty hours a day and suffered from neuralgia and dyspepsia. Deaf himself, he patented the first phonograph in 1877. Two years later he patented the carbon filament lamp, and went on to perfect a system for incandescent electric lighting and power. He produced a workable motion-picture camera. He became a folk hero of the new Age of Electricity. But it tells us much of that age to know that J. P. Morgan in 1892 did not hesitate to sell Edison General Electric out from under the inventor and to drop his name from the corporate title.

Edison's name remained in the titles of many utility companies, and in 1896 he journeyed to Long Island to the annual meeting of the Association of Edison Illuminating Companies. There he met Henry Ford, who had been employed for five years as an engineer at the Edison Company in Detroit. Ford had also been working on the use of an internal-combustion, gasoline-burning engine to power an automobile. Sitting beside Edison at the banquet table, he sketched out his ideas about ignition and piston-action on the back of a menu. At last Edison thumped the table and exclaimed, "Young man, that's the thing! You have it—the self-contained unit carrying its own fuel with it! Keep at it!"

Ford kept at it. Trained in the infant electrical industry, he did as much as anybody to show the manufacturing potential in discarding steam power in the factory and replacing it by the new electric motors to power individual machines. Ford benefited from other recent advances. Metal-cutting machines could be run much faster because of new harder high-speed steels such as that developed by Frederick W. Taylor in 1900. By that time many drills and lathes were so automatic that one man could oversee a battery of them.

The Ford Motor Company opened its first plant in 1903, with a paid-in capital of $28,500. A Detroit lawyer, Horace H. Rackham, invested $5,000. The coal dealer James Couzens took charge of the Ford office and invested $2,500. Within a decade Rackham and Couzens were millionaires. The new firm for a few months was hard-pressed to pay its bills, but by autumn receipts were comfortably above expenses. Thus the company was able to finance its enormous expansion without issuing stock to the public or resorting to bankers.

Ford's associates later said that he intended from the beginning to make a car that would retail for $500. But the company did not start out that way: its cheapest runabout the first year sold for $800. In the spring of 1906 the directors accepted Ford's view. He wanted to make a strong car that would hold up on the miserable American roads. He wanted a car that would ride high over muddy gulleys and ruts. To appeal to the great middle-class market of the United States, he wanted a car that could be mass-produced and sold cheaply. The first Model T was marketed in 1908, and Ford sold 10,000 cars. Marketing his cars through a few branches in big cities and through hundreds of dealers, the company in 1909 built its first branch assembly plant, at Kansas City. Also, to pay for the huge new Highland Park factory in Detroit, it raised the prices of the Model T.

Sales tended steadily upward, and the price steadily downward, as Ford abandoned production of all other models. To cut costs and speed production, he began painting all Model T's black. In 1913 the minimum price came down to $550, and sales were 168,000 cars. The next year sales jumped to 248,000, and the minimum price fell to $490. Henry Ford had reached his goal. And this during years when the cost-of-living index was rising from 88 in 1903 to 100 in 1914. Ford in 1914 produced 45 per cent of all the automobiles made in the United States.

By the systematic use of mass-production methods this large output was transformed into steadily falling costs. In 1913–1914 the Highland Park plant got the first moving assembly-line in any metal-working factory. "The idea came in a general way," wrote Ford later, "from the overhead trolley that the Chicago packers use in dressing beef." Before each job at Highland Park was minutely subdivided and carried past the workers on a continuously moving belt or chain, assembly of a chassis took 12½ man-hours of labor. In January 1913, it took 1 hour 33 minutes.

As the value of motor vehicles produced inched upward from $6 million in 1900 to $420 million in 1914, other major industries were transformed. Paint factories found a market for lacquers (especially black). Harvey Firestone in 1900 started a small plant

*Ford Motor Company's first moving assembly line, which was
located in Highland Park, Michigan, in 1913. This photograph shows
the exterior use of the Ford building for lowering the auto body
onto the chassis.* (Courtesy of Ford Motor Company.)

at Akron to produce solid rubber treads for wagons and buggies,
but in 1906 he took an order from Ford for 2,000 sets of pneu-
matic tires. Steel mills were called upon to produce a growing
variety of alloys for special purposes, and steel production went
from 5 million tons in 1892, to 10 million in 1900, to 20 million
in 1905, to 31 million in 1913. Output of electric power quadrupled
from 1902 to 1912. The petroleum industry, from its inception
producing chiefly kerosene, much of it for foreign markets, now
had a great new market at home. It also had a great new source
of supply to supplement the Lima-Indiana fields. In January 1901
the first of the Southwestern deposits was tapped. When the
Spindletop well at Beaumont, Texas, blew in and sent a tower of

pure crude 200 feet in the air, it "was the wonder and puzzle of the world." No previous well in the United States had been rated at more than 6,000 barrels a day, but Spindletop yielded 70,000. Henceforth the kings of cattle and cotton had to share power with the kings of oil, and American output of crude petroleum went from 63 million barrels in 1900 to 281 million in 1915.

The third of the great new clusters of industries to arise from new technologies after 1900 was industrial chemicals, and Du Pont was already pre-eminent. A century old in 1902, producer of gunpowder and other explosives, it had always been family owned and managed, but now the ruling generation of elders wanted to sell out. The company was bought for $12 million—by three young Du Pont cousins, none of them yet 40. Coleman, the eldest, was an engineer. Pierre was a chemist trained at the Massachusetts Institute of Technology who had worked on the development of smokeless gunpowder. Alfred was experienced in the manufacture of blasting powder.

The new management at once began to expand and diversify. For three decades Du Pont, working through the Gunpowder Trade Association, had controlled prices in the industry. But recent Supreme Court decisions suggested that existing arrangements might be illegal, and once again the Sherman Act of 1890 prompted steps toward a tighter monopoly. Du Pont bought out its only large rival in explosives, Laflin and Rand. It acquired more than sixty other companies and ventured far beyond the field of explosives—into nitrocellulose, into lacquers, into artificial leather. It shut down inefficient plants. It combined sales offices. More important for the future, it expanded its systematic research. A laboratory for explosives research was set up in 1902. Among its contributions to industrial blasting were developments in low-freezing dynamite. By 1906 the firm's research budget was $300,000 a year.

Du Pont also pioneered in systematic organization. In 1903 it set up one of the earliest corporate executive committees, which from the start included executives who were not members of the family. The task of this group of top executives was to stay free of details and to determine general policy. The function of accounting was re-thought, so that it was not simply a record of the past but a guide for the future. A special duty of the executive committee was to determine investment expenditures, so that not a dollar would be put into one part of the business if it could used more effectively elsewhere. Much attention was devoted to safety, to the psychology of employees, to personnel policy. A system of employees' bonuses was instituted in 1905.

Most skilled workers after 1898 were able to do well for themselves. The expansion of industry meant a brisk demand for carpenters and other construction workers, for printers, for locomotive engineers, for puddlers in steel mills, for machinists. Average earnings of workers in manufacturing rose from 15 cents an hour in 1890 to 22 cents in 1914, while the cost-of-living index went only from 91 to 100. The result was an increase of 37 per cent in average real hourly earnings. The favored situation of skilled workers also brought a great increase in trade union membership —from less than 500,000 in 1897 to more than 2½ million in 1914.

Many farmers too shared in prosperity. Ironically, they got the increase they had demanded in the monetary stock—but under the gold standard. After 1887 a flood of gold from the Rand fields in South Africa, the strikes in the Klondike, the new cyanide process for extracting gold from low-grade ores—from 1896 to 1914, the world's supply of monetary gold doubled. Even more helpful to farm prices was the combination of rapid urban growth with a marked slackening in the rate of growth of agricultural output. In the 16 years before 1898, farm output increased 46 per cent; from 1898 to 1914, only 22 per cent. The rural population rose less than 25 per cent from 1890 to 1910, while the urban population almost doubled. By 1920 most Americans lived in cities and towns. From these factors came sharp increases in the prices of farm staples. Cotton, less than a nickel a pound in 1894, sold steadily for at least twice that after 1903. Corn, 21 cents a bushel in 1896, hit 60 cents in 1903, and held high. Wheat prices edged up more slowly, but from 1907 to 1914 they did not fall below 80 cents a bushel, whereas they had been only 50 cents in 1895. It was with keen awareness of the realities that Ellen Glasgow in *Barren Ground* made Dorinda Oakley a success at farming whereas her father had failed at it a generation earlier. (And the novel is realistic too in showing a woman as a success in agriculture. Many were.)

Countless immigrants also began to climb the ladder. In 1900 the foreign-born and their children were 76 per cent of the population of New York, and East European Jews formed a majority of the students at the city's free colleges. Some parents had been instructed even before leaving their homelands on how to behave in the United States. *Di yuden in America,* a popular guidebook for Jewish immigrants published at Odessa in 1881, advised: "Forget your past, your customs, your ideals. . . . A bit of advice for you: Do not take a moment's rest. Run, do, work and keep your own good in mind." The formula could pay off.

Joseph Barondess landed in New York in 1888. He peddled, then worked in a paint factory, then a sugar refinery, then began to work his way up in garment trades—from pants, to shirts, to cloaks. He led the cloakmaker's strike of 1895 and served time in jail. Late in the decade he left the labor movement to enter the insurance business. In 1910 he was named to the city's Board of Education. The busy insurance agent declared: "Until the Ideal Society will be realized, I have certain duties to perform towards my clients, for which they pay." Some men found dazzling opportunities in real-estate deals. As the population of the Brownsville section of Brooklyn climbed from 10,000 to 60,000 between 1899 and 1904, lots in the five years rose in value from $200 to $5,000 and even $10,000.

Other traditional methods of making money could still work also—such as political influence. While Charles Tyson Yerkes was beaten in his effort to get a 50-year streetcar franchise from Chicago's aldermen, capitalists in Philadelphia proved that governments could still be bent to private ends. The city owned and operated a gas works. It furnished the city with free gas to light the streets. It also sold to residents, and its price had fallen from $3 a thousand cubic feet in 1866 to $1 in 1897. Its payroll was padded with political appointees, but in 1896 it showed net earnings after taxes and interest of more than $500,000. That year Mayor Charles F. Warwick and the common council agreed publicly that the gas works should be held forever by the city, with the mayor observing that "history shows that whenever such a property passes into private hands, it in time becomes an extortionate monopoly." Then agents of a private company began to infest the city council, and in November 1897 it leased the gas works for 30 years to the United Gas Improvement Company. Mayor Warwick signed the ordinance, now saying: "It is a grave question in my mind whether or not any municipality should operate any manufacturing industry."

Other firms were counting on aid from the Federal government in their operations overseas. But first the political issue had to be resolved. By the Treaty of Paris, signed 10 December 1898, Spain gave up her sovereignty over Cuba, and ceded the Philippines, Guam, and Puerto Rico to the United States. Almost as if conceding that the transfer of the Philippines was peculiar, the United States agreed to pay Spain $20 million. The President had his treaty, but it was by no means sure that he could get two thirds of the Senate to ratify it. Most Democrats were opposed to it. The Anti-Imperialist League which had been formed included such prominent Republicans as Andrew Carnegie, Charles Francis Adams, Carl Schurz, and Senator George F. Hoar. Mark Twain's "To a Person Sitting in Darkness" was only one of many attacks on imperialism by eminent writers. Louis F. Post of Chicago, who had managed Henry George's 1886 mayoralty campaign, pointed out in his weekly *The Public* that the Filipinos claimed that they had substantially liberated themselves from Spain without American aid. "If the Filipinos resist our aggression," Post wrote, "every American with the blood of the revolutionary fathers in his veins, with the principles of the declaration of independence in his heart, with Lincoln's immortal oratory in his memory, with President McKinley's reference to our code of morality on his conscience—every such American must pray for their triumph."

But the Democrats split on both principle and tactics. Bryan, tied up in his belief that the majority is infallible, said he wanted to see the Philippines freed, "not by a *minority* of the Senate but by a *majority* of the people." Therefore, he said, let us ratify the treaty in order to end the war and reduce military appropriations; then let us set the Philippines free. *The Public* endorsed this curious approach. Mayor Carter Harrison of Chicago and boss Richard Croker of Tammany Hall said we should keep the Philippines. With the opposition confused and divided, McKinley announced that hostilities against the Filipinos had begun on Luzon, with American casualties. He thought this made ratification certain. But the vote in the Senate was in doubt almost until the roll call on February 6, and the President got his way by the narrowest of margins.

Five days later, *The Public* reported the fighting in Manila on Sunday, February 5: "Hundreds of native huts were fired by the Americans to dislodge their occupants. One church, in which

Filipinos had fortified themselves, was set on fire by the Americans, and the escaping Filipinos were picked off with rifles as they were smoked out." Against such a background the Senate considered a resolution for the independence of the Philippines, and rejected it only by the casting vote of the Vice-President. Bitter fighting in the Philippines continued for years, while liberal American journals printed reams of stories about atrocities by the United States army.

American policy was clinched by the Presidential election of 1900. Declaring that imperialism was the "paramount issue," the Democrats again put up Bryan. Early in the campaign he centered his fire on militarism and the Philippines, but he found his audiences cold. Then he shifted his attack to the trusts and the money issues. Mark Hanna pointed to Republican prosperity and called on the voters to "let well enough alone." Theodore Roosevelt made a spirited race for the Vice-Presidency, and many customary Democrats rallied behind the Hero of San Juan Hill. Carnegie and Charles Francis Adams concluded that Bryan was more dangerous than imperialism. Many citizens showed no interest at all, and many others were confused by the multiplicity of issues. In four years the Democratic party had further solidified its hold on the South, and some voters in New England, New York, and Pennsylvania who had deserted in 1896 now returned to their traditional loyalty. But more portentous was the jump in Republican support west of the Mississippi; in 1900 McKinley and Roosevelt recaptured Kansas, Nebraska, South Dakota, Wyoming, and Washington. The Republicans got an even greater plurality than in 1896—861,000 votes. Nobody could say that a majority of Americans had endorsed imperialism, but they, for whatever reason, had returned to power an administration that favored imperialism. Men were more concerned about their own incomes than about the plight of the Philippines.

In May 1899, John Jacob Astor returned from Europe and predicted that the Continent would be ordering vast quantities of machinery and electrical goods from the United States. That autumn McKinley could announce that for the first time we were exporting more manufactured products than we were importing. A few months after his re-election he declared in a speech in Mississippi: "We want to send the products of our farms, our factories, and our mines into every market of the world; make the foreign peoples familiar with our products; and the way to do that is to make them familiar with our flag."

Raw materials also were sought abroad. The United Fruit Company made Guatemala into an adjunct of Boston banks. Mexico, under the pliable regime of dictator Díaz, was invaded by American crews prospecting for oil. Bethlehem Steel reached out to Cuba and Chile for iron ore. International Paper, formed in 1899 by the merger of nearly 30 firms, bought large tracts of timber in Canada. American capital in substantial amounts flowed to other countries. In 1897 the private foreign investments of the United States were only $700 million. By 1914, they had increased five-fold, and less than a quarter of the $3.5 billion consisted of loans; the rest was direct investments in railroads and ranches and mines and forests and factories. This country in 1914 was still a debtor nation in its international investment position, but only because foreigners had continued to invest substantial amounts of their wealth in the United States. And in every year from 1897 to 1914, the volume of American capital leaving this country was greater than the volume of foreign capital entering it.

Financier: J. P. MORGAN
(1837–1913)

John Pierpont Morgan (1837–1913) was a prominent lay member of the Protestant Episcopal Church. The first article of his voluminous will affirms: "I commit my soul into the hands of my saviour, in full confidence that having redeemed it and washed it in His most precious blood, He will present it faultless before my heavenly father, and I entreat my children to maintain and defend at all hazard and at any cost of personal sacrifice the blessed doctrine of complete atonement for sin through the blood of Jesus Christ once offered and through that alone."

His maternal grandfather, a passionate preacher, was among those who bequeathed to Morgan this sanctified tenet. The financier's legacies to his four children were largely tangible: substantial influence (control, some said) over perhaps half of the nation's railroads, many streetcar lines, Equitable Life Assurance, A. T. & T., U.S. Steel, General Electric,

International Harvester, a transatlantic shipping combine, the First National Bank of New York.

J. P. Morgan was the second generation of inherited wealth. He followed his father into banking, and there he stayed. Although he had strong rivals, for at least two decades he was pre-eminent in the re-organization of railroads and in the formation of the giant trusts that were coming to dominate manufacturing. His backing was needed to raise huge sums of capital because other bankers and investors agreed his word was good. He had almost a veto over the initiation of any mammoth corporation. His ambition was as expansive as his massive body. He had the eyes and the beak of a gull; it was appropriate that he should love the oceans and that his yachts should be named *Corsair*. But any inference that he was a buccaneer intent on loot would be mis-taken. He could be as ruthless as a herring gull, but lacked its in-dividualistic gluttony. Morgan sought accommodation, cooperation, peace.

In view of his power, his personal fortune seems rather modest, $118 million. His collections represented $50 million of his net estate. Agents bought for him rare editions, manuscripts (he owned Dickens' "A Christmas Carol"), Chinese vases, medieval illuminations, Renaissance paintings, bronzes, and fossils. A famous scientist at the Museum of Natural History was trying to write a definitive history of the evolution of the horse, since this was the species about which the geological record seemed the most complete. He knew that Morgan had left a sub-stantial number of fossilized horses to be stored in a locked wing of the Museum. The scientist asked permission to study the collection. In accord with the stipulations of the deceased, permission was refused.

CHAPTER 11

Frustration

If the automobile had been invented fifty years before the railroad, locational patterns in the United States would have been far different: surely the cities would not have developed as they did. Similarly it is amusing to speculate on what would have happened to Standard Oil had the electric light been invented fifty years before the automobile, rather than twenty. If Standard Oil was lucky in its relation to technological change, other combinations of 1900 were not. Such was the fate of the Theater Syndicate.

In the legitimate theater business, there were 250 touring companies by 1880, which had to be routed into 5,000 theaters in 3,500 towns. The producers thereafter were increasingly concentrated in New York and a few other centers, and the job of scheduling was done each summer in a mad scramble around Union Square. To simplify the problem and get better shows, theaters in a given region would band together into a circuit, but a gap between theater and acting company remained. It was closed by the evolution of booking agencies, which at first worked on a fixed-fee basis to the theater, but quickly converted to charging a percentage of the theater's receipts. By 1896 Charles Frohman, the leading producer of the time, and his partner Al Hayman had a virtual monopoly of all bookings into theaters west of the Mississippi. Klaw and Erlanger controlled any route through the South. Nixon and Zimmerman owned most of the major theaters in Philadelphia and had a string of houses through Pennsylvania and Ohio.

On August 31 these three partnerships united into the Syndicate. To get any bookings of a production controlled by the Syndicate, a theater had to give them control of its policies. A production had to put all its bookings in the hands of the Syndicate if it wanted any engagements in their theaters. Beginning with 33 theaters, the Syndicate within 5 years controlled 65. At the height of its power it managed the bookings of more than 700 theaters, including nearly every first-class house in the country. There were periodic rebellions by little groups of star actors, usually led by Minnie Maddern Fiske. The Syndicate stamped out these revolts mercilessly. First it would lure some rebels back by giving them higher percentages and other concessions. Then it would blacklist the others out of all its theaters. After a season or two of performing in second-class theaters or in tents, they came back.

The first effective opposition came from Sam Shubert and his younger brothers, who started reaching out from Syracuse, N. Y., to acquire theaters in other cities. When they invaded New York City in 1900, the Syndicate declared war. The Shuberts formed an alliance with Mrs. Fiske and with actor-producer David Belasco. They built more theaters with capital provided by Republican politicians in Cincinnati, including boss George B. Cox. By the spring of 1906 the Shuberts had fifty theaters, and their list of stars included Sarah Bernhardt and Ada Rehan in addition to Mrs. Fiske. The conflict continued sporadically for years. In 1909 the Shuberts shifted their emphasis from acquiring theaters to controlling productions. As they tied up more and more of the companies capable of doing one-night stands in smaller towns, the Syndicate had desperate trouble trying to provide such companies. But many theaters had to have them, and they began deserting the Syndicate in droves. At last, in 1913, the Syndicate and the Shuberts made peace—a peace of equals.

A worse enemy of the Syndicate had emerged from the wings even before it was formed. In April 1894 the Edison Kinetoscope, a peep show, was shown commercially for the first time. The first motion-picture show was projected by a Vitagraph machine in a theater on Herald Square on 23 April 1896. It was the 332nd anniversary of the birth of Shakespeare—and the 280th anniversary of his death. In 1908, as the Syndicate prepared for its biggest battle with the Shuberts, there were 337 touring companies in the United States. In 1934, there were 27.

Businessmen tried desperately to stabilize matters so that the future could be predicted with certainty. But it seldom can, and even J. P. Morgan made costly errors of judgment. One of the worst was his involvement in the formation of the International Mercantile Marine in 1902. Clement A. Griscom of Philadelphia wanted to merge his International Navigation Company with his only important American competitor, the Atlantic Transport Company. After complicated negotiations, the two merged with two major British lines—the Leyland Lines, and White Star—to form the I.M.M. The new firm was the largest shipping company in the world, with nearly 20 per cent of the nontramp tonnage in the North Atlantic. Morgan had advanced $11 million in cash that was needed to buy Leyland. He also formed a syndicate to raise $50 million in cash that was needed for various purposes. For the latter service he received a manager's fee of 50,000 shares of I.M.M. common plus 5,000 shares of preferred.

The deal went sour. Western opposition in the House of Representatives blocked a ship-subsidy bill that the promoters had counted on. They had expected that the consolidation would effect operating economies. They had expected a great increase in the demand for shipping in the North Atlantic. It did not come. In 1903 I.M.M. passed the dividend even on its preferred. Its securities sold in the market well below what had been anticipated. Morgan's money was tied up for years. Whereas in the U. S. Steel promotion the Morgan firm made $12 million, its I.M.M. losses were probably at least a million dollars. Even investment bankers took some risk.

But Morgan usually managed to come out with a profit, even when disaster was striking all around him. He did so during the panic of 1907. Except for minor fluctuations and localized troubles in some industries, the economy moved smoothly upward for nearly a decade after 1898. An alarming break on Wall Street came in March 1907, another in August. Morgan spent the summer in Europe, and then the first three weeks of October at the triennial Episcopal Convention, as was his custom. At accelerating pace, telegrams began to flow to Morgan, in Richmond, Va., from his office at 23 Wall Street. Morgan arrived in New York on October 20 knowing that trust companies managed by speculators were in serious trouble. Runs were on. Morgan appointed his own bank examiners to determine which institutions could be saved. He rallied the leading financiers to pool their reserves for loans to deserving banks. Even Rockefeller and Harriman followed his lead. Trust companies went to the wall. Westinghouse failed.

The Department of the Treasury made clear that it would advance cash for loans to deserving banks—to be designated by respectable New York bankers. Morgan reigned supreme. For two troubled weeks, other financiers met night after night in one room of his new mansion on 36th Street. He sat by himself in another room, nursing a severe cold, a 70-year-old autocrat playing solitaire and chewing a long black cigar. Occasionally somebody came to him with a proposal. Morgan said yes or no and went back to his solitaire.

The panic seemed to be abating when it became known that Moore & Schley, a big brokerage firm, might collapse, and carry others down with it. The firm had made large-scale loans against the collateral of stock in the Tennessee Coal & Iron Company. The stock had no ready market in the existing situation. Would U. S. Steel buy the stock, giving in exchange its bonds which could be marketed? Morgan approved. Judge Elbert H. Gary, chairman of U. S. Steel, objected. Morgan insisted. Gary surrendered. Would the acquisition by U. S. Steel of such a prominent competitor be prosecuted under the Sherman Anti-Trust Act? Judge Gary was sent to Washington to find out. The President did not object to the deal. It was made. In the midst of panic, one of Morgan's favorite companies became the dominant force in the iron and steel industry of the South, adding to its reserves an estimated billion tons of coal and 600 million tons of iron ore.

During the following depression, which lasted through 1908, U. S. Steel was able to protect itself. Judge Gary, having in 1907 seen the company spend $50 million to build a single mill at a new site (named for him) in northern Indiana, was not disposed to stand idle the next year when rivals began cutting prices. Such "unreasonable and destructive competition," he warned, might force an "application of the law of the survival of the fittest." For many years other firms in the industry were privileged to attend an annual dinner at which Gary announced the basic prices at which U. S. Steel would sell its output. They fell in line.

Most companies were more exposed. In 1894, North Carolina had 253 tobacco factories; only 33 in 1914. But in 1907 American Tobacco controlled a capitalization of $500 million. The cotton-textile mills of New England, with a majority of the active spindles in the country, could not keep them busy. The South by 1904 produced more cotton yarn than New England; by 1909 she outproduced the rest of the country. New England firms began to put millions of dollars into building cotton mills in South Carolina, Georgia, and Alabama. Some Southern promoters got New England financing in another way during and after the 1893 panic. They sold their stock to the Northern commission merchants who marketed their output. In lesser degree they used their own stock to pay for the machinery they needed. The Whitin Machine Works, one of the big textile-machinery manufacturers, first began taking substantial quantities of stock in Southern mills in 1895, and continued to do so through the next decade.

Owners of Southern factories did well after 1900, and their employees too were often better off than they had been on farms. But the labor force, by other standards, had little to cheer about. In tobacco factories most workers were women and children, who got little pay for long hours. Negroes were almost entirely excluded from textile mills, but the companies did not hesitate to exploit white men, women, and children. The program of the National Child Labor Committee was denounced by mill-owners as socialistic, un-Christian, meddling with parental authority over children, and a plot by New England textile manufacturers. Asa G. Candler of Atlanta, the founder of Coca-Cola, declared: "The most beautiful sight that we see is the child at labor; as early as he may get at labor the more beautiful, the more useful does his life get to be." Candler's brother, a Methodist bishop, meanwhile trumpeted for "great revivals" as "the cure for congested wealth and consuming poverty. This will extinguish the fires of socialism."

The fires of socialism were perceived by few of the 9 million Negroes in the United States in 1900. Nine of every ten Negroes were still in the South. A bare majority of employed Negroes worked in agriculture: 60 per cent of them as farm laborers, the rest as farmers. A half million children under 15 were listed as part of the labor force. If a Negro child went to school at all, it was without books or supplies, for only 8 or 10 weeks a year, to a squalid one-room school, where the teacher might know little more than he did. Probably one Negro in two could not read or write, and most literate Negroes got little to read but their Bibles.

The typical Negro farmer worked 20 or 30 acres. His cabin

might have only one room, but usually two. It was furnished with straw pallets or perhaps cots, a table, a few chairs or boxes to sit on, a fireplace or wood stove. It was lighted only by the fireplace and by daylight. The privy was close enough to be convenient and too close to be sanitary. The farmer worked his fields with a mule or two, a crude wagon, a wooden plow, a hoe and a spade, and little else. From dawn to dark he worked in heat over 100 degrees in the sun—and there was little shade. Nor any thermometers either, and he took the sun's measure with his muscles and his sweat and his exhaustion. In the dark he gulped his corn bread and fat pork and maybe some tea. As he lay sprawled on his bed his clothes dried, and the surface filmed up white as the salt was deposited.

Like as not he went to church on Sunday and sang Baptist or Methodist hymns. Saturday afternoon he might drive the lumbering wagon to the store to pick up the family's rations. If he was lucky he had an acre to use as a corn patch or a truck-garden: greens, watermelons, sugar cane. Even in the rural areas there was change, and more and more Negroes paid their rent in cash instead of being sharecroppers. But life for the typical farmer was endless work all by himself or with his family in a hot field, interrupted in winter by biting chill in his porous cabin.

Some Negroes gave up farming, to work in the turpentine camps, in the mines of Alabama and Tennessee, on the docks in ports. Often a Negro's chance for an industrial job came when white men went on strike; more than once a group of Negroes, upon learning that they were being used as strikebreakers, responded by walking off the job. Negroes in increasing numbers were drifting into small towns in the South or into cities. In nine Southern states the proportion of Negroes living in urban areas rose from 11.8 per cent in 1890, to 14.7 in 1900, to 17.7 in 1910 (the proportion of whites was only 18.9 per cent). By 1910, twenty-two cities had at least 20,000 Negroes each. Washington, New York, and New Orleans each had nearly 100,000.

Next to farming, domestic and personal service was the chief trade among Negroes, claiming three of every ten employed. Many in these occupations were women, who found it easier to get work in most towns and cities than did men. The man who did little work, or none at all, was common. Partly because they had no steady job, even more perhaps because slavery had prevented the growth of a tradition of family stability, many men simply walked off and left their women and children; in 1910, four of every ten Negro families in Charleston and Nashville were headed by a woman. In Birmingham, where the Negro population jumped from 17,000 in 1900 to 52,000 a decade later, half of the Negro men worked in industrial jobs, and the percentage of Negro families headed by women was much lower. In Negro ghettoes the rate of illegitimate births ran high. So did the rate of child mortality.

But the example of Zack Hubert and his twelve college-trained children is a reminder of Negro parents who worked wonders. It also suggests that the shibboleths of self-reliance and economic advancement were not pure delusion, even for uneducated ex-slaves. The heroic successes of men living by those shibboleths were early fashioned into a creed by the founder of Tuskegee Institute, Booker T. Washington. Soon after Frederick Douglass died in 1895, Washington leaped into the vacancy. On September 18 he gave a speech before white men at the Cotton States and International Exposition in Atlanta. Chiefly repeating themes that he had preached for fourteen years to students at Tuskegee, he laid out the famous Atlanta Compromise. Washington believed that Negroes belonged on the land rather than in cities, in the South rather than in the North. Now he called upon Negroes to "cast down your bucket where you are." Southern whites, he said, would find his people "the most patient, faithful, law-abiding, and unresentful people that the world has seen." In return for economic opportunity, he implied, Negroes would accept for the time being an inferior social status.

Thus he seemed to endorse the doctrine of "separate but equal." The next year the Supreme Court of the United States endorsed it too. Louisiana had a law requiring separate coaches for Negroes and whites on railroads. Such a statute, ruled the Court in *Plessy* v. *Ferguson*, did not deprive Negroes of the equal protection of the laws required by the Fourteenth Amendment if the coaches provided to the two groups were equal in quality. Justice Harlan, who again found himself alone in dissent, wrote bitterly: "Our Constitution is color-blind. . . ." But the majority held smugly that "legislation is powerless to eradicate racial instincts. . . ." Two years later in *Williams* v. *Mississippi* the Supreme Court upheld the Mississippi provisions for disfranchising the Negro.

Under slavery the rulers had tried to prevent slaves from congregating by themselves: even separate Negro churches were forbidden. After emancipation, as long as conservative ex-slaveholders held political power, Negroes were not rigidly segregated, and they had voted in large numbers in the South until 1890 and after. But even before 1860, as Richard C. Wade has pointed out to me, the decay of slavery in Southern cities had led to increasing demands for segregation. After 1898 this tendency was sharply accelerated. Not only did the opposition to segregation of Southern conservatives become much weaker, so did that of Northern liberals. For three decades the ardor of the North for rights of Negroes had been waning. The Republicans no longer needed Southern Negro votes to win the Presidency. And imperialist sentiment helped to swing Northerners into the anti-Negro camp.

"If the stronger and cleverer race is free to impose its will upon 'new-caught, sullen peoples' on the other side of the globe, why not in South Carolina and Mississippi?" asked the *Atlantic Monthly*. Of the Northern reaction to Southern disfranchisement of Negroes, the New York *Times* commented on 10 May 1900: "The necessity of it under the supreme law of self-preservation is candidly recognized." "No Republican leader, not even Governor Roosevelt," exulted Senator Ben Tillman, "will now dare to wave the bloody shirt and preach a crusade against the South's treatment of the Negro. The North has a bloody shirt of its own. Many thousands of them have been made into shrouds for murdered Filipinos, done to death because they were fighting for liberty."

As governor in 1895, Tillman led South Carolina in disfranchising the Negro. Louisiana followed in 1898; North Carolina in 1900; Alabama and Virginia in 1901; Georgia in 1908; Oklahoma in 1910; all by some type of constitutional amendment. Senator James K. Vardaman of Mississippi declared he would just as soon give the vote to "the coconut-headed, chocolate-colored, typical little coon" who shined his shoes for him as to Booker T. Washington. The Democratic party was converted into a white man's club by provisions for statewide Democratic primaries. All of the former Confederate states passed laws requiring each voter to prove he had paid his poll tax. A variety of suffrage requirements caused the number of registered Negro voters in Louisiana to fall from 130,000 in 1896 to 1,342 in 1904.

By 1900 every Southern state had a Jim Crow law applying to trains. In that year only Georgia had a similar provision for streetcars, but it was joined by ten other states by 1907. In 1905 Georgia adopted the first law requiring segregation in parks. Birmingham required that any public place should separate Negroes from whites "by well defined physical barriers." A young professor of sociology at Atlanta University led a Negro delegation in 1902 to protest against their exclusion from the city's public library. W. E. B. DuBois complained again at the National Negro Conference in 1909, "I am taxed for the Carnegie Public Library of Atlanta where I cannot enter to draw my own books."

In the intervening seven years DuBois had become the leader of the opposition to Booker T. Washington's program of accommodation. Elegant in attire and manner, haughty in personal relations, DuBois was a passionate and well-trained scholar with a Ph.D. from Harvard and a style of attack that ranged from statistics to poetry. He used the first to guide a series of careful studies of the status of Negroes. The second as well went into *The Souls of Black Folk* (1903), in which his politeness did not conceal his rejection of Washington's policies. Washington fought back, showing himself a ruthless—and powerful—opponent. His power came in large measure from the influence he gained among whites by his conservatism. He was the funnel through which most money from whites flowed into Negro education. By guiding the placement of white advertising, he lined up Negro newspapers for his program. Most important of all, especially after Theodore Roosevelt became President in 1901, he was the chief adviser on Federal patronage for Negroes. He and the Federal officials he had helped to place in the nation's capital wrote Republican propaganda and placed Republican (paid of course) advertisements in the Negro press during election campaigns.

Nothing did more to sap Washington's position than the lynchings and race riots that occurred from 1898 to 1908. In November 1898 at Phoenix, S. C., during a reign of terror that lasted for weeks, a white mob killed six Negroes and wounded or lashed many others. The same year Wilmington, N. C., suffered two days and nights which saw nine Negroes massacred. (A Negro private from Indiana wrote home from the Philippines that a little boy had asked him: "Why don't you fight those people in America that burn the Negroes, that make a beast of you, that took the child from its mother's side and sold it?") In 1906 conservative Democrat Hoke Smith abused Negroes freely during his race for governor of Georgia, and the Atlanta *News* exclaimed on September 23: "Vicious blacks are sounding the doom of their race. The wonder is that white men do not begin in earnest a real warfare on the blacks." The warfare came at once; two whites and ten Negroes were killed. When Booker T. Washington cautioned Negroes not to retaliate, the son of Frederick Douglass commented scornfully: "Our people must die to be saved and in dying must take as many along with them as it is possible to do with the aid of fire-arms and all other weapons."

Vast areas in the South also evolved a contract-labor system that differed hardly at all from the discredited convict-lease arrangements. The new tactic was found in turpentine camps as well as on cotton plantations. An Alabama law of 1885 made it a crime to sign a contract, accept an advance against wages, and leave the job before working off the debt if, but only if, the employee's "intent" on signing the contract was to defraud. This loophole, from the employer's view, was plugged in 1903. In 1907 Alonzo Bailey signed a contract to work for twelve months, and received a $15 advance. A month later, he quit. He was jailed. After legal play that lasted for more than two years, the Supreme Court of the United States declared the Alabama statute unconstitutional; obviously it had been merely a cover for reinstating imprisonment for debt behind the smokescreen of calling an occurrence "fraud." The decision greatly reduced the amount of peonage in Alabama, but the practice continued in Georgia and in Florida. Only during World War II did the Supreme Court invalidate the contract-labor laws of those states.

Already in 1905 DuBois and other prominent Negroes had started the Niagara Movement to press their straight-out program: Complete equality, in all spheres of life—Now. (Washington suggested that spies be planted in the organization to disrupt it.) White liberals were rallied to the Negro cause by a race riot in the summer of 1908 in Lincoln's home town of Springfield. Of the 53 persons who signed the call for the National Negro Conference, only six were Negroes; the whites included social workers Jane Addams and Florence Kelley and Mary White Ovington, writers Lincoln Steffens and William Dean Howells and William English Walling, publisher Oswald Garrison Villard, philosopher John Dewey. Events led to the founding of the National Association for the Advancement of Colored People in May 1910, and in

Immigration, 1899–1914

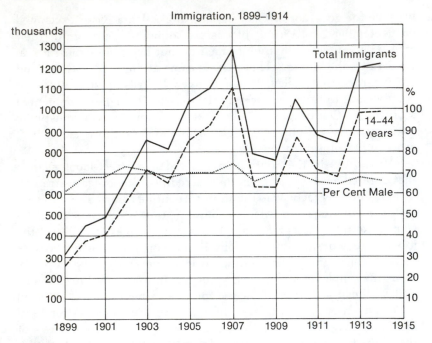

November the organization launched *The Crisis* with DuBois as editor. Conciliation was giving way to militance.

Not the least of Washington's faults was his addiction to racial thinking, as when he wrote in 1911 that immigration here from southern Europe might lead to "a racial problem in the South more difficult and more dangerous than that which is caused by the presence of the Negro." Thus Washington joined the opposition to a group often as badly off as Negroes. In the 14 years after 1900, nearly a million immigrants a year came to the United States. The number of foreign-born rose from 10.2 million in 1900 to 13.3 million in 1910; at that time foreign-born and Negroes together were a quarter of the population.

The new flood set out from southern and eastern Europe: 200,000 Russian Jews a year; 200,000 Slavs; 200,000 Italians, but the shift in sources of immigration was far from complete. As late as 1917 most copper miners at Butte were Irish-born, and, in spite of a law banning immigration of contract labor, many were recruited in the Old Country and brought straight to the mines. A story popular in Butte reflected the fact. Under the legal pretext of the so-called apex law, the companies regularly pirated each other's claims (since the ore was 50 per cent copper, the temptation was great). One day a gang was working in one of Heinze's stopes, and just above them in another stope was an Amalgamated Copper crew. The Amalgamated men planted too much powder and blew a hole in their floor. One of them fell through to the stope below. The Heinze shift-boss demanded, "Where did you come from?" The dazed miner replied, "County Galway."

Of 28 million immigrants from 1865 to 1915, perhaps a third went back to Europe. Our picture here of the South Slavs is fairly clear. Most intended to go back home, but did not. They started coming to America around 1880 when the extinction of the *Zadruga* (communal household) forced the division of lands. Many came from the relatively prosperous eastern counties of Croatia-Slavonia, even though they seemed to have no economic reasons for leaving. They said, "Mi idemo traziti ima li jos pravice na svietu." ("We are going to find out if there is still justice in the world.") Among the Yugoslav immigrants, males were much more numerous than females. Even as late as 1940, the sexual ratio was 154 males to 100 females among foreign-born Yugoslav-Americans. This was close to the ratio for Danish-Americans. Far higher, however, was the proportion among Greek-Americans—255:100.

The new reality was apparent by 1904, when 15 carloads of Austrian, Slavic, and Hungarian laborers arrived together in South Chicago. They were reportedly bound for Montana to work in the mines of Senator William Clark, who had been having labor troubles. Slavs did the heavy low-paid labor in the mines and mills of Pennsylvania. Jews swarmed into the needle trades, where it was often other Jews who exploited them in sweatshops. Italians worked in gangs, and their *padrone* hired them out to farmers and railroads and ditch-digging projects and contrived to seize most of their earnings for himself. American steamship companies had hundreds of agents in Europe, passing out circulars to tell Italian peasants that they could make $3.50 a day in the Pennsylvania coal fields. It did not turn out that way.

In 1897, during an anthracite strike, about 150 Poles and Hungarians set out from Hazleton to persuade the men in a nearby town to join the strike. On the urging of coal owners that the march was illegal, the sheriff, a former mine foreman, assembled

102 deputies to stop it. He commanded the marchers to turn back. Somebody hit him. He ordered his men to fire. As the terrified crowd stampeded, 21 of them were killed and 40 wounded. The sheriff said the strikers had been "like wild beasts." The Austro-Hungarian government demanded indemnification. The State Department refused the claim.

Foreigners did not always break and run. In the big anthracite walkout of 1900, with the legendary Mother Jones rallying women to the cause of the United Mine Workers, the men who went on working at the Old Forge colliery found it necessary to run a gauntlet of the strikers' wives and sisters. One blackleg complained:

> I could hold my own against a man any time, but those Hungarian women are more than my match. They ate garlic every morning and spit in our faces. They threw rotten eggs and red pepper at us when we came out from work in the evening, and we could not lift a finger against them because of their sex. . . . The gang of women followed us, hooting and hissing, for nearly a mile.

About a third of the population of Cedar Rapids, Iowa, were Bohemians, and the manager of the local American Cereal plant foolishly said that he could hire as many Bohemian women as he needed. About 150 women in the wrapping department struck in 1898 for a pay raise and other reforms. Reported the press: "The girls visited the wrapping room and created a lively scene, overturning chairs, emptying paste pots, throwing brushes out of the windows, spilling oatmeal over everything, and scaring half out of their wits the few girls who had been employed to take their places." They won the strike. In St. Joseph, Missouri, 400 women made labor history in 1901 by staging a sit-down strike in an overall factory.

Nearly 20 per cent of the workers in manufacturing from 1890 to 1905 were women—more than a million of them by 1900—and their work was not always light. Kansas had 4,000 women farmers in 1899, and women worked in the harvest fields of Iowa and Nebraska and the Dakotas—as well as in the South. The Mc-Cormick Harvester office in Chicago was typical in installing its first typewriter, and hiring its first lady stenographer, in 1882, and increasing numbers of women held office jobs. In 1910, nearly 7.5 million women were in the labor force. And a careful survey in

Boston in 1907–1909 showed that, of all the major occupational groups open to women, only women in the professions were meeting their expenses or were earning the $500 a year deemed necessary for a decent standard of living.

Not only were working women exploited at their jobs and often coerced by want into slums or cheap boarding houses, many of them also suffered under the discrimination and abuse that confronted all immigrants. Strong nativist feelings had arisen by 1886 as a response to the domestic crisis, and after 1890 the racist sentiments of Senator Lodge and Theodore Roosevelt and other Eastern patricians had led them to call for a requirement that all immigrants must be able to read and write some language. The demand died down as the Spanish-American War and the new colonies gave Americans a heady confidence in their ability to Americanize anybody, and the prosperity that brought immigrants here prompted businessmen in need of labor to want them to come. The assassination of President McKinley by an anarchist was followed by the general immigration act of 1903. Although it did, for the first time since the Alien Act of 1798, impose a test of opinion by barring anarchists, it did not contain any blanket restriction on immigration.

Nativism began to rise again about 1905, as the changed nationality of the immigration affected reactions to it, especially in the South and Far West. Neither section had been a favorite destination for New Immigrants; both together had only half as many as New York City. But the number of New Immigrants in the South more than doubled from 1900 to 1910, to reach a mere 1 per cent of the white population, and that in the Far West more than tripled, to reach 5.6 per cent. The sight of swarthy skins inflamed sections that had long insisted upon "a white man's country," and the reaction of the Far West was intensified by its sullen realization that the expected great new field for American sales and investments in China was slow to appear: Japan's victory over Russia in 1904–1905 suggested that it might never appear.

The literacy test reappeared in Congress in 1906. In spite of the opposition of businessmen and of the increasing number of voters who were New Immigrants, it seemed likely to pass. But Speaker Joe Cannon, who came from a mining district making heavy use of foreign-born labor, blocked it in the House. At last Senator Lodge agreed to drop the literacy test in order to get a ban on Japanese immigration.

Many Protestants were incensed at the religions of the New Immigrants, who were overwhelmingly Catholic or Jewish. The American Protective Association in 1894 had enjoyed a brief vogue in the Midwest with its outburst against Catholicism, and this program now found advocates in the South. Tom Watson—a great Populist two decades earlier—began denouncing the Pope in 1910. The next year a little town with falling population in the Ozarks, Aurora, Missouri, saw Wilbur Franklin Phelps found *The Menace* on the single plank of hostility to Rome. The paper publicized an oath by which fourth degree members of the Knights of Columbus swore to exterminate and mutilate all heretics. People believed it. In 1914 *The Menace* had a circulation of 1 million copies, and, reports John Higham, "the devout could often be seen going to church with the Bible in one hand and *The Menace* in the other."

In 1914 nativism was near to hysteria. It had remained violent as the economy swung upwards after 1909. Its intensity as war broke out in Europe was due not to international tensions but to a slump in the domestic economy in 1913 which continued into 1914. A down-at-the-heels descendant of colonial Americans wrote to the New York *World:* "I see employment furnished to foreigners every day at good pay where Americans are not wanted. I have reached the limit, I have been out of work until I can stand it no longer."

In 1914 Tom Watson labored to effect a lynching. The dead body of 14-year-old Mary Phagan was found in April 1913 in an Atlanta pencil factory managed by Leo Frank, a Jew from New York. Frank was indicted for murder and, in a courtroom surrounded by a mob, a terrorized jury convicted him. Every appellate court that reviewed the case, including the United States Supreme Court, divided about it, but the conviction was not overturned. After keeping quiet about the case for nearly a year, Watson cut loose in his *Jeffersonian* with the charge that Frank was "the typical young libertine Jew" who had been motivated by "a lustful eagerness enhanced by the racial novelty of the girl of the uncircumcized." The filthy campaign went on right down to the scheduled day of execution, 22 June 1915. When the governor of Georgia finally screwed up his courage and commuted the sentence, an enraged mob forced him to flee the state. Two months later Frank was snatched out of the state penitentiary, driven halfway across Georgia, and hanged from a tree. "Let Jew libertines take notice," said the *Jeffersonian*. "Georgia is not for sale to rich criminals." In 1920 an admiring populace sent Watson to the United States Senate.

One of the chief forces in the anti-immigration agitation was the American Federation of Labor. It first endorsed the literacy test in 1897, but for some years thereafter it did not show much vigor on the issue. It was growing immensely, its affiliates having perhaps 400,000 members in 1897 and four times that number in 1904. Then it was sharply checked. The first city-wide employers' association to fight unionism appeared in 1900 in Dayton, and the idea spread rapidly. By 1902 the emphasis of the N.A.M. was anti-unionism rather than foreign trade. The employers' association depended to great extent on the strategy of "balancing nationalities" so they could be played against each other. It was an easy strategy to play—by 1909 a third of the labor force in the chief industries consisted of the great variety of New Immigrant nationalities, and so far the A.F.L. had grown chiefly by enlisting native Americans and Old Immigrants. Thinking that it might contribute to immigration restriction, Samuel Gompers cheerfully watched the rise of anti-Japanese agitation in California. The New Immigrants would have to take care of themselves.

No union had a better policy about immigrants than the United Mine Workers, with a constitutional proviso that nobody could be denied work "on account of race, creed, or nationality." But even the U.M.W. had trouble with the situation. In several areas of Illinois, locals were organized by immigrants who then barred all other nationalities. In 1903 the state convention prohibited any local from being composed solely of members of one nationality. President John Mitchell of the union charged that the mine owners of West Virginia, with the collusion of state officials, were trying to import miners from Britain and Europe to prevent unionization—even though American miners worked only 200 days a year. Claiming that the U.M.W. had members of twenty nationalities and twenty languages in addition to Negroes, Mitchell added: "The American element always controls. It is the most intelligent element, and intelligence rules." At a time when virtually all unions admitted only skilled workers on a certain craft, Mitchell headed an industrial union that accepted anybody employed in coal mining, from skilled miners to nine-year-old slate pickers in the anthracite fields.

So when an anthracite strike was called in May 1902, a great majority of the 150,000 workers in the fields walked out. But not everybody, and the six great railroads that controlled most of the anthracite fields did all they could to induce strikebreakers into northeastern Pennsylvania. The conflict dragged through the summer, punctuated by rioting, shootings, dynamiting of mine tipples. The approach of cold weather brought alarm to cities from Boston to Washington, which chiefly used anthracite as domestic fuel. The union proposed arbitration, but the operators refused it, with President George F. Baer of the Reading Railroad declaring, "The rights and interests of the laboring man will be protected and cared for— not by the labor agitators, but by the Christian men to whom God in His infinite wisdom has given the control of the property interests of the country."

Theodore Roosevelt, who had been in the White House for a year, was in a tight spot. His conservative advisers in the Cabinet said he had no legal authority to intervene. But frantic Republican Congressmen from the East warned him that their seats in the House might be lost in November if the strike continued. He invited the operators and the union officials to the White House on October 3, and for hours Baer and his colleagues refused even to speak to Mitchell. Then, with the President's approval, Secretary of War Elihu Root went to New York and saw J. P. Morgan, who had financed the reorganization of the Reading. Roosevelt had been in office only a few months when he attacked the Northern Securities Company, a piece of Morgan's handiwork, but the financier had no desire to see Democrats in Washington. Where the President had failed, Morgan succeeded, and the operators agreed to submit the dispute to a seven-man arbitration panel named by Roosevelt. After endless hearings that took all winter and filled 57 large volumes, the panel in March 1903 gave the miners a 10 per cent pay increase and reduced the workday to either eight or nine hours. But the union did not get the recognition that it sought. Although the U.M.W., which had hardly existed in 1897, had nearly 400,000 members in 1914, the anthracite operators had not officially recognized that it existed. But already the U.M.W., jointly with bituminous coal operators, had asked for amendments to the Sherman Anti-Trust Act to allow price agreements.

Many unions, in exchange for concessions about wages and working conditions, joined employers in efforts to drive out competition and raise prices. Leaders of the Amalgamated Association of Iron and Steel Workers appealed to Congress for a higher tariff on steel. Increases in railroad fares were sought by Brotherhood officials. Building trades' unions formed alliances with contractors' associations. Teamsters got together with coal dealers. The Chicago *Tribune* predicted editorially in 1901 that the formation of U. S. Steel would bring labor peace because the company would set up a board of conciliation and arbitration to handle relations with its 400,000 workers. But the company had other ideas. Its directors secretly resolved not to allow any extension of unionism in their plants. A strike in 1904 was lost. By 1908 the Amalgamated Association controlled only a few U. S. Steel mills. The company decreed in 1909 that henceforth it would operate all its mills without union contracts. The next year the president of Bethlehem, the biggest independent, announced that he would not deal with organized labor. In basic steel, trade unionism was dead.

The anti-union drive of employers was greatly aided by government actions, especially of courts. Cities had, unofficially, injunction judges who could be counted on to restrain strikes or boycotts. And if local and state courts were bad, from the union viewpoint, the Federal judiciary was worse, including the Supreme Court. By the Erdman Act of 1898, Congress had prohibited railroads from discriminating against employees because of their union membership and from requiring "yellow dog" employment contracts; that is, contracts in which the new employee pledged not to join a union. In *Adair* v. *United States* (1908) the Court struck down these provisions as unreasonable violations of freedom of contract. Then in the Danbury Hatters Case, *Loewe* v. *Lawlor*, it unanimously ruled that a union boycott of a manufacturer could be prosecuted under the Anti-Trust Act as being in restraint of trade. In *Gompers* v. *Bucks' Stove and Range Company* (1911), it upheld an injunction banning the A.F.L. from publishing the company's name on its "unfair" list.

If the United States was a constitutional republic, it seldom seemed so during a labor dispute. Strike after strike erupted into ferocious fighting. Streetcar strikes in New York and Chicago became civil wars. Colorado's governor during the Cripple Creek strike of 1904 declared martial law and ordered the militia to destroy the Western Federation of Miners. The governor of Nevada in the Goldfield strike of 1908 joined the mine owners in trying to drive all members of the union out of the state—and Federal troops sent in by President Roosevelt were used to subdue the strikers. In a strike against Rockefeller's Colorado Fuel and Iron Company in 1914, the militia raked the strikers' tent colony with machine-gun fire and burned it to the ground. Two women and eleven children were burned to death. Rockefeller soon hired public-relations man Ivy Lee to improve his public image.

Labor used force too. During a machinists' strike in Los Angeles in 1910, the building of the anti-labor *Times* was blown up. Twenty men were killed. When Secretary-Treasurer John J. McNamara of the Structural Iron Workers and his brother James B. were indicted, Clarence Darrow was hired to defend them. Evidence existed to tie them to dozens of earlier bombings; in the building trades, dynamite was a stock organizing tactic. On 1 December 1911 the McNamara brothers confessed. The A.F.L. leadership protested loudly that they had believed firmly in the defendants' innocence. They virtually boycotted Darrow thereafter for his part in allegedly tricking them. In the labor code of the day, it was proper even to deceive yourself about who was responsible for what.

Mill Girl and Her Father: PETER SISSCAK

Born in Hungary, Sisscak was digging anthracite for the Pennsylvania Coal and Iron Company at Dunmore when the big strike hit in 1902. His oldest daughter, of five surviving children, started work in the local silk mill when she was 12. Textile mills liked to locate in coal towns: the wives and daughters of the miners provided a captive pool of cheap labor. The mother in the family was ill. Sisscak's financial status is hard to determine. The company showed that his last paycheck had been $91 for two weeks. But he was a contract miner, paid by the ton of coal, who had to pay his own helpers. He said that his share for two weeks was only $26. Twenty-six dollars for twelve ten-hour days underground in the damp dark, gnawing like a mole at the bowels of a mountain. Never seeing the sun in winter, constantly threatened by cave-ins and the horror of coal gas. A face permanently bleached by life in the deep, and then blackened by years of coal dust, which no soap and water could now eradicate. A skilled man.

John Demko was another miner at Dunmore. In the five years preceding 1902, six of his offspring had died young. He too had a daughter in the silk mill. The oldest of five remaining children, she was 13. When she entered the factory, her family owed $76 at a private store, not a company store. Her mother was then in an asylum but had since been released.

By Demko's testimony, the girl had wanted to take outside employment: "When she see another girl dressed up, I cannot help it." The company showed that his last fortnightly check was $144. He replied that this sum had to be shared with two other miners and four laborers; the latter received $2 a day each for the twelve days.

Perhaps as many as half of the employees in anthracite mining could not speak English: Italians, Hungarians, Slavs. The more cautious companies excluded these men from the dangerous stopes.

CHAPTER 12

The Politics of Make-Believe

Historians have yet to work out a comprehensive account of the flight from reality of many Americans two generations ago, but some of its signs can be charted. The natural human tendency to delude oneself had long been stimulated in the United States by evangelical religion. Some consequences were amusing. During the very years when the campaign against liquor was winning legislative victories in states and towns, the alcoholic content of patent medicines was high; Peruna was 28 per cent alcohol, and at least one Peruna alcoholic was reported to be a member in good standing of the Women's Christian Temperance Union. In 1883 the Commissioner of Internal Revenue wrote to a nostrum maker: ". . . to draw the line nicely, and fix definitely where the medicine may end and the alcoholic beverage begin, is a task which has often perplexed and still greatly perplexes revenue officers, and especially where a preparation contains so large proportion of alcohol as yours does." Manufacturers who put their product in fancy bottles—shaped like pigs, Indian maidens, lighthouses, busts of George Washington— presumably thought they would be used as ornaments in the parlor. But few ornate bottles survived; purchasers destroyed the guilty evidence so they could buy more. Consider events in 1906 in Monroe, Wisconsin, a town with 26 saloons for its 5,000 residents. A Chicago evangelist during a 5-week revival saved 425 souls. But the ticket favoring low taxes on saloons won the fall election.

Self-deception came to shape not only religion and prohibition and sexual morality and views of human nature but also tastes in literature and the visual arts. Some of these manifestations will be sketched later; here let us look at the altered flavor of public affairs. A symptom of the new tone of diplomacy was the rising faith in arbitration treaties as a means of settling disputes between nations. President Taft and Secretary of State Knox, President Wilson and Secretary of State Bryan, all shared it. (The sardonic Lord Salisbury remarked: " . . . like competitive examinations and sewage irrigation, arbitration is one of the famous nostrums of the age. Like them it will have its day and will pass away, and future ages will look with pity and contempt on those who could have believed in such an expedient for bridling the ferocity of human passions.") Navy Secretary Josephus Daniels said in 1913 in his report to Congress: ". . . it ought not to be difficult to secure an agreement by which navies will be adequate without being overgrown and without imposing overheavy taxation upon the industry of a nation." Seven months later World War I started. Also in 1914 the Anglo-American Exposition opened in London. It was meant to celebrate a century of peace.

Aside from the realm of private morality, prior to 1898 prominent Americans were often brutal in their candor—Vanderbilt on the public, Platt on the Sherman Act, Olney on the Interstate Commerce Act, Reed on the Wilson-Gorman Tariff and the Spanish-American War. But the new concentrations of business power at home and the new dimensions of American policy abroad brought a hurricane of cant. People turned from reality, as if they could not bear to admit to themselves what the facts were. Monopoly, imperialism, socialism—these were denials of a creed that had been rooted in individual initiative. But it was dangerous to diagnose them.

McKinley was prone to believe his own twaddle. As the American army, in spite of its scorched-earth policy, was slow to subdue the Philippines, he went on thinking that only a small minority of Filipinos were opposed to American rule. He spoke of the need to "Christianize" them, even though nearly all were Roman Catholics. He dreamed a house in the clouds and moved into it. He even imagined that he could get the Senate to approve reciprocity treaties, but of the seven he submitted to the Fifty-sixth Congress not one was reported out of committee. On 5 September 1901 at the Pan-American Exposition in Buffalo, just before he was shot down by Leon Czolgosz, the President told a crowd of 50,000: "We must not repose in fancied security that we

can forever sell everything and buy little or nothing." But businessmen and their political allies also had delusions, and they persisted
in the one to which McKinley referred.

Mark Hanna in 1900 had wanted a safe candidate for Vice-
President, but the President had ordered strict neutrality, knowing that Roosevelt's military glory had made him governor of
New York and would go well in another campaign. Matt Quay
agreed. Thomas C. Platt, once more boss of New York, wanted
to get Roosevelt out of state politics. To Hanna's question, "Don't
any of you realize that there's only one life between that madman and the Presidency?," they were deaf. So at McKinley's
death the Presidency went to a man who called it a "bully pulpit"
and preached from it. Roosevelt quickly made the White House
into the chief flapdoodle factory in the nation, but this very
quality helped to promote his popularity. He brought to his role
a color and dash that it had not known for decades. Sensitive to
what the average voter demanded or would toterate, he had an
asset which could be made to serve statecraft as well as politics. If
his perpetual motion on domestic problems often consisted in
jumping up and down in one place, yet the new railroad legislation of his administration and his conservation policies were
advances. In foreign relations it is extreme to say that he "was
unalterably opposed to bluffing, to making threats that he did not
intend to keep," but in the conduct of some diplomatic negotiations he was both shrewd and patient. He knew how to keep a
secret, and some highly explosive confidences were safe with him.

But his wiser contemporaries knew that frequently his speed
was uncontrolled or aimed in the wrong direction. They knew
too that his self-righteousness concealed the truth from him. One
Roosevelt homily prompted Elihu Root to comment: "What I
most admire about you, Theodore, is your discovery of the Ten
Commandments." Lincoln Steffens, observing that "Roosevelt's
lies were unconscious," told how he had falsely denied that he
had called on Boss Platt in connection with his gubernatorial
campaign—but only after he had told himself the lie so often that
he believed it. Steffens went so far as to refer to Roosevelt's "old
rule": "Never to deny anything unless it is true." About 1905
Mark Twain told Andrew Carnegie: "Mr. Roosevelt is the Tom
Sawyer of the political world of the twentieth century; always
showing off; always hunting for a chance to show off; in his

frenzied imagination the Great Republic is a vast Barnum circus with him for a clown and the whole world for audience. . . ." ("Americans have no political ideas," wrote Thomas Beer; "they follow leaders who attract them or who know how to manage them. The kind of political leaders they like are human circuses.") The President, wrote Henry Adams, was "pure act."

The noisiest acts of the first term were in foreign affairs, and the key was a Big Navy. Naval operations in the Spanish-American War had shown that the servicing and fueling needs of a modern fleet severely limited its radius of operations. Thus technology made it difficult for American ships to operate far from their bases, and it made our coastlines invulnerable to navies from Europe or Asia. Further, Britain in 1900 was the only European power with a sizeable fleet in the West Atlantic, and the rise of German naval power after 1898 forced Britain to pull many of its vessels back to European waters. So the Big Navy advocates trotted forth a circular argument: We needed the Philippines—4,800 nautical miles from Hawaii—to service our navy, and we needed the navy to protect the Philippines.

In 1901 Roosevelt actually told Lodge that Britain "could take the Philippines and Porto Rico" but we could retaliate by seizing Canada. Ridden by fantasies about German threats to the Western Hemisphere, the President insisted that the Caribbean would not be safe until we had a navy second only to Britain's.

Congress from 1901 to 1905 voted funds for ten first-class battleships, and the naval appropriation went from $85 million to $115 million a year—a peacetime high. If the policy was ill-conceived, its execution was deplorable. The *Idaho* and the *Mississippi* were authorized in 1903. These 13,000 ton battleships, costing nearly $6 million each, were completed in 1907. Not only were they far inferior to Britain's new dreadnoughts, they were too slow to keep up with the American fleet—obsolete the day they were launched.

Imagined dangers in the Caribbean drew attention to Cuba. The war resolution of 1898 had declared that she would be allowed to govern herself. Morality also seemed to demand that the United States make tariff concessions to Cuban products. But now the United States forced Cuba to incorporate into her constitution the so-called Platt Amendment (named for an American), giving this country the right to intervene in the island, and promising the United States naval and coaling stations there. Restrained by American sugar interests, Congress in 1902 failed to make any tariff concessions. That autumn Roosevelt informed Secretary of State John Hay that, no matter what happened about the tariff, Cuba would have to cede the naval bases, "and in the near future." A tariff treaty was approved in 1903: American rates on imports from Cuba were cut 20 per cent, and Cuban rates on imports from the United States were cut 20 to 40 per cent. Reciprocity need not be equal.

We needed the naval bases to protect a still undug isthmian canal, and now we had a new reason for needing a canal—the Big Navy. When the Spanish-American War started, the new battleship *Oregon* was at San Francisco. It took 68 days to steam the 13,000 nautical miles through the Straits of Magellan to Key West, where it joined the fleet. To naval minds the event showed that protection of the United States required either a huge fleet in each ocean, or a Central American canal. But a canal would be a strategic handicap, urged men like Mahan, unless this country had naval control of the West Atlantic and the East Pacific. So we needed a canal for the Big Navy, and we needed the Big Navy to protect the canal.

Construction of a canal was blocked by the Clayton-Bulwer Treaty of 1850, which provided that neither Britain nor the United States would seek "exclusive control" over any Central American canal. By 1900 American furor about the Monroe Doctrine prompted many Senators to urge that the United States should just denounce this piece of paper. The first Hay-Pauncefote Treaty that year was ratified by the Senate, but with amendments that Britain would not accept. A successful agreement was reached in 1901, giving the United States the exclusive right to build and manage a canal, and providing for its neutralization according to certain rules.

There remained the problem of real estate; the United States owned none in Central America. More than twenty years earlier a French company had started to dig a canal across Colombia at Panama but had abandoned the project; the Third Republic had even been rocked in 1892 by scandals about the finances of the company. Now it was willing to sell its physical property to the United States for $40 million. But its concession would expire in October 1904, when Colombia would simply take the property and sell it to the United States. Meanwhile Congress was pressing Roosevelt. In June 1902 it passed a law directing him to get a right-of-way from Colombia across Panama, but if he could not do so "within a reasonable time and upon reasonable terms," he was to seek a route across Nicaragua, which was closer to the United States.

On 22 January 1903 the Hay-Herrán Treaty was signed in Washington, giving the United States a zone six miles wide across Panama in exchange for $10 million cash plus $250,000 a year. Three days later, Herrán was instructed not to sign by the government of Colombia, which might be able to get $40 million or even more if it waited 18 months. On 12 August 1903 the senate of Colombia unanimously rejected the treaty. "Those contemptible little creatures" made Roosevelt furious: he was intent upon being nominated for re-election in 1904, and Republican National Chairman Mark Hanna would be a strong competitor. Also Congress might force a Nicaraguan canal if quick results were not gotten at Panama.

The President reached out for a treaty and a warship. The treaty was one giving the United States the right to intervene to preserve "free transit" across Panama. The warship was the *USS Nashville*, sent to Colón, Panama, where it arrived 2 November 1903. The next day a thousand Panama patriots revolted, and the American naval forces prevented Colombian troops from landing. An independent republic was proclaimed on November 4, and recognized two days later by Roosevelt. The Hay-Bunau-Varilla Treaty was even more advantageous to the United States than its predecessor had been, and made Panama a virtual military outpost of this country. Roosevelt later said that "every action" of his administration had been conducted "in accordance with the highest, finest, and nicest standards of public governmental ethics."

At the University of California in 1911 Roosevelt declared that "I took the canal zone and let Congress debate, and while the debate goes on the canal does also." This boast was expensive. In 1914 the United States, by treaty with Colombia, expressed its "sincere regrets" for the events of 1903 and agreed to pay an indemnity of $25 million. Senator Lodge and his cohorts blocked ratification until 1921, when the apology was striken. The indemnity remained. The Assistant Secretary of State had said that the Panama revolution had been financed by a personal loan from

J. P. Morgan to the Washington agent of the French company, which was so close to losing its $40 million.

Morgan also was interested in the Far East; he had been in and out of and back into the American China Development Company since its formation in 1895. At the end of the century the expansion in China of Germany, France, Russia, and Japan had caused the United States and England to fear that their citizens might be crowded out. To each of the other five powers, John Hay in September 1899 sent a circular letter asking for guarantees that none of them would discriminate against the nationals of other powers in its sphere of influence in China. Many of the replies were evasive, but the dauntless Hay sent around another note stating that all of the powers had agreed. Soon thereafter the Boxer Rebellion erupted against foreigners in northern China, and the United States joined other powers in sending troops to the area. While the foreigners in Peking were under siege in the legation compound, Hay dispatched another note on 3 July 1900, declaring that American policy was to preserve the "territorial and administrative integrity" of China and to "safeguard for the world the principles of equal and impartial trade with all parts of the Chinese Empire." The Open Door policy was premised on a belief that American agriculture and industry were so efficient that they could undersell foreign competitors in the markets of the world. "Even protectionist organs are for free trade in China, where freedom is for the benefit of American manufacturers," commented the London *Times.*

But would the administration do anything to restore the Open Door at home? In his first annual message to Congress, Roosevelt said that the rise of large firms "has not been due to the tariff or to any other governmental action, but to natural causes in the business world. . . ." In this process the captains of industry had played a creative role. To harass them now would be to jeopardise the indispensable international commercial dominion of the United States. At the same time, grave evils existed, such as overcapitalization and stock watering. Only the Federal government could control these practices. Mr. Dooley summed up the President's attitude toward the trusts: "On wan hand I wud stamp thim undher fut; on th' other hand not so fast."

The Northern Securities Company gave Roosevelt a good target. Edward Harriman sought a route into Chicago for his Union

Pacific. James J. Hill wanted the same outlet for his Great Northern. The Burlington would be an ideal connection for each man. Hill, also in control of the Northern Pacific at the time, negotiated the purchase by that road of the Burlington. Harriman now set out to buy enough stock in the Northern Pacific to give him control of the outlet he wanted. In the struggle that followed, the price of Northern Pacific common stock was forced from about $100 a share to as high as $1,000. Men who had been selling it short could not deliver on their contracts. The resulting panic of 9 May 1901 was too much for J. P. Morgan, Hill's financial agent, and he arranged a community of interest. Northern Securities was formed as a giant holding company over the Great Northern, the Northern Pacific, and the Burlington. Harriman was given a seat on the board.

On 19 February 1902, Attorney-General Philander C. Knox filed suit against Northern Securities as a violation of the Sherman Anti-Trust Act. Businessmen gasped at the act, and Morgan paid a social call at the White House, where he said to the President: "If we have done anything wrong, send your man [Knox] to my man [Stetson] and they can fix it up." The following November the Republicans held control of Congress—owing their thanks not only to the President's attack on Morgan but also to Morgan's help in settling the anthracite strike.

Roosevelt had also instituted another program that proved popular with the voters. Beginning with President Harrison, and more rapidly under Cleveland, forests in the Federal public domain had been set aside for permanent parks and reserves. In the summer of 1901, 30 Western Congressmen had approved a plan to use part of the receipts of public-land sales in their states for dams and reclamation projects. Joe Cannon, soon to be Speaker, led the opposition, complaining that farm output was already too great. But with Roosevelt's vigorous aid the Newlands Act was passed, and under it some 3 million acres was irrigated in the next four years.

In 1903 Roosevelt got three minor laws supposedly aimed at corporate wrongdoing. A Department of Commerce and Labor was set up, with power to subpoena evidence and compel testimony about firms in interstate commerce. But it had no powers beyond publicity. The Expedition Act provided that any suit of "general public importance" brought by the United States under the Interstate Commerce Act or the Anti-Trust Act should be given precedence over other cases in the courts. The Elkins Act, seeking the end to rebates and other discriminations by railroads, made deviation by a road from its published rates the sole test of discrimination and declared guilty the receiver as well as the giver of a rebate. (That some railroads were glad to use Federal power to suppress unfair competition is suggested by the role of a lawyer for the Pennsylvania in drafting the Elkins Act.)

By 1904 Roosevelt had used the Federal patronage to consolidate his hold on the party's machinery, and his nomination for President in his own right seemed certain. But his chief rival, Senator Hanna, was nobody to laugh at. To improve his position the President asked Congress to declare that any Union veteran who had reached age 62 was half-disabled and thus eligible for a pension. Congress did not act. Writing to Elihu Root that of course the average man at 62 had lost "at least one-half" of his capacity for physical labor, Roosevelt inspired the Pension Commission to discover in April that it could make the desired change by administrative ruling. Men who had done no physical labor for decades more severe than handling a knife and fork were awarded $5 per month each.

Already, in February, Hanna had died of typhoid fever, and on March 14 the Supreme Court ordered the Northern Securities Company dissolved, by a vote of 5 to 4. Roosevelt was aggrieved that one of his two appointees to the Court, Justice Holmes, dissented with the comment that Harlan's interpretation of the Sherman Act in the decision "would make eternal the *bellum omnium contra omnes* and disintegrate society so far as it could into individual atoms." But when the Democrats put up for President a New York judge, Alton B. Parker, who wanted to leave the trust problem to the wisdom of state legislatures and the common law, Roosevelt could present himself to the public as a foe of evil trusts.

That the Northern Securities decision had been an annoyance rather than a cause for undying enmity became clear quickly. Morgan and his partners dropped $100,000 into the Republican national campaign fund. At the special request of Harriman, of all people, they gave another $50,000 to the New York state fund. When the New York *Times* said that the Republican national chairman was squeezing corporations by methods close to blackmail, the Democratic nominee repeated it. On the eve of the election, Roosevelt called Parker's charges "unqualifiedly and atrociously false." But in fact companies and their officers had contributed handsomely to the more than $2 million spent by the Republicans during the campaign.

Roosevelt scored an unprecedented victory, with more than 7.6 million votes to 5.1 million for his opponent. In 17 states Parker did not win a single county. Parker, said a humorist, "was defeated by acclamation." In both Senate and House, Republicans would outnumber the Democrats by nearly two to one. Here was a legislative majority that could do something.

But increasingly the Republican majority split into hostile factions. Most Congressmen belonged to the "regular" wing, symbolized by Aldrich and Cannon. But reform had begun on the city level about 1890. Then a number of reformers were elected governor: LaFollette in Wisconsin in 1900; Albert Cummins in Iowa in 1901; Joseph Folk in Missouri in 1904. Next the insurgent Republicans hit Washington—George W. Norris in the House after 1902; in the Senate, LaFollette after 1906, William J. Borah after 1907. The insurgents, chiefly from the plains and prairie states, contested bitterly for control of policy with the regulars from the East and the Midwest. A President who had been careful to get along with the conservatives in his party could write at the beginning of 1907 that he was "trying to keep the left center together."

On two issues voters demanded action. With the ICC gutted by Supreme Court decisions, the railroad consolidations brought sharp rises in freight rates. In 1903 a Commissioner stated that discrimination in rates was disappearing, and that extortionate rates had become the chief complaint of shippers. But a railroad official claimed in 1905 that, in spite of the Elkins Act, rebating was still "open and notorious." Out of the legislative pulling and hauling came the Hepburn Act of 1906, which drew only three negative votes in the Senate, only eight in the House. The law gave the ICC power not only to annul excessive rates but also to substitute reasonable rates for those it had condemned. The "commodities clause" prohibited a railroad from carrying any goods, except timber, produced by a company that the railroad controlled.

Aside from the Northern Securities indictment, Roosevelt during his first term had used the Anti-Trust Act only against the Meat Trust. The large packing houses were known to resemble cesspools; Harvey Wiley, chief chemist in the Department of Agriculture, and Senator Beveridge had long been calling for Federal inspection. In 1905 Roosevelt read and was shocked by the nauseating descriptions of the Chicago stockyards in Upton Sinclair's *The Jungle*. After an investigation of meat packing, the President informed Congress that the conditions reported were "hideous" and had to be "remedied at once." When conservatives blocked a bill he threatened to publish the whole "sickening report" on meat packing. At last he did release part of it and indicated that he might follow with the more damaging remainder. His efforts were a vital factor in securing the Meat Inspection Act and the Pure Food and Drug Act of 1906.

These laws together with conservation were the chief domestic achievements of the Roosevelt administrations, and they suggest just how limited those achievements were. LaFollette had tried to effect thorough railroad regulation by empowering the ICC to set a value on a carrier for purposes of rate determination, but his amendment got only six votes in the Senate. The Pure Food and Drug Act was an advance, but many abuses lingered; major producers of patent medicines did better than ever because many Americans took the existence of the law to mean that self-medication was safe. As Arthur Link has said of Roosevelt, ". . . the sum of his legislative accomplishments was small. . . . In brief, his chief contribution to the reform cause was the publicity he gave to it." George Mowry agrees: "And while he did little himself to solve the numerous questions he broached, he did create a national demand that these questions be met and answered. Roosevelt was the best publicity man progressivism ever had."

In many instances, the publicity was not *for* an answer; the publicity *was* the answer. Repeatedly it happened that important segments of the industry to be "regulated" would seek Federal supervision as a paper barricade against more effective manifestations of public displeasure. Major railroad executives supported the Interstate Commerce Act and subsequent legislation supposedly aimed at controlling them. Several life-insurance magnates campaigned in vain for Federal regulation as a desirable alternative to inchoate and often more radical rules and taxes decreed by the states. The conservation movement was supported often by the affected companies, which sought not so much the public welfare as a more efficient and profitable use of resources. Big bankers spearheaded the drive for "reform" that would culminate in the establishment of the Federal Reserve System, and it was no accident that the new arrangements strengthened the relative position of New York banks that had been losing ground to rivals in other sections of the country. Similarly major packing firms in 1906 favored a Federal meat-inspection law because they needed a government stamp to reassure their customers, especially their foreign customers. What they wanted, of course, was not a guarantee of pure meat but, as George W Perkins explained, "a government certificate for their goods." Much of the so-called regulation by the Federal government in the Progressive years was not a victory for democracy; it was not even neutral. It was actively sought by the interests at whom it was supposedly aimed. And frequently the solution it achieved was not so much efficacious as ceremonial.

By 1906 many voters were distinguishing symbolic answers from real ones, and the Republicans were threatened by losses in the elections that year. Although since about 1900 they had been cutting into Democratic majorities in Northeastern cities by building contacts among New Immigrant voters, now the Socialists were gaining among these groups. Especially threatening was the strong campaign by Democrat William Randolph Hearst, who was well equipped to publicize his demands for drastic reform, to become governor of New York. With reports coming to the White House on the eve of the election that Hearst might sweep the Jewish districts of New York City, the President acted. By naming the head of Macy's, Oscar Straus, as Secretary of Commerce and Labor, he put a Jew in the Cabinet for the first time and gave him control over the bureau that supervised immigration.

At a dinner presided over by Jacob H. Schiff, the head of Kuhn, Loeb, the President explained how he had selected Straus. Indifferent to race, religion, and national origin, he said, he had cared only to find the best man for the job. This could be confirmed by Schiff. Schiff, who was deaf, nodded and said: "Dot's right, Mr. President. You came to me and said, 'Chake, who is der best Jew I can appoint Secretary of Commerce?' "

In New York City the Negro vote was important too. About 1 August 1906 three companies of the Twenty-fifth Infantry, Negro,

were transferred to a fort on the Rio Grande just outside Brownsville, Texas. Several incidents took place between townfolk and
Negro soldiers. On the night of August 13, some men, never
identified, shot up Brownsville, and a white citizen was killed.
An investigator for the Inspector General's Department of the
Army concluded that some of the Negro troops must be guilty,
although he could not name them. He also felt sure that other
Negroes must know who the guilty ones were, and he insisted
that anybody with such knowledge had a duty to reveal it. The
three companies contained men who had been in the army for 25
years; they contained six wearers of the Congressional Medal of
Honor. But Roosevelt ordered everybody in the three companies
discharged without honor. The decision was made public on
November 7, the day after the Congressional election. Two weeks
later the President wrote a friend that since the case was "of
vital concern to the whole country, I will not for one moment
consider the political effect."

The Republicans kept control of Congress by wide margins,
but the regulars were able to block the President's domestic program. Roosevelt could win the electorate, but he could not win
the Senate and the House. His autocratic methods, as with the
revision of pensions in 1904, were no substitute for leadership.
Even more infuriating to many Congressmen were his policies
and techniques regarding conservation. James R. Garfield, Secretary of the Interior, and Gifford Pinchot, head of the Forestry
Bureau in the Department of Agriculture, reserved over 2,500
water-power sites by designating them as ranger stations. In 1907
Congress added to the appropriations bill for the Department of
Agriculture a rider that required the approval of Congress for
any additions to the forest reserves in six Western states. With
the bill on his desk, Roosevelt created or increased 32 forest reserves. Then he signed it.

But LaFollette was right when he said that conservation was
the chief achievement of the Roosevelt administration. Against the
bitter opposition of Westerners who had always thought of the
public domain only as a source of private wealth, he increased
the total Federal reserves from 50 million acres to nearly 200
million. He broadened the meaning of conservation to include
mineral lands, oil reserves, and power sites. In his annual message
of 1907 he set forth a concept that, 26 years later, would be

realized in the Tennessee Valley Authority. He called the National Conservation Congress of 1908, which led to a yearly meeting of governors and prompted more than 40 states to set up their own conservation commissions. The *Report* of the Country Life Commission named by him in 1908 was the first searching study of the status of farmers in the industrial age. But by the time the investigation was finished, Congress was so hostile that it would not appropriate funds to circulate the *Report* widely.

Roosevelt could not get new laws from Congress, but he could enforce the ones on the books, and he made effective use politically of the Anti-Trust Act. In his second term, 42 firms were indicted under it, including such unpopular companies as American Tobacco, Standard Oil, and DuPont. Significantly, in no instance did the administration bring a criminal indictment against a corporation official. But in 1907, when a leader of the Western Federation of Miners was on trial in Idaho for murder, Roosevelt did not hesitate to compare law-breaking businessmen to "the so-called labor leader who clamorously strives to excite a foul class feeling on behalf of some other labor leader who is implicated in murder." Later, under attack, he said that he had not implied that defendant Bill Haywood was guilty. The jury found Haywood innocent.

Relations with Latin America were marked by the same high-handedness. Having proclaimed that he would "show those Dagos that they will have to behave decently," Roosevelt tried to do so in Venezuela. Cipriano Castro's government had defaulted on the greater part of its international debt, much of which was held in Europe. Britain, Germany, and Italy tried to force a satisfactory settlement with their nationals who held defaulted bonds by conducting operations against the Venezuelan navy and then declaring a blockade of all its ports. The parties were willing in principle to arbitrate. While American opinion became inflamed at the threat to the Monroe Doctrine, the terms of arbitration were negotiated, and in February 1903 a protocol was signed stipulating that the dispute would be submitted to the Hague Court. Roosevelt later claimed that he had forced Germany to arbitrate by saying that he would resort to military force if she did not. Historians for years thought that the story was his own invention. But recently Howard K. Beale after a searching investigation concluded that Roosevelt had firmly but politely warned the

Kaiser and that he had backed up his warning by sending a naval detachment under Dewey toward Venezuela.

After the episode, plus an outbreak of disorder in Santo Domingo in 1904, came the Roosevelt Corollary to the Monroe Doctrine. British policy in Venezuela had sought to compel the United States either to recognize the British right to take punitive action against offending Latin American nations, or to herself take responsibility for their behavior. Roosevelt accepted the latter alternative, which he set forth in a letter made public by Elihu Root in May 1904. That December in his message to Congress the President said:

> Chronic wrongdoing, or an impotence which results in a general loosening of the ties of civilized society, may in America, as elsewhere, ultimately require intervention by some civilized nation, and in the Western Hemisphere the adherence of the United States to the Monroe Doctrine may force the United States, however reluctantly, in flagrant cases of such wrongdoing or impotence, to the exercise of an international police power.

A doctrine which had begun as a barricade to European meddling was now twisted into a justification of American meddling. The practical meaning was made clear in Santo Domingo, which, pressed by European holders of its defaulted bonds, had asked the United States to intercede. In February 1905 a protocol was signed by which an American would be collector of customs in Santo Domingo and would allocate receipts among the various claimants. While the protocol was being negotiated, Roosevelt had two American warships in the harbor of Santo Domingo. He kept war vessels in that nation's waters and instructed them to put down any revolt that might arise.

Roosevelt also intervened in a threatened war in Europe. France was determined to dominate Morocco. For recognizing her preeminence there, she had "compensated" Italy by acknowledging her claims to Tripoli and she had "compensated" Britain by giving her a free hand in Egypt. German prestige was slighted. When in 1904 France hinted that she meant to intervene in Moroccan politics, the Kaiser's reaction was explosive. Germany in May 1905 urged upon Roosevelt that unless an international meeting about Morocco was held, she would have to choose between waging war upon

France or a bilateral conference to settle the dispute. The outlook for the latter was not good. Then Roosevelt, working deftly through the French and German ambassadors, managed to overcome French objections to a conference. When it met in January 1906 at Algeciras in Spain, the United States was represented, but for weeks it took no stand. At the conference there emerged for the first time the line-up that would fight the World War: Italy drifted away from the Triple Alliance; Germany was isolated except for Austria-Hungary. France got what she wanted in Morocco. After the issue was as much as settled, the United States provided, in A. J. P. Taylor's words, "a curious, almost absurd, epilogue." Roosevelt came up with a new plan for control of the police in Morocco. It was not acceptable to anybody else at the conference, and he was persuaded to drop it. But he had helped to stave off a possible European war.

In the Far East too, the United States, at times unwittingly, furthered Britain's aim of building an anti-German alliance in Europe. After 1902 the British were formally allied with Japan, hoping to use that power to check the expansion of Russia into the Far East. Thus Russia could be turned back into Europe, and her power also would be available to offset Germany. Japan in February 1904 made a successful surprise attack on the Russian fleet at Port Arthur in Manchuria. By the summer the Japanese had won victories on land at Port Arthur and Mukden, and had about wiped out the Russian navy in the Pacific. Roosevelt's initial reaction to the war was to hope that the combatants would fight until both collapsed; thus the United States would not confront "either a yellow peril or a Slav peril." But he soon came to believe that both of the warring nations could play useful roles in a Far Eastern balance of power that would save the Open Door in China, and he began a patient series of moves to bring about a negotiated peace. By the summer of 1905 the Russians, in addition to their military reverses, were beset by revolution, and the Japanese faced financial exhaustion. The opponents met at Portsmouth, New Hampshire, on 9 August 1905. Roosevelt put most of his pressure on Russia to give in to Japan. Skillful maneuvering by the Russian delegation avoided the imposition of an indemnity, but Japan did gain many benefits in the treaty of September 5. She acquired the Russian leasehold at Port Arthur and Talien. She got the section from Port Arthur to Changchun of the Russian-built Chinese Eastern Railway. She got the southern half of Sakhalin. She got a protectorate over Korea.

The Portsmouth Conference and Roosevelt's related actions in the Far East reveal several basic weaknesses in his approach to foreign relations. Having divided the world in his own mind into "civilized" and "barbarous" nations, he repeatedly overestimated the power of Britain (he thought that Australia, occupied by whites, was more important than India). He had only contempt for the potential of China, and he had organized a conference at which Japan and Russia drew up a peace for China without Chinese participation or consent. In trying to contain Russia he wanted Anglo-Japanese-American control of East Asia, under which Japan would control Korea and have the major voice in Manchuria while Britain and the United States would dominate the Yangtze valley. This thinking produced the Taft-Katsura Agreement which had two main points. With Japan indicating a desire to take over Korea altogether, the United States made no objection, and Korea disappeared as an independent nation. Even more breathtaking, the President secretly entered a commitment with Britain and Japan under which each nation was obligated to go to war in defense of the others if any was attacked by an outsider.

Japan's victory over Russia, following her triumph a decade earlier over China, set off wild anti-Japanese agitation in the Western states. The Pacific Coast gushed with rumors of invasion. Immigrants from Japan were regarded as soldiers or spies. When San Francisco in October 1906 segregated Asian children in its public schools, Japan made diplomatic protests. Roosevelt was annoyed at the Californians for precipitating an international crisis, but some of their premises came to be his.

"America's geographical position on the Pacific is such as to insure our peaceful dominion of its waters," the President had said in 1903. But in 1905, when Congress was showing reluctance in voting funds for the four battleships he had requested, he was beset by fantasies of a Japanese attack on the Pacific states. From the gross exaggeration that we can dominate the Western Pacific, he came to the gross exaggeration that Japan was a threat in the Eastern Pacific. In December 1907, as the struggle in Congress neared a climax, Roosevelt sent the American fleet on an around-the-world cruise. If he really feared Japanese attack, it was a strange move: What if she had attacked the fleet itself in

Japanese waters—by surprise? Congress in April 1908 voted two battleships.

The dispute about immigration was settled that year by the so-called Gentlemen's Agreement. Japan agreed to discourage emigration by laborers to the United States. This country agreed that Japanese former residents and close relatives of residents were entitled to entry permits. Already in December 1907 Japan had proposed to Roosevelt a joint declaration of friendship, and in November 1908 the Root-Takahira Agreement pledged both nations to maintain the *status quo* in the Far East, including the Open Door in China. Such was American friendship for China: together with Japan, we had proclaimed without Chinese consent a policy that chiefly concerned China.

Roosevelt picked his own successor in the White House: his former Governor of the Philippines, Secretary of War William Howard Taft. Taft sent Bryan to his third defeat by a majority of 1,260,000 votes, and the Republicans maintained their edge in both Houses of Congress. The new administration could be expected to continue Roosevelt's policies, and it seemed to have the political power to do so.

But the Senate refused to ratify treaties with both Honduras and Nicaragua which provided for the appointment of an American as director of the national revenues and for the transfer to American banks of national debt which had been held in Europe. To carry out his policy of dollar diplomacy, Taft was compelled to rely on his executive powers as Commander-in-Chief of the armed forces; before he left office in 1913 he sent American marines to occupy Nicaragua as well as Santo Domingo. But the great failure of Taft's aggressive policies came in his efforts to enhance American governmental and business power in China and especially in Manchuria.

Here Morgan and Kuhn, Loeb were in the picture as well as the State Department. In 1905, when Morgan controlled the American China Development Company, its concession to finance a railroad from Hankow to Canton had been cancelled by China. He considered selling his interest in the company. On July 18, President Roosevelt wrote to Morgan: "I cannot expect you or any of our big business men to go into what they think will be to their disadvantage." But, continued Roosevelt, if Morgan was considering giving up the project because of fear that his government would not support him, he could be sure that the administration would "do all that in its power lies to see that you suffer no wrong whatsoever from the Chinese or any other power in this matter." For himself, said the President, "My interest of course is simply the interest of seeing American commercial interests prosper in the Orient." But Morgan agreed with China to cancel the concession—in return for a heavy indemnity. Then for four years Secretary Root followed a cautious policy, and Roosevelt, after he got embroiled with the Japanese, was cautious too. But with the change of administration Philander Knox took over at the State Department, and caution fled.

In 1909 the United States by pressure on China forced the admission of American capital to a British-German-French consortium to construct railroads from Hankow to Canton and from Hankow to Szechuan. On 2 October 1909 a representative of the American Group that included Morgan and Kuhn, Loeb signed a preliminary agreement for the construction of a railroad in Manchuria from Chinchow to Aigun. The validity of the contract depended on the issuance of an imperial edict confirming it by China. On November 6, Knox sent a note to Great Britain stating confidentially that the edict had been issued. He also proposed that all railroads in Manchuria should be neutralized: an international syndicate of private bankers should be formed to purchase them on behalf of China and to control them during the term of the loan.

The scheme depended on a false notion of American power in Manchuria, and it came to grief quickly. When Knox informed Britain that the Chinchow-Aigun contract had been ratified by China, the wish was father to the fact; it had not been. It never was. Japan objected to a proposal that would reduce the profitability of her South Manchuria Railway. Russia was angered at the idea that China might approve a new railroad that would intersect the Russian-owned Chinese Eastern Railway. On 4 July 1910 the former enemies announced a pact in which they pledged cooperation in the development of Manchurian railroads and in protection of the *status quo*. By a secret clause they agreed to each other's spheres of influence in Manchuria and Mongolia.

By now, Morgan was ready to give up hope for the Chinchow-Aigun scheme because of the opposition of other powers. The American Group was threatening to withdraw from all activity in China. The American drive had been beaten. But in September, Taft sent Knox to New York to plead with the American Group not to "take the final step which will defeat entirely our international purpose." The President turned to Roosevelt for advice, and was warned that economic leverage in the Far East depended on military strength there. The American public would not stand for a large army and navy in Manchuria. Therefore, wrote Roosevelt, the Open Door was empty words if a military power such as Japan chose to violate it.

But Taft and Knox would not quit. They dragged out the game until they left office in 1913, but the chief result for American financiers was wasted effort. The four-power consortium in May 1911 did sign an agreement with China for a $30 million loan to help build the two projected railroads from Hankow. Issued in full, the loan fed Chinese anger at foreign domination and helped to bring about the revolution that overthrew the Manchu dynasty. Two years later, when American bankers were considering participation in a proposed loan of $125 million to the new government, they told President Wilson that they would take part only if he asked them to do so. He refused, saying such an action might ultimately impose on the American government the responsibility to interfere forcibly in "the financial, and even the political, affairs of that great oriental state. . . ."

Taft tried to continue his predecessor's Big Navy policy, but he had even more trouble with Congress than had Roosevelt. Funds for two battleships were voted in 1910, for two more in 1911, for only one in February 1913. This cutback in construction did not imply a cutback in naval appropriations, which were increased by $60 million a year over those of Roosevelt's second administration. In 1909, when Germany held three government navy yards and Great Britain six, the United States had eleven. Thinking that the navy existed for the sake of the navy yards rather than vice versa, Congressmen from the favored districts fought bitterly against any effort to consolidate the yards. The arrangement was a precursor of cradle-to-grave social security.

Although Taft's foreign policies led from preposterous premises to ludicrous conclusions, it was in domestic policy that he found the knives to puncture his own jugular vein and bleed to death politically. The first issue Taft bobbled was the tariff, which Roosevelt had refused to handle at all. Indeed Roosevelt was able to persuade himself that the setting of tariff schedules was a matter of "expedience and not of morality," and cheerfully watched Congress delegate to protected industries its power to tax American consumers. But Taft called a special session as soon as he took office for the sole purpose of reducing the tariff. In less than a month the House passed the Payne bill, and the President thought its rates were "substantial reductions" even though they were not as low as he wished. On April 12 a revised bill, with more than 800 amendments to the Payne clauses, was put before the Senate by Aldrich. It sharply hiked rates on many iron and steel products, textiles, and lumber; the inheritance-tax clause of the Payne bill was deleted.

The opposition to this Republican bill was led by six insurgent Republicans from the Midwest, including LaFollette and Beveridge. In addition to dissecting the measure in detail, they denounced the regular Republicans as tools of the trusts and referred to themselves as progressives. But they could not prevent passage, and a conference committee took up the measure. Although the final law set up a tariff commission and imposed a Federal tax on corporations in interstate commerce, the general level of tariff rates it set was little lower than those of the Dingley Act. Worse, because of Taft's insistence on free raw materials, it made sizeable reductions in the duties on hides, coal, iron ore, and boots and shoes—further benefiting the East at the expense of the Midwest. Seven Midwestern Republicans voted against the final Payne-Aldrich Act in the Senate, as did 20 in the House. With such papers as the Chicago *Tribune* and the Kansas City *Star* keeping their readers inflamed against the law, Taft took the road in September to defend it. At Winona, Minnesota, he even called it "the best tariff act" ever passed.

Conservation was the next problem to trip the President. At his direction the Secretary of the Interior, Richard A. Ballinger, returned more than a million acres to the public domain on the ground that his predecessor had exceeded his legal authority in putting them into Federal reserves. The progressives had other questions about Ballinger, and Gifford Pinchot, still head of the Forestry Bureau, raised the issue with Taft. Just before starting on his tour to defend the tariff act, Taft ruled for Ballinger on all points. Pinchot then forced Taft to fire him by attacking Ballinger publicly as a foe of conservation. Pinchot was an intimate friend of Roosevelt, and, although a carefully packed Joint Congressional Committee exonerated Ballinger, many progressives and Roosevelt admirers went on thinking that Taft's man differed from them on conservation policy if he was not actually dishonest.

When Congress assembled in 1910, insurgent Republicans joined Democrats in the House to end the dictatorial control of Speaker Joe Cannon, high-tariff man and arch conservative. After a dramatic battle led by George Norris, the Rules Committee was enlarged from five members to 15, and it was made elective by the House instead of being appointed by the Speaker. Soon after this revolt Congress passed the Mann-Elkins Act, which enlarged the powers of the states and of the ICC to regulate railroads. By deleting the phrase "under substantially similar circumstances and conditions" from the long-and-short-haul clause of the Interstate Commerce Act, it made that provision effective for the first time since the Supreme Court had gutted it in 1897.

The catastrophe worked by Taft's actions became apparent in November. Only the Pacific Coast went Republican. In several usually Republican states—Massachusetts, Connecticut, New York, New Jersey, Ohio, Indiana, Nebraska, Colorado—Democratic governors were elected. The Democrats won a majority of 67 in the House. Although they had only 41 members in the Senate, they could control it by uniting with insurgent Republicans. The same combination in many states after 1910 passed law after law regulating labor and factory conditions, or establishing commissions to fix rates of public utilities.

Taft continued to drive away support. In January 1911 his Secretary of State sent to the Senate a reciprocity treaty with Canada. Onto the free list of each nation would go most farm products, some minerals, paper pulp, iron, and steel plate. Farmers, East as well as West, called it a sell-out to the industrialists. But the industrialists in the Iron and Steel Institute denounced it as a first attack on the principle of protection. For once the Republicans in the Senate were united, and they stopped the treaty from coming to a vote. The President called a special session, and relied on Democratic support to get the treaty ratified. But, having alienated American voters on every hand, he saw ratification defeated in Canada by a combination of manufacturing interests plus fear of domination by the United States.

As a final irony, it was his anti-trust policy that sealed Taft's fate. In four years he started more prosecutions under the Anti-Trust Act of 1890 than all of his predecessors combined. In nearly eight years, Roosevelt brought 44 indictments; in four years, Taft brought 65. The Attorney-General on 26 October 1911 announced a suit against U. S. Steel. Apparently Taft did not know until the charges were made public that they relied heavily on the acquisition by U. S. Steel of Tennessee Coal & Iron during the 1907 panic; even then, he seemed unconscious that Roosevelt might react explosively. But the former President was quite sensitive about his part in the event in question. He regarded the suit as a final betrayal by the successor he had chosen, a last outrage to cap the rejection of his advice on Manchuria, on the tariff, on conservation.

Roosevelt the preceding June had stated that he would not seek the Republican nomination for President nor would he endorse anybody else, but his views shifted rapidly after the U. S. Steel suit was announced. Already in January 1911 the National Progressive Republican League had been set up to push reform legislation. Reform had been thwarted by "the special interests," as shown by the fate of the campaigns for effective railroad regulation, conservation, curbing the trusts, and revision of the banking laws. The League included influential citizens, eight Republican Senators, several Representatives, six governors. Early in 1912 the governors of 7 states publicly asked Roosevelt if he would be the Republican candidate for President if asked to do so. On February 24 he said yes.

LaFollette had expected that he would get Progressive support for the Republican nomination, and he continued in the race. But the outcome of the struggle was foregone, for neither contender could overcome Taft's control of the party machinery including especially the national committee. Patronage paved the way for the administration steamroller at the national convention, and the President was renominated. At Roosevelt's direction, most of his followers bolted the convention. Six weeks later they met in Chicago, formed the Progressive party, and named Roosevelt to run against Taft. When the Progressive nominee trumpeted at the convention that he felt like a Bull Moose, he gave his party its popular name.

In the interim the Democrats, smelling victory, had put forward a man who was even more given to preaching than Roosevelt. Woodrow Wilson was a Presbyterian, a native of Virginia, an admirer of the English system of government, and a historian. Scotch-Irish himself, he remarked: "A Scotch-Irishman *knows* that he is right." A colleague at Princeton, where Wilson was president from 1902 to 1910, commented that he "romanticized" the practical world. Wilson also showed a marked ability to pretend that he was doing one thing while doing something else. When Dean Andrew F. West wrote a report calling for the creation of a new graduate school, Wilson stated in his introduction that the plans were "in every way admirable." Some years later a dispute between Wilson and West came before the Princeton trustees, and a member asked Wilson why he had earlier praised West's proposal for a graduate school if he now opposed it. Wilson's reply was that he had not read the report at the time he wrote his laudatory introduction. West's original manuscript was subsequently found—revised in Wilson's handwriting.

Wilson resigned from Princeton under fire in October 1910, but already he was the Democratic candidate for governor of New Jersey. He promptly turned on the machine that had chosen him, and the Democratic surge in November carried him into office by a 50,000 majority. Beginning in January 1911 he jammed through the legislature, against the opposition of the bosses, a good bit of the reform program—direct primaries, legislation against corrupt practices, state control of railroads and public utilities, workmen's compensation for occupational injuries. But the New Freedom that he championed in the 1912 campaign was essentially a demand to take the Federal government out of economic affairs. Repeal all laws that give special privileges to anybody, Wilson urged, and let business problems be settled by competition. Meanwhile Taft was defending his record, and Roosevelt was calling for a federal trade commission to exercise sweeping control over business.

Conservation was an important issue in the campaign. Perhaps even more important was pure food, dramatized when the lifelong Republican Harvey Wiley bolted his party. Since 1906 Wiley had been deciding issues with the intent of giving maximum protection to consumers. But any specific ruling was likely to bring protests from the company involved. When, for instance, Wiley objected to sales of glucose, unpopular under that name, as "Karo corn sirup" by the Corn Products Refining Company, he brought the administration into conflict with a firm permeated by Standard

Oil men and money. That was hardly the way to get campaign contributions. After six years of internecine war, Wiley quit his job and supported Wilson because he thought the Republicans were so tainted by big business that only a defeat could purify them.

Some of Wilson's troubles were of his own making. In his *A History of the American People* (1902), having abused immigrants from Italy, Poland, and Hungary, he had concluded: ". . . the Chinese were more to be desired, as workmen if not as citizens, than most of the coarse crew that came crowding in every year at the eastern ports." The remark acted on the anti-Asian prejudice of voters, stirring a Polish-American priest to denounce it as "an insult to the white race." While the Hearst papers gave wide publicity to Wilson's sentences, he wrote to an Italian-American editor:

> I beg that you will judge the passage . . . in connection with its full context, and not by itself. I yield to no one in my ardent admiration of the great people of Italy, and certainly no one who loves the history of liberty should fail to accord to Italians a great place in the history of political freedom.

Arthur S. Link in his biography of Wilson comments: "Reading the derogatory passages in their 'full context' does not change their meaning," and questions Wilson's sincerity in writing such "fawning letters."

But Wilson was in tune with the times, and the most votes went to the man with the best pulpit manner and the least realistic economic program. The Democratic total of 6,300,000 made Wilson the first minority President since 1889. Bull Moose and Republicans together beat him by well over a million votes. Taft became the first President in history to run third in a campaign for re-election. For every four Republican votes, Eugene Debs got one on the Socialist ticket.

The Democratic platform had accused Republican tariff bills of making "the rich richer and the poor poorer," and on this issue Wilson was both prompt and effective. On inauguration day Congress was called into special session, and on April 8 Wilson became the first President since John Adams to make a personal appearance before it. The House quickly passed the Underwood bill by a majority of more than two to one, reducing rates to half the Payne-Aldrich level. On the expectation that customs receipts would decline by $100 million a year, the bill also instituted an income tax—made constitutional by the recently ratified Sixteenth Amendment. But the decisive test came in the Senate, where the Democrats had a majority of only six.

Wilson had insisted that raw sugar and raw wool should be placed on the free list, and the provision was obnoxious to Democratic Senators from Louisiana and the wool-producing states of the West. The President argued and beseeched. Then he publicly denounced the "industrious and insidious" lobbyists seeking to influence Congress. LaFollette suggested that all Senators disclose their holdings of any property that might be affected by tariff changes, and the result was a full-scale revelation of Senatorial interests. Gradually Democratic resistance collapsed, and in the end only two Democrats from Louisiana voted against the bill. The Underwood-Simmons Act brought the general level of duties down to about 25 per cent—the first real tariff reduction since 1857. Besides wool and sugar, food and other farm products went on the free list. So did wood pulp and paper and farm machinery and iron and steel products and clothing and shoes. Whereas rates were reduced on 958 classifications, they were raised on only 86, mostly in chemicals. (Although DuPont had been indicted under the Anti-Trust Act, it had, as will be seen, friends in Washington.)

The new income-tax clause made it clear that most Congressmen did not design to redistribute the wealth. All incomes of more than $4,000, individual or corporate, were taxed 1 per cent—this at a time when a factory worker earned perhaps $1,000 a year. In addition, incomes of $20,000–50,000 were subject to a surtax of 1 per cent; $50,000–75,000, of 2 per cent; $75,000–100,000, of 3 per cent; $100,000–250,000, of 4 per cent; $250,000–500,000, of 5 per cent; over $500,000, of 6 per cent.

Public opinion, jolted by the 1907 panic and outraged by the findings of the Pujo Committee in 1912 and 1913 that large spheres of the economy were dominated by a few financial groups, also demanded a new monetary system to replace that of the National Banking Act. Progressives called for decentralized reserve banks ultimately dominated by the government. The business community divided sharply in its outlook, as it did on railroad regulation and on control of trusts. Bankers fought each other. City financiers outside of New York wanted to legalize branch banking; they also wanted a decentralized but banker-controlled reserve system to issue currency based upon liquid assets of the commercial banks rather than upon United States bonds. Country bankers opposed branch banking. Instead of the scheme for currency based on liquid assets, which did not recognize some assets important in rural areas, they wanted authorization of emergency money issued by local clearing houses. Wall Street wanted a centralized system under its control. Such conflicts gave the administration considerable leeway in advancing its own program, and Congress approved the Federal Reserve Act two days before Christmas in 1913. Twelve reserve banks, "bankers' banks," were founded in major cities to hold monetary reserves and to rediscount the assets of commercial banks. The governmentally controlled Federal Reserve Board that topped the system was empowered to adjust the rediscount rate. Although the arrangement later proved to have serious defects, it perhaps deserves to be described as "the greatest single piece of constructive legislation of the Wilson era" and it was surely a big advance over the National Banking Act.

Other new laws were supposedly intended to curb the trusts and to protect trade unions. The Clayton Act amended the Anti-Trust Act to ban tie-in contracts, outlaw price discriminations that would tend to aid a monopoly, and prohibit interlocking directorates between large firms that would otherwise be competitors. By declaring that labor was "not a commodity or article of commerce," the act enabled Samuel Gompers to delude himself into thinking that unions had been exempted from the antitrust laws, but the courts disabused him of the notion. Another law set up a Federal Trade Commission with the power to issue restraining orders against several practices designated as "unfair competition," including boycotts, false advertising, and combinations to maintain retail prices. Even before these two laws were enacted in the autumn of 1914, Wilson had abandoned his notion that the proper course was to destroy all special privilege and restore competition. Under pressure of the growing depression, he began trying to woo business, and he named wealthy conservatives to both the Federal Reserve Board and the Federal Trade Commission. In November he claimed that the American economy had now been fundamentally reorganized by the Democrats, that the job was done, that the future gleamed with promise. He had taken over the platform for Federal regulation of business of his 1912 rival, Theodore Roosevelt, but the Roosevelt admirer Herbert Croly denounced his claims. Wilson, wrote editor Croly in the *New Republic*, possessed "a mind which is fully convinced of the everlasting righteousness of its own performances and which surrounds this conviction with a halo of shimmering rhetoric. He deceives himself with these phrases, but he should not be allowed to deceive progressive popular opinion."

Wilsonian phrases were even more in evidence in foreign affairs; Abraham Flexner wrote of the President: "The man cannot pass an ink bottle without sitting down to pen a note." And at the head of the State Department Wilson placed another rhetorician, William Jennings Bryan, who had fluttered the crowd at his party's convention of 1912 by putting forward a resolution attacking any candidate who spoke for "the privilege-hunting and favor-seeking class." The move played little or no part in securing Wilson's nomination, but Bryan got his reward anyway.

Wilson has often been credited with repudiating the dollar diplomacy of Taft and Knox, but he did so only in a special sense. True, he refused in 1913 to ask American bankers to take part in the Six Power Loan to China. But Bryan said the action was taken because Americans would "not have a controlling voice" in the consortium. Wilson thought that American democracy depended more on exports of goods than of capital. By giving foreign powers more influence in China, the loan might lead them to intervene directly and to exclude Americans altogether.

Back in 1902 Wilson had claimed for the United States the power to "command the economic fortunes of the world." Five years later he declared: "Concessions obtained by financiers must be safeguarded by ministers of state, even if the sovereignty of unwilling nations be outraged in the process. Colonies must be obtained or planted, in order that no useful corner of the world may be overlooked or left unused." He entered the White House looking forward to "many sharp struggles for foreign trade." In nothing, he said, was he "more interested than the fullest development of the trade of this country and its righteous conquest of foreign markets." The spreading depression made this task urgent. In May 1914 the National Council of Foreign Trade met in convention in Washington. Secretary Bryan appeared the first day to remind the audience that Wilson had made clear the aim of his administration to "open the doors of all the weaker countries to an invasion of American capital and enterprise." He added: "My Department is your department; the ambassadors, the ministers, and the consuls all are yours. It is their business to look after your interests and to guard your rights." The following day a special meeting was held in the White House itself, and the President assured those present of his full support. Markets abroad were soon found, for some American companies at least. Without the aid of Morgan, Bethlehem Steel, and DuPont, testified the Director-General of British Explosive Supplies, the British and French armies could not have survived in 1915. And with the new markets in Europe came improved markets at home.

Right through the Wilson years the marines stayed in Nicaragua, where Taft had sent them, and where in 1912 they helped to suppress a revolt. Elsewhere in Latin America, Wilson and Bryan embarked on what Arthur Link has aptly called "missionary diplomacy." On 27 October 1913, with the Panama Canal almost completed, the President went to Mobile to give a speech. "I believe that by the new route that is just about to be opened," he said, "while we physically cut two continents asunder, we spiritually unite them. It is a spiritual union which we seek." In Mexico he sought it by any means that came to hand.

The corrupt regime of Porfiro Díaz had been overthrown by Francisco Madero in 1911, and in 1913 Madero was murdered by his chief general, Victoriano Huerta. Calling the Huerta crowd "a government of butchers," Wilson abandoned the traditional American policy of recognizing de facto governments. He withheld recognition. He tried for some months to bring the Mexican factions together for a free election, going on the baseless assumption that Huerta had promised that he would not be a candidate in such an election. From November 1913 to April 1914, the United States encouraged Venustiano Carranza and his Constitutionalists in their efforts to depose Huerta. In August, Carranza overthrew Huerta. Wilson, however, schemed to replace Carranza with his general, Francisco Villa, who had tricked Wilson into thinking he would be amenable to American control. At last, in October 1915, the United States recognized the Carranza regime.

But the end was not yet. Villa, unable to whip Carranza, began raiding across the border to provoke American intervention. Already, in April 1914, Wilson had sent the United States navy to occupy Vera Cruz briefly in retaliation for the arrest of American seamen (who had been released two weeks before the occupation). Now he sent a Punitive Expedition of more than 6,000 soldiers into Mexico. Mexico protested, and an armed clash with Carranza's troops occurred in June 1916. Wilson drew up a virtual war message to Congress—in which he disclaimed any intent of interfering in the internal affairs of Mexico. This after he had been ceaselessly interfering for three years. Then it turned out that the message was premised on a false view of how the clash in Mexico had occurred, and Wilson never sent it to Congress.

In dragooning a reluctant Britain into backing his opposition to Huerta, Wilson assured her that he would "teach the South American republics to elect good men." But the assumption that he could control the government of Mexico was just another bit of fantasy.

Perhaps the crowning product of an age of cant came from Elihu Root, who during his tenure in the Cabinet found occasion to refer to "the supreme governing capacity of America." In the Philippines the assembly in 1914 passed resolutions urging Congress to provide for the independence of the islands at its current session. In Puerto Rico the affiliate of the AFL urged government action to relieve the widespread unemployment and distress. Times were not good in the United States either.

CHAPTER
13

Beliefs They Lived By

In a society that is corrupt, opined Henry George, democracy is a worse form of government than autocracy; for if free elections exist, the ruling groups can keep their power only by perverting the voters. His own age produced interesting evidence on this thesis. Although we have no sure way of knowing what the majority of Americans then thought, it is possible to stake out an incoherent assortment of ideas that moved large numbers of men to action. One—the belief that great results can follow from picayune means —contributed tangibly to the air of intangibility, of unreality.

This air hangs over much of the Progressive crusade. The movement did achieve worthwhile reforms in many states and cities: restrictions on labor by women and children, workmen's compensation for industrial accidents, some effective commissions for the regulation of business. Probably the most important spurt of state reform, both for its direct impact and for its influence in other states, occurred in New York in the four years up to 1915. On 26 March 1911 the Triangle Waist Factory in Manhattan was stricken by a flash fire that trapped 850 employees behind locked doors. It killed 146 of them. The resulting State Factory Investigating Commission recommended and secured over 50 labor laws, and the consequent model factory code was widely copied elsewhere. But along with such achievements of Progressivism went the illusion that political tinkering would lead to utopia. The world would be saved by woman suffrage, or by restoring rule to the people through the devices of direct democracy: the initiative, the referendum, the recall.

The studies that have been published of Progressive leaders suggest that most were city men of the upper middle class. They tended to be independent businessmen or professionals, without experience in coping with the giant institutions of contemporary life. They were individualistic and conservative. Their political training was limited to local affairs. And the program they devised had little appeal for farmers while such demands as prohibition were vehemently rejected by most immigrants among urban workers.

It was not even clear that their political reforms would under all circumstances result in an extension of democracy. A prosperous businessman and conservative Democrat in Cape Girardeau, Missouri, protested against the institution of direct primaries to nominate candidates on the ground that it would increase dependence of voters on the advice of big-city bosses. He much preferred the old way of making nominations through a hierarchy of conventions based on delegates chosen in "a systematic and orderly way by the people of the several townships. . . ." Robert LaFollette, a shrewd machine politician, remarked to a colleague that if they could get a direct-primary law in Wisconsin they could "hold this state forever." While many Progressives were campaigning for the election of judges, W. E. B. DuBois was charging that Southern judges were "at the absolute mercy of the white voters" and would seldom convict a white man for a crime against a Negro. Some reformers wanted to increase the direct power of the voters; others like Woodrow Wilson sought to concentrate responsibility by reducing the number of elective jobs. Former Mayor Seth Low of New York even thought the politics of Boston had been reformed when the number of elective officials there was reduced from 97 to 10 in 1909, but men like James Curley proved him mistaken.

While great if sporadic efforts went into campaigns for dubious changes in the political machinery, the American tax system remained a jungle of deception. "Our revenue laws as a body," wrote Henry George, "might well be entitled: 'Acts to promote the corruption of public officials, to suppress honesty and encourage fraud, to set a premium upon perjury, and to divorce the idea of law from the idea of justice.' That is their true character, and they succeed admirably." Taxable values of real estate were often laughable. In Chicago assessments were fixed by a man elected by the district that he assessed. The results were inevitable. In 1898, when the population of the city was more than 1,500,000, the total assessed valuation was less than in 1867 when the population was only 250,000. An even greater joke was furnished by the supposed taxation of personal or intangible property. In West Virginia in 1884, reported the state tax commission, payment of taxes on personal property had come to be "considered pretty much in the same light as donations to the neighborhood church or Sunday school." Three years later the governor of Ohio told the legislature: "The great majority of personal property of this State is . . . entirely and fraudulently withheld from taxation." In Connecticut that year a special commission on taxation pointed out that during the decades when residents of the state had been investing heavily in public and corporate securities or in Western mortgages, the proportion of intangible property to all taxable property had fallen steadily. "As the law stands," said the report, "it may be a burden on the conscience of many, but it is a burden on the property of few. . . ."

Taxes were levied less to raise funds to pay government bills than for other and essentially private purposes. License fees were a way to hinder new competitors trying to enter a field. For the same reason, distillers opposed reduction of the whiskey tax. Duties on imports protected the American producers and also raised the value of inventories in this country. The income tax did have the virtue of aiming chiefly at raising government revenue, but for many persons it too left few scars on property.

With the tax collector, as with everybody else, Americans held to the doctrine of individualism and self-help. "Godliness is in league with riches," declared William Lawrence, the Episcopal bishop of Massachusetts, in 1901. A fuller statement came from the pastor of the Temple Baptist Church in Philadelphia and the founder of Temple University, Russell H. Conwell, in his address "Acres of Diamonds." Conwell assured his audience that virtually all of them could get rich without ever leaving their native towns. It was their duty to become wealthy, for "to make money honestly is to preach the gospel." Godliness and success in business both followed from the same maxim: Live and let live. If you sell a man something he needs, you have no more right to do so without making a profit than you have to overcharge him.

> Let me say here clearly. . . . ninety-eight out of one hundred of the rich men of America are honest. That is why they are rich. That is why they are trusted with money. That is why they carry on great enterprises and find plenty of people to work with them. It is because they are honest men.

By giving this talk more than 6,000 times, Conwell himself became rich.

In its extreme form the creed of competitive individualism turned up as social Darwinism—as the doctrine that social progress and individual justice consist in the *bellum omnium contra omnes*, in the law of tooth and claw, in endless war leading to the survival of the fittest. This creed could be congenial to a businessman seeking to justify his destruction of a competitor or his exploitation of wage earners and consumers, and Carnegie and Judge Gary were only two of the many who had recourse to it. But the typical American capitalist was not an educated man of the sort to read Darwin or Herbert Spencer, and social Darwinism had its chief vogue among intellectuals: historian John Fiske, sociologist William Graham Sumner. For every businessman who cited "the survival of the fittest" there were perhaps ten others who buttressed their behavior by talking about "the right to manage."

More frequent still were the resorts to Scripture. John Wesley had presented the required note in his sermon, "The Use of Money":

> Gain all you can, without hurting either yourself or your neighbor,
> . . . save all you can, by cutting off every expense which serves only to indulge foolish desire; . . . waste nothing, living or dying, on sin or folly, whether for yourself or your children;—and then, give all you can, or, in other words, give all you have to God.

The benefactions of W. W. Corcoran give substance to his testament to his grandchildren: "Blessed by kind Providence with larger possessions than commonly fall to the lot of man, I have regarded them as a sacred trust for the benefit of knowledge, truth and charity," while those of Jacob H. Schiff reflect his sincerity in affirming, with Jewish overtones, the stewardship of wealth. Russell Conwell warned his listeners not to seek wealth for its own sake; rather they should use it for the public good. George F. Baer in 1902 pictured himself as a surrogate of the Almighty; so did John D. Rockefeller in 1907: "I am a trustee of the property of others, through the providence of God committed to my care." Success in business was a reward for good character, for "industry, frugality, and sobriety—simple moral virtues that any man could cultivate," as Irvin G. Wyllie has said. The man who acquired wealth should never forget that he held it as God's steward. Often men got rich, of course, by seeking a monopoly in their own industries, but the business world as a whole they pictured as an endless array of Open Doors. "Opportunities for success, like opportunities for salvation, were limitless; heaven could receive as many as were worthy."

Religious faiths felt some impact from the Social Gospel preached by men like Rabbi Stephen S. Wise and the Congregational minister Washington Gladden. Besides his religious duties Gladden served on the city council of Columbus, Ohio, and helped to found the local nonpartisan Municipal Voters League in 1903. He advocated public ownership and operation of all natural monopolies, including telegraph, railroads, mines, all public utilities. He insisted that industrial education for Negroes was not enough, that they should be given higher education equal to that for whites. Looking back over the religious history of his long life, Gladden thought ministers in 1909 were appealing less to fear, more to love, that they were stressing altruism instead of selfishness as the chief motive of men. The time was drawing near, he hoped, "when the Christian church will be able to discern and declare that simple truth that Religion is nothing but Friendship; friendship with God and with men."

The year 1908 saw the formation of the Federal Council of the Churches of Christ in America, but Gladden and his kind remained exceptions. Whether among the more populous Protestant sects, or among Catholics, who grew in number from 8 million in 1891 to 16 million in 1914, or among Jews, most clergymen emphasized personal conduct in this world that they thought conducive to salvation in the next. Even some of the best minds of the time were stricken by supernaturalism. Not only is Selah Tarrant in *The Bostonians* a mesmeric healer, but the King in *Huck Finn* runs a temperance revival and the Duke tries his hand at "mesmerism and phrenology when there's a chance . . ." William James wrote respectfully of Mary Baker Eddy and her new Christian Science, and was keenly interested in accounts of religious visions. *Progress and Poverty* ends with an argument for human immortality. It was reported that Leland Stanford put a good deal of money into spiritualism after his only son died at age 16. Lyman J. Gage, Chicago banker, champion of amnesty for the Haymarket survivors, Secretary of the Treasury under McKinley, took up spiritualism and theosophy. J. P. Morgan often asked his librarian to read aloud from Scripture, and he believed the story of Jonah and the whale. If he could not trust every word in the Bible, he said, he could not trust any of it.

Social Darwinism seemed to die down after 1900, save in the writings of novelists like Dreiser and Jack London, and so did the onslaughts of religious literalism against the theory of evolution. But in 1910 appeared the first of *The Fundamentals*. As a touchstone for Christians this series of ten little pamphlets set forth the Five Points: the literal truth of the Bible, the authenticity of all its miracles, the Virgin Birth of Christ, His Resurrection, His substitutionary atonement for the sins of man. From this creed *The Fundamentals* concluded that "no possible points of contact" could exist between Christianity and Darwinism. Constant assertion of the Five Points during World War I and after helped greatly to stimulate the obscene campaign that culminated in the Scopes trial of 1925.

Although among urban wage earners and even in small towns there was a counter trend toward secularism and indifference to religion, the various sects engaged in wild-eyed drives for members. Said a saw of the time:

> I'd rather be a Baptist, and wear a shining face,
> Than for to be a Methodist and always fall from grace.

One result of ecclesiastical imperialism was great waste of physical as well as spiritual resources. Bellville, Ohio, for instance, had only 913 residents in 1917. But its five churches, with a combined annual income of $4,500, had 1,675 seats. Small wonder that many impoverished ministers were so ignorant that they could offer only appeals to superstitious revivalism. Small wonder too that ministers often advanced social doctrines that might appeal to large donors. Said *Harper's Weekly* of the famous evangelist Dwight Moody in the crisis year of 1896: "He is the enemy of sectionalism and all hostility of class to class. His mission is to arouse the conscience and awaken the spiritual side of men, to make them patient, long suffering, diligent."

Much of what passed for education was close to revivalism. Some 100 million copies of McGuffey's Readers were sold to school children in the half century after 1850, and the Sixth Reader typically declared:

> If you can induce a community to doubt the genuineness and authenticity of the Scriptures; to question the reality and obligations of religion; to hesitate, undeciding, whether there be any such

thing as virtue or vice; whether there be an eternal state of retribution beyond the grave; or whether there exists any such being as God, you have broken down the barriers of virtue, and hoisted the floodgates of immorality and crime.

The stories in the Readers set forth a simple code. First, they praised blind obedience to authority. The 13-year-old boy Casabianca is assigned by his father to a post of duty during a sea battle. When the deck catches fire, he dies in the flames rather than leave his post. Second, they slobbered. A chimney sweep working in a wealthy home emerges from a chimney into the lady's bedroom where his eye is caught by "a fine gold watch." His desire for it fights his conscience, and conscience wins. The next day the lady rewards his honesty by adopting him. "One great beauty of the lessons which our childhood readers taught," recalled Clarence Darrow of his youth in northeastern Ohio, "was the directness and certainty and promptness of the payment that came as a reward of good conduct. Then, too, the recompense . . . was always paid in cash, or something just as material and good. . . . Everything in the universe seemed always ready to conspire to reward virtue and punish vice." Darrow wondered how the publishers "reconciled themselves to the hypocrisy they must have felt when they sold the books." But how far did they believe the rubbish themselves? Third, while William Dean Howells was insisting that the job of a novelist is to restore perspective, McGuffey utterly lacked it. A small boy who snitches a big piece of cake behind his mother's back is threatened with Hell everlasting. "Do you think the angels will want a liar to enter Heaven and be associated with them? No! No liar can enter the kingdom of Heaven." We may ask whether the self-deceiving self-righteousness of men like Roosevelt and Wilson was conditioned by a belief that trivial derelictions could bring eternal punishment.

When Wilson, during World War I, called on his countrymen to make the world safe for democracy, he was appealing to the prejudices instilled by the McGuffey Readers. In presenting the war in terms of liberty against despotism and ignoring the autocracies among the Allies, he used a simple-minded belief in a moral order. By exaggerating the power of the United States, he called again on the hoary doctrine of Manifest Destiny.

Colleges too left much to be desired—even before President

Charles W. Eliot instituted the elective system at Harvard and started them down a path that would leave many indistinguishable from supermarkets. But some universities made improvements, the most substantial ones being in post-graduate facilities. By 1900 a half dozen schools—first Johns Hopkins, then Harvard, Yale, Clark, Chicago, Wisconsin, Michigan—were offering graduate training in many departments to match the best available in Europe. Perhaps the greatest changes of all were made in medical schools, and they stemmed in large part from the investigations of a man without medical training, Abraham Flexner, who had been headmaster of a boys' school in Louisville.

At the behest of the new Carnegie Foundation for the Advancement of Teaching, Flexner in a year visited every one of the 155 alleged medical schools in the United States and Canada. His report of 1910 called the schools "essentially private ventures, money-making in spirit and object." By his calculations the two owners of the parent school of osteopathy at Kirksville, Missouri, were getting net profits of more than $60,000 a year. At Louisville the entrance requirement was less than two years of high school. Of Birmingham Medical College, opened in 1894, Flexner wrote: "A stock company, paying annual dividends of 6%;—the hospital is largely given over to surgical patients—gunshot and other wounds being decidedly abundant; the dispensary service is as yet unorganized." In general, anybody who could pay his expenses in a medical school was admitted and was almost sure to graduate. His diploma was his license to practice. In the United States and Canada combined, wrote Flexner, only Johns Hopkins was giving sound medical training. His report made the front pages and hit the medical profession like a tidal wave. The number of medical schools in Louisville quickly declined from seven to one; in Chicago, "the plague spot of the country in respect to medical education," from 15 to 3. With the success of the report, the Foundation raised Flexner's salary, to $5,000 a year. Possibly no foundation ever did so much good by such modest expenditures.

The men who set out to improve academic work had a hard row to hoe. The scholar Andrew D. White, president of Cornell, blurted to the literary historian Moses Coit Tyler: "Moses, if any man ever offers you a college presidency, shoot him on the spot!" Perhaps fortunately, the lamentable nature of most schools did not destroy the American faith in education. Altgeld and Darrow might question that college made a student more sensitive to the needs of others, but Theodore Roosevelt asserted that the intervening two millenia of education had made the typical American better than the Athenian in "moral cleanliness, family life and self-control."

Emphasis on physical as well as moral purity was stimulated by the growth of slums with their filth and lack of sanitation to go with their white slavery and saloons and Catholic lotteries. Respectable Protestants exclaimed in horror that "cleanliness is next to Godliness." The ranking of sins is suggested by the ordinances of Lawrence, Kansas, in 1880, which stipulated that the keeper of a bawdy house was to be fined not less than $25 but which set a minimum fine of $50 for keeping a saloon open on Sunday. Midwestern and Southern states allowed local option in the admission of liquor; towns and counties banned it altogether; and some weeks Clarence Darrow spent more time speaking against prohibition than practicing law.

There were dissenters. Many upper-class persons refused to admit a necessary connection between pleasure and sin. Catholics and New Immigrants and Germans and Irish saw no harm in a barrel of beer and a little gambling. Lower-class idlers like Huck Finn's Pap ignored the code except for a few hours or days after a revival. For many, the new puritanism involved a scuttling between the revival and the brothel, and newspapers featured detailed news about divorce trials and bordelloes.

In the arts, audiences increasingly wanted romantic melodrama and sentimental moralizing. James D. Hart, in his study of popular books in America, lists 53 books for the period 1877 to 1893, including five by Twain, two each by Hardy and Tolstoi, Grant's *Memoirs*, *Progress and Poverty*, and *Looking Backward*. But of the 73 books popular from 1898 to 1914, only three had literary merit. Frank Luther Mott, defining a bestseller as a book with total sales equal to 1 percent of the United States' population in the decade of publication, lists 24 books for the years 1880–1889. Among them are *Looking Backward*, *War and Peace*, and two of Twain's books. But the flight from reality was such that the 21 books for 1900 to 1909 do not include a single piece of realism. Typical are kegs of corn syrup like Gene Stratton-Porter's *Freckles* and *A Girl of the Limberlost*.

"My formula for a book was damned by three of our foremost

publishers in the beginning, and I have never changed it a particle," Mrs. Porter admitted. The publisher Henry Holt complained in 1903 about the way a popular writer had reacted to his advice about revisions in a manuscript. The author admitted that the changes would improve the book, but, since other publishers would accept it in its present form, he refused to make them. "All I care for," he said, "is to turn out the greatest amount of work in the shortest time, and get the most pay that I can." Far different was the attitude of a hard-working Virginian, Ellen Glasgow, when asked if she would write an "optimistic novel about the West" and get into a juicy market. She replied, "If there is anything I know less about than the West, it is optimism." Her success, and her best work, came after World War I when the mood had changed.

Although the East held a leisure class seeking culture or pleasure, in the Midwest only the wives of well-to-do businessmen were an audience for art, and nationally women formed the great bulk of the audience for literature. The standards they set are apparent in the report of Charles Dawes after he had taken his mother and mother-in-law to see the folksy "David Harum" on the stage: "They were much pleased with this quaint, clean and wholesome play." President Cleveland said of the theater: "When I come I want to see something to make me laugh!" Postmaster General Wilson almost agreed: "Indeed, when I go to theater after a hard day's work, or a hard day's experience of mingled work and interruptions, I prefer a good mirth provoking play to anything less than a thoroughly first class tragedy—which latter one seldom sees." Men endorsed the female idea of decency. President Roosevelt thought Chaucer "altogether needlessly filthy," and was pleased when Anna Karenina's adultery was followed by her suicide. Anthony Comstock used the League for the Suppression of Vice to impose his prudery on New Yorkers. Chicago in 1904 had a police sergeant cruising the city in search of salacious paintings. He had a simple way of discriminating pornography from art. "If a picture or statue costs $50," he held, "it is beyond all question a work of art. If an artist devoted sufficient time to make it cost $50 it stands to reason that his motive was high."

Cities were regarded as sewers of vice, of immorality, of political corruption. A boy who wanted to make good, so it was said, would be well-advised to be born in the country. In 1883 a Brooklyn pastor reported that of 500 successful men he had surveyed, 57 per cent were from rural areas, only 17 per cent from cities. This was myth. Recent studies by C. Wright Mills and others have concluded that fewer than one in four business executives were farm boys.

Except for a few years during the free-silver struggles, when even Frederick Jackson Turner apologized for the barbarism of frontiersmen, it was thought that God had smiled on the farmer, especially in the West. Whereas earlier there had been warnings about the Great American Desert east of the Rockies, now land promoters (abetted by the state geologist of Nebraska) claimed scientific proof that "rain follows the plow." To a prospective investor in Philadelphia worried about drought in Kansas, a land-mortgage broker there wrote: "We are satisfied that the rainless belt has retreated before the march of civilization and that wherever civilization has pressed hardest there the limit is farthest west." The company claimed that skies were bluer, children better educated, and insanity less common in Kansas than elsewhere. A land pamphlet about Kansas claimed that low rainfall was beneficial: "One good lung here is worth a pair in the damp heavy air of the older states. Western Kansas is pre-eminently THE PARADISE OF THE LUNGS." An English minister wrote in *The Christian World* a story about an old resident of Kansas who found the climate so healthy he couldn't die. At last, having stipulated that he should be buried on his Deer Creek farm, he went to Illinois, where he succeeded in dying. But when he was buried the contact with Kansas soil brought him back to life, "to the disgust of his heirs and the confusion of those who had doubts about Kansas."

From Henry George in 1879 to Lord Bryce in 1914, eminent men contended that the cities were a threat to democracy and good government. "Whence shall come the new barbarians?" asked *Progress and Poverty*. "Go through the squalid quarters of great cities, and you may see, even now, their gathering hordes!" In *The Iron Heel* (1907), a vivid prediction that democracy in the United States will be replaced by the dictatorship of an oligarchy, Jack London shows a working-class mob in Chicago which will compare for animality with the wolf packs of *The Call of the Wild* (1903). Theodore Roosevelt in 1885 reported from his experience in the New York legislature that the worst of his colleagues came from the great cities. A few of the city representatives were educated and ethical men, "but the bulk are very low indeed. They are usually foreigners of little or no education, with exceedingly misty ideas as to morality, and possessed of an ignorance so profound that it could only be called comic, were it not for the fact that it has at times such serious effects upon our laws."

Such statements show how the notion of rural purity and urban corruption was fed by the racial thinking of the times—to which every President from Cleveland to Wilson contributed. At a time when Cleveland supposedly wanted above all else to stamp out the threat of free silver, he expressed his great sympathy for Southerners in the Cabinet who might feel constrained to support even a Silver Democrat for President in order to maintain the one-party system and white supremacy in their home states. Not only did McKinley stimulate racism by his foreign policies, he rescinded an order sending Negro troops to Little Rock when confronted by local protests. As to Theodore Roosevelt, Brownsville did not lead him to justice. Taft averred that he would not appoint Negroes to office in any region where white citizens objected, thus barring Negroes from new Federal jobs in those places where virtually all Negroes lived. Wilson, with Southerners holding most of the key positions in Congress, allowed the organization of segregation in several bureaus in Washington itself. When Federal officials in the South were given a free hand to fire or downgrade Negroes, the Collector of Internal Revenue in Georgia said: "There are no Government positions for Negroes in the South. A Negro's place is in the cornfield." Liberal protests brought the campaign to a stop and in places reversed it, but in September 1913 the President wrote the editor of the *Congregationalist:* "I would say that I do approve of the segregation that is being attempted in several of the departments." Wilson contended that Jim Crow had been adopted for the good of the Negroes.

If racism embodied a host of errors, so did the accompanying explanation of political corruption. The contention that immigrants were dependent on political bosses because they had been peasants in Europe and were untrained for urban life might be answered by saying migrants to cities from rural areas in the United States were at least as badly trained for urban life. Indeed, with their traditions of unrelenting individualism, they suffered from what Veblen called trained incapacity, and the great influence of Irish-Americans in city politics may well be due to the fact that they were much better trained to act in an organized fashion. In politics as in war, Bryce wrote, organization is all. Second, corruption was by no means confined to cities. New Hampshire, a rural state, was notoriously boss-ruled. Rhode Island's governor said in 1903 that nobody tried to conceal the purchase of rural votes, so common was the practice. The Democrats won New York in 1910, and some politicians said the Republicans had lost because they had not paid the rural voters. In Adams County, Ohio, almost the entire population was native-born whites; farming was the chief occupation; and the county seat was the only one in the state with neither railroad nor telegraph. Most people were quite poor. After the Civil War the two major parties were evenly balanced, and the sale of votes began. By 1885 it was public and well established. A clean-up finally came after the 1910 election, under a law requiring that anybody convicted of selling his vote should be disfranchised for five years. In the county, more than one voter in four was stricken from the election rolls. That the vote sellers regarded the system as a form of social security was reflected in verses printed in the *Literary Digest:*

> Many people sold their vote
> For to buy an overcoat,
> Or to buy a sack of flour,
> Thinking it a prosperous hour.

Yet, confronted with this clear evidence of the social roots of corruption, Theodore Roosevelt wrote in the *Outlook* that neither "capital" nor "labor," but the individual, was responsible for dishonest government.

A third defect of the notion that urban immigrants were the chief source of corruption was that, especially in the Midwest, many immigrants did not live in cities. North Dakota, 70 per cent rural and with an economy wholly dependent on farming, was dominated until 1906 by the regular Republican machine of Alexander McKenzie, who protected banking, railroad, and milling interests controlled from Minneapolis and St. Paul. More than half the state's population was foreign-born or first-generation Americans, often living in colonies that preserved the ways of the Old Country. Much of McKenzie's voting strength came from his shrewd selection of candidates to appeal to these local nationality

groups. But in 1906 insurgent Republicans combined with Democrats to elect John Burke governor, and he was re-elected in 1908
and 1910. His victories came from heavy majorities in the populous
eastern counties; wheat farmers in the rural western areas cared
little about freedom from boss rule and went on voting as before.
Conversely, Burke and the Progressives did nothing to lower railroad rates or to give the farmers a state-owned terminal grain elevator. Their program bore little relation to the needs of North
Dakota; what they did was to copy the political and social reforms
of Progressives elsewhere, particularly in Wisconsin. Even in a rural
state, Progressivism was the abstract and legalistic creed of urban
middle-class reformers. Its impact on North Dakota proved to be
slight.

Blubbering about rural virtue could expand into general optimism about human nature. Due to "the lessening intensity of
religious belief" in this country, wrote Henry George, "the distinction between Jew and Gentile is fast disappearing." William I.
Thomas, sociologist, said in 1904 that, with changes in communication that brought groups in contact, race prejudice would
become unimportant. William Allen White tooted over "the essential nobility of man," and Booth Tarkington closed a popular
novel by calling Midwesterners "the beautiful people." Mayor
Samuel "Golden Rule" Jones of Toledo said that he didn't want to
rule anybody: "Each individual must rule himself."

Beside the sentimentality was cruelty. In 1884 in Missouri the
Sedalia *Bazoo* scheduled a special train to carry curious folks 100
miles to the town of Nevada to see a public execution. The placard
giving the time-table and round-trip fares announced the train
would start back "thirty minutes after the death-scene at the gal-
lows." Often, as Mark Twain had so acutely seen, the sentimental
were also the cruel. Cole Blease, the white-supremacy governor
of South Carolina, did not scruple to encourage lynching. Neither
did he scruple to pardon whites convicted of all manner of crimes.
"I love the pardoning power," he said. "I want to give the poor
devils a chance. I hope to make the number an even thousand before
I go out of office." His actual total of pardons exceeded 1,500.

The American mind, then, was like my grandmother's attic,
crammed with junk: an old four-poster Victorian code of behavior,
educational furniture from Louis Quatorze to *chic moderne*, ethics

carved by cave men. It held everything from baby curls to bowie knives. The baby curl might even be knotted daintily about the bloody knife.

Empty words, illogic, and self-contradiction permeated the constitutional law of the period. "The great difficulty in the future," wrote Chief Justice Morrison R. Waite to another judge in 1877, "will be to establish the demarkation between that which is private and that in which the public has an interest." The chief agency to make this demarcation was the legislative. Admitting in *Munn* v. *Illinois* (1877) that a legislature might abuse its power to regulate property "affected with a public interest," Waite wrote for the Court: "For protection against abuses by Legislatures the people must resort to the polls, not to the courts." This doctrine of judicial self-restraint was rejected by a minority of the Court who wanted the judiciary to wield a Big Stick in defense of property. Most prominent in this faction was Justice Stephen J. Field, who had been attorney for and intimate of the Central Pacific executives. When Field complained that, although he stood with the majority in a case involving the Union Pacific, another justice had been assigned to write the decision, the Chief Justice called Field's attention to "the excited state of feeling" about the railroad's relation to the government: "It seemed to me, therefore, especially important that the decision should come from one who would not be known as the personal friend of the parties representing these railroad interests."

Personnel changes and shifts of opinion brought new supporters to the Field view, especially after the advent of Chief Justice Melville W. Fuller in 1888. Whereas Waite's doctrine of "public interest" sanctioned regulation of any firm that vitally affected the public, Field's decision in *Georgia Railroad* v. *Smith* (1888) upheld state regulation of a railroad on the ground that it had obtained special concessions from the state—a charter, the right of eminent domain—and thus had incurred an obligation to the public. Here was a narrowing of state regulatory power, but more significant was the emergence of "substantive due process" under first the Fourteenth Amendment, then the Fifth. Historically "due process of law" had mattered chiefly in criminal law, as requiring certain procedural safeguards: exemption from arrest without a warrant, right to counsel, trial by jury, and so on. Now came the dogma that the results of the procedures must be reasonable, and in many cases the idea of judicial self-restraint went into cold storage. During the argument in *Santa Clara County* v. *Southern Pacific Railroad* (1886), the Chief Justice stated that the Court unanimously thought that corporations as well as individuals were protected by the 14th Amendment's prohibition of state action that would "deny to any person within its jurisdiction the equal protection of the laws." In 1890 the Court held unconstitutional a Minnesota law giving a commission final and conclusive power to set intrastate railroad rates. Presumably the decision was an attack on faulty procedure, since the statute had not allowed the railroad the right of appeal. But what if a legislature should set rates directly? And if a legislature could fix rates, asked Justice Bradley for three dissenters, why could it not delegate that power to a commission? The question of reasonableness of railroad charges, wrote Bradley, was "pre-eminently a legislative one. . . ."

Not so, ruled the Court in *Smyth* v. *Ames* (1898), striking down a Nebraska law on the ground that it set intrastate freight charges so low that they were confiscatory and a deprivation of property without due process of law. The decision held that rates must be based on the "fair value" of the property:

> And, in order to ascertain that value, the original cost of construction, the amount expended in permanent improvements, the amount and market value of its bonds and stock, the present as compared with the original cost of construction, the probable earning capacity of the property under particular rates prescribed by statute, and the sum required to meet operating expenses, are all matters for consideration, and are to be given such weight as may be just and right in each case. We do not say that there may not be other matters to be regarded in estimating the value of the property.

A public authority following these prescriptions would be fortunate to set one rate a year, and would then find it reviewed by a series of courts. And under the doctrine of *Smyth* v. *Ames*, pro-railroad judges in depression years based the "fair value" of a railroad on its original cost, but in prosperous years they focused on its current reproduction cost.

In the Minnesota Rate Case of 1890 the Court also worked magic on its definition of property. In the Slaughter House Cases of 1872 the majority had held to the common-law definition of property as the use value of physical objects. Thus when the

Fourteenth Amendment said "nor shall any State deprive any person of life, liberty, or property, without due process of law," it meant that his physical possession or legal title could not be lifted without just compensation. Justice Swayne of the dissenters held on the contrary that property "is everything which has an exchangeable value . . ."; if the exchange value of a man's labor is reduced, for instance, he is deprived of his property. In 1890 the Court extended its definition to accept Swayne's view: expected earning power became property. Marketable assets obviously depend upon access to markets; *Allgeyer* v. *Louisiana* (1897) saw a solid Court hold that the liberty of the Fourteenth Amendment meant the right of a person to "live and work where he will" and to make all contracts necessary to "the enjoyment of all his faculties . . ." The changed meaning of property was in fact a reversal. It had been producing power to increase the supply of goods; now it was also bargaining power to restrict the supply of goods in order to raise their price.

While restricting the power of states over railroads, the Court also construed the Interstate Commerce Act so that the ICC was without power. Although the Commission in 1887 did not assume that it had authority to set rates *de novo*, for a decade it did act as if, having set aside a given rate as unreasonable, it could substitute an alternative. In the Social Circle Case (1896) and the Maximum Freight Rate Case (1897), the Court ruled that nothing in the Act gave this power to the Commission. The Act also prohibited a railroad from charging more for a short than for a long haul "under substantially similar circumstances. . . ." In 1897, in an Alabama case involving rates that favored Montgomery over Troy, the Court ruled that the presence of railroad competition between two points might justify a lower charge for a long haul than for a short one. The dissenting Justice Harlan declared with reason that the Supreme Court had rendered the ICC "a useless body for all practical purposes," and it remained so until the Hepburn Act in 1906.

In interpreting the Sherman Anti-Trust Act, the Supreme Court for a time seemed to retreat from its position in the Knight Case of 1895. The decision in the Addystone Pipe Case (1899) held that at least some combinations among manufacturing firms might be violations of the law. Holding in the Trans-Missouri Freight Association Case (1897) that a pool of railroads to fix rates was illegal, the Court explicitly, if by a 5 to 4 majority only, held that "the plain and ordinary meaning" of the Sherman Act banned all combinations in restraint of interstate trade, not merely "unreasonable" ones.

But in the Standard Oil Case in May 1911, the Rule of Reason became the law of the land. Under the decision the holding company was forced to divest itself of control over 33 affiliates with 57 per cent of its net worth. But the Standard Oil Company of New Jersey remained by far the largest oil company in the country; the only industrial firm that was larger was U. S. Steel. And by 1927 Jersey Standard would have assets more than twice what they had been before the dissolution decree, while several other firms split off by the decision were also giants. For years after 1911 it was almost impossible to bring a prosecution successfully under the anti-trust laws, for the alleged monopoly could appeal with telling effect to the Rule of Reason. When Chief Justice White put the shibboleth forward in 1911 in the American Tobacco Case and said it "was in accord with all previous decisions of this court," Justice Harlan pointed back a mere 14 years to the 1897 ruling and scoffed at White: ". . . this statement surprises me quite as much as would a statement that black was white or white was black." Make-believe was a mark of the era.

Also revealing in its implications for anti-trust policy was the Du Pont Case of 1907–1912. A Federal court in 1911 directed the company and the government to suggest how to reorganize the firm. At once the United States army and navy protested that the national interest would suffer if Du Pont were stripped of its monopoly in making military smokeless gunpowder. Under a plan for reorganization that took effect in 1912, Atlas Powder and Hercules Powder were split off from Du Pont as independent companies and shared with it the business in industrial explosives and sporting gunpowders. But Du Pont remained the biggest producer of explosives and the only producer of smokeless military gunpowder.

If the Interstate Commerce Act and the Anti-Trust Act were hardly effective against large corporations, they could be used to impede trade unions. In the Ann Arbor Case of 1893, Circuit Judge William Howard Taft enjoined the Brotherhood of Locomotive Engineers from enforcing its rule that banned its members from handling the property of a railroad against which the union was on strike; Taft held that the rule violated the Interstate Commerce Act and thus made "the whole brotherhood a criminal conspiracy against the laws of their country." In the Danbury Hatters Case (1908) the Supreme Court unanimously ruled that the Sherman Act could be brought to bear against a trade union that instituted a secondary boycott; that is, asked its members not to buy the products of a firm that was not their employer.

When Congress tried to legislate for the protection of wage earners, the Court scrutinized the statute carefully. A law of 1906 made all common carriers in interstate commerce liable for industrial injuries to their employees, and set aside as a defense the fellow-servant doctrine under which a firm was not responsible for injuries suffered because of the carelessness of a fellow workman. Holding that the statute was so worded that it applied even to employees working solely in intrastate commerce, the Court in 1908 held it unconstitutional. The same year the Court struck down part of the Erdman Act of 1898 which had banned railroads from requiring yellow-dog contracts under which their employees had to agree not to join a union. The provision, held the Court in *Adair* v. *United States*, violated the Fourteenth Amendment because it was an unreasonable infringement on freedom of contract.

State laws to regulate working conditions might fall under the same doctrine. In 1898 the decision in *Holden* v. *Hardy* allowed a Utah law restricting the hours of labor in mines to eight a day, and in *Muller* v. *Oregon* (1908) the Court took account of sociological data in upholding as a reasonable exercise of the police power a statute prohibiting women from working more than ten hours a day in certain places of employment. But the Court in *Lochner* v. *New York* (1908) by the narrowest possible margin disallowed a law banning bakers from working more than ten hours a day, declaring that the public interest was in no way affected by the provision and therefore it invaded freedom of contract. In a brilliant dissent Justice Holmes asserted the right of the legislature to experiment within a broad scope, and called for a return to judicial self-restraint.

But time after time constitutional questions were decided by resort to the fetish of "class legislation." In 1893 a Missouri law banning the payment of wages in company scrip was knocked over in *State* v. *Loomis* by the state supreme court as class legislation and improper infringement of freedom of contract, while in *Braceville Coal Co.* v. *People* the same fate on the same grounds befell an Illinois law requiring corporations to pay wages weekly. The income tax was widely denounced as class legislation, although nobody in history has ever drafted a tax law that did not bear more heavily on some social groups than on others. When in 1913 Congress attached to an appropriation law a provision that none of the funds provided in the bill could be used to prosecute trade unions or farm organizations, Taft vetoed it as "class legislation of the most vicious sort." The next year a bill setting up land banks to extend long-term credit to farmers provided that, if private investors did not buy the bonds of the banks, the Federal government should do so. Wilson opposed the proposal for government aid on the score that "it is unwise and unjustifiable to extend the credit of the Government to a single class of the community." Prior to 1900 laws excluding aliens from employment on public works had been held unconstitutional as class legislation, but under the depressed conditions of 1914 the Supreme Court allowed such a statute, to be used against unnaturalized Italians building the New York subways.

Some of the wildest doctrines evolved by the Court came in cases to determine what rights the overseas colonies and their residents had under the Constitution of the United States. That document required customs duties to be uniform throughout the country, and forbade the imposition of export taxes on goods leaving any state. But Congress wanted to tax imports from Puerto Rico. In *Downes* v. *Bidwell* (1901) the Court held it could do so because the Constitution did not apply until Puerto Rico had been "incorporated" into the United States by Congress. Thereafter, in each case the Court decided whether a given territory had been incorporated or not. A majority also discovered, more than a century after the adoption of the Bill of Rights, that some of its guarantees, such as the procedure by means of grand jury and common-law trial jury in criminal trials, were not "fundamental rights" enjoyed by all under American jurisdiction but were required only in "incorporated" territories. Substantive due process was rising, but procedural due process was falling.

How to explain this constitutional jumble, under which a court could decide a case in diametrically opposite ways by choosing to strike it with one rather than another of the untidy array of arrows in the judicial quiver? The answer lies in the reigning view as to the function of the courts and, more broadly, of the government. Justice Holmes was quite explicit in defining "the most perfect government": it would register "the actual equilibrium of force in the community—that is, conformity to the wishes of the dominant power . . . the proximate test of a good government is that the dominant power has its way." By this reasoning, for instance, it was inevitable that the government would find a way to frustrate the desire of Eastern farmers for railroad legislation to ban disproportionately high charges for short hauls, because lower rates for long hauls were wanted by Western farmers, by Eastern employers who desired cheap raw material, and by Eastern consumers who wanted cheap food.

Holmes legitimized the wealthy as "the dominant power" in the United States. Asked "Whether a man can render services entitling him to a fortune as great as some of ours in America," he wrote: "My practical answer is that a great fortune does not mean a corresponding consumption, but a power of command; that some one must exercise that command, and that I know of no way of finding the fit man so good as the fact of winning it in the competition of the market." Already in 1897 the Justice was pointed in indicating the special pressures that had been playing on the courts:

> When socialism first began to be talked about, the comfortable classes of the community were a good deal frightened. I suspect that this fear has influenced judical action both here and in England, yet it is certain that it is not a conscious factor in the decisions to which I refer.

These remarks "came close" to the main reason for the changing attitudes of lawyers and judges from 1887 to 1895, Arnold M. Paul has recently concluded. And American socialism was still in its infancy in 1897; its electoral strength grew swiftly after the Socialist party was formed in 1901.

By 1904, when Eugene Debs received 420,000 votes for President, Theodore Roosevelt was alarmed. The growth of Socialism, he wrote the following February, was "far more ominous than any populist or similar movement in the past." A year later he told Taft: "The dull, purblind folly of the very rich men; their greed and arrogance and the corruption in business and politics, have tended to produce a very unhealthy condition of excitement and irritation in the popular mind, which shows itself in the great increase in the socialistic propaganda." While Roosevelt drifted leftward in his effort to hold the loyalty of wage earners and restless members of the middle class, the Socialist vote went on growing. It passed 900,000—nearly 6 per cent of the total—in 1912.

That result came to Debs in his fourth race for the White House. But in reality his life had become one continuous agitation to replace the existing social order with a better one: against the Spanish-American War; against the trials of Bill Haywood in 1907 and of Jim McNamara in 1911; against Wilson's policies in Mexico; against private ownership of the means of production; for strikers here and there; for the creation of a new world that would bring joy in the morning.

Evangelist: DWIGHT L. MOODY

Eminence in the Protestant ministry is a telling index of historical change in America. In the first generation of Puritans, Thomas Hooker had steadfast purpose and a splendid sense of metaphor. Jonathan Edwards a century later was cool, seemingly aloof, a dogged Calvinist who brooded over original sin, and a brilliant student of psychology. Of the pre-Revolutionary generation, Jonathan Mayhew directly contradicted Edwards by his advocacy of freedom of the will and the rights of man. At midpoint in the nineteenth century Charles Grandison Finney was a fervent abolitionist and author of *Lectures on Systematic Theology* (1846). Dwight Lyman Moody (1837–1899) felt no need to shoulder such a weighty burden. One story about him, however apocryphal it might be, sums up his shallowness. At the end of a revival meeting a lady approached him from the audience to say that, although she loved to hear him preach, she was not sure that she agreed with his theology. "My theology?", he supposedly replied. "I didn't know I had one."

Nominally a Unitarian, Moody applied for church membership at age 18 to an evangelical congregation in Boston. He was rejected. According to his Sunday School teacher, Moody "could not tell what it was to be a Christian; had no idea of what Christ had done for him . . ." A year later he passed, and soon removed to Chicago. There he was zealous for advancement. He clerked for a boot and shoe retailer, dabbled in real estate, was traveling salesman for a wholesaler. He got caught up in the religious revival of 1857, and through the YMCA and another evangelical church he took up the cause. By 1859 he had started a mission school on the north side of Chicago; he was off and drooling. His message was jejune: He was nondenominational. Insofar as he mentioned social problems at all, his formulas were those of the businessman's ethic. He was less individualistic than Finney less than two generations earlier. To Jonathan Edwards, only God, by his free grace, could redeem a man. Finney urged that each man must save himself. Moody said that we must save each other: "Instrumentally men are to be Saviours of one another."

He became the most successful "enthusiastical" of his times, precursor to Billy Sunday and Billy Graham. Although he had scored elaborate gains from his mission in Chicago, he became a sensation at home only with a tour of Great Britain in 1873–1874. His countrymen were proving in many ways their dependence on foreign indulgences: by marrying Continental nobility, by reading alien novels. Xenophobia was accompanied by adulation of the exotic outlanders. Only when they saw on his shank "European Inspected" did his native land place its trust in an American aboriginal.

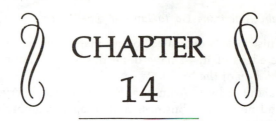

CHAPTER
14

Eye, Mind, and Spirit

Way back when Debs was buoyantly beginning his career in socialism, Mark Twain had already despaired of mankind. Jay Gould (to Twain a chief factor in the "moral rot" of America) left his fortune to his daughter Helen, and in 1898 she gave the United States government $100,000 as her contribution to the Spanish-American War. In far-off Vienna, where Twain was, the newspapers applauded her act. "We all belong to the nasty stinking little human race," wrote Twain to Howells, "& of course it is not nice for God's beloved vermin to scoff at each other; but how can I help it when the Abendblatt pukes another mess of Helen-Gould adulation onto me. . . . Oh, we *are* a nasty little lot—& to think there are people who would like to save us, continue us. It won't happen if I have any influence."

The venom of his late years never carried Twain to the imaginative heights of *Huck Finn,* nor did any of Howell's novels after 1900 reach the level of *Silas Lapham.* Many critics profess to find the best work of Henry James in three late novels, but to me they seem turgid and marred by a philosophy verging on solipsism. The old generation waned in the new century, but an even larger group of lasting writers was looming up. Most incredible of all was the first real birth of poetry in the United States. In spite of isolated accomplishments—Edward Taylor, some Emerson, Whitman at his best, the prodigious if almost unknown Emily Dickinson—the quality of American verse had been generally contemptible. Then the modern American movement was presaged by a slight volume that was privately published in 1896 in Gardiner, Maine. The whimsical and charming beginning has, I believe, remained safely a secret confined to the few copies of the original edition: "This book is dedicated to any man, woman, or critic who will cut the edges of it.—I have done the top." The perverse title was *The Children of the Night*.

Much about Edwin Arlington Robinson was perverse. In a practical land he scorned business and scraped together the barest living until Theodore Roosevelt gave him a sinecure in the usual spot—the New York Customhouse. In a land that scorned tradition Robinson insisted that to create is to transmute an inheritance, and he went to the Bible and Shakespeare and Emerson and Browning and Tennyson. The latter two had shown the poetic possibilities of the dramatic monologue, and Robinson in "The Night Before" pioneered for Americans with the literary form that would be used so deftly two decades later by Robert Frost. Robinson's long monologue, uttered by a man about to be hanged for killing his wife's lover, is a failure, but even as a failure it holds passages that are vintage poetry:

> For a conscience
> He carried a snug deceit that made him
> The man of the time and the place, whatever
> The time or the place might be.

What Robinson did was to revivify traditions by revising them. All poetic forms are shackles that the poet voluntarily accepts. To the challenge they pose, he says in effect: Even if I willfully scrap most of the resources of the English language, I can find other resources that will enable me to express myself precisely. More, I can still express profound truths precisely. Here is Robinson's early proof:

> Because he was a butcher and thereby
> Did earn an honest living (and did right),
> I would not have you think that Reuben Bright
> Was any more a brute than you or I;
> For when they told him that his wife must die,
> He stared at them, and shook with grief and fright,
> And cried like a great baby half that night,
> And made the women cry to see him cry.

And after she was dead, and he had paid
The singers and the sexton and the rest,
He packed a lot of things that she had made
Most mournfully away in an old chest
Of hers, and put some chopped-up cedar boughs
In with them, and tore down the slaughter-house.

The traditional elements are clear enough. It is a sonnet, having fourteen lines, with a section of eight lines followed by a section of six. It is in the most common metrical scheme for sonnets— iambic pentameter. Each verse has five measures or metrical feet, and each foot has an unaccented syllable followed by an accented one. But only a bold poet could have accepted the additional limitations that Robinson imposed on himself, and only a mature poet could have conquered them. Abjuring entirely the vocabulary and syntax regarded as "poetic," Robinson used the speech of his home town of Gardiner, Maine. The sentences and words are ruthlessly simple. Two words have three syllables; thirteen have two syllables; 108 have one syllable only. Only the word *sexton* derives from a Latin root, and that is so corrupted from *sacristan* that a reader might well think it the most Anglo-Saxon word in the poem.

Every mention of Mrs. Bright (*she, hers*) is an accented beat; all mentions of Reuben (*he, him*) save one fall on an unaccented beat. The sole exception is in the ninth line, when *he* pays the singer and the sexton and the rest. By this emphasis Robinson sustains to the very last clause in the poem the tone of the first section. As the sonnet opens Reuben is a butcher; that is, a man whose relation to death is mediated by money; this notion is repeated by stressing that he pays for the funeral. The only other knowledge we have of him is that he is capable of the sentimental reaction to death that was conventional at the time: He weeps, he packs her things away in a chest. But when he tears down the slaughter-house, we are slashed with the news that a single death has altered Reuben's relation to the universal phenomenon of death, that even the soul of a most common man can be plowed to its depths. In poem after poem Robinson dealt with the realities that men experience—love, jealousy, death, fantasy, faith in God and doubt of God. And the "lives of quiet desperation" to which Thoreau had pointed.

Whenever Richard Cory went down town,
We people on the pavement looked at him:
He was a gentleman from sole to crown,
Clean favored, and imperially slim.

And he was always quietly arrayed,
And he was always human when he talked;
But still he fluttered pulses when he said,
"Good morning," and he glittered when he walked.

And he was rich,—yes, richer than a king,—
And admirably schooled in every grace:
In fine, we thought that he was everything
To make us wish that we were in his place.

So on we worked, and waited for the light,
And went without the meat, and cursed the bread;
And Richard Cory, one calm summer night,
Went home and put a bullet through his head.

Robinson's prying into escape mechanisms—fantasy, alcoholism, suicide—would have seemed to many contemporaries his most perverse and morbid trait. Isn't the "Progressive era" often called an "age of optimism," a time when men believed in progress and looked on the smiling side of life? But the imaginative literature of the time shows many instances in which society, having in large measure shaped a person's desires, frustrated them so repeatedly and so deeply that he kills himself. Defining a free society in these terms, American writers saw their own land as in great degree servile. In one major work after another, suicide is a factor:

> *Maggie: A Girl of the Streets*, by Stephen Crane (1896)
> *The Damnation of Theron Ware*, by Harold Frederic (1896)
> *Sister Carrie*, by Theodore Dreiser (1900)
> *The Pit*, by Frank Norris (1903)
> "Paul's Case," by Willa Cather (1905)
> *The House of Mirth*, by Edith Wharton (1905)
> *Martin Eden*, by Jack London (1908)

Of all those who consider suicide, the only one we might dislike is Theron Ware. In the first American novel to probe deeply into the relations of immigrant Catholics to the underlying Protestant stock, Frederic sets forth the moral decay of a young Methodist minister in a small town in upstate New York. Although a married man, Ware becomes infatuated with Celia Madden, who is Irish, Catholic, rich, and "emancipated" in the most exotic ways she can dream up. Ware also becomes infatuated with the learning of the urbane priest Father Forbes and his atheistic friend Dr. Ledyard. Sneering now at the faith in which he earns his bread, Ware is moved by vanity to one villainy after another. He conspires with two professional fund-raisers to palm off songs by Chopin as Methodist hymns. He conspires with two trustees of his church to take advantage of a third and defraud the church. Projecting his own faults on those closest to him, he accuses his innocent wife of improper conduct with the victimized trustee, and even suspects Celia of improper conduct with Father Forbes. He deceives others freely, and his lack of real virility lets him deceive himself. He builds a dream world in which he resigns his ministry, runs away with Celia, and lives off her money. And he believes his romantic inventions up to the minute she tells him bluntly: "What you took to be improvement was degeneration." The story builds beautifully to the end, and it is loaded with characters seen in the round. But Frederic was a journalist, and he had the fault common in that trade of reaching for the handy word instead of seeking for the right word. So his phrasing is sometimes clumsy, but it is often delicious, as when he writes that Theron's imagination drew "pictures of whole weeks of solitary academic calm, alone with his books and his thoughts. The facts that he had no books, and that nobody dreamed of interfering with his thoughts, subordinated themselves humbly to his mood."

Similar remarks must be made about another journalist who wrote novels—Dreiser. Stilted phrasing, banal passages. But already in *Sister Carrie*, his first book, he created in George Hurstwood one of the most moving characters in American fiction, and the over-all structure of the book is solid and complex and neatly fitted. The manuscript won the instant admiration of a young reader at Doubleday, Frank Norris, who was himself learning to write novels. But Norris had a long way to go. His first two tries, both focusing on the ways that biological traits affect human behavior, were frequently dull, and so was *The Octopus*, the first volume of a proposed trilogy dealing with the relations between mankind and wheat. Far better was *The Pit*, which gets real excitement into descriptions of speculation in grain futures on the

Chicago Board of Trade. In this story of the efforts of a big operator to corner the market for wheat, Norris wrote one of the few alleged "business novels" to actually deal with the business career as well as the personal life of its hero.

But Norris died young, without writing his masterpiece. He cannot even be credited with getting Dreiser before an audience, for, although *Sister Carrie* was accepted by Doubleday on his recommendation, it was virtually suppressed by the publisher when his wife complained that it was immoral. The book was not really available to American readers until 1908, and three years later Dreiser showed that neither its literary merit nor its objectionable theme was an aberration by duplicating both in *Jennie Gerhardt*. Each of the novels is titled after a young woman who becomes successively the mistress of two men, but the characters and the plots are entirely different. Although Carrie Meeber becomes a star of the stage, she is a vapid and even silly woman, and the book belongs to Hurstwood rather than to her. But however much our interest is caught by William Gerhardt and by Archibald Kane and his son Lester, it is the story of Jennie's life—her behavior that society outlawed, and her emotions that Dreiser revered—which makes the novel outstanding.

Working as a hotel maid in Columbus, Ohio, Jennie becomes acquainted with Senator Brander, who helps her needy family. When Jennie's brother is arrested for stealing coal from a railroad yard, she turns to the Senator, and he has the brother freed. Dreiser saw that a young woman in the grip of despair and then of gratitude was available for seduction, and Jennie becomes pregnant. Brander dies before he can marry her, and she has the child. When she comes under the eye of the heir to a huge carriage-manufacturing firm in Cincinnati, Lester Kane (who also helps her family), she fears to tell him of her earlier liaison with Brander. He cannot make up his mind to marry her because of her class position, but they set up housekeeping together in Chicago. After some years Lester discovers that Jennie has a daughter, and, in an exquisitely written section, Dreiser comments:

> That a man of Lester's temperament should consider himself wronged by Jennie merely because she had concealed a child whose existence was due to conduct no more irregular than was involved in the yielding of herself to him was an example of those inexplicable

perversions of judgment to which the human mind, in its capacity of keeper of the honor of others, seems permanently committed.

A study of codes of honor, as was *Huck Finn, Jennie Gerhardt* also is saturated as was Twain's book with awareness of the human ability to just drift along. Lester will not marry Jennie, and he cannot leave her. Again as in *Huck Finn, Jennie Gerhardt* sees society as menacing. The placid cohabitation of Jennie and Lester is disrupted by his family. In a confrontation the old manufacturer Archibald Kane tells his son: "I began to see through my business connections how much the right sort of marriage helps a man. . . ." Dreiser has already made clear that the liasion under attack is the right sort of marriage—right because Jennie and Lester are easy with one another. Archibald's definition is different: ". . . what the world considers as right and proper."

But if society is evil, its human agents are not. In the novel there is nobody to dislike, not Lester nor his father, not Jennie nor her father. Cruelty happens, but nobody wills it. And even cruelty cannot mar the generosity and courage of Jennie Gerhardt. As Lester watches Jennie's grief at the funeral of her father, he thinks, "Well, there is something to her. There's no explaining a good woman." But he left her anyway, for reasons that Dreiser understood and even condoned.

In Edith Wharton's *The House of Mirth*, society is savage. Lily Bart's world respects only money, and she is destroyed because she has none. She is born wealthy and cultured, but when she is nineteen, her father fails in business. She depends on the support of an aunt until the aunt dies, then on invitations to the house parties of wealthy friends. Blackballed by a ruler of society who falsely implies that Lily has had an affair with her husband, she becomes a social secretary to newly rich women. She has a chance to re-enter proper circles by marrying Simon Rosedale. Although high society is anti-Semitic, neither Rosedale's Jewish birth nor his vulgarity would bar them after their marriage, for Lily has no doubt of the influences that are thwarting her:

> That influence, in its last analysis, was simply the power of money: Bertha Dorset's social credit was based on an impregnable bank-account. Lily knew that Rosedale had overstated neither the difficulty of her position nor the completeness of the vindication he offered:

once Bertha's match in material resources, her superior gifts would make it easy for her to dominate her adversary.

But Lily lets the chance slip away, and winds up a seamstress in a hat shop. As Veblen had suggested in *The Theory of the Leisure Class* (1899), the lower classes copy the values of the leisure class, and Lily causes little stir among her fellow workers: "She had fallen, she had 'gone under,' and true to the ideal of their race, they were awed only by success—by the gross tangible image of material achievement."

While Wharton and Dreiser and Ellen Glasgow were starting their careers as novelists, Willa Cather and Stephen Crane were writing notable short stories. Of the seven stories in Cather's *The Troll Garden* (1905), "Paul's Case" moves in a weird light comparable only, so far as I know, to that of D. H. Lawrence's "The Rocking-Horse Winner." Her "A Wagner Matinee" is a fugue woven of the themes of Eastern culture and Western squalor. A woman, teacher of piano at the Boston conservatory, marries, moves west, and spends 30 years helping to subdue a Nebraska farm. Back at last in Boston, she is taken to a concert by her nephew, now a cultured resident of the city but once a boy the aunt had helped to rear on that Western farm. The *Tannhäuser* overture brings to him keen images:

> With the battle between the two motives, with the frenzy of the Venusberg theme and its ripping of strings, there came to me an overwhelming sense of the waste and wear that we are powerless to combat; and I saw again the tall, naked house on the prairie, black and grim as a wooden fortress; the black pond where I had learned to swim, its margin pitted with sun-dried cattle tracks; the rain-gullied clay banks about the naked house, the four dwarf ash seedlings where the dishcloths were always hung to dry before the kitchen door.

Lawlessness and society, frontier violence and the stability suggested by marriage, these are the antipodes in Stephen Crane's fine story "The Bride Comes to Yellow Sky." But nowhere does Crane's craft show to better effect than in "The Open Boat," a tale of four shipwrecked men in a 10-foot dinghy who try to ride through a storm to the Florida coast. The symbols revolve around traditional American themes: the comradeship of men when confronted by a common foe and a common job to be done; the sea as menace and the land as safety—Melville's "insular Tahiti" again; Nature's indifference to man, painted by Eakins into his Crucifixion. In Crane's ironic formulation: "When it occurs to a man that nature does not regard him as important, and that she feels she would not maim the universe by disposing of him, he at first wishes to throw bricks at the temple, and he hates deeply the fact that there are no bricks and no temples."

Most Americans went on seeing mirage temples. They boasted of their Presidents, who were not impressive men; they were proud of the American genius at self-government, for which the evidence was gaunt; and they largely ignored the cultural riches pouring forth from artists and musicians and writers. Nobody can know how much the country was hurt by this neglect. As Edward Alsworth Ross pointed out in his *American Journal of Sociology* series on "Social Control" in 1898, many of the techniques by which societies had controlled their members were becoming emaciated and wan: etiquette and ceremony, custom, religion, a sense of kinship and community. What was available to do the job in the future, to prevent men from breeding anarchy or tyranny? In his novel *The Iron Heel* in 1908 Jack London with terrifying power predicted that they would breed both. But Ross had already pointed to writers as a source of hope:

> Art is one of the few moral instruments which, instead of being blunted by the vast changes in opinion, have gained edge and sweep by these changes. So far as the eye can pierce the future, there is nothing to discredit it. The sympathies it fosters do not, it is true, establish norms and duties; but they lift that plane of general sentiment out of which imperatives and obligations arise. If there is anyone in this age who does the work of the Isaiahs and Amoses of old, it is an Ibsen, a Tolstoi, a Victor Hugo, or a Thomas Hardy.

In some places in the United States a sense of community still existed at the turn of the century, and nowhere was its persistence more important than in New Orleans, for there it fed the first important body of instrumental music to be created in the United States. Also contributing to the birth of Dixieland jazz were musical traditions that Negroes had brought from Africa and modified in this country. An example is the rhythmical "snap," by which the last beat in a measure is split in two. As rhythm instruments there was the washtub, which in Africa had been a hole in the ground covered by a skin, serving as a sounding chamber. A cord from the skin ran up to a pole, the other end of which was rested on the ground beside the hole. Raising or lowering the upper end of the pole adjusted the tension of the cord, which was plucked or bowed. The washtub was replaced in jazz bands by the bass viol. Also for rhythm was the jawbone of a large animal with the teeth loosened; a stick was scraped across the teeth. Replaced by the guitar. And drums, not replaced at all. The melodic tradition from Africa was antiphonal, part singing. This was reinforced in America by the harmonica, a cheap and organ-like instrument readily available to Negroes, and eventuated in the jazz melody section of cornet, clarinet, and trombone. The kazoo, a sort of pipe, accustomed them to an instrument that only partially instrumentalized the human voice. And for melodies the Negroes had not only their spirituals and hymns but also work songs and shouts.

Country Negroes with these traditions and instruments came to New Orleans in large numbers after the Civil War. They felt close together emotionally, united by a sense of shared injustice and misery, by religion, by habit of seeking release in gaiety and liquor and sex. In New Orleans, a cosmopolitan city, a great seaport, a port second only to New York, in New Orleans they came against a third element in the birth of jazz—the European instrumentation of brass bands. After 1890 Negro lodges began to set up their own brass bands to play for street parades and funerals. Then Negro bands moved indoors to play for dances, and the standard Dixieland band came to be three rhythm instruments—drums, bass, and guitar—plus three melody instruments, the cornet or trumpet usually playing the melody, with the clarinet playing variations in a higher register and the trombone playing variations in a lower. As in poetry, a firm structure to each song set the limits for improvisation.

The spirit that animated Dixieland bands has been recalled by drummer Baby Dodds:

> With all the outfits I played, I felt that I was just as essential in the outfit as any other instrument in it. I knew I had to do my part. . . . Of course, I never worked any place where I felt I was

the whole thing. I felt that all the other instruments were needed too. No one can do anything by himself. If there are more than two it's a group, and I feel that all members are essential. In playing music I always felt that I was part of the group and not an individual performer.

Better, listen to the George Lewis record, "Jazz in the Classic New Orleans Tradition." Or get Bessie Smith's first recording, "Downhearted Blues," and hear the generosity with which Clarence Williams puts the rhythm of his piano underneath the young singer's voice and carries her through the song. The latter performance was in 1923, and by that time the striving for overall ensemble effects was dying out as the bands drifted out of the community that had spawned them. Baby Dodds and his brother Johnny were in Chicago with Louis Armstrong, and men who had learned to play their horns in a New Orleans orphanage were using their talents on soloes. It was the day of the star performer, and the day of the buffoon lay ahead.

An important factor in the decline of group solidarity was the great geographical and social mobility, which in turn was facilitated by the rapid applications of science. But, paradoxically, the United States was not an eminent country in science. Leading American scientists, such as the physiologist Jacques Loeb, were born and trained in Europe. Another, the mathematical physicist J. Willard Gibbs, testified that in a lifetime of teaching at Yale he had only a half-dozen students capable of understanding his work. A Du Pont official claimed that even after World War I this country was a "Science Sahara." Thomas Edison, upon reading of Hertz's experiments with radio waves, had said to an associate: "Well, I'm not a scientist. I'm an inventor. Faraday was a scientist. He didn't work for money. . . . Said he hadn't time to do so. But I do. I measure everything by the size of the silver dollar. If it don't come up to that standard then I know it's no good."

The American talent ran to making science practical and profitable. Edison's many inventions, Ford and the automobile and the assembly line, the pioneer flights in 1903 by Orville and Wilbur Wright at Kitty Hawk. Other Americans excelled at projects requiring not only engineering skill but also esthetic judgment and social dedication—and, often, organizational ability. Brooklyn Bridge was opened in 1883, a monument to the bravery of many men and to the genius of John A. Roebling and his son Washington Roebling. It was the longest suspension bridge in the world, and prominent engineers had declared it impossible. It was soaring spidery magical beauty that shamed its shabby surroundings. It was still adequate to the demands of traffic a century after it was conceived. The 16-year struggle to build it, which cost the father's life and the son's health, was far longer, more heroic, and more useful than the Spanish-American War.

Technical innovation combined with artistic and social vision also shaped the unbelievable career of Frank Lloyd Wright, which began in 1887 at a drafting board in the Chicago office of Louis Sullivan and Dankmar Adler. For the Larkin Building of 1904 in Buffalo, a hermetically sealed and fireproof office building in which the floors were balconies opening into a central gallery, Wright invented the hanging partition. His Universalist Church near Chicago was "the first total building designed for and completed in the wooden forms into which it was poured as concrete." By 1914 the Midwest was graced by several examples of his basic prairie house, with its sweeping horizontals emphasized by the hovering roof.

The graphic arts after 1898 produced nobody comparable to Eakins or Homer or Ryder, but the general level of art improved considerably. Painters drew together for comfort and stimulation into informal groups such as the Ashcan School. One of its abler

Robie house, designed by Frank Lloyd Wright. (Courtesy of University of Chicago.)

members, Robert Henri, took as a pupil the young George Bellows, who trumpeted: "What this world needs is art. Art and more art." Himself a star baseball player at Ohio State, Bellows left canvases of polo games and swimming and tennis. His "Stag at Sharkey's" is a better rendering of a prize fight than any that Eakins did, and his best portraits would have been worthy of the American painter he idolized.

Bellows was among the 25 artists who in 1912 set out to organize a New York showing of the experimental American work which was largely banned from museums and galleries by the conservative taste of the National Academy of Design. But the president of the sponsoring group had become an enthusiast for European post-impressionists and cubists, and due to his influence the show that opened on 17 February 1913, at the 69th Infantry Regiment Armory, was dominated by contemporary work from France. Marcel Duchamp's "Nude Descending a Staircase" got a great stir in the press, and in four weeks the Armory Show was visited by some 300,000 people. The 1,600 works on exhibition included many worth seeing. Statues by Lehmbruck and Brancusi. Picasso and Van Gogh and Cézanne and Monet and Manet. Seurat. It was the introduction of Americans to the French moderns, and it brought into American art influences and aims far different from those that had animated native realism. The Ashcan School and Bellows followed Eakins and Homer in trying to represent and analyze objects and to reveal their emotional meaning. They were repelled by the crassness and money-making of their country, but they were drawn to its vigor and natural beauty and humanity. In the new currents from Europe, rejection of the outside world could seem total. The duty of the artist was to reach inside himself for ideas and visions, and then to capture the subjective in paint or stone. The Armory Show was, for American art, a step down the road to abstract expressionism.

Whatever else may be said about that creed, it repudiated the balance of and interplay between the personal and the social that Henry Demarest Lloyd had in mind when he wrote: "There must be independence as well as interdependence. . . . We must be men as well as members." Nearly all of Lloyd's *Wealth Against Commonwealth* in 1894 was an account of the history of Standard Oil, but he closed with two chapters of impassioned eloquence on "The Old Self-Interest and the New." He did not call on men to be altruistic or to sacrifice themselves; he saw into the problem deeper than pious injunctions:

> We have overworked the self-interest of the individual. The line of conflict between individual and social is a progressive one of the discovery of point after point in which the two are identical. Society thus passes from conflict to harmony, and on to another conflict. Civilization is the unceasing accretion of these social solutions. . . . The man for himself destroys himself and all men; only society can foster him and them.

Lloyd saw that too much wealth or the wrong kinds of wealth were dangerous, that the mere fact that something is technologically possible does not mean that it is socially or personally desirable: "A thorough, stalwart resimplification, a life governed by simple needs and loves, is the imperative want of the world." He called for an end to cant and a concentration on changing the world's institutions: "The world is too full of amateurs who can play the golden rule as an aria with variations. All the runs and trills and transpositions have been done to death. All the 'sayings' have been said. The only field for new effects is in epigrams of practice."

Lloyd's friend Jane Addams lived his maxim fully; to a lifetime in settlement work she added untiring labors for world peace. She and her associates at Hull-House were perhaps the most constructive group of women ever to assemble in the United States, so great were their contributions to the new field of social welfare. Alice Hamilton virtually founded the science of industrial medicine in this country. Alzina Stevens was the first probation officer of the first juvenile court in America, and eight years after the court was founded, Julia Lathrop led it to pioneer in psychiatric diagnosis and counseling. Miss Lathrop became the first director of the United States Children's Bureau, and was succeeded by Grace Abbott. Grace's sister Edith was dean of the new School of Social Service Administration at the University of Chicago. Florence Kelley headed the National Consumers' League which campaigned against child labor.

John Dewey perceived that the divorce of children from material production was not pure gain. In a farming society the child worked with his father or mother, and thus was trained in industry, in discipline, in the responsibility to do useful work. But in a modern industrial city, the typical child seldom encounters economic processes. Instead he sits in school and chants back to the teacher traditional but irrelevant lessons that he has memorized. Education must be reshaped so that the child will learn a spirit of service and can play his role in co-operative activities; thus it can help to re-create society into a "worthy, lovely, and harmonious" whole. In his Elementary School at the University of Chicago, Dewey experimented with a curriculum based on the history of occupations, of man's unfolding efforts to solve his persistent central problems: "how to master and use nature so as to make it tributary to the enrichment of human life." Small children studied a primitive tribe dependent on hunting and fishing. They learned the fibers and processes for making cloth. They built their own smelting oven to study the Iron Age and metallurgy. Education derived in this way from the "psychology of occupation" was a far cry from training for a trade, which aimed only at external utility; what Dewey sought was the internal growth of each student, the development of his ability to plan and to verify.

Here was the essence of DuBois's position, which he stated in a succinct note in 1910: "Are you training the Negro for his own benefit or for the benefit of somebody else? If he has a right to be trained for his own benefit then he may demand the highest training to which his best minds are capable. If he is to be trained for usefulness to other people then his training depends, of course, on how they want to use it." In *The Souls of Black Folk*, a unique and beautiful book, DuBois insisted that the "Talented Tenth" among Negroes be provided with classical and scientific training. To those who urged that trade schools should be established first, then grammar schools, and finally colleges, he replied that the only historically possible procedure was just the reverse. Southern whites would not educate Negroes, and Northern whites in sufficient numbers could not be obtained. Therefore Negroes must teach Negroes:

> Progress in human affairs is more often a pull than a push, a surging forward of the exceptional man, and the lifting of his duller brethren slowly and painfully to his vantage-ground. Thus it was no accident that gave birth to universities centuries before the com-

mon schools, that made fair Harvard the first flower of our wilderness. So in the South: the mass of the freedmen at the end of the war lacked the intelligence so necessary to modern workingmen. They must first have the common school to teach them to read, write, and cipher; and they must have higher schools to teach teachers for the common schools.

By 1900 some 2,500 Negroes had graduated from college, and 53 per cent of them had become teachers.

Just as the influence of DuBois was enhanced by his editorship of *The Crisis* after 1910, so did John Dewey's ideas reach a wider audience after the *New Republic* was started in 1914. Walter Lippmann, one of its editors, referred to Dewey as "the finest and most powerful intellect devoted to the future of American civilization." Whereas Dewey had criticized traditional education for instilling in pupils a spirit of competitive selfishness and individualism, Lippmann in *Drift and Mastery* (1914) made a similar charge against the American mother and the 19th-century home. Children were taught to look inward toward the family, not outward toward society. The home did little "to bring the child into contact with the real antidote to acquisitiveness—a sense of social property." The man who feels pride in the public parks and museums and libraries is much more civilized than he who wants to own a private art collection or a fenced-in estate. The conservation movement showed a growing attachment to collective property, but "that attachment is something that almost everyone to-day has had to acquire after he was grown up."

Whether property was to be personal or collective was a matter of law, and the law is "prophecies of what the courts will do in fact. . . ." Thus spoke Oliver Wendell Holmes, Jr., a justice of the highest court in Massachusetts, in an address on "The Path of the Law" in 1897. Pointing out that the rise of socialism had created discomfort among "the comfortable classes" and had pushed judges in a conservative direction both in the United States and in England, he argued that a judge could not help being influenced by his views of what was best for society. The least any jurist could do, he urged, was to ask consciously when advancing a rule of law what social advantage would be served by it.

But the crux of the matter, wrote Thorstein Veblen in *The Theory of Business Enterprise* (1904), is that judges trained to follow precedent must often be unaware that a traditional concept is no longer applicable; much of law is make-believe. To illustrate, from about the time in the 18th century when freedom of contract became a dominant legal principle, it had been made obsolescent by a new economic fact—the machine process—which the law had never recognized. Modern industry existed in fact, but not in law, whereas liberty of contract existed in law, but not in fact. "The material necessities of a group of workmen or consumers, enforced by the specialization and concatenation of industrial processes, is, therefore, not competent to set aside, or indeed to qualify, the natural freedom of the owners of these processes to let work go on or not, as the outlook for profits may decide. Profits is a business proposition, livelihood is not."

The essence of business enterprise is profits, and profits are made by buying and selling. Therefore they depend on prices. But the level of prices was continuously being undermined by the machine process, which had developed to the point where technological advance was automatic. Suppose a company built a factory to make textiles. But within a few years a newer factory could operate with more efficient machinery, and make its goods at lower costs. Therefore it could sell at lower prices. The older plants, unable to sell at prices that were profitable for them, would go bankrupt; they would suffer "the penalty of taking the lead." In this sense of being able to produce more than could be sold at profitable prices—the United States had been plagued by excess capacity for nearly three decades. "It may, therefore, be said, on the basis of this view, that chronic depression, more or less pronounced, is normal to business under the fully developed regime of the machine industry." One result was the rise of "the socialistic bias" and of "materialistic skepticism" in the stead of romanticism and supernaturalism.

Within the limits of a system of production for profit, two solutions were possible. One was the trust movement: combining into monopolies in order to keep the price of your output up to profitable levels. The other was massive waste of resources in nonproductive ways, and for that job the government was best fitted.

The quest of profits leads to a predatory national policy. The resulting large fortunes call for a massive government apparatus to secure the accumulations, on the one hand, and for large and conspicuous opportunities to spend the resulting income, on the other hand; which means a militant, coercive home administration and something in the way of an imperial court life—a dynastic fountain of honor and a courtly bureau of ceremonial amenities. Such an ideal is not simply a moralist's day-dream; it is a sound business proposition, in that it lies on the line of policy along which the business interests are moving in their behalf. . . . Habituation to a warlike, predatory scheme of life is the strongest disciplinary factor that can be brought to counteract the vulgarization of modern life wrought by peaceful industry and the machine process, and to rehabilitate the decaying sense of status and differential dignity. Warfare, with the stress on subordination and mastery and the insistence on gradations of dignity and honor incident to a military organization, has always proved an effective school in barbarian methods of thought. . . . Such is the promise held out by a strenuous national policy.

Thus Veblen to President Theodore Roosevelt.

Novelist: EDITH WHARTON

Mrs. Wharton (1862–1937) was born into an aristocratic line of New York merchants that had been founded in colonial times. She was raised to glide easily among the leisured class of Europe, especially in Italy and France, and at Newport, Rhode Island. Both her father and her husband were independently wealthy.

As a girl she wrote poetry—a harmless enough pursuit, to her associates. A yacht trip in the Aegean soon after her marriage in 1885 seems to have led her back to writing; her short stories began to appear in leading magazines. But neither family nor friends welcomed her artistic bent. To them, a lady should be as glittering and useless as the epergne on her own dinner table, and Mrs. Wharton was committing the sin of bad form. Annoyed by her books or indifferent to them, they did not mention them. She repaid her peers by reflecting their silly taboos in the mirror of her scorn, and displaying the artificial mandarinate in which the best people of American Society spent their aimless days. One of her characters referred to Manhattan's Washington Square, a center of the Four Hundred, as the Reservation, predicting that "before long its inhabitants would be exhibited at ethnological shows, pathetically engaged in the exercise of their primitive industries."

Added to the hostility of her class was the growing instability of her husband's psyche. They wandered rather restlessly from western Massachusetts to France, where he had to be placed in a sanatorium. She divorced him in 1913. Already she had firmly established herself with the best-seller *The House of Mirth* (1905). It was the first of four notable novels, which included *Ethan Frome* (1911), *The Custom of the Country* (1913), *The Age of Innocence* (1920). Mrs. Wharton, along with Ellen Glasgow and Willa Cather, proved to the discerning mind for the first time that North American women could make enduring contributions to fiction.

Edith Wharton's defects were refracted from her background. Her heroes are usually fatuous, sometimes foppish, although Ethan Frome does not suffer from this weakness. Further, Mrs. Wharton could be obsessed by the pretended demands of "good taste." But her best works are majestic and gripping. She wrote: "My last page is always latent in my first." Such an approach might have produced novels in which the "inevitability of fate" tediously unraveled itself. It did not; her stories are studded with climaxes; her pages crackle with drama. Good fiction, she added, must seek "the disengaging of crucial moments from the welter of existence."

CHAPTER 15

The Faulted Core

The upsurge in the productive capacity of the American economy from 1877 to 1914 was awe-inspiring, and it contributed to a standard of physical comfort that might serve as the basis for the most deeply human society in world history. But the price paid for material progress was great.

The Theory of Business Enterprise, with its coiled prose and its ironic wit which cut deeper into the period than any other book, made predictions that came true. The American economy was tied to government outlays for nonproductive purposes, especially to military expenditures. It is hardly an exaggeration to say that for a century we have enjoyed sustained prosperity only in times of war, preparation for war, or recovery from war. The spread of depression in the United States in 1914 was halted by war in Europe, and the next year the House of Morgan and other bankers began selling war bonds for Allied governments. Money borrowed here by England and France was spent here for munitions—and on an unprecedented scale. In October 1914, Du Pont had the capacity to produce 8,400,000 pounds of smokeless gunpowder a year. By April 1918 its capacity was 455,000,000 pounds a year. The firm in four years supplied the Allies with 1,500,-000,000 pounds of military explosives, and at its peak it had more than 100,000 employees. Of its wartime profits it spent $3,350,000 on research and chemical control, resulting in new civilian products that further enhanced its size and profits after the war. Another piece of the Du Pont earnings went to acquire control of General Motors.

Everywhere the old society of independent men, which still had existed in great degree in 1877, was being transmuted into a world of bureaucracy. As the president of the N. A. M. told its convention in 1911: "We are living in an age of organization; an age when but little can be accomplished except through organization; an age when organization must cope with organization. . . ." Power was being gathered into fewer hands, and fewer persons had scope to exercise their personal preferences or private judgment in economic affairs. To some extent of course the new corporate bureaucracies were essential to economic efficiency; they were needed to make use of the possibilities of modern technology. But it was not a contribution to the public welfare for a handful of men to direct such a huge portion of the total resources of America. The Du Ponts had a congeries of empires. So did the House of Morgan. So did Henry Ford. The earnings of Standard Oil moved hither and yon. This centralization of control was not needed for efficiency; it came about because wealth meant power, and thereby gave men of wealth the chance to get more power, and they did.

Wealth gave political influence to the barons of business, including the barons of publishing such as Hearst and Pulitzer and Frank Munsey. By the early 20th century the process had carried so far that Lincoln Steffens could observe in his autobiography: "What Boston suggested to me was the idea that business and politics must be one; that it was natural, inevitable, and—possibly —right that business should—by bribery, corruption, or—somehow get and be the government." The most important question about a government, he insisted, was not whether it was corrupt, or whether it held elections regularly, but what social and economic groups did it represent. His indictment of political bosses was directed against their disloyalty to the people:

> Natural leaders were born to lead the people, who really need loyal leaders. They could not solve their own problems; they wanted their leaders to represent them and take care of their social interests. They gave those leaders their faith and their votes, all they had. . . . So the business men who wanted to get from the people part of their common wealth had to deal with the people's leaders, and the people's leaders sold out the people, betrayed the pitiful faith of the masses in their weakness, and—hence our American government is no longer a democracy, but a plutocracy.

The problem went deeper than just a few evil men; the problem was that the typical American had no far-reaching vision of what kind of society he wanted: "It was vision that made men honest, devoted (to a cause), courageous—heroes; like the early Christians, when Christianity was a vision of world salvation."

The ideal of abiding by the rules of the game was weakened. Only success counted, and the game had no rules. To contend for fair play was to expose yourself as weak and effeminate. In 22 years up to 1907, more persons were lynched in the United States than were legally executed. But the general exemption from morality was never granted to Jews. If a Jewish businessman relied on the practices of his gentile competitors, he inevitably reinforced the notion that all Jews were grasping and not to be trusted. Anglo-Saxons were allowed to behave like mere Christians, but every Jew was obligated to behave like Christ.

A book steeped in anti-Semitism, *The Education of Henry Adams* (1904), made the ultimate charge against Americans by asserting that they did not worship anything, not even money. Europeans and Asians worshipped money, as they worshipped God or any other concrete form of power. But the American spent more money "to less purpose than any extravagant court aristocracy; he had no sense of relative values, and knew not what to do with his money when he got it, except use it to make more, or throw it away." For Americans the problem was that they had been absorbed in the pursuit of wealth for so long that they could not abandon themselves to any other values. They were more ignorant of history than any people had ever been. Ideals moved them to distrust and dislike. The mind of the time is revealed in the remark of writer Hamlin Garland after he met Henry Ford: "He is a colossal genius, I am merely an industrious writer of obscure books; and yet he did not appear to despise me for my failure to make money."

It was Garland's *A Son of the Middle Border* (1917) which found words for a crucial and often misunderstood characteristic of American life. His father, selling a farm in western Wisconson in 1868 to move to Iowa, predicted that soon his brother-in-law would follow him. The father-in-law exclaimed: "I hope ye're wrong. I'd like to spend me last days here with me sons and daughters around me, sich as are left to me. It's the curse of our country—this constant moving, moving. I'd have been better off had I stayed in Ohio, though this valley seemed beautiful to me the first time I saw it." The Garland family, having started in

New England, moved on from Iowa to Dakota. In a society where clergymen thought that progress meant more parishioners and a new and larger building, the Garland children as they grew up could not even worship in a church that reminded them of their parents. When Hamlin Garland returned to the Midwest after six years in Boston, "I clearly perceived that our Song of Emigration had been, in effect, the hymn of fugitives!"

Even dead Americans had to keep moving. In *A Hazard of New Fortunes*, Howells wrote of an old German in Indiana who became wealthy when natural gas was discovered on his farm. Moving to New York, he invests in a new magazine. On a trip back West he authorizes the sinking of gas wells in the woods pasture on the old farm, even though it will require moving the graves of his two children who died young. His wife wails: "It does seem too hard that they can't be let to rest in peace, pore little things. I wanted you and me to lay there too, when our time comes, Jacob. . . . Jacob, I wonder you could sell it!" He consoles her by saying that he will buy a cemetery lot for the children— and a monument with two lambs on it.

We may doubt that the bribe assuaged her grief. Surely it would have been rejected by Wellamotkin, head of a band of Nez Percé Indians who had lived peacefully for generations in a valley in Oregon. Just before he died in 1871 he told his son, soon to be Chief Joseph: "A few years more, and the white man will be all around you. They have their eyes on this land. My son, never forget my dying words. This country holds your father's body. Never sell the bones of your father and mother." Few whites felt any attachment to a given spot of land. They moved repeatedly, gleefully. Rising land values prompted farmers to clear a strip, sell at a profit, and move on, to repeat the process elsewhere. The typical philosophy was "Settle and sell, settle and sell." The moving van became a great American symbol. Neighborhoods were incredibly fluid. A study of Rochester suggests that fewer than 60 per cent of its residents in 1894 were still there five years later. In one of Boston's streetcar suburbs the Baptists built a huge church. It soon became a Jewish temple. Later it was used by a Negro congregation.

For progress, a heavy price. The United States surely was, in many ways, the Land of Progress. But to that image we should counterpose another—America as the Land of Flight. Millions of persons did not know where they wanted to get to; they only knew that they wanted to escape from their origins. Names were abandoned in favor of more "American" ones. As Jewish immigrants in New York sought to follow the advice imbibed from *Di yuden in America*, it was reported: "Names are changed as easily as shirts"; a writer in 1913 even said it was "a matter of common knowledge" that "a majority of the prize-fighters in New York are really Jews who operate under Irish names," and Republican ward captain "Stitch" McCarthy had been born Sam Rothberg.

The consequences could be shattering: "psychical instability, even liquidity of character among the Jews."

The craving to "get ahead" was manifest in geographical mobility and in lust for wealth as the tool of social mobility. Men who prospered changed their religions: Episcopalianism was the creed of the wealthy. City-dwellers scorned their ancestors still on the farm. Second-generation Americans felt contempt and shame for the outlandish ways of their parents. The United States became a country of men in flight, running over unmarked fields without traditions to guide them or visions to serve as beacons, with no havens for rest and no end but the grave, with no goal but wealth, and of wealth there is never enough.

In a nation on the run, Negroes ran too. In 1900 in Dougherty County, Georgia, where Negroes outnumbered whites by five to one, only 10 per cent of all adults had been born in the county. Of 10 million Negroes in the United States in 1910, 1,600,000 did not live in the state of their birth. W. E. B. DuBois pointed to the steady drift from farms into Southern towns. Booker T. Washington called on his fellows: "Cast down your bucket where you are." In 1879, at the time of the Great Exodus from Louisiana, Frederick Douglass warned:

> Three moves from house to house are said to be worse than a fire. That a rolling stone gathers no moss has passed into the world's wisdom. . . . The habit of roaming from place to place in pursuit of better conditions of existence is by no means a good one. A man should never leave his home for a new one till he has earnestly endeavored to make his immediate surroundings accord with his wishes. . . . No people ever did much for themselves or for the world, without the sense and inspiration of native land; of a fixed home; of familiar neighborhood, and common associations. . . . It

is a more cheerful thing to be able to say, 'I was born here and know all the people,' than to say, 'I am a stranger here and know none of the people.'

In any small Midwestern town an "old family" was one that had lived there for a generation, and in cities men felt even more isolated and exposed. In Chicago in 1905 five bachelors got together to found Rotary, the first modern "service organization" for men, which tried to make the idiotic practice of calling strangers by their first names into an adequate substitute for a feeling of community. Thus the American habit of being always on the move reinforced the changes that were being wrought by technology and urbanization. "All of us are immigrants spiritually," proclaimed *Drift and Mastery*:

> We are all of us immigrants in the industrial world, and we have no authority to lean upon. We are an uprooted people, newly arrived, and *nouveau riche*. As a nation we have all the vulgarity that goes with that, all the scattering of soul. . . . We make love to ragtime and we die to it. We are blown hither and thither like litter before the wind. Our days are lumps of undigested experience. You have only to study what newspapers regard as news to see how we are torn and twisted by the irrelevant: in frenzy about issues that do not concern us, bored with those that do. Is it a wild mistake to say that the absence of central authority has disorganized our souls, that our souls are like Peer Gynt's onion, in that they lack a kernel?

Even the relations between the sexes were different. Henry Adams tried to puzzle out the changes, saying that without such an effort the study of history was "mere pedantry." The American woman was obviously a failure. She had not even held her traditional place in church or at court. She could not keep her children about her, and the family was "extinct like chivalry." The traditional tasks of women had been undermined by modern technology. Woman was free, and knew not how to use her freedom. With sparkling wit and glittering jewels, she found no men fit to admire her and had "no place but the theater or streets to decorate." Like American men, she had married machinery. She was surprised when anybody regarded her as sexual.

In place of sexuality, by the evidence of popular songs, came a harsh sexiness. Up to 1890 song hits in this country were marked by pre-Raphaelite sentimentality and reflected male dominance and female chastity. Then came a timid hedonism, showing women as frail rather than sinful: "She is More to be Pitied Than Censured (a Man was the cause of it all)." But by 1910, as woman in the new image became predatory, standards of attitude and behavior were not so different for men and women: My Gal Sal was simultaneously pictured as wild and "an all 'round good fellow."

The pretended sexual morality was strict, but newspapers gloried in prurience, stories of white slavery were spread across front pages, and the press in Washington daily carried such advertisements as these: "WANTED—A FURNISHED ROOM in a quiet family, for gentleman and lady; board for lady only; no questions." Or: "PERSONAL—a widow lady desires a gentleman to assist her financially." Marriage ties were slipping, and divorce in some states was perhaps easier than anywhere else in the Western world. Although Indiana supposedly stopped being a divorce mill in 1873, a joke popular a decade later makes one wonder. Before a train stopped at a depot in Indiana, so the story ran, the porter always came through calling: "Ten minutes for refreshment and five for divorces." Advertisements in the Legal Notices columns of New York newspapers regularly read: "ABSOLUTE DIVORCES, QUIETLY, WITHIN A MONTH: Incompatibility, all causes; legal everywhere; no money required until granted." A society hostess in *The House of Mirth* remarks: "Some one said the other day that there was a divorce and a case of appendicitis in every family one knows."

American women were failures, said Henry Adams, because American men were failures. In many of the best novels of the time, the women are strong, the men are ineffectual. Edith Wharton pictured an immensely wealthy man who nonetheless "was a mere supernumerary in the costly show for which his money paid"; another male character is "almost bridal in his own aspect. . . ." Madeleine Lee in *Democracy* "regarded men as creatures made for women to dispose of, and capable of being transferred like checks, or baggage-labels, from one woman to another, as desired." Dorinda Oakley in *Barren Ground* is a successful farmer; her lover is a drunken weakling. Theron Ware under provocation cannot muster "any manly anger." Willa Cather built her novel *O Pio-*

neers! (1913) around the stalwart nature of Alexandra Bergson: "In his own daughter, John Bergson recognized the strength of will, and the simple, direct way of thinking things out, that had characterized his father in his better days. He would much rather, of course, have seen this likeness in one of his sons, but it was not a question of choice." We can assume that Basil Ransom in *The Bostonians* is speaking to some extent for his creator when he exclaims: "The whole generation is womanised; the masculine tone is passing out of the world; it's a feminine, a nervous, hysterical, chattering, canting age, an age of hollow phrases and false delicacy and exaggerated solicitudes and coddled sensibilities, which, if we don't soon look out, will usher in the reign of mediocrity, of the feeblest and flattest and the most pretentious that has ever been."

American boys and young men were, reported upper-class English observers, much better mannered than their own compatriots. "But," continued an Englishman who taught modern history at Cornell, "they have not the same sense of honour as English boys; they make excuses; you can't trust them; they are always adapting themselves to you, instead of letting you get some real influence over them. All comes from being brought up by women; living at home with their mothers and sisters; being taught by women teachers, and sitting next little girls at schools. It improves their morals and manners and lowers their sense of honour and public spirit." Beatrice Webb, while agreeing that American men were deficient in civic spirit, added another note: "And these good manners do not mean effeminacy. No race exceeds the American in physical courage. If nervous will-power and sheer delight in using it, if love of risks—at any rate physical and financial risks, are the test of virility, the American has no peer." But Henry James insisted on a quite different test of "the masculine character, the ability to dare and endure, to know and yet not fear reality. . . ."

It was to an extent the new bureaucracies that promoted timidity and self-delusion; a man becomes courageous and forceful only if his world encourages him to pursue his own aims and to wrestle out decisions with his own mind. But also women had a vastly enlarged scope for imposing their standards on growing boys. A farm boy in 1880 spent most of his time with his father in the fields, doing man's work, or in the livery stable, with its earthy concerns; during his brief tenure in school his teacher might well be a man. But whereas 43 per cent of the teachers in the United States in 1880 were men, only 20 per cent were men in 1914. A much larger proportion of boys were growing up in cities, where they spent more time in school, and in their remaining hours they were seldom far from some censorious female witness.

The new position of women was having great influence on public affairs, and in *Sin and Society* (1907) Edward Alsworth Ross suggested that some of the effects were baneful. Men, he wrote, are touched when they see injustice; women, when they see suffering. Therefore men bridle at sin; that is, at behavior that injures somebody else. But women are stirred by actions that harm the actor, by vice. "Now, the rise of great organizations for focusing the sentiments of millions of women has lately brought about a certain effemination of opinion." Most church-goers were women, and ministers framed their arguments chiefly for women. Therefore the clergy had lost moral influence with "the virile, who see in graft and monopoly and foul politics worse enemies than beer, Sunday baseball, and the army canteen. . . . Our moral pace-setters strike at bad personal habits, but act as if there were something sacred about money-making; and, *seeing that the master iniquities of our time are connected with money-making,* they do not get into the big fight at all." Thus the church made its contribution to self-deception.

If we seek to grasp why the American voter gave his support to political preachers like Roosevelt and Wilson, we should recall Thomas Beer's characterization of Roosevelt as a "figure in warm clay, with its female tact and childish tempers and its sense for crowds . . ." And we can perhaps find enlightenment in an entry on "The Mentality of Woodrow Wilson" in the diary of his Secretary of State, Robert Lansing:

> In fact arguments, however soundly reasoned, did not appeal to him if they were opposed to his feeling of what was the right thing to do. Even established facts were ignored if they did not fit in with this intuitive sense, this semi-divine power to select the right. Such an attitude of mind is essentially feminine.

Men tried to cleave to the old moral creeds and the shibboleths of individualism even when they were beaten upon by the on-

going Industrial Revolution and its consequences. Our grand-
fathers lived amid changes so swift and so basic that nobody
could grasp more than a fraction of what was happening. Their
problems were so urgent and complicated as often to overwhelm
them. However forceful and intelligent a man might be, he frequently could not foresee the implications of his own behavior.
Thus Andrew Carnegie might seem to be a prototype of the clear-
minded and determined man, but his career brims over with contradictions. Himself benefiting greatly from the tariff, he called it
"trifling." From his company emerged the biggest oligopoly of
all, but he called the trust problem a "bugaboo" on the ground
that no firm could long shield itself from competition. A pro-
fessed sympathizer with workingmen, he sanctioned union-smash-
ing of the most calculated and ruthless sort at Homestead. He
was prominent in the Anti-Imperialist League in 1898; two years
later he supported the imperialist McKinley because Bryan was
even more dangerous. Having tried to use the Venezuela crisis
to get orders from the United States navy, he put up $10 million
in 1910 to establish the Carnegie Endowment for International
Peace. He gave funds to erect thousands of buildings for public
libraries, but in such a way—making the recipient provide the
real estate, all equipment, and maintenance—that New York City
rejected part of his gift rather than accept the financial burden.
While Carnegie was truly modest about his important achievements,
reported Mark Twain, he constantly displayed a "juvenile delight
in trivialities that feed his vanity." The former messenger boy
and self-proclaimed democrat dilated no end about his acquaintances
with royalty, owned a Scottish castle, and liked to be called "the
Laird."

Did the individual and his personal qualities matter? By 1900
even a Carnegie needed to be reassured that he amounted to something, that he was "independent." The typical American had
trouble now regarding himself as "a definite, coherent . . .
whole. . . ."

Black Laborer: HENRY JOHNSON

Johnson was born about 1845 in Patrick County, Virginia. When interviewed by a black woman for the Federal Writers' Project under the New Deal, he said: "I was only sold twice." He never met his parents until he was more than twenty years old. His last name he borrowed from one of his owners.

His father (supposedly) picked him out by his appearance one day after the Civil War in Danville, Virginia. His family were sharecroppers, getting half of what they raised. By the time that the white landowner died after they had been with him for five years, they had saved enough to buy a pair of oxen and have money to jingle besides. On their next farm, where they stayed for two years, they got two thirds of the crop, the owner only one third. Then Henry's father sold the oxen and bought his own land for $200. He stayed there about five years.

Henry left home to wander. He learned to play a violin, which gave him a living for "a long time." He never did learn to write. His schooling consisted of three days. A black friend taught him to read out of a blue-back spelling book.

He quit playing the violin and went to work for the railroads as a gandy dancer. After eight years at that exacting task, he drifted along to Decatur, Alabama, where he helped to lay pipe. This pursuit lasted only three months. He got married and moved to Tennessee.

By 1895 Henry Johnson, then some fifty years old, was in St. Louis. In an industrial accident he "got scalded almost to death." His injury cost him eight months in a hospital; it also brought him $500 from a damage suit. He bought a horse and wagon out of it and did light hauling. Later he spent sixteen years doing landscaping. At last he could no longer do heavy work. "I got a garden but I can't make any money from it, 'cause all de other folks out here got gardens too."

CHAPTER
16

Life-Styles in 1914

The counterthemes of history are permanence and change. My aim now is to trace out the ways in which these opposing thrusts operated to produce a cluster of subcultures by the outbreak of World War I that was insidiously similar to—yet vastly different from—the nation at the end of Reconstruction. Chapter 1 chose to operate at the lowest level of abstraction that the historian knows —an individual at a precise point in time and space. Even though each of these persons was picked as being representative of a significant group, the procedure here will be reversed; that is, the purpose will be to reach as high a level of abstraction as current knowledge will permit. It has been indicated that the typical American gained considerably in his material standard of living during these thirty-seven years. But what close-knit processes led to this culmination? Four seem to stand out: (1) He moved from a farm to a city or larger town. (2) He worked in industry or commerce rather than in agriculture. (3) He used more efficient equipment. (4) His wife or daughters could find gainful employment outside the home.

Take the fourth assertion first. "This country is fine for men and dogs, but it's Hell for women and horses." Thus ran a frontier saying. It was the abundance of free land that gave American men their freedom from landholders, but females had to wait, and a mighty tiresome and abusive wait it was, for the slow work of urbanization to take hold. Perhaps the chief agent yet for women's liberation was the typewriter. It was mechanically workable by 1874, but only after 1900 did it become common in offices. This oppression of women on the frontier was not a willful tyranny exerted by men; it was an expression of reality in a situation where physical force counted for more than any other virtue. The fact can be seen in many countries. A recent Australian novel says of settlement in the outback around 1907, "Must have been hard going in those days, especially for women." An American farm woman stated, "My washings are so hard to do, it tires me completely out for a day or so." Said Senator Preston Plumb of Kansas: "Pioneering is hard enough under the most favorable circumstances. There is always disappointment. The burden falls first and hardest upon the wife." Henry George described the "monotonous existence" of a farm woman: "its lack of recreation and excitement, and of gratifications of taste, and of the sense of harmony and beauty, its steady drag of cares and toils that make women worn and wrinkled when they should be in their bloom. Even the discomforts and evils of the crowded tenement-house are not worse than the discomforts and evils of such a life."

But the load fell on men too. The psychic drain was lessened if a man moved to the frontier as part of an established group, a new region, and stayed put. These migrant communities were almost always tied together by ethnic and linguistic or by religious bonds, or all three. This type of movement, fairly common in 1877, had almost died out by 1914. Further, men found that they had to keep moving; of those living in Kansas in 1885, barely half remained a decade later, scarcely 40 per cent in 1905. The patterns are appalling: one boy moved from Kentucky to Missouri, 1850 to California in the gold rush, returned eastward via Panama, joined the Pike's Peak miners in 1858–1859, went to Nebraska in the early 1870's, thence to Texas, and just before he died he was thinking of going to Oregon to raise prunes. These solitary wanderers often paid a heavy psychological price. Their first remove westward tore them loose from family and friends. Having been hurt once, they hesitated to form other deep associations in a new place. Each move increased their resistance. We read about neighborly barn-raisings and such, but how many close friendships were formed?

In ways that will be explored further below, women benefited more than men by the growth of cities. But the average male surely got ahead in absolute terms. Within a city, the proportions of the labor force in manufacturing as against service industries (trade, transportation, utilities, finance, professional, personal) remained about the same from 1870 to 1910. But since the service industries were relatively more important in urban areas than in rural, the shift in population densities brought a shift in occupations. Surprisingly, in the rural workforce the percentage in service trades was growing more rapidly than the total. But the two crucial shifts were these: the movement to cities, and the rising proportion of urban populations that were part of the labor force. Of every hundred rural residents, the number in the workforce grew only from 31.9 in 1870 to 33.6 by 1910. In the same period in urban areas, the rise was from 36.2 to 45.4. This gain chiefly reflected the increasing role of women in gainful employment outside the home.

To quote a recent scholar, "The most significant aspect of America's transformation in the post-Civil War era was the relative shift of population from the countryside into cities of increasing size." Even so, and data have been given (more will be given) to delineate the impact of that shift. But why did it happen at all? Because cities are the centers of creation. They generate new forms of work. Innovations occur in cities for two reasons. An urbanite knows about more different types of inputs, and therefore the number of combinations available to him is greatly enhanced. Second, he has more information from which to estimate the flow to him of future incomes if he succeeds in making some specific innovation. A portion of the new kinds of work results in additional goods or services that can be exported from the city. (Even changes in rural techniques and behavior are chiefly the consequence of urban innovations.) These added exports facilitate the purchase of more imports. The city learns to replace many of these imports by its own products. Thus it frees the productive factors to devise further exports. This process of almost self-sustaining expansion puts in perspective the comment of Frederick Law Olmsted: ". . . only the poorest, who cannot find employment in the city, will come to the country, and these as soon they have got a few dollars ahead, are crazy to get back to town."

The growth of cities meant more than the transfer of persons into service industries that paid more than farming. It meant a huge increase in the efficiency of available techniques. In antebellum days, power came from animals, including human beings, or from waterfalls. This limitation restricted the location of factories to a few sites, and it prevented concentration of industry in large cities because waterpower could not be sent over long distances. Then came mechanical energy and electrical transmission. Energy consumption

Population and Labor Force, 1865–1915

rose fivefold from 1865 to 1915. Mineral fuels, mainly coal, had provided less than a fifth of the total in 1865, but furnished 85 per cent by 1915. Along with this growth of energy production went a surge of population. Although, as has been seen, immigration played a crucial part in the nation's increase of output, natural population growth was more significant. Further, the labor force grew faster than population; in 1870 one American in three had a job or was looking for one, by 1910, four out of ten.

As the proportion of income-earners increased, so did their gains. Average Gross National Product per capita in 1905 was about 50 per cent higher than in 1880. But for each gainfully employed person, the rise was probably about 30 per cent, or scarcely more than 1 per cent a year. Consequently, expenditures on consumption were far too low, the rate of savings was far too high, and overproduction inevitably followed. Moreover, the gains were not equally distributed among the regions of the country. The Northeast and North Central states held their positions in relation to the country as a whole. The West, as its mining booms lost momentum, fell backward rapidly. Readers may be astounded to know that the section that gained ground was the South, especially from 1900 to 1920.

What was the human import of these statistical trends? A farm girl in Nebraska in 1877 could expect the isolation and drudgery of marriage and motherhood; by 1914 she could leave for Chicago and a sales job at Marshall Field. A youth in 1877 could expect to dig potatoes all his born days if he lived in the Aroostook valley; in 1900 he travelled to many towns in the interest of Singer Sewing Machine. The heir to the neighboring tract had drifted off to Detroit and worked as a machinist's helper. The miner's son from Leadville had moved to Denver and ran a general store. But how did such geographical and occupational moves affect the balances of their lives?

Let us begin at the center. Anthropologists have long studied kinship systems and family structures. Psychologists have been concerned with child-rearing. Only recently have historians begun systematically to take these subjects within their view. The findings to date are fragmentary, but some are astounding. Earlier scholars had asserted that the American norm had been the extended family (parents plus children plus other relatives) until the twentieth century when it was replaced by the nuclear family (only parents and children). Evidence now available suggests that the nuclear family has been the American Way ever since Plymouth. The tragedy started there.

With parents, identification with the family was the be-all and end-all. As a Yankee prayer would have it: "God save me and my wife, My son John and his wife, Us four and no more." But with children the story was often the opposite. A brilliant historian has written of the epoch that concerns us here:

> Revolt against the father by a young man is one thing; rejection of the father by an infant is something else. Revolt asserts a male role; rejection declines to adopt a male role. Revolt seeks to seize authority; rejection expresses an aversion to the exercise of authority by oneself or anyone else. Revolt is an expression of confidence in one's identity; rejection is a failure to attain identity.

As Reconstruction ended, the dominant figure in the typical family was the father. He gave his children leadership in religion, in ethics, and in the rough and tumble of life. His wife followed the marital dictum to "love, honor, and obey." His children were budding adults who had to be disciplined to the ways of the external world. Within a generation, especially in the exploding cities, particularly among the middle clases, this syndrome was shattered.

Our best data, while based on a distressingly small sample, are reliable. They derive from a Chicago neighborhood that was changing during these years from upper class to middle class. In a city that was literally booming, doubling in population every decade, the businessmen and professionals were lucky to hold their own; indeed, many were losing ground financially. Defeated by the outside world, the father retreated to the shelter of his fireside. Inside his home, he was secure. His family became an isolated unit. As it did so, emotional ties within it became more intense. An indifferent success in his vocation, having no social ties outside his household, the father lavished his atrophied energies on his offspring. He demanded that his sons succeed at the very tasks that had thwarted him.

As women came to see their husbands as weaklings, the wife drew back. She too turned from sire to siblings. The norm in sexual relations must have been a nightmare; as Tolstoi said, "The worst tragedies of all take place in bedrooms." In regard to the relations of man to woman, material reasons reinforced psychological ones: children in a city are not a help but a handicap. They cost money. Add to those obstacles the combined pressure of the law arguing that sexual intercourse was criminal, and the church contending that it was sinful except for procreation, and everybody's parents yammering that it wasted your body and your nervous energy without earning any money, and the country produced what it wanted—a frustrated, if not castrated, populace. Add further that even persons who desired to practice birth control did not know where to go for reliable information about the devices that were available. No course remained except abstinence. Heaven help us all. A recent article is entitled "The Progressive Era Revolution in American Attitudes Toward Sex." The title is misleading; the revolution never happened. True, a few doctors did try to introduce more liberty of discussion, but their efforts were met by the objection that the entire topic was "attended with filth," and the actual behavior of Americans was, if it changed at all, backsliding.

This ambience developed some weird children (including males and females who would steer the nation's course until after World

War II). One recent study based on a severely limited sample indicates that sons who rebelled against the discipline of their fathers were more likely to be aggressive when they became adults. But the pattern in our Chicago neighborhood was quite different. In the proper middle-class home, the mother did not work. The father was the family's sole contact with economic endeavor. He retreated from it. His home became a refuge, almost a bomb shelter. He was not fit to be a model for any son. Alienated from his work, he next became alienated from his family. The commodity economy had whipped him; now the commodity family would whip him even worse. These insights into the emergent middle-class household add pungency to the warning by Fritz Pappenheim: "There is no short-cut in our struggle against the forces of alienation. If we really want to triumph over them, we must accept the challenge to strive for a new foundation of society, for the development of economic and social institutions which will no longer be dominated by the commodity structure."

As the status of the father declined, that of the mother grew. Nobody could say ill of the Star-Spangled Banner, apple pie, or Mother. Listen to a typical bit of maudlin about the newly enthroned head of the home:

> She was companion and friend, job, solace and delight to every member of her family, and when in 1878, after a long life devoted to their happiness, at the ripe age of seventy-four, she died surrounded by her children, calm, fearless and triumphant, something was taken from their lives which changed the tenor of their thoughts forever.

Common sense tells us that many women who bore children were jealous, envious, neurotic, incompetent, and often cruel. But they were never publicly presented in those shades.

Or were women the new rulers of the home? Was it not rather the children? Before about 1870, the child-dominated family would have been unthinkable. A demographic fact must be noted. In another work I have printed a gravestone in Gloucester, Massachusetts, that reports the deaths of three infants in one family between 1876 and 1880. Not one had lived to be eight months old. Under such conditions, a parent simply could not afford to make a total emotional commitment to any baby. Then came a true revolution in medical science. As chances for survival zoomed, so did complete emotional dedication to "my Willie." Infant mortality fell from 273 per thousand in 1885 to fewer than 100 in 1915. Other indices can be used. New York City in 1887 got a new ordinance calling for small parks with playground equipment. Nothing was done. As late as 1900 the Park Board, when asked for sandboxes and basketball courts, recommended a large restful park "for the hard-working people of the neighborhood." Parks were for adults. In less than a generation, a total reversal occurred. Parks were for kids. A major complaint against saloons was that they might lead to the corruption of the young. A common litany held that if society guarded and nurtured its youth, the whole world might be saved. Incredibly, this catechism was used to teach English to grown-up immigrants in Cleveland on the eve of World War I:

Oh baby, dear baby, Whatever you do,
You are the king of the home, And we all bend to you.

Ironically, at the very time when more parks for the kiddies were being built, middle-class children were denied by their parents the freedom to use them. Returning again to our Chicago district, we find that in 1865 when the area was upper class the entire family, including the father, customarily went to Union Park or Jefferson Park on Sunday. A generation later, middle-class children were forbidden to go there. Pupils were escorted by their parents to school in the morning, and picked up when classes ended. The unspoken goal was to insulate the offspring from the temptations and dangers of the external environment. The outcome was horrendous. More than half of the children in the neighborhood were still unmarried at age 29, living at home with their parents. Since women married much younger than men, the typical male did not marry until he was well past 30. Nor did he spend those years in school; only 2.5 per cent of the boys got a high-school diploma. He suffered later as a result. It was common for the elder son of a professional or businessman to slip back into a blue-collar trade.

Contrary to common expectations, it was not the favored sons of small nuclear families who were most likely to progress in their careers. The probable winners came from homes of five or six people, who thus gained some competitive experience early in life.

Further, they came from extended households, where an uncle or a grandparent also worked at a gainful job, so that talk about the workaday world was a common exposure in the home. At this point, we encounter a striking obtuseness among both contemporaries and later analysts; namely, that the presence of boarders within a family was necessarily harmful. In the words of the *Federal Strike Report* after the Pullman boycott, "a roomer can not go to his own room without going through the private rooms of the family, which breaks into the sanctity of the family." The truth is that families, for boys at least, were too sanctified. The presence of an outsider within the home may have been the greatest boon that budding males could hope for. As for the blooming females, it is hard to say. The fears that they might be violated are obvious. But did the "augmented household" (nuclear family plus non-relatives) pose more dangers than its simpler variations? My guess is that incestuous relations of father or uncle or brother to daughter were far more common than is usually admitted.

Until the twentieth century, the most important training institution was the family. Next most significant was the peer group; boys learned their cues from their buddies in the gang. Churches and ministers made their weight felt. In North America, an apprenticeship in a trade was crucial to the growing up of many a young man. Limping weakly along behind came the schools. But as other heuristic forces abdicated or were deserted by their parishioners, formal schooling was expected to replace them. It could not do so; it did not do so. Nonetheless, American society persisted in the illusion that a schoolmarm could inculcate all of the knowledge and all of the motives that had earlier been derived from many teachers. The schools can hardly be faulted, nor can the taxpayers, because both citizen and pedagogue made quite an effort. Of children aged five to seventeen, 63.9 per cent were enrolled in public schools in 1877, and 73.7 per cent were in 1914. Whereas only 2.5 per cent of seventeen-years-olds were graduated from high school in 1880, 8.8 per cent had been by 1910. The problem is rather that teachers were being asked to provide for pupils a vast range of instruction that other agencies, especially parents, had previously given during their leisure time.

The whole concept of leisure changed its meaning. Of course Americans had always had recreations: horse racing, wrestling, marksmanship matches, gambling. Girls had dolls, and boys had balls made of rags. At the turn of the century, however, three major changes were taking place, and two of them weakened the original meaning of re-creation. Never before had leisure been so sharply split away from productive activities. Hunting, fishing, knitting—were they work or play? Nobody worried his head over the question. Now the Gospel of Work of the older middle class was being replaced by the values of leisure. Formerly the heroes of popular biography had been figures from the everyday world, such as business magnates or generals; now they wore the glamorous aura of actresses and centerfielders and playboy millionaires. Closely related to this transmutation was the growth of mass-spectator entertainment. Earlier sports had called for personal participation, even the notorious turkey shoots of the Old Northwest; in the twentieth century a man could, for a fee, simply sit and watch. The first Sunday baseball game at Philadelphia took place in 1888. It was in 1882 that John L. Sullivan was proclaimed the first heavyweight champion of the world. Other branches of athletics were seeing parallel developments about the same time, and none of them was possible until people had been congested into cities. But while the city was making possible the growth of professional sports, that change was relegating ordinary men from the playing field to the sidelines.

Paradoxically, it was a distinctly urban ritual that perhaps best preserved the rural fusion of work with play. When a man speculated on the stock market or the commodity exchanges, what was he doing? Was it deadly serious or was it fun? For many, including some of the strongest, it was a game, hopefully a fame. By the end of the century, the number of bushels and bales being traded on the exchanges was seven times greater than the annual crop.

Also paradoxical was the conversion of certain leisure-time rituals into vocations. This happened notably among women. It seems certain that their status, including their portion of spare time from household duties, was growing rapidly. In the town of Pullman, for instance, it was widely believed that women had benefited more from the model town than had any other group of its denizens. Housekeeping had become easier, life had become more varied. Their husbands had no opportunity to stop at the saloon on the way home to deliver their paycheck (saloons did not exist). Few contemporaries wrote down how heavily the scales had been weighted in favor of women by the local demography. No large society can exist for long with a population such as the one for Pullman in July 1885:

men	3,752
women	1,945
children under 16	2,906

Add to this imbalance the pronounced mobility of Pullman's residents. One woman in 1884 said that although she had lived in the town only two years, only three families of her acquaintance had been there when she arrived. Asked, "It is like living in a great hotel, is it not?", she answered, "We call it camping out."

But patterns among working-class and middle-class women, with their new mobility and their new leisure (increasingly squandered on their children) did not apply to large numbers of women in the social stratosphere. In these ranks, what had been "church work" or "charity" was reclassified into "social work." An even more devastating redefinition came shortly. In the words of a Negro leader, "social work was born in an atmosphere of righteous indignation, of divine discontent," but swiftly it was mutated by the urge to declare oneself a "professional." Emotional ties no longer bound one to his clients, but rather to his fellows in the trade. Poor folks were not friends to be helped, not even charges to be succored, they were enemies to be fended off. Case workers on the Lower East Side were warned by their supervisors never to admit that they spoke Italian or Yiddish, because such a bond of solidarity would encourage their clients to "take advantage of us."

Such a sense of sorority would have distressed (angered?) such founders of settlement houses as Lillian Wald at the Henry Street Settlement in New York or Jane Addams at Hull-House in Chicago. In their weaker moments, they helped to found national associations of social workers, and at times they spoke in the guise of do-gooders. Their deeper senses, however, went far beyond these infantile predilections; they wanted to promote fraternity, and their feeling for many immigrants amounted to love, even though they might occasionally try to "Americanize" everybody. But others soon perceived the sympathetic impulses of potential donors as the carpet to a career. Figures tell the story: six settlement houses in 1891, more than 100 by 1900, over 200 by 1905, more than 400 by 1910. These statistics deliberately omit most Roman Catholic so-called settlements, which were counted as high as 2,500 by 1915, for the simple reason that they were more proselytizing agencies than welfare institutions.

Even though some men were early standouts in social welfare, at the beginning of the century this type of endeavor was dominated by women. Settlements did not appeal to men, even in the role of customers; as one immigrant said, "The social settlement here meant nothing to us men, we went there for an occasional shower, that was all." However, the contribution to women and children of these founders of settlement houses cannot be exaggerated. At a time when many private dwellings did not afford comfortable means for keeping oneself clean, the solace of a heated bathhouse must have been enormous. How many of us today can look at the analogs in modern Montreal without seeing an anachronism? But do we see truly? When the first public bath was started in the South End of Boston in 1895, indoor plumbing was not common. The population showed 50,000 people per square mile. You figure it out. A recent study suggests that, from the viewpoint of society as a whole, the most profitable investments in the United States in the late nineteenth century were those in public health: pure water, sewage disposal, clean streets. They paid better, from the perspective stated already, than money put into factory buildings, machinery, or education.

The settlement houses were adept at launching a project, then putting the burden for continuing it onto the shoulders of the taxpayers. When Hull-House was started, the Chicago public schools were doing nothing to promote the visual arts. So the settlement started its own art exhibits, used them to found a committee of citizens, and pressured the schools to take over the task. Settlements did not begin the idea of kindergartens, but they promoted it vigorously. A handicraft shop at Greenwich House in New York became a private venture after three years. Many neighborhood houses had theater groups, which, in addition to their obvious benefices, helped immigrants to learn English. (Jane Addams, astute as usual, commented, "The number of those who like to read has been greatly over-estimated.")

These new leisure-time activities were outside reality for most American men. They, literally, worked themselves to death. Life was the job, sleep, eating, sometimes copulation. Beyond that, nothing. Mainly, life was toil; the work week in steel mills until after World War I was eighty-four hours, twelve hours a day seven days a week. Men did not read, or go to the theater, or even go to church. Their few encounters with religion were likely to expose them to some old fool like Dwight Lyman Moody (page 309). Wage earners and clerks and small merchants were smart enough to stay away. Parishes and congregations, a generation earlier the domain of priests or elders and other male communicants, became female turf.

When a man's habits, including his religion, came in conflict with the demands of a strange industrialized society, untold anguish could result. Orthodox Jews from eastern Europe had an "occasion of much rejoicing" on the eighth day after the birth of a son. Inevitably, that day by American standards was normally a workday, so the celebration was shifted to the next following Sunday. Now the joyous day became a sad day, because everybody would "know it is not the right day." This pressure of the time-clock reinforced the original animus of many immigrants who came with the intention of building up a small capital to carry back to their home country. From 1908 to 1910, for every hundred immigrants from eastern and southern Europe, forty-four left. As one young man in Rochester phrased it:

> Nothing job, nothing job,
> I return to Italy;
> Comrades, laborers, good-bye;
> Adieu, land of "Fourth of July."

Religion had been the chief tie of most Americans to the products of the intellect. That tie was cut. The typical citizen now knew nothing about the creations of the brain. The pity of it all was augmented because those creations were more indigenous than ever before. Emerson had tried to conjure up "The American Scholar," but had not succeeded. With few exceptions—Jonathan Edwards, Franklin, Whitman, Melville, Lincoln—native thought had derived from foreign origins. Now, instead of following alien leads in a specific area, theology or the novel or philosophy, the greatest Americans were relying on inferences from the society around them. They were less traditionalists than inductionists.

They differed from their preceding countrymen in another dimension as well. They were more theoretical. They wrote essays on vastly abstract subjects:

The Energies of Men
The School and Social Progress
The Path of the Law
The System of Social Control

Even Jamie Madison, pondering the relevance of geographical dimensions in the operation of a republic, even Alexander Hamilton, dissecting the functions of government in the operations of an economy, even Abraham Lincoln, thinking about the relation of free land to social equality, had never soared so high into the ionosphere.

The third major alteration in the meaning of "leisure" was the growing conviction that government should play a part in filling the spare time of its citizens. Municipal parks had been started in a few places before the Civil War. But in the nation as a whole, this movement was trivial until the end of the century. Then states and the Federal government began to use their authority. The first national park was Yellowstone in 1872, then Yosemite in 1890; now there are three dozen. These recreational areas were not used by the typical American until after World War II, but when he wanted them, they were there.

While state and nation surged forward in the provision of parks, cities moved haltingly. Reasons for this laggardness can be inferred from evidence for Chicago already noted, and we now have even better data for Cincinnati, where the mayor in 1893 boasted that his city had an acre of park for every 770 persons, "nearly twice that of any large city in the country." In most cities, if not in Cincinnati, word was getting around that the park was not a safe place to go. Four decades would pass before this claim won virtually universal assent, but already by 1914 it was sufficiently widespread to sap the strength from citizens' demands for more and better urban parks. Cincinnati did, however, witness the changing notions of the uses of parks. As late as 1895 the city government was bragging that it had kept athletics out of the parks, that it had maintained the restful quality of these "rural" oases. But a decade later the mayor, responsive to the accents of the new child-oriented culture, was trumpeting in favor of sports fields and playgrounds.

For more than twenty years, George B. Cox was the Republican boss of Cincinnati. But he could remain in that status only by shifting his party to conform to changes in the locale. In 1890 he relied on the lowest circles of the electorate: immigrants, saloons, and gamblers. As the suburbs grew, he found it expedient to wear pinstriped suits and silk neckties. To keep the reins in his hand, he had to move with the team. Starting out on the edge of the Basin—the flats along the Ohio River where the casual laborers lived, he tried to migrate his power upwards toward the Hilltops. He failed in the end, and was turned out, but for twenty years he ran a model political machine. His failure came from the enhanced position of his original constituency, as governments and official social workers took over more of the functions that the local boss had once furnished. To cite another transformation, the budding government bureaus also displaced the settlement houses; Hull-House in 1940 was a relic of the vibrant neuron of 1900.

In the American's stance toward civic affairs, the most important change in these thirty-seven years was in his attitude toward the rest of the world. He had always been aggressive toward weaker neighbors. He had never felt any sympathy for Indians. One writer characterizing the thought of the Southwest has said, "Hatred of Mexicans is total—and totally in the service of American expansion." But with regard to stronger outsiders, Americans had been cautious. In regard to Canada, the government of the United States had not tried to bullyrag its northern neighbor before the twentieth century. Private Americans had screeched for annexation, even some prominent Federal officials had done so, but the full power of the Federal government had never been launched on such an expansionist course. Events had gone, indeed, in the opposite direction. After a treaty of 1910 had fixed a maritime line of a mere 25.2 miles to the Bay of Fundy, the British minister could truthfully report to the governor-general of Canada, ". . . our frontier from the Atlantic to the Pacific is fixed and settled."

But in discussing American-Canadian relations, a historian of this period must be wary. It was Canada, not the monster to the south, that rejected reciprocity in 1911. The moving force was not a bitter hostility to the United States, but rather a quiet determination to resist Americanization and annexation; for many it meant also a resolve to keep and even to strengthen the British connection. Tantalizing is the fact that one of the clearest expressions of this attitude came from a woman who was half-English, half-Mohawk:

> The Dutch may have their Holland, the Spaniard have his Spain,
> The Yankee to the south of us must south of us remain;
> For not a man dare lift a hand against the men who brag
> That they were born in Canada beneath the British flag.

This Canadian insistence upon independence from the neighboring ogre was felt deeply and broadly. A Tory MP from Montreal proclaimed, "Let us be an independent nation rather than the backyard of the United States." Robert Borden, whose Conservatives made him Prime Minister upon winning the Federal election of 1911, had attacked the reciprocity treaty by saying that Americans thought it to be "the first step towards annexation."

The complications do not end there. A carriage maker in Indiana, also former president of the National Association of Manufacturers, had declared in 1907 that the country required more foreign markets, and that the obvious place to seek them was Canada. A year earlier, James J. Hill, a native Canadian converted into an American railroad mogul, had announced: "Canada is merely a portion of our own western country, cut off from us by accident." Hill logically was in favor of reciprocity in 1911. His companion among railroad moguls, William Cornelius Van Horne, an American turned Canadian, was logically against it. Van Horne had explained how an American thought Canadian while a Canadian thought American, "patriotic sentiments have never in the history of the world stood long against the pocket book." Patent laws, in addition to import duties, prompted many American manufacturers to start branch plants in Canada; by 1912 more than 200 such operations existed. Apart from minor accessions like the Philippines and Puerto Rico, U.S. corporations had opted for informal empire and the open door rather than legalized colonies.

This inference helps us to see the importance of William A. Williams' *The Roots of the Modern American Empire* (1969). A few earlier historians had defined the interests of specific groups of American farmers in foreign markets: George Rogers Taylor, Norman A. Graebner, Paul W. Gates. But Williams presents them as the lancers in the phalanx of overseas expansion. His evidence is most persuasive, even though most of it cannot possibly be reprinted there. The *Western Rural*, for instance, commented on the possibility of a war in Europe in 1885: "We will do the best we can to feed the people at the best price we can get." As Jefferson had said long before, The United States can fatten on the follies of the Old World. This attitude saturated agricultural thought all through the nineteenth century, whether we want to talk about the Napoleonic Wars or the Spanish-American War. The dramatic change in 1898 came not because farmers had changed their ideas, but because businessmen and politicians had changed theirs. Americans now became conscious of alternatives: Did they want to be models, standing aloof from foreign entanglements but striving to set an upright example? Or did they want to be missionaries and merchants, striving to capture the moneys and the minds of the whole world? By and large, they plunked for the latter. This *bouleversement* would haunt them for a century.

Part of the dilemma, of course, came from their definition of the good life. They may have flipped their attitudes toward peoples on other shores. But their posture toward their countrymen changed hardly at all. Americans were committed to life as a series of episodes that were enacted under floodlights. The central problem was to wear your mask successfully. Living in a society so fluid that your face-to-face encounters lasted for five minutes at a time, you came to think it foolish to suppose that anybody else would ever know what you were really like. There was no real Ray Ginger; he became a sequence of hypocrisies. He was, however, always the hero, for in his moral drama he was destined to reform all aliens. Only Americans had snatched the true message from the Almighty. This had not been the traditional mode until about 1870. Let us close with two key terms of the American creed. The common meaning of each had ended in turmoil and egocentric cruelty. Individualism, except for rare people like John Quincy Adams and his parents, had not meant individuality; it had not meant realizing your private potentials; it had not meant personal distinction. It had not offered singularity. The ideal of the frontier was not separatism, but self-reliance to be replaced by cooperation as soon as you had neighbors. To cite another glorious frontier phrase, this one from Jacksonian times, "this is a free country, and every man does as he pleases, and if he don't, we make him do so."

The common man worshipped equality as much as he worshipped individualism, but he was just as foggy about what he meant by it. In the first place, it is not nearly so congenial to Liberty as Jefferson and Lincoln had said. But true believers continued to deny that the two policies might clash. Liberty guaranteed your right to enter the Race of Life. Equality guaranteed that each individual should have the same chance in the starting gates; even infants whose birth pangs were already tainted by deprivation, such as females or blacks, were not entitled to "special privileges." Is the rise of spectator sports connected to the general American notion of equality as an athletic contest?

Lawyer: CLARENCE DARROW

The name of Clarence Seward Darrow (1857–1938) conjures up the Monkey Trial and Leopold-Loeb. He is remembered as the foremost defense lawyer of his generation, spokesman for the accused in dozens of murder trials. This view is badly distorted. It offers only a courtroom advocate in his waning years, whereas the truth is far more complex. Darrow found his springboard into the Chicago bar in the practice of civil law, not of criminal. His friendship with John Peter Altgeld made him the corporation counsel of Chicago, representing the city in such mundane actions as land titles and tax assessments. Next he was general attorney for the Chicago and Northwestern Railroad, trying to fend off the regulatory efforts of municipalities and legislatures and the Federal authorities. It was his appearance as attorney for Eugene Debs in the Pullman boycott of 1894 that projected him onto a larger and more brilliantly lighted stage. For the next twenty years his best-known clients were a cross-section of the trade union officials of the nation.

Even after he became a famous labor lawyer, Darrow continued to represent large corporations—if they would pay his fee. His friends in the settlement houses sometimes challenged the contradictions in his behavior. He replied thus, probably in 1895, to one of them:

> I undertook to serve this company or these people, believing they had an ordinance, procured by the aid of boodle. Judged by the ordinary commercial and legal standard of ethics I did right. . . . I am satisfied that judged by the higher law, in which we both believe, I could not be justified, and that I am practically a thief. I am taking money that I did not earn, which comes to me from men who did not earn it, but who get it,

because they have a chance to get it. . . . I came to Chicago about eight years ago, before I came I lived in a small country town. . . . I determined to take my chance with the rest, to get what I could out of the system and use it to destroy the system. I came without friends or money. Society provides no fund out of which such people can live while preaching heresy. It compels us to get our living out of society as it is or die. I do not choose yet to die although perhaps it would be the best. . . .

Darrow was in a quandary. The lawyers he knew as a youth were private practitioners, each his own man, picking his own clients, serving in a wide spectrum of causes. But the legal firms on the ascendant in 1900 were bureaucratic teams of experts. Not only was each attorney a victim of the division of labor, so were most firms (specialists in municipal bonds, or railroad reorganizations, or land development). Darrow was the marginal man, teetering between these ways of life. Over the long haul, he liked the old ways better than the new.

ESSAY ON SOURCES

In the following remarks, I have discussed each work in relation to that chapter or those chapters where its data proved most valuable in writing this book. But inevitably some studies that I have evaluated as business and economic history also contain material bearing on political or social or intellectual or diplomatic matters. Therefore, readers interested in the secondary sources on the United States in the late 19th and early 20th centuries are asked to read this essay straight through from front to back.

A recent attempt to deal in an over-all way with the early part of this period, to about 1890, is H. Wayne Morgan, ed., *The Gilded Age: A Reappraisal* (1963). Unfortunately the essays, by ten scholars, vary greatly in quality, ranging from a careful and original study of the status of industrial workers in various types of communities by Herbert G. Gutman to a very poor chapter on literature. I have brought together 36 primary sources to illustrate many phases of American history in *The Nationalizing of American Life, 1877–1900* (1965).* Besides a 10,000-word general introduction, each document is preceded by an evaluation of its meaning.

GENERAL BIBLIOGRAPHIES

Invaluable are Philip M. Hamer, ed., *Guide to Archives and Manuscripts in the United States* (1961); George Frederick Howe and others, eds., *American Historical Association's Guide to Historical Literature* (1961); and Oscar Handlin and others, eds., *Harvard Guide to American History* (1954). U. S. Bureau of the Census, *Historical Statistics of the United States: Colonial Times to 1957* (1960) is both an indispensable 800 large pages of tables and also a superb guide to other statistical sources.

GLIMPSES INTO THE HISTORY OF A YEAR, 1877

(Chapter 1)
The material used here has been taken mainly from primary but published sources. Mari Sandoz, *Crazy Horse* (1942)* is a

* An asterisk after a title indicates that a paperback edition is now available.

classic; see also George E. Hyde, *Red Cloud's Folk* (1957 edition). A generally reliable summary is Alvin M. Josephy, Jr., *The Patriot Chiefs: A Chronicle of American Indian Leadership* (1961). The conditions of farm wives in Indiana are described in Myron W. Reed to Mrs. William O. Carpenter, 8 January 1879, in Myron W. Reed Papers, Chicago Historical Society. Material has been taken from Theodore C. Blegen, ed., *Land of Their Choice: The Immigrants Write Home* (1955); Henry E. Lucas, ed., *Dutch Immigrant Memoirs and Related Writings* (1955); Charles Morley, ed., *Portrait of America: Letters of Henry Sienkiewicz* (1959); Jacob R. Marcus, ed., "An Arizona Pioneer: Memoirs of Sam Aaron," *American Jewish Archives*, vol. 10 (1958), 95–120; and Ward Thoron, ed., *Letters of Mrs. Henry Adams, 1865–1883* (1936). The other Henry Adams, ex-slave of Shreveport, testifies in *Senate Report 693*, 46th Congress, 2nd Session, Part II, pp. 101–111. Frances Cornwall Hutner, *The Farr Alpaca Company* (1951) is solid. Material on other Southerners is from Albert D. Kirwan, *Revolt of the Rednecks: Mississippi Politics, 1876–1925* (1951); Henry W. Grady's article in *Harper's Monthly*, vol. 63 (1881); and William Gibbs McAdoo, *The Crowded Years* (1931). For an enlightening contemporary view of Thomas Eakins see William C. Brownell, "The Art Schools of Philadelphia," *Scribner's*, vol. 18 (1879), 737–750.

Allan Nevins, *Study in Power: John D. Rockefeller, Industrialist and Philanthropist* (1953); and Ralph W. Hidy and Muriel E. Hidy, *Pioneering in Big Business, 1882–1911: History of Standard Oil Company (New Jersey)* (1955), are based on wide-ranging research in primary sources. But both of these works seem to me to come to one-sided, overly favorable conclusions because of their selective reporting of data. Each of them, for instance, skips over the efforts of the Company to influence American foreign policy—a topic on which considerable evidence is now available in other scholarly studies that will be discussed later. A less partisan analysis is Harold F. Williamson and Arnold R. Daum, *The American Petroleum Industry, 1859–1899: The Age of Illumination* (1959).

BUSINESS AND ECONOMIC HISTORY

(Chapters 2, 3, 10)

Obviously no individual could hope to examine more than a tiny fraction of the primary sources possibly relevant to this study, and I cannot claim to have done so. If works so broad in scope are to be written at all, they must be constructed chiefly from the findings of other scholars. But I have not used the research of another unless it was manifest that he or she had worked thoroughly and carefully through the pertinent primary materials. Thus, while I have relied mainly on secondary sources, I have spurned tertiary and quaternary ones.

Nearly every issue of the *Business History Review* since 1954 contains relevant data. I wish to acknowledge my especially heavy debt to the following articles in that journal: Thomas R. Navin and Marian V. Sears, "The Rise of a Market for Industrial Securities, 1887–1902," vol. 29 (1955), 105–138, which sheds much light on the origins of the separation between ownership and control in manufacturing companies; Marian V. Sears, "The American Businessman at the Turn of the Century," vol. 30 (1956), 382–443, an excellent summary; Richard C. Overton, "Charles Elliott Perkins," vol. 31 (1957), 292–309; and Alfred D. Chandler, Jr., "The Beginnings of 'Big Business' in American Industry," vol. 33 (1959), 1–31, a model study.

Although most of its space is devoted to non-American studies, the *Journal of Economic History* was also very valuable, especially Douglass C. North, "Life Insurance and Investment Banking at the Time of the Armstrong Investigation in 1905," vol. 14 (1954), 209–228, and Allan G. Bogue and Margaret B. Bogue, " 'Profits' and the Frontier Land Speculator," vol. 17 (1957), 1–24. *Agricultural History* holds surprisingly few useful articles.

Three volumes of *The Economic History of the United States* survey the period in detail, and each of them contains a massive bibliography. Fred A. Shannon's classic *The Farmer's Last Frontier: Agriculture, 1860–1897* (1945) shows that migration to farms was not a safety valve for discontent in the East. But while this is true, "farms" is not identical in meaning with "the West," which held cities from the beginning and which in various ways did stimulate economic prosperity and social mobility. Edward C. Kirkland's *Industry Comes of Age: Business, Labor, and Public*

Policy, 1860–1897 (1961), while seeming to imply that excess capacity was no more central in developments of the times than, say, trade unionism, contains a wealth of data. The succeeding volume, Harold U. Faulkner, *The Decline of Laissez Faire, 1897–1917* (1951), is far inferior.

A few sectional studies are outstanding. C. Vann Woodward, *Origins of the New South, 1877–1913* (1951) is an overwhelming book that sets economic factors into the total context. John S. Spratt, *The Road to Spindletop: Economic Change in Texas, 1875–1901* (1955) and Leonard J. Arrington, *Great Basin Kingdom: The Economic History of the Latter-Day Saints, 1830–1900* (1958) are good local studies. A little-known phase of the technical revolution in agriculture is well treated in Reynold M. Wik, *Steam Power on the American Farm* (1953).

Many publications of the National Bureau of Economic Research were helpful. I am particularly indebted to Rendigs Fels, *American Business Cycles, 1865–1897* (1959), a detailed work making use of economic theory, statistical analysis, and qualitative historical data. Another probing study is Albert Rees and Donald P. Jacobs, *Real Wages in Manufacturing, 1890–1914* (1961). Contrary to the view widely held previously, Rees and Jacobs conclude that the average hourly real earnings in manufacturing rose 37 per cent in the period.

Also deserving attention is Edward Chase Kirkland, *Dream and Thought in the Business Community, 1860–1900* (1956). This little book devotes a chapter each to examining the ideas of businessmen on (a) the worries of being in business in this period, (b) their own mansions, (c) public schools, (d) universities, (e) government, and (f) the contributions of businessmen to civilization in general.

Three notable studies take broad approaches to railroad history. Unlike recent works that, although allegedly historical interpretations, have tended to substitute sociological hypotheses for research in historical documents, Thomas C. Cochran has made a pioneering effort to use such concepts as "role" to make sense of a great mass of data. In his *Railroad Leaders, 1845–1890: The Business Mind in Action* (1953), an invaluable appendix holds nearly 300 pages of extracts from the letters of 60 executives. Edward Chase Kirkland, *Men, Cities, and Transportation: A Study in New England History, 1820–1900* (1948) is sweeping, as is Julius Grodinsky, *Transcontinental Railway Strategy, 1869–1893: A Study of Businessmen*

(1962). See also Grodinsky's *The Iowa Pool: A Study in Railroad Competition, 1870–1884* (1950) and his *Jay Gould: His Business Career, 1867–1892* (1957). Other useful works on individual railroads or executives include Joseph Gilpin Pyle, *The Life of James J. Hill* (1917); George Kennan, *E. H. Harriman: A Biography* (1922); Richard C. Overton, *Gulf to Rockies: The Heritage of the Fort Worth and Denver-Colorado and Southern Railways, 1861–1898* (1953). Robert W. Fogel, *The Union Pacific Railroad: A Case Study in Premature Enterprise* (1960) is noteworthy for its use of rather simple analytical tools to refute its own subtitle. George Rogers Taylor and Irene D. Neu, *The American Railroad Network, 1861–1890* (1956) carefully elucidates the physical integration of the network, especially the standardization of gauge, and contains admirable maps.

On the oil industry, in addition to works already cited, see Arthur Menzies Johnson, *The Development of American Petroleum Pipelines: A Study in Private Enterprise and Public Policy, 1862–1906* (1956). Matthew Josephson, *Edison: A Biography* (1959) is very good; and Harold C. Passer, *The Electrical Manufacturers, 1875–1900: A Study in Competition, Entrepreneurship, Technical Change, and Economic Growth* (1953) is stunning in its simultaneous grasp of technology, business, and historical data. The two major firms in another metal-working industry are well handled in George Sweet Gibb, *The Saco-Lowell Shops: Textile Machinery Building in New England, 1813–1949* (1950); and Thomas R. Navin, *The Whitin Machine Works since 1831: A Textile Machinery Company in an Industrial Village* (1950). William T. Hutchinson, *Cyrus Hall McCormick: Harvest, 1856–1884* (1935) is superb. Allan Nevins and Frank Ernest Hill, *Ford: The Times, the Man, the Company* (1954) is derived from a great mass of company records but it is sometimes careless. On DuPont see Williams Haynes, *American Chemical Industry: A History*, vol. 6 (1949); Ernest Dale, *The Great Organizers* (1960); and the trail-blazing study by Alfred D. Chandler, *Strategy and Structure: Chapters in the History of the Industrial Enterprise* (1962). If anybody wonders why I have neglected to mention Frederick W. Taylor and "scientific management" he should treat himself to the subtle and ironic study by Hugh G. J. Aitken, *Taylorism at Watertown Arsenal: Scientific Management in Action, 1908–1915* (1960).

Our knowledge of manufacturing in the late 19th century has

been growing fairly rapidly as a number of careful studies have been done based chiefly on company records, which in general are far more reliable than government reports, daily newspapers, or trade journals. In comparison, we still know relatively little about what Marian V. Sears has called "the distribution revolution." In her words: "Taking our clue from the observations of the contemporary businessman himself, we apparently need to know much more about the department store, the mail-order house, the wholesaler; about advertising, warehousing, packaging, catalogues, direct selling, sales administration; and about how these institutions and functions evolved." A solid start is made in Ralph M. Hower, *History of Macy's of New York, 1858–1919: Chapters in the Evolution of the Department Store* (1946); Boris Emmet and John E. Jeuck, *Catalogues and Counters: The History of Sears, Roebuck and Company* (1950); Robert W. Twyman, *History of Marshall Field & Co., 1852–1906* (1954); and Ralph M. Hower, *The History of an Advertising Agency: N. W. Ayer & Son at Work, 1869–1949* (1949).

On the semi-arid West the best book is Walter Prescott Webb, *The Great Plains* (1931).* The most penetrating study of ranching is Lewis Atherton, *The Cattle Kings* (1961), in which the notes are a good guide to other literature. Joe B. Frantz and Julian Ernest Choate, Jr., *The American Cowboy: The Myth and the Reality* (1955) disappointed me, but I trust nobody will be disappointed in Andy Adams, *The Log of a Cowboy* (1902).*

Milton Friedman and Anna Jacobson Schwartz, *A Monetary History of the United States, 1867–1960* (1963) has an indispensable 200 pages on the years to 1914. Lewis Corey, *The House of Morgan* (1930) is based on public records and the contemporary press. In addition to these sources Frederick Lewis Allen interviewed several Morgan partners and used a limited amount of manuscript material made available by the firm in writing *The Great Pierpont Morgan* (1949). The result, in spite of many failings, is the best biography of the biggest banker of them all. It is thickened and corrected at several places by John A. Garraty, *Right-Hand Man: The Life of George W. Perkins* (1960). On the head of the largest rival house see Cyrus Adler, *Jacob H. Schiff: His Life and Letters* (1928). A suggestive article is Barry E. Supple, "A Business Elite: German-Jewish Financiers in Nineteenth-Century New York," *Business History Review*, vol. 31 (1957), 143–178. A superior look into the banking world is provided by Fritz Redlich, *The Molding of American Banking: Men and Ideas* (1951), and a major source of funds is studied in Morton Keller, *The Life Insurance Enterprise, 1885–1910: A Study in the Limits of Corporate Power* (1963). Edward G. Campbell, *The Reorganization of the American Railroad System, 1893–1900* (1938) should be read with John F. Stover, *The Railroads of the South, 1865–1900: A Study in Finance and Control* (1955).

Sigmund Diamond, *The Reputation of the American Businessman* (1955) is an imaginative effort to get at the changing stances from which business magnates have been evaluated by dissecting the obituaries of six of them, including Vanderbilt and Morgan. Thomas C. Cochran's *The American Business System: A Historical Perspective, 1900–1955* (1962 ed.) * is compressed and informed. Samuel P. Hays, *The Response to Industrialism, 1885–1914* (1957) * is not only brief but thin, an effort at synthesis that just does not come off.

SOCIAL HISTORY

(Chapters 4, 5, 8, 11, 13, 15)

Robert V. Bruce, *1877: Year of Violence* (1959) gives a detailed and exciting account of the great railroad strikes. Henry David, *The History of the Haymarket Affair* (1936) is excellent. The three candidates for mayor of New York in 1886 are studied in Henry F. Pringle, *Theodore Roosevelt: A Biography* (1931)*; Allan Nevins, *Abram S. Hewitt, with Some Account of Peter Cooper* (1935); and Charles Albro Barker, *Henry George* (1955). I have relied particularly on Thomas J. Condon, "Politics, Reform and the New York City Election of 1886," *New York Historical Society Quarterly*, vol. 44 (1960), 363–393. Perhaps the best study yet made of any American labor dispute is Donald L. McMurry's exhaustive *The Great Burlington Strike of 1888: A Case History in Labor Relations* (1956), based in large part on the railroad's archives. Henry David, "Upheaval at Homestead," in Daniel Aaron, ed., *America in Crisis: Fourteen Crucial Episodes in American History* (1952) is the latest extended account of the violence and tumult of 1892. Almont Lindsey's *The Pullman Strike* (1942) is standard. Other reliable studies of the industrial labor force and of unionism are Vernon H. Jensen, *Heritage of Conflict: Labor Relations in the Nonferrous*

Metal Industry up to 1930 (1950); Lloyd Ulman, *The Rise of the National Trade Union* (1955); and David Brody, *Steelworkers in America: The Nonunion Era* (1960). Philip Taft, *The A.F. of L. in the Time of Gompers* (1957), seems to me far more admiring of the Federation and its titular head than the facts warrant.

The works already cited by Shannon, Spratt, and Woodward are invaluable on the problems of farmers. Much of the best recent work in agricultural history has been done by Paul W. Gates and his students. See Gates, *Fifty Million Acres: Conflicts over Kansas Land Policy, 1854–1890* (1954), which was important for my purposes chiefly for its argument that railroad land policies played a greater role in provoking the agrarian uprising than has usually been realized, and Margaret Beattie Bogue, *Patterns from the Sod: Land Use and Tenure in the Grand Prairie, 1850–1900* (1959). I owe a special debt to Allan G. Bogue, *Money at Interest: The Farm Mortgage on the Middle Border* (1955), a superb monograph based almost entirely on business manuscripts. Two generations of historians had written about the exploitation of farmers by loan sharks; now Bogue has provided solid evidence on the crucial problem of agricultural credit from 1870 to 1900. His study analyzes: first, the activities of two brothers in upstate New York who invested heavily in Midwestern farm mortgages; second, the operations of the large firm of J. B. Watkins in Lawrence, Kansas, which served as middleman between Western farmers and Eastern or English investors; third, the incidence of the farm mortgage on a township in eastern Nebraska and on another in central Kansas. An investigation following Bogue's lead of a broker in Portland, Maine, and New Haven, Connecticut, is Glenn H. Miller, Jr., "The Hawkes Papers: A Case Study of a Kansas Mortgage Brokerage Business, 1871–1888," *Business History Review*, vol. 32 (1958), 293–310. Again, as was true of J. B. Watkins, we encounter an interesting connection between religion and business: most of the loanable funds placed by Hawks came from local societies in the East of the United Society of Believers (the Shakers). Joseph Cannon Bailey, *Seaman A. Knapp: Schoolmaster of American Agriculture* (1945) is useful.

Attitudes toward Negroes are fitted into the over-all psychology of Southern whites in W. J. Cash's classic *The Mind of the South* (1941),* a book that nobody should miss. The most stimulating recent effort to see the Negro problem in the entire South in this period is C. Vann Woodward, *The Strange Career of Jim Crow* (revised edition, 1957).* Although Woodward incisively shows the intensification and legalization of segregation in the late 19th century, I suspect he may have minimized the segregation that existed earlier, enforced either by custom or by local ordinances. Some fascinating items are contained in Herbert Aptheker, ed., *A Documentary History of the Negro People in the United States* (1951).* E. Franklin Frazier's *The Negro Family in the United States* (1939)* remains standard.

Not only is W. E. B. DuBois' *The Souls of Black Folk* (1903)* a mine of information and a revelation to read, but also its stance can conveniently be compared to that of E. Davidson Washington, ed., *Selected Speeches of Booker T. Washington* (1932). See also Booker T. Washington, *Up from Slavery: An Autobiography* (1901).* Helpful scraps can be found in Samuel R. Spencer, Jr., *Booker T. Washington and the Negro's Place in American Life* (1955), but it seemed thin and based on a faulty or even prejudiced outlook when it was published; it seems more so today. Francis L. Broderick, *W. E. B. DuBois: Negro Leader in a Time of Crisis* (1959) and Elliott M. Rudwick, *W. E. B. DuBois: A Study in Minority Group Leadership* (1960) are not wholly satisfactory. DuBois has been simultaneously a scholar, a literary artist, and a leader of protest movements, and no facet of his career should be slighted. We greatly need thorough biographies of Washington and DuBois. *The Negro's Progress in Fifty Years* (1913), by DuBois, Washington, Kelly Miller, and others, is a valuable collection of essays including statistical material on occupations, rural and urban residence, and so on.

Rayford W. Logan, *The Negro in American Life and Thought: The Nadir, 1877–1901* (1954) surveys the attitudes and actions of national leaders and of the press bearing on the roles of Negroes in American society, but it is disappointing for its failure to give a picture of how Negroes actually lived. On the latter point see the outstanding Chapters 6 and 7 in George Brown Tindall, *South Carolina Negroes, 1877–1900* (1952), another of the best recent works on this period. Other useful state studies are Vernon Lane Wharton, *The Negro in Mississippi, 1865–1890* (1947); Emmy Lou Thornbrough, *The Negro in Indiana: A Study of a Minority* (1957); and Charles E. Wynes, *Race Relations in Virginia, 1870–1902* (1961). In contradiction of the widely held view that it was the "poor whites" who demanded segregation, Wynes concludes: "The Virginia legislators who disfranchised the Negro and segregated him by statute *were not* led by representatives of that class of white men who competed directly with the Negro economically and who were more likely to be thrown with him socially. Instead, men of good family and social prestige led the fight." (p. 149) Tindall found that in South Carolina such upper-class whites as Wade Hampton were willing in a paternalistic way to accord the vote and some other rights to Negroes. But whereas the Federal Civil Rights Act was declared unconstitutional in 1883, South Carolina had a largely similar state law until 1889. Another nine years elapsed before a statute required segregation on trains—and then only on first-class carriages where the wealthier citizens rode. The delays were caused chiefly by railroad opposition, but they were also influenced by the "inertia of white public opinion . . ." (p. 300).

Oscar Handlin, *The Uprooted: The Epic Story of the Great Migrations That Made the American People* (1951)* is a highly regarded effort to portray the psychology of immigrants, but I still prefer to get at this aspect of immigration by means of diaries and letters such as I have cited or by means of fiction. Relevant novels that are outstanding include Willa Cather, *O Pioneers!* (1913); her *My Antonia* (1918)*; and O. E. Rolvaag, *Giants in the Earth: A Saga of the Prairie* (1927). In Rowland Tappan Berthoff's superior study, *British Immigrants in Industrial America, 1790–1950* (1953), I prefer the first part on economic adjustments to the second part on social adjustments, but Berthoff emphatically dissents from my preference. The overall quality of the work is suggested by the fact that the author learned Welsh to do research for it. Only one other nationality has received comparable treatment; see Theodore C. Blegen, *Norwegian Migration to America* (1931, 1940). A splendid study of opponents of immigration is John Higham, *Strangers in the Land: Patterns of American Nativism, 1860–1925* (1955).

In Moses Rischin, *The Promised City: New York's Jews, 1870–1914* (1962), massive research has yielded much useful data (I was intrigued, for instance, by such touches as the impact of the numerically small Society for Ethical Culture). But I wish that Rischin had consigned to tables or appendices the lists of occupations, of periodicals, of speakers at meetings, that make parts of his text almost unreadable. And at time, as in referring to the "populist rhetoric" of anti-Semitism (p. 260), his generalizations seem ill-adjusted to his evidence. I doubt the wisdom of making poor farmers in the 1890's responsible for the ban against Jewish members imposed by the Greek letter societies at the College of the City of New York in 1878 (p. 261). Roy Lubove, *The Progressives and the Slums: Tenement House Reform in New York City, 1890–1917* (1962) does much to firm up the picture drawn by Lillian D. Wald, *The House on Henry Street* (1915).

On Chicago see the works of Jane Addams; the remarkable *Hull-House Maps and Papers: A Presentation of Nationalities and Wages in a Congested District of Chicago* (1895); Ray Ginger, *Altgeld's America: The Lincoln Ideal versus Changing Realities* (1958); Wayne Andrews, *Battle for Chicago* (1946); and Bessie Louise Pierce, *A History of Chicago*, vol. 3 (1957). Sam B. Warner, Jr., has done outstanding work in *Streetcar Suburbs: The Process of Growth in Boston, 1870–1900* (1962). It seems incredible, but he analyzed the permits for more than 23,000 buildings. Thus he is able to show how the metropolitan area was segregated economically into slums and suburbs; how in the suburbs community life was fragmented and meaningless; and how extreme decentralization of decision making led to dreary uniformity in suburban lots and buildings. See too Warner's edition of Robert A. Woods and Albert J. Kennedy, *The Zone of Emergence* (1962).* Another facet of Boston's history is deftly told in Arthur Mann, *Yankee Reformers in the Urban Age* (1954). E. Digby Baltzell, *Philadelphia Gentlemen: The Making of a National Upper Class* (1958) is a standout. Works on other cities can be located by means of Blake McKelvey's handy if plodding survey, *The Urbanization of America, 1860–1915* (1963). It is indeed unfortunate that, with the partial exception of urban history, local history in this country should have been left almost exclusively to the antiquarians; the great possibilities in this area when it is attacked with imagination and diligence can be seen in Paul M. Angle's *Bloody Williamson: A Chapter in American Lawlessness* (1952) and in James C. Malin's account of "the poet laureate of Kansas" in his whimsically titled *Confounded Rot about Napoleon: Reflections upon Science and Technology, Nationalism, World Depression of the Eighteen-Nineties, and Afterwards* (1961).*

The flavor of contemporary society is communicated by Frank

G. Carpenter, *Carp's Washington* (1960), a scintillating volume edited by Frances Carpenter from a reporter's dispatches to the Cleveland Leader, 1883–1889. The tone of the following decade saturates Thomas Beer's impressionistic *The Mauve Decade: American Life at the End of the Nineteenth Century* (1926).* It contains many mistakes of fact, but such sketches as the one of Tammany boss Richard Croker are priceless. Beer was a keen observer of men; too, he had gotten considerable inside information from his father who was an executive of New York Life. See also Beer's *Hanna* (1929).

For insight into the values of the proper middle classes there is no substitute for poking about in magazines of the period: the *Atlantic Monthly, Harper's,* the *North American Review, Century Magazine, Scribner's, McClure's, Collier's,* and so on. Diaries also are very illuminating, and some have been published: see Charles G. Dawes, *A Journal of the McKinley Years,* ed. Bascom N. Timmons, (1950); and Festus P. Summers, ed., *The Cabinet Diary of William L. Wilson, 1896–1897* (1957). Both give glimpses into life in Washington and elsewhere, and the latter reveals the total inability of an educated and civilized if conservative Gold Democrat to see how anybody could favor the free coinage of silver unless he was a fool or a knave.

Ideas and values are discussed in Lewis Atherton's excellent study of small towns in the Middle West, *Main Street on the Middle Border* (1954). Irvin G. Wyllie's *The Self-Made Man in America: The Myth of Rags to Riches* (1954) is a concise and beautifully written account of Russell H. Conwell and other propagators of the myth. Richard Hofstadter, *Social Darwinism in American Thought, 1860–1915* (1945)* is standard; a useful corrective is Irvin G. Wyllie, "Social Darwinism and the Businessman," *Proceedings of the American Philosophical Society,* vol. 103 (1959), 629–635.

On religion Washington Gladden, *Recollections* (1909) is useful. Among the careful studies are Charles H. Hopkins, *Rise of the Social Gospel in American Protestantism, 1860–1915* (1940), Aaron I. Abell, *Urban Impact on American Protestantism* (1943), Henry F. May, *Protestant Churches and Industrial America* (1949); Thomas T. McAvoy, *The Great Crisis in American Catholic History, 1895–1900* (1957); and William G. McLoughlin, Jr., *Modern Revivalism: Charles Grandison Finney to Billy Graham* (1959). Along with other topics, the impact of traditional religion on the schools can be seen in Harvey C. Minnich, *William Holmes McGuffey and His Readers* (1936); and Richard D. Mosier, *Making the American Mind: Social and Moral Ideas in the McGuffey Readers* (1947).

Lawrence A. Cremin, *The Transformation of the School: Progressivism in American Education, 1876–1957* (1961) is a documented study drawn from a multitude of sources. Richard Hofstadter and Wilson Smith have edited *American Higher Education: A Documentary History* (1961); see also George Paul Schmidt, *The Liberal Arts College: A Chapter in American Cultural History* (1957). Edward A. Krug, ed., *Charles W. Eliot on Education* (1962)* is handy. Some of the best sources deal with specific institutions, as Samuel Eliot Morison on Harvard (1930, 1936); William Fuller Dunaway on Penn State (1946); Merle Curti and Vernon H. Carstenson on the University of Wisconsin (1949); George Wilson Pierson on Yale (1952); James B. Sellers on the University of Alabama (1953); Hugh Hawkins on Johns Hopkins (1960); and Charles M. Gates on the University of Washington (1961). The Flexner Report of 1910 is discussed, with substantial extracts, in *I Remember: The Autobiography of Abraham Flexner* (1940). Thorstein Veblen, *The Higher Learning in America* (1918)* is caustic and often hilarious.

Frank Luther Mott's *Golden Multitudes: The Story of Best Sellers in the United States* (1947) and James D. Hart's *The Popular Book: A History of America's Literary Taste* (1950) are carefully researched and very helpful. Of the two, Mott's work was the more useful to me because he is explicit in his definition (A bestseller is a book with sales equal to 1 per cent of the U. S. population for the decade in which it was published). See also Mott's standard *A History of American Magazines, 1885–1905* (1957).

Henry Nash Smith's *Virgin Land: The American West as Symbol and Myth* (1950) is one of the ten best books on American history to be written in this generation. My view of this topic was strongly influenced by my browsing through dozens of old land pamphlets in the Snyder Collection of the library of the University of Kansas City. For evidence that political machines and corruption were not limited to cities or to immigrants see Charles N. Glaab, "Failure of North Dakota Progressivism," *Mid-America*, vol. 39 (1957), 195–209; Genevieve B. Gist, "Progressive Reform in

a Rural Community: The Adams County Vote-Fraud Case,"
Mississippi Valley Historical Review, vol. 48 (1961–1962), 60–78;
and Winston Churchill's novel, *Coniston* (1906).

James Harvey Young, *The Toadstool Millionaires: A Social
History of Patent Medicines in America before Federal Regulation* (1961) shows how research on a subject that may superfi-
cially seem unpromising can, in the hands of a first-rate historian,
throw searchlights in many directions. One of its fascinating
features is the insight afforded into the high alcoholic content of
many nostrums and the contribution it made to American self-
deception in private morality. Incisive remarks on make-believe
in the fiscal policies of American governments were made by Henry
George in *Progress and Poverty*. Such comments are also common
in the reports of British visitors such as Lord Bryce, *The American
Commonwealth* (1921 edition); and David A. Shannon, ed., *Beatrice
Webb's American Diary, 1898* (1963).

The best statistics on geographical mobility are given by Simon
Kuznets and Dorothy S. Thomas, *Population Redistribution and
Economic Growth, United States, 1870–1950* (1957, 1960); this
study is summarized in Everett S. Lee and Anne S. Lee, "Internal
Migration Statistics for the U.S.," *Journal of the American Statisti-
cal Association*, vol. 56 (1960), 664–697. A major factor contribut-
ing to mobility is discussed in David M. Potter, *People of Plenty:
Economic Abundance and the American Character* (1954),* which
is especially provocative in its remarks on Turner's frontier hy-
pothesis and on child-rearing. Rowland T. Berthoff, "The American
Social Order: A Conservative Hypothesis," *American Historical
Review*, vol. 65 (1959–1960), 495–514, and George W. Pierson,
"The M-Factor in American History," *American Quarterly*, vol. 14
(1962), 275–289, are splendid efforts to work out the implications of
various types of mobility. A special type is described in Nelson
Manfred Blake, *The Road to Reno: A History of Divorce in the
United States* (1962), which is narrower than its subtitle suggests.
This brief book focuses on legal aspects, particularly in New York
State, but the research is meticulous as far as it goes, the writing is
good, and Blake's attitudes are sensible. There is still an enormous
need for solid historical studies of the American family.

POLITICAL HISTORY

(Chapters 6, 8, 12)

All statistics on Presidential elections in this book are taken from W. Dean Burnham, *Presidential Ballots, 1836–1892* (1955), or Edgar Eugene Robinson, *The Presidential Vote, 1896–1932* (1934). Each of these compilations is based almost entirely on the official county returns and is therefore as authoritative as we can expect. On specific campaigns see C. Vann Woodward's path-blazing *Reunion and Reaction: The Compromise of 1877 and the End of Reconstruction* (1951)*; Herbert J. Clancy, *The Presidential Election of 1880* (1958); and George Harmon Knoles, *The Presidential Campaign and Election of 1892* (1942). Although it needs to be corrected at several places by more recent studies, Matthew Josephson's *The Politicos, 1865–1896* (1938)* is generally sound and is written with zest. It is still the best analytic survey of three decades of national politics. Josephson's sequel, *The President Makers: The Culture of Politics and Leadership in an Age of Enlightenment, 1896–1919* (1940) is less good.

Richard Hofstadter, *The Age of Reform, From Bryan to F.D.R.* (1955)* is not as bad as might be inferred from Norman Pollack, "Hofstadter on Populism: A Critique of 'The Age of Reform,'" *Journal of Southern History*, vol. 26 (1960), 478–500, but neither is it as good as has been widely claimed. On three major points it seems to me basically right: (1) Jingoism and imperialism were so rampant in Populist regions in the years leading to the Spanish-American War that the notion of an "isolationist" Mid-west at that time is highly suspect. (2) Make-believe was a major element in the Progressive era; on crucial problems what the movement sought was "a purely ceremonial solution" (Hofstadter, p. 243); and Roosevelt's success in satisfying that mood was central to his popularity. (3) Very probably most Progressive leaders were white middle-class Protestants in the cities.

Minor matters aside, *The Age of Reform* has major defects. Its analysis depends on minimizing the economic problems of both the Populist and Progressive periods. (a) Hofstadter: The Populists failed to realize that their plight was a result of world-wide overproduction of certain staples. True, but it was also a result of Federal policy. For Populism as "farm interest politics," see C. Vann Woodward, "The Populist Heritage and the Intel-

lectual," *American Scholar*, vol. 29 (1959–1960), especially p. 63.
(b) Having barely noted the devastating squeeze on farmers in
a period of "rubber money and iron debts," Hofstadter presents
them as a parochial bunch (they were) beset by status anxieties
(a doubtful point) that were manifested in anti-Semitism and
other types of xenophobia. He writes: "It is not too much to say
the Greenback-Populist tradition activated most of what we have
of modern popular anti-Semitism in the United States." (p. 80).
In contrast David M. Potter has written: ". . . the evidence of a
high correlation between Populism and anti-Semitism is flimsy."
I agree; see Norman Pollack, "The Myth of Populist Anti-
Semitism," *American Historical Review*, vol. 68 (1962–1963), 76–
80, and Walter T. K. Nugent, *The Tolerant Populists: Kansas
Populism and Nativism* (1963).

(c) Hofstadter: Progressivism was provoked chiefly by a status
revolution that lowered the position in society of white Protestant
Anglo-Saxons among the urban middle classes. He writes:
"Curiously, the Progressive revolt—even when we have made allowance for the brief panic of 1907 and the downward turn in business
in 1913—took place almost entirely during a period of sustained
and general prosperity." (pp. 134–135) Compare Cochran, *The
American Business System*, pp. 22–23: "The Progressive movement,
for example, reached its height during the years 1908 to 1914
when for nonagricultural sectors of the economy recession or depression was more the rule than prosperity." Both statements are
exaggerated. The best statistics we have shown that real Gross
National Product on a per capita basis was growing from 1907 to
1911, but at less than half as rapid a rate as from 1902 to 1906. In
the Progressive era millions of Americans lived in extreme poverty.
Many middle-class persons suffered losses in income as well as in
status from the combination movement: for small businessmen the
point is obvious, and in *Altgeld's America* I tried to show how
ordinary lawyers—important in the leadership of any political
movement—lost sizable portions of their law practices because of
changes in the business world. (d) Neither Chandler nor Mowry,
the students on whom Hofstadter relies in describing the traits of
Progressive leaders, used a control group in his study; that is,
neither proved that the same traits would not characterize the
leadership of, say, the Old Guard Republicans. Surely a demonstration of this point would be useful in showing that a "status revolu-

tion" was correlated with Progressivism. (e) Hofstadter implies that the same social group that produced Progressive leadership also provided its mass support among voters. No compelling evidence on this point has been produced, and I think we should heed the warning in another connection about "the confusion that has come often from interpolating from its leadership the nature of the Federalist party as a party." (Shaw Livermore, Jr., *The Twilight of Federalism* [1962], p. 6). (f) Hofstadter: "In politics, then, the immigrant was usually at odds with the reform aspirations of the American Progressive." (pp. 180–181) Here again *The Age of Reform* seems to be coarse-grained, aimed more at working out the implications of certain psychological and sociological assumptions than at working into the historical record; see J. Joseph Huthmacher, "Urban Liberalism and the Age of Reform," *Mississippi Valley Historical Review*, vol. 49 (1962–1963), 231–241. The insistent demand now current in some historical circles for "revisionism" is not a valid reason to brush aside older scholarship in order to embrace ideas that are startlingly original but mistaken, and evidence contrary to much of Hofstadter's argument is available in many careful studies.

Eric Goldman, *Rendezvous with Destiny* (1952)* focuses on the varieties of "liberalism" since the Civil War. Roughly 200 pages relate to the years from 1877 to 1914, and the account is thin on economic developments and governmental responses. Goldman tries to show how certain ideas in Social Darwinism (Conservative Darwinism, he calls it) were undermined by the thinkers of Reform Darwinism and how the latter ended in a "relativism" that he considers dangerous. These broad categories bother me; I doubt that we gain in understanding by putting a single label on thinkers as diverse as Henry George, Veblen, Rauschenbusch, and Holmes; and Goldman's analyses of some thinkers seem misleading or even false. For instance, how can it be argued that "William James expanded Peirce's fragmentary suggestions into a system . . ."? (p. 155).

For the best biography of each of the Presidents in this period, see Harry Barnard, *Rutherford B. Hayes and His America* (1954); Theodore Clark Smith, *Life and Letters of James Abram Garfield* (1925); George Frederick Howe, *Chester A. Arthur* (1934); Allan Nevins, *Grover Cleveland: A Study in Courage* (1933); Harry J. Sievers, *Benjamin Harrison* (1959); Margaret Leech, *In the Days of*

McKinley (1959); Pringle, *Theodore Roosevelt**; Henry F. Pringle, *The Life and Times of William Howard Taft* (1939); and Arthur S. Link's first three volumes on Woodrow Wilson (1947, 1956, 1960). It is hardly too much to label as great the works by Nevins, Pringle, and Link. The volume by Margaret Leech makes clear that McKinley was not a pliant tool of Mark Hanna, but it surely did not deserve the Pultizer Prize that it received. Organized in a way that is baffling and often irritating, it adds little to our understanding of the period and it seems to me dull in its concern with trivia. Published excerpts from the works of some of these Presidents are very illuminating, especially Charles Richard Williams, ed., *Diary and Letters of Rutherford Birchard Hayes* (1922, 1924, 1925, 1926); Allan Nevins, ed., *Letters of Grover Cleveland, 1850–1908* (1933); Elting E. Morison and others, eds., *The Letters of Theodore Roosevelt* (1951, 1952, 1954); and Ray Stannard Baker and William E. Dodd, eds., *The Public Papers of Woodrow Wilson* (1925, 1926, 1927). Several other prominent politicians of the period left enlightening memoirs.

Many of the richest studies of this era have been biographies. Since the older ones can be readily located through the previously cited *Harvard Guide to American History* (1954), I will not mention them here unless they seem so outstanding as to be indispensable. First-rate works on Southern politicians are Francis Butler Simkins, *Pitchfork Ben Tillman: South Carolinian* (1944); Robert C. Cotner, *James Stephen Hogg: A Biography* (1959); Dewey M. Grantham, Jr., *Hoke Smith and the Politics of the New South* (1958), which can be set against C. Vann Woodward's surging study of Smith's adversary in Georgia, *Tom Watson: Agrarian Rebel* (1938); and Kirwan, *Revolt of the Rednecks*.

Horace Samuel Merrill's *Bourbon Leader: Grover Cleveland and the Democratic Party* (1957), and his *Bourbon Democracy of the Middle West, 1865–1896* (1953) are chiefly valuable as systematic reviews of data already known but do add some new facts; Merrill shows that even in his first administration, Cleveland turned the distribution of Midwestern patronage over to conservative Democrats. This wing of the party also gets incisive treatment in James A. Barnes, *John G. Carlisle: Financial Statesman* (1931); John R. Lambert, *Arthur Pue Gorman* (1953); and Herbert J. Bass, *"I Am a Democrat": The Political Career of David Bennett Hill* (1961). Bass found that the touchy issues for a man seeking state office in New York in the years around 1888 were not the great problems of national politics—not the tariff or monetary legislation or anti-trust policy—but ballot reform and the liquor question. The major leaders of the Silver Democrats are treated in Harry Barnard's superlative *"Eagle Forgotten": The Life of John Peter Altgeld* (1938)* and Paul W. Glad's thin and uncritical *The Trumpet Soundeth: William Jennings Bryan and His Democracy, 1896–1912* (1960). The great need for a solid study of Bryan remains, but see my selection from his works (1967).*

Standing out among the biographies of conservative Republicans are Philip C. Jessup, *Elihu Root* (1938); John A. Garraty, *Henry Cabot Lodge* (1953); Edward Younger, *John A. Kasson* (1955); and Leland Sage, *William Boyd Allison* (1956). Belle Case LaFollette and Fola LaFollette, *Robert M. LaFollette* (1953) is longer than *LaFollette's Autobiography: A Personal Narrative of Political Experiences* (1913),* but less exciting, and hardly more judicious. Arthur Mann, *LaGuardia: A Fighter against His Times* (1959) is excellent.

Paul H. Buck, *The Road to Reunion, 1865–1900* (1937),* although containing many statements that now seem wide of the facts or biased against Negroes, is a mine of information on the reconciliation of Northern and Southern whites. It must be read beside two recent works. Vincent P. De Santis, *Republicans Face the Southern Question, The New Departure Years, 1877–1897* (1959) is a solid study of the Republican party in the South. Stanley P. Hirshson, *Farewell to the Bloody Shirt: Northern Republicans and the Southern Negro, 1877–1893* (1962) dredged much useful data out of a wide search in the sources. But it also poses a difficulty that is suggested by comparing the title to the subtitle: namely, its analysis does not gain in clarity by glossing over the distinction between (a) waving the bloody shirt; that is, refighting the Civil War to win votes, and (b) urging Negro suffrage. Some Republicans (John Sherman in 1887) simultaneously advocated both policies, but they are different in logic; the latter aimed chiefly at strengthening the Republicans in the South, the former at solidifying their ranks in the North; and in some circumstances they could contradict one another.

Ari Hoogenboom, *Outlawing the Spoils: A History of the Civil Service Reform Movement, 1865–1883* (1961) is too eager to mock Matthew Josephson's analysis of the significance of the reform in re-structuring party politics. But Hoogenboom does show that the movement was led largely by professional men, that the outcome of the 1882 elections was vital in converting reluctant Congressmen to vote for the Pendleton Act, and that for years it did more to protect job-holders than to protect job-seekers. Useful related works are Paul P. Van Riper, *History of the United States Civil Service* (1958) and Leonard D. White, *The Republican Era, 1869–1901: A Study in Administrative History* (1958), the latter being part of a massive four-volume study of this aspect of the Federal Government from its beginnings.

My account of the road that led to passage of the Interstate Commerce Act rests heavily on a model monograph, Lee Benson's *Merchants, Farmers, & Railroads: Railroad Regulation and New York Politics, 1850–1887* (1955); also see James W. Neilson, *Shelby M. Cullom: Prairie State Republican* (1962). I. L. Sharfman, *The Interstate Commerce Commission: A Study in Administrative Law and Procedure* (1931, 1935, 1936, 1937) is standard. An outstanding state study is James F. Doster, *Railroads in Alabama Politics, 1875–1914* (1957).

John D. Hicks, *The Populist Revolt* (1931)* remains the ruling over-all treatment, even though it needs to be modified at many points. Probably the most important contribution since Hicks wrote is the demonstration, especially by C. Vann Woodward in works already cited, that the Southern branch of the movement was more important than the Midwestern one. See also Theodore Saloutos' sprawling *Farmer Movements in the South: 1865–1933* (1960). Norman Pollack, *The Populist Response to Industrial America: Midwestern Populist Thought* (1962) is right in arguing that there were "radical dimensions to Populism" (p. 89) that resembled aspects of Marxism; many supporters of this position became Socialists after 1896. But I think that Pollack exaggerates the numerical importance of this viewpoint; that it was definitely a minority position in the Midwestern movement; that most Populists in that section came out of the Republican party and went back to it. I also think that Henry Demarest Lloyd was right when he wrote in October 1896: "The People's Party is a fortuitous collection of the dissatisfied"; that the main cause of their dissatisfaction was the low prices of certain staple crops; and that Pollack errs in contending that endorsement of Bryan in 1896 was a continuation of radical Populism.

The foremost Populist in Minnesota, although announcing that he would support Bryan, bitterly denounced fusion with the Democrats at the national level: "The Democracy raped our convention while our own leaders held the struggling victim." Martin Ridge, *Ignatius Donnelly: The Portrait of a Politician* (1962), p. 357. This first biography of a long and tortured career is rooted in monumental research. It concludes that the unrest of farmers "centered on immediate economic needs." (p. 268) I think it also constitutes an effective answer to allegations that Donnelly was anti-Semitic; certainly it shows that Donnelly was a leader in the campaign for Negro rights.

Roy V. Scott, *The Agrarian Movement in Illinois, 1880–1895* (1962) shows that independent political action by farmers in that state had collapsed long before 1896. When two of its three representatives in the 1891 legislature helped break a long deadlock by voting to send Democrat and corporation lawyer John M. Palmer to the Senate, "damnable treachery" and corruption were widely charged, and farmers by the thousands quit their organizations. Other aspects of the situation in Illinois are brilliantly treated in Chester M. Destler, *American Radicalism, 1865–1901* (1946).

Indispensable articles on Populism and its antecedents are James A. Barnes, "Myths of the Bryan Campaign," *Mississippi Valley Historical Review*, vol. 34 (1947–1948), 367–404; Paul M. O'Leary, "The Scene of the Crime of 1873 Revisited: A Note," *Journal of Political Economy*, vol. 68 (1960), 388–392; and Gilbert C. Fite, "Republican Strategy and the Farm Vote in the Presidential Campaign of 1896," *American Historical Review*, vol. 65 (1959–1960), 787–806.

Years of patient digging into manuscripts and periodicals are apparent in George E. Mowry's *Theodore Roosevelt and the Progressive Movement* (1946)* and his *The California Progressives* (1951). The same sources inform his *The Era of Theodore Roosevelt, 1900–1912* (1958). Since this is the handiest one-volume survey of the Progressive period, it is especially unfortunate that the book contains some mistakes on major facts and has quite a few misspelled names. For the engrossing memoirs of a Tammany major, see Harold C. Syrett, ed., *The Gentleman and the Tiger: The Autobiography of George B. McClellan, Jr.* (1956). The approach of a Tammany leader is expounded in the priceless monologues compiled by William L. Riordan in *Plunkett of Tammany Hall*

(1905)*; the philosophies of many other professionals can be studied in Lincoln Steffens' *The Shame of the Cities* (1904)* and in *The Autobiography of Lincoln Steffens* (1931), a masterpiece that nobody should miss. A rather flimsy inside view of the Federal Government is given by Joseph L. Bristow, *Fraud and Politics at the Turn of the Century: McKinley and His Administration as Seen by His Principal Patronage Dispenser and Investigator* (1952). Helene Maxwell Hooker, ed., *History of the Progressive Party, 1912–1916* by Amos R. E. Pinchot (1958) is an account by a participant which gives flavor and tone.

The same purpose is filled by anthologies published recently, of which my favorite is Arthur and Lila Weinberg, eds., *The Muckrakers* (1961). Harvey Swados, ed., *Years of Conscience: The Muckrakers* (1962) seems too much a collection of snippets; Otis Pease, ed., *The Progressive Years* (1962) veers toward the opposite extreme.

Special aspects of the period have recently gotten incisive treatment. Robert H. Wiebe, "Business Disunity and the Progressive Movement, 1901–1914," *Mississippi Valley Historical Review*, vol. 44 (1957–1958), 664–685 shows that on three major issues—banking reform, regulation of railroad rates, and control of trusts—sharp cleavages occurred within the business world. This important article seems, strangely, better than Wiebe's more extended *Businessmen and Reform: A Study of the Progressive Movement* (1962). Gabriel Kolko, *The Triumph of Conservatism: A Reinterpretation of American History, 1900–1916* (1963) is often lopsided and even pretentious; some of its more startling conclusions are backed by little or no evidence. These defects do not destroy its importance. The author worked through a great many sources, and he shows that several famous reforms were initiated by companies supposedly to be regulated. He is right too to say that Federal regulation of business was in fact and was intended to be conservative in the sense that its aim was, in Kolko's words, "to preserve existing power and social relationships" (p. 2). J. Leonard Bates, "Fulfilling American Democracy: The Conservation Movement, 1907 to 1921," *Mississippi Valley Historical Review*, vol. 44 (1957–1958), 29–57, declares: "The organized conservationists were concerned more with economic justice and democracy in the handling of resources than with mere prevention of waste" (p. 31). Conversely, Samuel P. Hays, *Conservation and*

the Gospel of Efficiency: The Progressive Conservation Movement,
1890–1920 (1959) insists that the campaign must be seen primarily
"from the vantage point of applied science, rather than of democratic protest" (p. 2). Surely both motives were at work, but Hays
seems to have the better of the dispute in regard to such leaders as
Roosevelt and Gifford Pinchot, who were not averse to government aid to Weyerhaeuser and other giants so long as they would
cooperate in scientific forest management; see also M. Nelson
McGeary, *Gifford Pinchot: Forester-Politician* (1960). Other studies
of limited but significant topics are Clayton S. Ellsworth, "Theodore
Roosevelt's Country Life Commission," *Agricultural History*, vol.
34 (1960), 155–172; James H. Timberlake, *Prohibition and the
Progressive Movement, 1900–1920* (1963); and William Preston,
Jr., *Aliens and Dissenters: Federal Suppression of Radicals, 1903–
1933* (1963), which sustains its thesis that Federal attacks on dissenters during and after World War I were rooted in earlier attempts
to restrict the civil liberties of aliens.

A key figure in the harassment of dissenters was Theodore
Roosevelt, who needs a further word. Recently several efforts
have been made to redeem his reputation, but a striking feature
of this literature is that even the scholars who in general respect
Roosevelt have reached some extremely damaging conclusions.
Mowry, *The Era of Theodore Roosevelt*, p. 128, writes: "Whenever Roosevelt could argue himself into believing that morality
was not involved in a question, the right thing to do was usually
the expedient thing; and in the general tariff issue, by far the
most expedient thing was to do nothing." William Harbaugh,
*Power and Responsibility: The Life and Times of Theodore Roose-
velt* (1961), p. 164, says of an episode in 1902: ". . . the President
characteristically deluded himself." John M. Blum in his remarkable
little *The Republican Roosevelt* (1962 edition),* p. 32, declares:
"Roosevelt had built an eclectic intellectual home . . . designed to
provide security for a man whose personality compelled him to act,
whose profession required him to compromise, and whose moral
beliefs forced him to justify everything he did." And, p. 141: "The
awful suspicion ever lingered that he cared as much for fighting
as for right." A man whose awe-inspiring research enabled him
to set the record straight on several important episodes, Howard K.
Beale, goes even further in his *Theodore Roosevelt and the Rise of
America to World Power* (1956), p. 36: "Actually Roosevelt was

confused about the whole problem of war and peace. He and his associates came close to seeking war for its own sake."

The Socialist movement, at least on the national level, has been carefully studied in the last two decades; see Donald D. Egbert and Stow Persons, eds., *Socialism and American Life* (1952); Ira Kipnis, *The American Socialist Movement, 1897–1912* (1952); Howard Quint, *The Forging of American Socialism* (1953); David A. Shannon, *The Socialist Party of America: A History* (1955); and Ray Ginger, *The Bending Cross: A Biography of Eugene Victor Debs* (1949).*

MILITARY AND FOREIGN AFFAIRS

(Chapters 9 and 12)

Probably no scholar will ever be inclined to rework exactly the ground covered by David M. Pletcher's *The Awkward Years: American Foreign Relations Under Garfield and Arthur* (1962)— nearly 400 pages on foreign affairs during four rather uneventful but nonetheless revealing years. If the word "exhaustive" has meaning, it seems to apply here.

A. T. Mahan, *The Interest of America in Sea Power, Present and Future* (1897) is a convenient collection of his periodical pieces since 1890; see also his *The Influence of Seapower upon History, 1660–1783* (1890)* and Theodore Roosevelt's unsigned review, *Atlantic Monthly*, vol. 66 (October 1890), 563–567. The most detailed study is William E. Livezey, *Mahan on Seapower* (1947). Harold and Margaret Sprout, *The Rise of American Naval Power, 1776–1918* (1946) is clearly written but is based chiefly on published official records. A highly official view can be found in E. B. Potter, ed., *Sea Power: A Naval History* (1960). On military aspects of the Spanish-American War, Frank Freidel's vivid *The Splendid Little War* (1957) is a pictorial history with a text woven from eyewitness accounts.

Armin Rappaport, in *The Navy League of the United States* (1962), makes clear that the organization did little and had little influence from its founding in 1902 until 1909. But the study is not only written from the records of the League, it is also written from the viewpoint and values of the League. Rappaport is at great pains to imply that while big money was going into anti-militarism, the Navy League was backed by ordinary citizens with a legitimate patriotic concern for national security. Two of its five original officers were Herbert Satterlee and his father George. The chairman of the Executive Committee in 1916 was Robert L. Bacon. Nowhere does Rappaport mention that Bacon or Herbert Satterlee was connected with J. P. Morgan, although Satterlee was his son-in-law and Bacon was a partner in his firm. The League's Committee on Legislation in 1913 was composed of Robert M. Thompson, Perry Belmont, and William Gibbs Mc-Adoo. The first was chairman of the board of International Nickel. The second was a brother of banker August Belmont. The third was a New York corporation executive who would soon become Secretary of the Treasury and son-in-law of President Wilson. And so on.

Dexter Perkins, *The Monroe Doctrine, 1865–1907* (1937) is a comprehensive and often penetrating survey of the diplomatic correspondence. But its texts of documents are not infallible and it frequently needs to be supplemented by other sources that show the larger context of an episode. A corrective is provided in three excellent articles by Walter LaFeber, "The American Business Community and Cleveland's Venezuelan Message," *Business History Review*, vol. 34 (1960), 393–402; "The Background of Cleveland's Venezuelan Policy: A Reinterpretation," *American Historical Review*, vol. 66 (1960–1961), 947–967; and "American Depression Diplomacy and the Brazilian Revolution, 1893–1894," *Hispanic American Historical Reveiw*, vol. 40 (1960), 107–118.

Julius W. Pratt, *Expansionists of 1898: The Acquisition of Hawaii and the Spanish Islands* (1936) remains the standard effort to tell the whole story. The evidence now available, including my own research on Boston and Chicago, suggests to me that Pratt was right in concluding that most big businessmen opposed the declaration of war in 1898. I also suspect that he was wrong in writing: ". . . business interests in the United States were generally opposed to expansion, or indifferent to it, until after May 1, 1898." (p. 22) Pratt's own book contains interesting evidence to the contrary although he fails to recognize it as such; he reports that W. F. Draper on 3 February 1894 gave the major speech in the House of Representatives favoring annexation of Hawaii and other bases and construction of an isthmian canal. But Pratt fails to note that this W. F. Draper was chief spokesman in the House for New England textile interests and was himself president of the large textile-machinery manufacturer, George Draper & Sons of Hope-dale, Massachusetts. Again, Pratt notes that James J. Hill came to support retention of the Philippines even though he had opposed the declaration of war. But Pratt's source—a private letter of 26 March 1898 written from Wall Street by the father of Thomas Beer —gives a quite different impression: "Nothing but war talk. Hill seems to be the only prominent railroad man who is fighting for peace. The Pennsylvania crowd say that nothing can be done to stop it since C. K. Davis and Alger are pushing the President. It cannot be stopped from this end and I do not think Hanna can stop it in the Senate." The reference to Davis (of Minnesota) and Alger (of Michigan) is an interesting commentary on the stereotype of an "isolationist" Midwest. If Pulitzer's New York *World* and Hearst's New York *Journal* were "yellow" for war, so was the Kansas City *Star*.

I am not satisfied that we now have a solid picture of the attitudes of American business to colonialism. What we need is studies based, not on the few trade journals on which Pratt relied so heavily, but on the correspondence of business executives, Congressmen, and consuls and other diplomats. There is also useful published evidence in such volumes as *Reports from the Consuls of the United States on the Commerce, Manufactures, Etc., of Their Consular Districts* (1881). It is particularly unfortunate that business historians have seldom reported the views of their subjects on foreign affairs.

The general interpretation given by Richard Hofstadter, "Manifest Destiny and the Philippines," in Aaron, ed., *America in Crisis*, finds an extended development in Ernest R. May, *Imperial Democracy: The Emergence of America as a Great Power* (1961). Research in the archives of a half-dozen governments brought May to some important findings, particularly that Spain and the United States were not on the verge of a negotiated settlement when war was declared: Spain was still not willing to grant Cuban independence while nothing less would have satisfied key elements in Congress. But *Imperial Democracy* suffers from what might be called temporal solipsism in its failure to recognize that the war followed 25 years of persistent and general excess capacity and that probably by 1898 a majority of American businessmen believed that prosperity at home depended on greater sales abroad. For an incisive long critique of May's book, see the review by

William Appleman Williams in *Studies on the Left*, vol. 3 (1963), 94–99.

After writing the preceding two paragraphs, I read Walter LaFeber's *The New Empire: An Interpretation of American Expansion, 1860–1898* (1963). This splendid study goes far toward providing what was needed. That nearly all major segments of the American economy were characterized by excess capacity after 1873 was the chief thesis of a paper that I presented to the Mississippi Valley Historical Association in 1962 (It is still unpublished, but the chief conclusions are given above, especially Chapters 4 and 9). Now LaFeber has turned up copious evidence that leading politicians and businessmen at the time saw the country's problems in terms of this condition and constructed foreign policies grounded on this perception. He shows further that such men as Cleveland and Olney shared the view that foreign markets and increased exports were essential to American prosperity, and thus undercut their opposition to the acquisition of colonies. It can be emphatically said that the general interpretation advanced by Julius Pratt and accepted for a generation by most historians, including Ernest May, is not tenable on the basis of what we know today.

The late Howard K. Beale's *Theodore Roosevelt and the Rise of America to World Power* is surely the most comprehensive analysis yet of the pertinent evidence. While I do not share the general appreciation of Roosevelt that Beale manifested, his evidence has changed my mind on several points; perhaps the most important is his showing that the President did make polite but firm naval gestures against Germany in the Venezuela episode of 1902–1903. But again there are signs of carelessness. For example, Senator Lodge is quoted as writing to an American diplomat about joint action with England and Japan against the Boxer Rebellion: "If we act properly together, we can prevent the absorption of China by Russia and keep the Empire open for our trade and commerce, which is all we want." (p. 185) But earlier in the book (p. 76) the same sentence is quoted without the final phrase—hardly a trivial one—and with no indication that words had been deleted.

A key element in Roosevelt's foreign policy has been treated well in Lionel M. Gelber, *The Rise of Anglo-American Friendship: A Study in World Politics, 1898–1906* (1938) and especially in Charles S. Campbell, Jr., *Anglo-American Understanding 1898–1903* (1957). Campbell has also contributed the superb *Special Business Interests and the Open Door Policy* (1951). For the evolution of the latter policy see Raymond A. Esthus, "The Changing Concept of the Open Door, 1899–1910," *Mississippi Valley Historical Review*, vol. 46 (1959–1960), 435–454; Paul A. Varg, *Open Door Diplomat: The Life of W. W. Rockhill* (1952); and particularly Charles Vevier, *The United States and China, 1906–1913: A Study of Finance and Diplomacy* (1955). Having searched through a multitude of archives and manuscript collections, Vevier concluded that the Open Door Policy was in large measure unrealistic.

On various aspects of relations with Mexico see four carefully researched monographs: David M. Pletcher, *Rails, Mines, and Progress: Seven American Promoters in Mexico, 1867–1911* (1958); Robert E. Quirk's *The Mexican Revolution, 1914–1915* (1961), and his *An Affair of Honor* (1962); and Clarence C. Clendenen, *The United States and Pancho Villa: A Study in Unconventional Diplomacy* (1961). On Wilson's Mexican policy I have followed the superlative account in Arthur S. Link, *Woodrow Wilson and the Progressive Era, 1910–1917* (1954). My general view of Wilson was influenced by two outstanding brief interpretations: John A. Garraty, *Woodrow Wilson* (1956), and John Morton Blum, *Woodrow Wilson and the Politics of Morality* (1956).* The recent literature is keenly dissected in Richard Watson, Jr., "Woodrow Wilson and His Interpreters, 1947–1957," *Mississippi Valley Historical Review*, vol. 44 (1957–1958), 207–236.

INTELLECTUAL HISTORY

(Chapters 7 and 14)

I know no more spacious and revealing window into the American mind of the 19th century than F. O. Matthiessen, *The James Family, Including Selections from the Writings of Henry James, Senior, William, Henry, & Alice James* (1947). Virtually every subject worthy of discussion crops up in this beautiful volume that remains entrancing throughout its 700 pages. Matthiessen interlarded his own lengthy and incisive commentaries into this unique anthology of four of the century's best American writers. Anybody who is captivated by novelist Henry James or psychologist William James should become acquainted with their father, who was perhaps even more charming than they.

Twelve outstanding essays written about 1900 are reprinted in Ray Ginger, ed., *American Social Thought* (1961),* which also cites major books by the authors. Morton White, *Social Thought in America: The Revolt against Formalism* (1957 edition)* is intellectual history of the best sort. Concentrating on the most significant ideas of five important thinkers, it probes deep into their assumptions, possible meanings, and implications. Morton White and Lucia White, *The Intellectual versus the City, From Thomas Jefferson to Frank Lloyd Wright* (1962), dealing mainly with persons active between 1877 and 1914, is less happy.

Although it contains deftly written passages, Daniel Aaron's *Men of Good Hope: A Story of American Progressives* (1961 edition)* does not seem to add up into a book. Charles B. Forcey, *Crossroads of Liberalism: Croly, Weyl, Lippmann, and the Progressive Era, 1900–1925* (1961) is more satisfying than David W. Noble, *The Paradox of Progressive Thought* (1958). Robert H. Bremner, *From The Depths: The Discovery of Poverty in the United States* (1956) is a solid survey, while Sidney Fine, *Laissez Faire and the General-Welfare State: A Study of Conflict in American Thought, 1865–1901* (1956) operates from blunted philosophical categories that are sometimes unfair to the man whose thought is being summarized.

By far the outstanding over-all survey of the relations between the visual arts and society is Oliver W. Larkin, *Art and Life in America* (1961 edition). One later effort to encompass the same facts was published as a multi-volume work at various dates. *The Arts in America* is also multi-author, and the result, almost inevitably, is a hodgepodge, some strong sections, some weak. Edgar P. Richardson, *Painting in America* (1956) has some superb commentaries, while Alexander Eliot, *Three Hundred Years of American Painting* (1957) records the right anecdotes. Lloyd Goodrich's excellent studies, *Thomas Eakins* (1933), *Winslow Homer* (1945), and *Albert P. Ryder* (1959), yielded most of the biographical facts I have used. The reactions to the paintings are my own. The Indian art I have discussed is in the William Rockhill Nelson Museum in Kansas City. On the Armory Show and its delayed impact on American painting see Charles Hirschfeld, " 'Ash Can' versus 'Modern' Art in America," *Western Humanities Review*, vol. 10 (1956), 353–373.

Discrimination of the great from the shoddy in American

building of this era can be said to have begun with Lewis Mumford, *The Brown Decades: A Study of the Arts in America, 1865–1895* (1931).* Several excellent works have continued the evaluation: Wayne Andrew's richly sympathetic *Architecture, Ambition and Americans: A History of American Architecture, from the Beginning to the Present, Telling the Story of the Outstanding Buildings, the Men Who Designed Them and the People for Whom They Were Built* (1954); Carl W. Condit, *American Building Art: The Nineteenth Century* (1960); John Burchard and Albert Bush-Brown, *The Architecture of America: A Social and Cultural History* (1961); and James Marston Fitch, *Architecture and the Esthetics of Plenty* (1961). Henry-Russell Hitchcock, Jr., has written the standard *The Architecture of H. H. Richardson and His Times* (1936) and *In the Nature of Materials, 1887–1941: The Buildings of Frank Lloyd Wright* (1942). Hugh S. Morrison, *Louis Sullivan: Prophet of Modern Architecture* (1935) is still in general the best study. One of my favorite books on this epoch is D. B. Steinman, *The Builders of the Bridge: The Story of John Roebling and His Son* (1950 edition). Thorough in his research, bringing to his job the unique qualification of being himself the outstanding bridge designer of his generation, Steinman wrote with gusto. He also wrote with the admirable conviction that hero-worship is unobjectionable if the object of adulation deserves it.

My remarks about novels, plays, and so on are based on my own reading of the works. Donald Sheehan's *This Was Publishing: A Chronicle of the Book Trade in the Gilded Age* (1952) is especially reliable and useful for having used the office files of four major firms (Harper; Scribner's; Holt; and Dodd, Mead). Aubert J. Clark, *The Movement for International Copyright in the Nineteenth Century* (1960) is helpful; see also Gordon Milne, *George William Curtis & the Genteel Tradition* (1955). In general I have shied clear of critical studies, but two recent works are landmarks. Henry Nash Smith's *Mark Twain: The Development of a Writer* (1962) brilliantly traces out the creation of the literary strategy, especially in the use of a first-person narrator, that culminated in *Huckleberry Finn*. Smith and William M. Gibson have edited *Mark Twain-Howells Letters: The Correspondence of Samuel L. Clemens and William D. Howells, 1872–1910* (1960). This definitive edition includes every known communication, 681 of them, between two great writers, and the editors have supplied splendid annotations. The result is truly a joy to read as well as a flawless piece of scholarship.

Nearly all of the mountain of material published about Dixieland jazz is sensationalistic and seems to me trashy, but I am indebted to two splendid articles: Russell Roth, "On the Instrumental Origins of Jazz," *American Quarterly*, vol. 4 (1952), 305–316, and Chadwick Hansen, "Social Influences on Jazz Style: Chicago, 1920–30," *American Quarterly*, vol. 12 (1960), 493–507.

CONSTITUTIONAL HISTORY

(Chapters 8 and 13)

Again I have relied chiefly on my own reading of the decisions, but a few secondary works are helpful. Arnold M. Paul, *Conservative Crisis and the Rule of Law: Attitudes of Bench and Bar, 1887–1895* (1960) is a first-rate monograph resting chiefly on a comprehensive search in law journals and in reports of bar-association meetings. Bruce R. Trimble, *Chief Justice Waite: Defender of the Public Interest* (1938) is corrected and fleshed out by C. Peter Magrath, *Morrison R. Waite: The Triumph of Character* (1963), which gives new data on the inner workings of the Supreme Court. Willard L. King, *Melville Weston Fuller: Chief Justice of the United States, 1888–1910* (1950) gives a great deal of information in the course of arriving at much too flattering an estimate of the man who was perhaps the worst Chief Justice ever to sit. Useful biographies of other members of the Supreme Court in this period are Carl Brent Swisher, *Stephen J. Field: Craftsman of the Law* (1930); Charles Fairman, *Mr. Justice Miller and the Supreme Court, 1862–1890* (1939); and George Shiras, *Justice George Shiras, Jr., of Pittsburgh* (1953).

ESSAY ON SOURCES

Supplement for Second Edition

These remarks deliberately focus on works published since 1965, so that readers can have a concentrated view of the progress that historians have made in their understanding in the last decade. In my judgment, the gains have been imposing. While I have not felt inclined to alter many of the interpretations or conclusions that I stated originally in this book, I can substantiate many of them with a better display of evidence. To advance in any field of inquiry, the researcher must take the wisdom available at the time and try to make it more solid and more refined. Many of my colleagues have been doing exactly so. If I now wrote a review of *Age of Excess* (1965), I would make some caustic remarks. Hence this revision.

BUSINESS AND ECONOMIC HISTORY

(Chapters 2, 3, 10, 16)
By far the most useful work is Robert Higgs' *The Transformation of the American Economy, 1865–1914: An Essay in Interpretation* (1971). Concise, perceptive, it should find its way into many classrooms. Higgs has fresh insights about the fate of immigrants in the marketplace, about urbanization, about "the economics of information." But some of his generalizations seem silly. If he looked, he could find a lot of farmers (whether dairy in New York, corn-hogs in Iowa, wheat in Montana) who would boggle at the statement, "farming is generally a constant-cost industry." Nor is it true that "The market for land was everywhere highly competitive." Paul Gates was correct in remarks about "land monopoly": an acre at State and Madison is not an acre in Kansas at 120° W 40° N. In spite of these flaws, Higgs has given us a book that both provokes thought and is a valuable guide to other literature.

Some articles have been especially stimulating: Thomas Weiss, "The Industrial Distribution of the Urban and Rural Workforces:

Estimates for the United States, 1870–1910," *Journal of Economic History*, vol. 32 (1972), 919–937; Lewis C. Solmon, "Opportunity Costs and Models of Schooling in the Nineteenth Century," *Southern Economic Journal*, vol. 37 (1970), 66–83; Mary Yeager Kujovich, "The Refrigerator Car and the Growth of the American Dressed Beef Industry," *Business History Review*, vol. 44 (1970), 460–482; Pete Daniel, "Up from Slavery and Down to Peonage: the Alonzo Bailey Case," *Journal of American History*, vol. 56 (1971), 654–670. Charles Hoffmann's *The Depression of the Nineties* promises to be helpful but isn't; the copyright date (1970) momentarily obscures the fact that the book was finished by 1953.

SOCIAL HISTORY

(Chapters 4, 5, 8, 11, 13, 15, 16)

Ray Allen Billington's *America's Frontier Heritage* (1966) is the most important work on the subject since Turner. Learned, judicious, it winnows a huge hopperful of grain to extract kernels from chaff.

One of the few strides toward comprehension of American family structures is Richard Sennett, *Families against the City: Middle Class Homes of Industrial Chicago, 1872–1890* (1970). Although this fine study tells a lot about how weak fathers rear flabby sons, and about how the fathers became weak, it neglects some of its own opportunities. Why not follow up, for instance, the report by David Potter in *People of Plenty* (1954) about the significance of a separate bedroom for each child?

In Justus D. Doenecke, "Myths, Machines and Markets: The Columbian Exposition of 1893," *Journal of Popular Culture*, vol. 5 (1971–1972), 535–549, the most original paragraph discusses the Women's Building and its claims. Allen F. Davis, *Spearheads for Reform: The Social Settlements and the Progressive Movement, 1890–1914* (1970 edition) concentrates not on claims but on achievements. It emphasizes what Steffens and Frederick Howe had noted: that reformers were driven beyond their neighborhoods to more encompassing governments. The second chapter is a persuasive profile of settlement workers: mainly middle class, educated far beyond the contemporary median. We learn much about the movements for playgrounds, child-labor laws, compulsory attendance at school. The weakest chapters deal with city reform (Be wary of his talk about Chicago, 1895–1906). The only really annoying part of the book is the prefatory remark by Richard C. Wade: "In rescuing the settlement movement from scholarly neglect Mr. Davis has also enriched our knowledge of city life at the turn of the century." He owes apologies to Arthur M. Schlesinger, his wife Louise Wade, Jane Addams, me, Roy Lubove, Robert H. Bremner, and quite a few other folks. Does editorship in a series drive you to advance your own children by denigrating all others? Another author in the same series, Stanley Buder, had access to more than three score scrapbooks, mainly clippings, kept by the Pullman family and Company. But his *Pullman: An Experiment in Industrial Order and Community Planning, 1880–1930* (1967) adds little. His best contribution softens the harshest portrayals of the coercion over politics by the oligarch and his henchmen.

The vital area of family structures and feminine roles—and *it* has suffered "from scholarly neglect"—is barely touched by John C. Burnham, "The Progressive Era Revolution in American Attitudes Toward Sex," *Journal of American History*, vol. 59 (1973), 885–908. Whether there was a Progressive Era remains doubtful, and Burnham's evidence does not move me at all in favor of believing that a revolution in American attitudes toward sex occurred. Far more meaningful, although based on terribly fragmentary data as he admits, is Murray G. Murphey's "An Approach to the Historical Study of National Character," in Melford E. Spiro, ed., *Context and Meaning in Cultural Anthropology* (1965), 144–163. He worked from the memoirs of twenty-three men born in New York, Pennsylvania, New Jersey, or Delaware between 1794 and 1830. The fathers of fifteen of these men were farmers (although most of the sample were themselves professional). Another work that might be regarded as a study of national, or at least of regional, character is Alexander Saxton, *The Indispensable Enemy: Labor and the Anti-Chinese Movement in California* (1971). This painstaking and thoughtful study shows how efforts to achieve class unity were repeatedly undercut by the white worker's contempt and hatred of Asians.

A work hard to classify is Jane Jacobs, *The Economy of Cities* (1970). The best American social scientists have been model-builders: Jefferson, Madison, Hamilton, Van Buren, Clay, Turner, Veblen. Jacobs has provided the most fetching paradigm that I have read since 1965. Flaws can be found; even her definition, never explicit, of "city" seems flabby. But for originality and insight, her book is great. It expands and bolsters the contention of my 1965 edition that cities are the centers of creativity.

POLITICAL HISTORY

(Chapters 6, 8, 12)

Our comprehension of the national party struggles has not advanced greatly in the last ten years. Among the better works are Robert D. Marcus, *Grand Old Party, Political Structure in the Gilded Age 1880–1896* (1971) and David J. Rothman, *Politics and and Power: The United States Senate 1869–1901* (1966). For the Mugwumps see an excellent study by Geoffrey T. Blodgett, *The Gentle Reformers, Massachusetts Democrats in the Cleveland Era* (1966). A convenient guide to recent literature is offered by Lewis L. Gould, "New Perspectives on the Republican Party, 1877–1913: A Review Article," *American Historical Review*, vol. 77 (1972), 1074–1082, which comes to evaluations that are markedly more favorable than my own.

My favorites from the past decade are considerably more specialized monographs. Two deal with municipalities. Roger Lane, *Policing the City: Boston, 1822–1885* (1967) tackles only one phase of municipal government, and its evidence lies largely outside the time span of this book, but it is revealing. Zane L. Miller, *Boss Cox's Cincinnati: Urban Politics in the Progressive Era* (1967) holds more insight into the civic affairs of a locality than any book since Steffens and Plunkett (and V. O. Key?). It gives the most succinct description that I have seen of the techniques of an efficient machine that reached beyond the county to influence state and Presidential elections. More than one glib theory might be shaken by Miller's claim that the chief determinant of political behavior in Cincinnati was not ethnicity nor religion nor party affiliation but rather the neighborhood where you lived. However, the subject of ethnicity is forcibly raised by Thomas N. Brown, *Irish-American Nationalism, 1870–1890* (1966), which tells sometimes more, sometimes less, than we really want to know.

FOREIGN AFFAIRS

(Chapters 9, 12, 16)

Far and away the most important addition in this sector is William Appleman Williams, *The Roots of the Modern American Empire: A Study of the Growth and Shaping of Social Consciousness in a Marketplace Society* (1969). Williams' finest effort to date, this book copiously documents my earlier contention that overseas expansion was spurred onward by a widespread recognition that the United States could produce more than home markets could absorb. Moreover, it plugs the major gap in LaFeber's study (1963) by showing that farmers shared this general malaise. According to Williams, agrarians as early as 1840 were the spearhead of a drive to gain new markets abroad because of their own overproduction in relation to the domestic economy. Only after about 1884 did "metropolitan leaders" (the undefined meaning to this phrase is a serious ambiguity in Williams' work (begin to hurl their substantial weight behind an expansionist policy.

Although more slight, Stephen Scheinberg's "Invitation to Empire: Tariffs and American Economic Expansion in Canada," *Business History Review*, vol. 47 (1972), 218–238, is truly notable. Perhaps persons like Scheinberg, Americans but long-time residents in Canada, are most likely to savor the lovely remark by James H. Hill quoted in an earlier chapter. Two articles in the *Canadian Historical Review* illuminate other aspects of America's relation to its northerly neighbor: A. C. Gluek, "The Passamaquoddy Bay Treaty, 1910," vol. 47 (1966), 1–21, and W. M. Baker, "A Case Study of Anti-Americanism in English-Speaking Canada: the Election Campaign of 1911," vol. 51 (1970), 426–449.

INTELLECTUAL HISTORY

(Chapters 7, 14, 16)

If you believe, as I do, that intellectual history should be approached through the original writings of the strongest and most coherent minds of a given era, it stands to reason that you will not put a lot of stock in the works of later commentators. Therefore, by your own ground rules, you are not likely to find, sixty years after 1914, many new insights into pulsations of the mind before that date. But happily, there have been some. I might add that pertinent

396 Essay on Sources

tributes to other contemporary scholars are made below under "Chapter 16."

In Russel B. Nye's *This Almost Chosen People: Essays in the History of American Ideas* (1966), two chapters were most useful to me. "The American as Nationalist" specifies clearly how our domestic version differed from all European varieties. It should be linked with the subsequent essay, "The American Sense of Mission." Together, they dovetail rather neatly with Williams' investigation cited above. Thus we can reach a better perspective—derived on a much longer sweep of time—of the grotesque reversals in American foreign relations at the turn of the century.

Readers will doubtless wonder why I include here the monumental biography by Joseph Frazier Wall, *Andrew Carnegie* (1970). If you check the Index under "libraries," you might understand how I can claim that my education came more from Carnegie Libraries, where you could go voluntarily, than from public schools with their infernal compulsory-attendance laws. In brief, we need to scrutinize closely the categories with which we work. Is the steel tycoon more a part of business and economic history than of intellectual history? Probably so, but it is worthwhile to ask the question. Similarly with another new study. Simultaneous publication in one magazine of *The Bostonians*, *Huck Finn*, and *Silas Lapham* is awesome, but do not neglect James F. Findlay, Jr., *Dwight L. Moody* (1969). Maybe the evangelist had as much influence on the mental-emotional climate of the times as the three great novelists put together.

LIFE-STYLES IN 1914

Unquestionably the work that stimulated me most in writing this addition is Don E. Fehrenbacher, ed., *History and American Society: Essays of David M. Potter* (1973). Of the sixteen pieces collected, five had not been published earlier. For my purposes, these five manuscripts revealed more probably than all the others together—and I emphatically do not denigrate the other eleven; they simply pertain chiefly to an earlier epoch than the one that is my concern. Potter's key terms are now cant words in the social sciences: alienation, civilization, cohesion, community, nationalism. He digs deep into the meaning that "individualism" has had to Americans, suggesting that through the nineteenth century it meant self-reliance. In my quotation from Jacksonian times, we find no hint of individuality. But by the generation of Clarence Darrow and Lincoln Steffens, the word had taken this vastly different twist. Among the other provocative themes in this assortment: "What happens to law based upon the norms of the community if there is no prevailing community but only a multiplicity of conflicting communities?"

Herbert G. Gutman, "Work, Culture, and Society in Industrializing America, 1815–1919," *American Historical Review*, vol. 78 (1973), 531–588 is almost a monograph, and it is more useful than almost any monograph you can name. This remarkable study does more to unite history to the social sciences than a bundle of "methodological" polemics on the topic. Gutman focuses on tensions between immigrants' cultures (values, attitudes, and patterns of behavior that have been internalized) and the society they met up against in the United States. When pre-industrial sets are injected into an industrial setting, when foreign ores are injected into a Bessemer converter, sparks fly in unforeseen orbits.

Judith Mara Gutman, *Lewis W. Hine and the American Social Conscience* (1967) collects nearly a hundred pages of well-reproduced photographs by Hine. Here are vivid glimpses into the reality of specific immigrants, of individualized child labor, plus an extended introduction by Gutman. Her zeal tracked down hundreds of these masterpieces in caches that nobody had ever explored. Two different approaches are used by Kevin Starr, *Americans and the California Dream, 1850–1915* (1973) and by Michael Lesy, *Wisconsin Death Trip* (1973). Starr's study, while thoughtful, is inclined toward the conventionalities. Lesy's sojourn is extraordinary. It holds materials about Black River Falls, Jackson County, Wisconsin, in the decade after 1890. Photographs by one Charles Van Schaick plus excerpts from the *Bay State Banner* add up to a sordid portrait of the underbelly of American life. This project was conceived with imagination and executed with care; the exhibits are presented artfully. With two reproaches. The notion of omitting pagination from the book was a frightful mistake. An index would be helpful.

PRIMARY SOURCES

Four selections of documents might be useful: Sigmund Diamond, ed., *The National Transformed: The Creation of an Industrial*

Society (1963); John A. Garraty, ed., *Labor and Capital in the Gilded Age* (1968); Ray Ginger, ed., *The Nationalizing of American Life, 1877–1900* (1965), and F. J. Jaher, ed., *The Age of Industrialism in America* (1968).

Table of Cases

FEDERAL COURT DECISIONS

STATE DECISIONS

Index of Subjects

accounting, importance of, 52, 222–23, 224, 231–32; methods of, 12; *see also* corporate organization, "trusts"

advertising, 19, 24, 28–29

agrarian myth, 64, 87–89, 152, 167, 297–99

agriculture, 4–7, 13–14, 22–25, 32, 62–72, 82, 87–89, 97, 104, 113, 118, 122, 129–30, 182, 183, 232, 242–43, 250, 269, 298–301, 342; *see also* farmers

Algeciras Conference, 273

anarchists, 59–60

Anglo-American friendship, rise of, 196, 199

anthracite strike of 1902, 253–54

anti-Catholicism, 82, 100, 111, 195, 252

anti-Semitism, 80, 82, 252–53

arbitration treaties, international, 259

architecture, 142–44, 322

arts, American weakness in, 136–37, 144; graphic, 17–18, 93–94, 138–42, 322–23

automobile manufacturing, 228–30

Big navy policy, 191–92, 201–202, 259–61

blackmail, industrial, 33–34, 50, 115

Bland-Allison Act of 1878, 103, 124

"bloody shirt," waved by Republicans, 74–75, 119

blue laws, 59

book publishing, 138, 156–57

business administration; *see* corporate organization

business cycles, 41–45

cattle ranching, 67–68, 86–87

chemical industry, 227, 231–32, 305

child labor, 242

child-rearing practices, 345–50

cities, alleged sources of corruption, 297–301; as centers of opportunity, 297–98, 342–43

civil-service reform, Federal, 104–109, 113, 119

"class legislation," 306–307

coal mining, 40, 87–88, 170–71, 250, 253–54

colonies, desire for, 191–94, 211–14, 216, 234–36, 356–57

Columbian Exposition of 1893, 167

company towns, 10

competition, cut-throat, 48–49, 55–56; intercity, 105, 113; theory of, 36; *see also* overproduction

conservation, Federal, 265, 270–71, 278–79, 281

construction, 39, 40, 95, 227

convict-lease system, 33

copper, 14, 26–27, 248–49

copyright, international, 156–57

corruption; *see* political corruption 52–53, 96, 222–23, 231–32, 236–37, 320–21, 359

corporations, growth of 45–53 327–28, 330–31

corruption, *see* political corruption

cotton manufacturing, 40, 41, 205, 241–42

credit, need for, 9–10, 16, 24, 42–45, 63–69, 98, 129, 130, 169–70, 241

Crime of '73, 27

criminal law, 32–33, 167, 270, 302, 307

crop-lien system, 68–69, 129, 130

cruelty, 150–53, 294, 301–302; *see also* Negroes, violence

Cuban crisis, 11, 200–210, 212

cultural center, absence of, in U.S., 136

cut-throat competition, 48–49, 55–56, 113, 115–16, 163, 220, 241, 327

401

Index of Proper Names

Ginger, Ray
  Age of excess

973.8

G.A.R. MEMORIAL LIBRARY
WEST NEWBURY, MA